Critical Readings on Pure Land Buddhism in Japan

Volume 1

Critical Readings on Pure Land Buddhism in Japan

VOLUME 1

Edited by

Galen Amstutz

BRILL

LEIDEN | BOSTON

The Library of Congress Cataloging-in-Publication Data is available online at http://catalog.loc.gov
LC record available at http://lccn.loc.gov/2020936996

Typeface for the Latin, Greek, and Cyrillic scripts: "Brill". See and download: brill.com/brill-typeface.

ISBN 978-90-04-40140-2 (hardback, set)
ISBN 978-90-04-40137-2 (hardback, vol. 1)
ISBN 978-90-04-40138-9 (hardback, vol. 2)
ISBN 978-90-04-40139-6 (hardback, vol. 3)
ISBN 978-90-04-40150-1 (e-book, vol. 1)
ISBN 978-90-04-40151-8 (e-book, vol. 2)
ISBN 978-90-04-40152-5 (e-book, vol. 3)

Copyright 2020 by Koninklijke Brill NV, Leiden, The Netherlands.
Koninklijke Brill NV incorporates the imprints Brill, Brill Hes & De Graaf, Brill Nijhoff, Brill Rodopi,
Brill Sense, Hotei Publishing, mentis Verlag, Verlag Ferdinand Schöningh and Wilhelm Fink Verlag.
All rights reserved. No part of this publication may be reproduced, translated, stored in a retrieval system,
or transmitted in any form or by any means, electronic, mechanical, photocopying, recording or otherwise,
without prior written permission from the publisher.
Authorization to photocopy items for internal or personal use is granted by Koninklijke Brill NV provided
that the appropriate fees are paid directly to The Copyright Clearance Center, 222 Rosewood Drive,
Suite 910, Danvers, MA 01923, USA. Fees are subject to change.

Brill has made all reasonable efforts to trace all rights holders to any copyrighted material used in this
work. In cases where these efforts have not been successful the publisher welcomes communications from
copyright holders, so that the appropriate acknowledgements can be made in future editions, and to settle
other permission matters.

This book is printed on acid-free paper and produced in a sustainable manner.

Contents

VOLUME 1

Introduction: Brill Critical Readings on Pure Land Buddhism
in Japan   1

PART 1
Useful Overarching Perspectives

1   Buddhism as a Religion of Hope: Observations on the "Logic" of a
Doctrine and Its Foundational Myth   17
Luis O. Gómez

2   Pure Land Buddhism as an Alternative Mārga   36
Mark L. Blum

PART 2
Early Presence in Japan

3   The Development of *Mappō* Thought in Japan (I)   79
Michele Marra

4   The Development of *Mappō* Thought in Japan (II)   109
Michele Marra

5   The Growth of Pure Land Buddhism in the Heian Period   127
Robert F. Rhodes

6   *Ōjōyōshū, Nihon Ōjō Gokuraku-ki,* and the Construction of Pure Land
Discourse in Heian Japan   159
Robert F. Rhodes

7   With the Help of "Good Friends"
Deathbed Ritual Practices in Early Medieval Japan   182
Jacqueline I. Stone

VI CONTENTS

PART 3
Turn to the Nembutsu as the Sole Solution

8 Hōnen on Attaining Pure Land Rebirth: the Selected Nenbutsu of the
Original Vow   223
Allan A. Andrews

9 Hōnen and Popular Pure Land Piety: Assimilation and
Transformation   241
Allan A. Andrews

10 Socio-Economic Impacts of Hōnen's Pure Land Doctrines: an Inquiry
into the Interplay between Buddhist Teachings and Institutions   255
Martin Repp

PART 4
*Shinran's More Radical Turn to the Enlightenment Gift as an
Involuntary Emergent Property*

11 Faith: Its Arising   305
Alfred Bloom

12 "Rely on the Meaning, Not on the Words"
*Shinran's Methodology and Strategy for Reading Scriptures and Writing
the* Kyōgyōshinshō   322
Eisho Nasu

VOLUME 2

PART 5
*Formation of a Major Institution: Honganji and Its Negotiations
with Popular Consciousness*

13 From Inspiration to Institution
The Rise of Sectarian Identity in Jōdo Shinshū   349
James C. Dobbins

CONTENTS VII

14 Shin Buddhist Attitudes towards the Kami
From Shinran to Rennyo 363
Robert F. Rhodes

15 Popular Pure Land Teachings of the Zenkōji Nyorai and Shinran 388
Eisho Nasu

16 Stand by Your Founder
Honganji's Struggle with Funeral Orthodoxy 398
Mark L. Blum

17 Steadied Ambiguity: the Afterlife in "Popular" Shin Buddhism 430
Galen Amstutz

18 Ambivalence Regarding Women and Female Gender in Premodern
Shin Buddhism 449
Galen Amstutz

PART 6
The Alternative Field: Pure Land Striven for in This World

19 Ippen and Pure Land Buddhist Wayfarers in Medieval Japan 483
James H. Foard

20 The Shingon Subordinating Fire Offering for Amitābha, "Amida Kei Ai
Goma" 509
Richard K. Payne

21 Breath of Life: the Esoteric Nembutsu 530
James H. Sanford

22 Jōkei and the Rhetoric of "Other-Power" and "Easy Practice" in Medieval
Japanese Buddhism 561
James L. Ford

PART 7
Pure Land Fellowships in War and Peace

23   The Life of Rennyo
      A Struggle for the Transmission of Dharma   603
         Yasutomi Shin'ya

24   The Dilemma of Religious Power
      Honganji and Hosokawa Masamoto   628
         Michael Solomon

25   Shin Buddhism and *Burakumin* in the Edo Period   645
         Galen Amstutz

26   Precepts in Japanese Pure Land Buddhism
      The Jōdoshū   695
         James C. Dobbins

27   Exemplary Lives
      Form and Function in Pure Land Sacred Biography   712
         Michael Bathgate

28   Preaching as Performance
      Notes on a Secretive Shin Buddhist Sermon   746
         Clark Chilson

29   The *Nianfo* in Ōbaku Zen: a Look at the Teachings of the Three
      Founding Masters   759
         James Baskind

30   Extreme Asceticism, Medicine and Pure Land Faith in the Life of
      Shuichi Munō (1683–1719)   778
         Paul Groner

VOLUME 3

PART 8
*Meiji and Modernity: Political Resettlement and Realignment,
Moments of Intellectual Hybridization, Emigration,
Collaboration, Postwar Progressivism, Lingering Conservatism*

31   Shin Buddhism in the Meiji Period   805
     Mark L. Blum

32   Against Buddhist Unity: Murakami Senshō and His Sectarian
     Critics   875
     Ryan Ward

33   The Honganji: Guardian of the State (1868–1945)   908
     Minor L. Rogers and Ann T. Rogers

34   Shinran's Thought in Present-Day Japan   931
     Gerhard Schepers

35   Propagation, Accommodation and Negotiating Social Capital:
     Jōdo Shinshū Responses to Contemporary Crises   954
     Jørn Borup

36   Family Temples and Religious Learning in Contemporary Japanese
     Buddhism   978
     Jessica Starling

37   Shin Buddhist Studies and Secularization   993
     Mitsuya Dake

38   Amida and Pure Land within a Contemporary Worldview:
     From Shinran's Literal Symbolism to Figurative Symbolism   1005
     Kenneth K. Tanaka

39   The Medieval and the Modern in Shin Buddhism   1033
     James C. Dobbins

40	Rethinking Acculturation in the Postmodern World 1082
	Michihiro Ama

41	Nenbutsu and Meditation: Problems with the Categories of Contemplation, Devotion, Meditation, and Faith 1089
	Lisa Grumbach

Index of Personal Names 1103

Introduction: Brill Critical Readings on Pure Land Buddhism in Japan

The leading Pure Land scholar James Dobbins stated the following in a 2006 review of an innovative book which already at that time aimed to disrupt certain reified ideas of what was supposed to constitute the Pure Land aspect of Buddhist traditions:

> In some cases it [Pure Land] has appeared as a clearly defined and distinct tradition with parallels to the Hōnen-Shinran model. In other cases Pure Land has operated as an amorphous and open-ended collection of themes without a cohesive center. It is as if the Pure Land discourse can function as an open semantic field in which a wide variety of beliefs, doctrines, and religious claims can plant their meaning. And yet, for all its definitional problems, we still seem to recognize Pure Land Buddhism when even a few of its symbols or motifs appear in proximity to each other.[1]

As Dobbins explicated, the latest scholarship has illuminated Pure Land traditions—best understood in the plural, like other aspects of Buddhism(s)—as a layered, convoluted arena of imaginaries and practices, a cloud of texts, languages, concepts, ideas, persons, and institutions, held together only by a number of floating signifiers. Pure Land is, in other words, a diffuse polyvocal semantic field, situated inside the similarly diffuse polyvocal semantic field which might be called the Buddhosphere. It is the dimension of variability and interpretive flexibility which the selections for this Brill series aim to accentuate.

Before overviewing the contents, several preliminary reminders might be helpful. Pure Land traditions were extremely important to people in many southern and eastern parts of premodern Asia for nearly two millennia. However, they have a history of being relatively poorly intelligible to non-Asians (especially "Westerners," i.e. observers from the Euro-American

---

1 James C. Dobbins, review of Richard K. Payne and Kenneth K. Tanaka, eds., *Approaching the Land of Bliss: Religious Praxis in the Cult of Amitābha* (Kuroda Institute Studies in East Asian Buddhism 17) Honolulu: University of Hawai'i Press, 2004), in *Japanese Journal of Religious Studies* 33.2 (2006): 417–18. The Kuroda Institute volume contained three essays which already represented the movement to complicate perceptions of Pure Land in Japan (by Stone, Sanford and Jaffe) which in deference have not been selected for reprinting here.

© KONINKLIJKE BRILL NV, LEIDEN, 2020 | DOI:10.1163/9789004401501_002

traditions), because in addition to the general problems these non-Asians may have with appreciating Buddhist onto-epistemologies and psychologies, Pure Land lays traps for the unwary:

1) Appreciation of Pure Land challenges some problematic and unresolved conventions in modern Buddhist studies as a whole: limited attention to issues of semiotics, rhetoric, discourse, and sociological imaginaries, as well as aspects of recent psychology which do not line up with mindfulness theory; and in comparison, over-attention to approaches rooted in (Western) religious studies and analytical philosophy. Such preconceptions contribute to insufficient attention being given (with tantric studies as a partial exception) to the inconsistencies which appear almost anywhere under the conventional heading "Buddhism," conflicts which were reflected in ancient controversies within the Buddhosphere itself about the extent to which it is unified. (A related net of issues occurs around *upāya*, the educative forms of communication which mediate between the worlds of ordinary and enlightened consciousnesses.) The concept of the floating signifier is particularly useful: in the formulation of critical theorist Fredric Jameson, this refers to a term "susceptible to multiple and even contradictory interpretations," lacking a specific meaning itself, but functioning "primarily as a vehicle for absorbing meanings that viewers want to impose upon it."[2]

2) Pure Land, at least before the nineteenth century arrival of Christian missionizing in East Asia, had nothing to do with Near Eastern monotheisms at all. Although the notions of an "agency" in some kind of cosmic realm providing hope and help have a surface resemblance to Christianity or Islam, they were (at least for Buddhist elite thinkers) instead entirely rooted in Buddhist philosophical and imaginative fields and assimilated to Mahāyāna theories of knowledge concerning ultimate non-duality and non-discrimination.

3) Unfortunately, however, in the "gift" mode especially (see below), the structure of the Pure Land mythos has left it vulnerable to textbook caricature along the lines of "salvation in Amida's Paradise" which can be misleading about the deeper meanings. In modern Western-language presentations, literal translationese such as "paradise," "faith," "salvation," and so on has become widely routinized, often creating an impression that the mythopoetics and symbolics of Pure Land rhetoric were received by Asians quite literally. Consequently Pure Land has been brought confusingly into ongoing Christian-based debates about whether the term

---

2 See entry on "floating signifier" in Oxford Reference's *A Dictionary of Critical Theory*, (2019), accessed online February 2019.

INTRODUCTION 3

"faith" can effectively serve as a meaningful cross-traditional category among religions, whether "religion" is a Western construct or not, how far religions are actually comparable with each other, and so on. The selections chosen for these Brill volumes cannot escape these embedded conventions either, and so readers are encouraged to grit their teeth and to try hard to look past the normal English semantics of such terminology.

4) Superficial caricature about "birth in paradise" or even "Buddhahood in this body" also leads to under-appreciation of the complexity of the developments which come under the Pure Land heading. Certainly there is a corpus of relatively distinctive "purely doctrinal" material in this sphere of Buddhism, which draws in classical Buddhological disciplines such as philology. Above that, however, emerges a not-so-easily-coherent range of other themes, including institutional formations, power politics, socioeconomic evolution, historiographical prejudices, visual arts, multiple effects of modernization, and even "diasporic" Japanese Buddhism. The "bare" original mythos hints at only a fraction of how these phenomena evolved.

5) In Japan there is a vast amount of Pure Land material, composed in registers academic and popular, new and old, and both insider and outsider, and accumulated over the entire history of the country. Modern Japanese academic scholarship in Pure Land, as in other branches of its Buddhist studies, has been stimulated since the Meiji period by contact and challenge from Western research into traditions of several kinds, in areas ranging from the philology of the texts to institutional history to sociology. Thus, although less well recognized by the non-Japanese-language world public than other streams of Buddhism(s), the range and importance of Pure Land in Japan has made it the subject of a substantial body of academic literature in Western languages (especially English). At present, however, this material tends to be scattered and inadequately consolidated, in ways which limit an improved comprehension of Pure Land. Perception is also conditioned by embedded Japanese historiographical orientations, particularly the persistent modern cultural nationalist tendency to construct Japanese Culture in ways that over-unify or homogenize it and underrepresent its diversity. For such reasons Pure Land studies in the West have found themselves confined within a bit of an academic island (or ghetto) out of the mainstream. On the Japanese side this has produced a thread of running complaints in the twentieth century about "Western" relative disinterest to Pure Land, constituting almost a genre in itself! Still, it seems accurate to note that one of the paradoxes of world Buddhism over the last century is that the aspect of Buddhism which modern Japanese themselves have continued to treat as

probably the most vital and interesting—the Pure Land imaginary represented in the Shin school—has been found by non-Japanese to be the least important and interesting.

6) The special historical size and success of one particular phenomenon—the tradition(s) under the heading of Jōdoshinshū (for short known as Shinshū or Shin)—have long tended to overpower perceptions of the other aspects of what can be called Pure Land in Japan. These institutions had more members and influence, gathered more money, produced more literature and scholarship, interacted more heavily with government, and in the twentieth century even spread overseas more. This school has had a long tradition of distinctive self-consciousness (loosely "sectarianism") and self-promotion, and a long-developed proprietary personality including a "guild"-like leadership class and a unique intellectual system replete with abstract thought and terminology whose relationship to the larger world of Buddhism(s) is not necessarily transparent.

7) This Shin dominance has contributed to a characteristic pattern of hermeneutical pressures in the presentation of Pure Land. In the purely academic realm, where Japanese scholarship (which is generally followed by Western scholarship) excels in historical research and "first order" description and rendition of material, the representation of Pure Land has had difficulties taking distancing critical steps. Apologist insiders have often not been their own best exponents, for their conventions of literal exposition of doctrinal language outside original contexts have a tendency to get caught up in textualism and scholastic detail, imposing an insider perspective even when addressing general audiences in non-Japanese languages. While no one would label Shin Buddhism a "cult," it tends to be committed to a "proprietary universalism" based on its own sense of unique language which can be willing to minimize modern intellectual hybridization and larger (trans-Japanese) intellectual accessibility. As with the translationese problem, the selections chosen for these Brill volumes cannot escape these environments, implicit or explicit; readers are encouraged to keep them in mind.

Introducing the Thematic Categories

While emphatically recognizing Dobbins's comment about an "open" semantic field, still for heuristic purposes two loose primary clusters in Pure Land can be identified: one dealing with the sensibility of "gift" (either deferred or involuntary); and one in tantric-like mode typically proposing the possible "availability of Buddhahood in this very body."

INTRODUCTION

Buddhist Transformation as a "Gift" (Especially of Deferral): For millennia Buddhisms usually thought "enlightenment" (cognitive disentrapment) was hard—exceedingly hard, and extraordinarily rare. From a very early stage arose a sense that somehow gifts of help were needed: the present activity of some Buddhas. (For outsiders to the traditions, the symbol "Pure Land" in this context is itself somewhat of a misnomer, a misdirection pulling attention away from the core underlying issue of "gift.") A widespread vision of obtaining this help emerged as an orientation to some "rebirth" (karmic transfer) over to a realm, other than this present Earth, where the influence of Buddhas would be available. The commonest version involved the concept of a Pure Land presided over by a Buddha named Amitābha, who had, according to the relevant mythos presented in three central Pure Land sutras, made a series of conditions relating to how the "persons" (karmic streams) of followers could be "born" (transferred) to a "place" in which the eventual achievement of full enlightenment under favorable circumstances was promised. One Sanskrit term for this hope was *buddhānusmṛti* (recollection of the Buddha, thinking on the Buddha, keeping the Buddha in mind), a term rendered into Chinese as "*nienfo*" (念仏) which was eventually pronounced "*nembutsu*" or "*nenbutsu*" in Japanese. As this form of Buddhist imaginary developed, the sensibility regarding some kind of hopeful (or realized) "gift" along these lines remained broad, serving as only the beginning of discussion and controversy about technical detail and interpretation, lineages of authority, psychological nuances, and inner contradictions. There was a historical shift, especially in East Asia, toward simplification and popularization of practice (especially toward the notion of *nembutsu* as a mere vocal recitation of the Buddha Amitābha's name), but the exact nature of best practice remained a source of debate. In terms of social history the Pure Land "gift" idea created openings for Buddhist practice that was relatively more open to householder nonmonastics, but in other cases could remain ritually engaged, contemplatively active, or even discipline-focused. For the intellectual elites, these ideas remained related to neither Christianity nor some kind of ontological reification, but concerned deferral, meditation, or involuntariness within purely Buddhist notions of conventional versus ultimate realities.

Western expectations have tended to resonate with a generalized authority claim—one which tends to be pervasive throughout non-Pure Land worlds of Buddhist discourses even in Asia—that the disentrapments with which elite Buddhisms are ideally concerned are matters which can be more or less controlled or directed by conscious or structured intention. Although the issues of control and authority embedded in this claim only simmer below the surface through most of the Buddhosphere, they explicitly rose above the surface in the "gift" sectors of Japanese Pure Land. Though it can be mentioned only in passing (it remains so far an undeveloped area of comparative study), skepticism regarding the extent of intentional authority over consciousness is congruent with sectors of modern cognitive psychology which offer perspectives alternative to mindfulness research.

It should be emphasized that partial agnosticism about the Pure Land mythos is widely characteristic of its interpretation in *modern* Japan under the influence of common-sense science. Since the twentieth century, it is one matter to take Buddhist philosophical issues seriously or to tangle with psychological conundrums about intentional control over the mind, but it is something different to continue to work with an *upāya* according to which the ultimate solution is karmic transfer to an imaginational realm inhabited by an Amida Buddha who will eventually show the way. Contemporary intellectuals in Japan, no less than non-Japanese would be, are aware that this tension must be dealt with by an agnosticism in which older visions of the Pure Land as an in some sense "real" transitional realm decline in significance, along with premodern classical notions of life-to-life karmic continuity.

The Pure Land as a This-Worldly Possibility: The other major cluster of interpretations, associated variously with T'ien-tai (Tendai) philosophy, or Chan or Zen "mind-only" teachings, or tantrism and esotericism, instead incorporated the Amitābha or Amida Buddha less as a figure from the three major Pure Land sutras than as another generalized or alternative representation of Mahāyāna Buddhist teaching. For these versions of the imaginary, the vision of some transformation into a Pure Land was typically situated in this present world. They had wide-ranging interaction with popular or folk modes of religion in Japan.

In any case, Japan was the locus of an at least to some extent distinctive historical evolution which appeared out of this pan-Asian aspect of Buddhism(s). For these volumes, the compiler has made choices about what can be seen as key foci, with some eye to identifying a few of the important writers and scholars, but recognizing that any single selection can only offer one more or less idiosyncratic, fragmentary tranche. Furthermore, some areas remain neglected in scholarship despite the expanding English literature, such as the Tokugawa period, or the Pure Land traditions outside the Shinshū, or the collaborations with the Japanese governing regime in the early half of the twentieth century. Other topics are shortchanged for reasons of space, such as a focus on original Pure Land texts themselves or the influences of the Pure Land imaginary on medieval Japanese literature or on visual arts. Also, the inner complexities of the particularistic Shinshū doctrinal tradition have been mostly set aside here: while this plays a weighty role for a significant number of Japanese, as previously hinted it is also scholastic, easily opaque for outsiders, and full of

INTRODUCTION

persistent linguistic challenges involving language, text and translation. Users of these volumes will speedily find paths into that world if they so desire.

1 Useful Overarching Perspectives

Although hardly in the mainstream of modern Western religious studies thought, a number of non-Japanese scholars have intensely engaged with Pure Land. The best of these have long recognized that Pure Land is a loose mythic family which is not a "simplification" of Buddhism. Instead, rather than being an analytical philosophy, it has been instead about narrativity and hope, described as a transfer of "merit" from the Buddha. (Item #1 Gómez) Within Buddhist traditions themselves, despite being diffuse as a "school," Pure Land could be seen as a class of path (*mārga*) reflecting rich give and take regarding subitist ("sudden," uncontrolled) versus gradualist (accumulative, discipline-oriented) versions of transformation towards awakening. Its developments in China, with their elements of inconsistency and contradiction, became the grist for thought afterwards in Japan. (Item #2 Blum)

2 Early Presence in Japan

Pure Land in Japan had its origins as part of the mixed repertoire of practices and teachings that characterized the Chinese and Korean monasteries from which Japanese Buddhism was imported.

Both inside and outside the monastery, in the Heian period the notion of *mappō*—a conception of historical long-term decline in the quality of Buddhist tradition—had a major effect, in ways that became peculiar to Japan, in stimulating efforts to develop counter-solutions to overcome the alleged decline (Items #3 and #4 Marra) Scholars have excelled in historical and textual surveys of this period. (Item #5 Rhodes) From the standpoint of religious "imaginaries," it is helpful to view Pure Land as a constructed discourse which was successful because it operated in varied registers or cognitive modes, including the logico-scientific and the narrative, the former including the famous *Ōjōyōshū* and the latter the biographies of individuals thought to have experienced Pure Land "rebirth." (Item #6 Rhodes) The Pure Land orientations had a long history of special affiliation with death because of the belief that karmic rebirth could be shaped at the last moment. Out of that interest, Pure Land became part of a whole medieval culture of deathbed practices, containing significant diversity including assimilations to esotericism. (Item #7 Stone)

3   Turn to the Nembutsu as the Sole Solution

Beginning in the Heian period certain lines of Pure Land started to break off from the conventional mixed programs of monastic-lay participation, producing interpretive shifts which made Japanese developments unique. In the modern period, and especially under the influence of the Shin school, Japanese historians trying to put a "progressive" spin on these developments in "transmission" have tried to view the changes through a populist teleological lens leading towards the later Shin position, but recent historians recognize that events were not so perfectly straightforward or linear. Each of the main characters—Genshin, Hōnen and Shinran—had complex and ambiguous relations with the doctrines which preceded them.

Hōnen (1133–1212) promoted the superiority of a vocal recitation of the Buddha Amida's name (*nembutsu*) as a kind of solution in the age of *mappō*. However, the discontinuity with his predecessor Genshin (942–1017) was significant. In its details, Hōnen's thought left numerous problematic, contradictory issues unresolved about the nature of the recitation he promoted. (Item #8 Andrews) Furthermore Hōnen's thought synthesized not only influences from the larger scriptural canon proper and the major Chinese Pure Land thinker Shantao, but also Buddhist popular piety as it was evolving inside Japan in the Heian period. (Item #9 Andrews) Regardless of doctrinal variations, historians have reached a consensus that the emergence and reception of Hōnen's thought reflected and then reinforced, albeit at first only very gradually, a kind of ground-bass authority-dispersing shift in the socio-economic environment of Japan. (Item #10 Repp)

4   Shinran's More Radical Turn to the Enlightenment Gift as an Involuntary Emergent Property

The eventual success of the Shin tradition, which originated in the ideas of Shinran (1173–1262), has tended to overpower other representations of Pure Land Buddhism in Japan and garner the largest amount of attention, even though Shinran's inventive semantics can be viewed as idiosyncratic against the larger field of historical Buddhism(s). In an effort to establish a different balance, it has seemed justified to underplay the representation of Shinshū among these selections.

Shinran's innovative idea of *nembutsu* has been the linchpin of that tradition and is reviewed in virtually every discussion of the doctrines. Shinran seemed to follow Hōnen on the surface, but the former held that self-consciously

INTRODUCTION

intentional recitation was not the point, since the speaking-out by the practitioner needed to express a spontaneous, involuntary upwelling of changed consciousness due to the "working" of Amida Buddha. The writings of the American scholar Alfred Bloom (1926–2017) established one kind of language for the expression of Shin teaching in English which has been a standard hermeneutical marker. (Item #11 Bloom) What must be emphasized is that behind Shinran was a particularly creative relationship with preceding thought which eventually led to an extensive body of distinctive Shin scholasticism (Item #12 Nasu).

5 Formation of a Major Institution: Honganji and Its Negotiations with Popular Consciousness

Shinran's biography and the formation of the Honganji institution based on him have been extensively presented in Japanese religious studies, as in the pioneering work of James Dobbins (Item #13 Dobbins). Spotlighted here is how even within the Honganji tradition(s), which developed into a relatively tight Japanese Buddhist lineage of ideas, negotiation with popular consciousness was necessary from an early stage. There was a significant degree of semantic floatiness below the level of the doctrinal elites despite a tendency in the twentieth century to make Whiggish representations which exaggerate the "modernity" of the earlier traditions. Despite Shinran's aversion, negotiation with the world of Shintō allowed the evolution of a number of accommodative attitudes towards kami among the early leadership. (Item #14 Rhodes) From the start, Shin memberships coexisted with, and often interacted with, popular cultic sites such as Zenkōji, thought to be the site of an actual living Amida Buddha mediating the Pure Land. (Item #15 Nasu) Shin Buddhism in practice depended economically on funeral ritual although the actual doctrinal status of death ritual was contradictory or situational. (Item #16 Blum) Below the elite levels, it has been often ambiguous what participants think concepts like the "Pure Land" really even mean. (Item #17 Amstutz) And it is similarly ambiguous what the doctrinal message to women, and their range of understandings, really was. (Item #18 Amstutz)

6 The Alternative Field: Pure Land Striven for in This World

Although the gift/hope/deferral cluster of Pure Land semantics has tended to obscure the view, the Tendai/Zen/tantric cluster also had a major presence at least in premodern Japanese history. Various scholars have demonstrated that the twentieth century notion of "progressive" Reformation-like Kamakura Buddhist movements was an exaggerated retrojection of twentieth century interests which underestimated both the persistence of earlier monastic Buddhism and how elements of the Pure Land imaginary were infused polymorphically into other aspects of Japanese religions. From the early days the monastic institutions had possessed a fringe element of itinerant Buddhist characters (*hijiri*) who performed various services for the population or for the monastic centers. Among the best known of these was Ippen (1234–1289), associated with a kind of popular dance and recitation which revealed the Pure Land as this very world. (Item #19 Foard) Pure Land elements were present in the Shingon sphere: explicitly tantric (*mikkyō*, *vajrayāna*) was a *goma* ritual formally classified as Shingon but devoted to the Buddha Amida/Amitābha (Item #20 Payne) Similarly there existed a hidden (*himitsu*) version of *nembutsu* teachings led by Shingon priests who appropriated Pure Land recitation to an immanentist, tantric practice monistically assimilating the Vairocana and Amida Buddhas to a vision of this world itself as the Pure Land (Item #21 Sanford) Thus it is easy to understand why in Hōnen's time, there were polemics against him from the monk Jōkei (1155–1213) who maintained that any hard oppositional rhetoric of self-power/easy practice (*tariki*, the gift/hope/deferral nexus) versus self-power/difficult practice (*jiriki*, intentional gradualism) was a dichotomizing oversimplification of the nuanced, blended thought which was actually cultivated in the older monastic schools. (Item #22 Ford)

In any case, diversity within this dimension of Buddhism was intrinsic and manifests fundamental internal contradictions: psychological discontinuities between the *tariki* and *jiriki* accounts, and qualitative gulfs between varying notions of the Pure Land. Yet one thing surely illustrated is a political principle: that whether a given Buddhist imaginary lives together with its contradictions in some kind of coexistence, or instead draws out, highlights, and expresses them via distinct institutions, depends on when participants historically come to feel that differences have to be shown in new forms of organization.

7 Pure Land Fellowships in War and Peace

The influential Honganji's teachings on "gift" had a corollary: a "political" semantics involving a distinctive sense of equal followership (*dōbō*) and institutional esprit de corps within its communities. The well-studied explosive growth of the institution began with the later proselytizer, organizer and adapter Rennyo (1415–1499), who along with Shinran has been one of the

INTRODUCTION

major figures in Pure Land history in Japan, described here by a mainstream scholarly insider. (Item #23 Yasutomi)

The combination of Rennyo's ideas and socio-economic change led to a following century-long episode involving *ikkō-ikki* (fighting fellowships seeking local autonomy in an anarchic period of governmental transition). The strengthening of the headquarters institution under militarized conditions in this period led to new ambiguities and inconsistencies as the emphasis on Honganji power per se became layered on top of the more idealized goals of the teachings of Shinran, so that the notion of Pure Land acquired a yet additional semantics of corporate identity. (Item #24 Solomon) Although this sociopolitical history can seem only tangentially "religious," it was the strength of the original Pure Land imaginary in the background which held the membership networks and communities together.

Institutionally speaking, the Tokugawa period was the most important for all Buddhist lineages in Japan including the Pure Land ones because of that era's officialized consolidation and mandatory membership performed under a kind of delimited surveillance by the bakufu government. Yet although participation in and influence of Pure Land was historically highest at this stage, it has also been the least represented in scholarship because of lack of historiographical consensus on the validity or quality of the Buddhist life in the period. Nevertheless, the Tokugawa was a crucial era of energy and diversity, shaped less by top-down government control than by the society-wide pattern of partition into compartmentalized functional roles (the *mibun* or "status" system) which characterized the regime, combined with Buddhist localism. Multiple such issues come together in the ways *eta* or burakumin communities interacted with Shin Buddhism (Item #25 Amstutz) By the end of the seventeenth century, Pure Land of various lines had reached a position of majority among the types of Buddhisms in Japan. Very importantly, a variety of non-Shin schools evolved post-Hōnen, including the Chinzei; these pursued various interpretations of *nembutsu* but unlike the Shinshū continued the organizational rule of monastic precepts. (Item #26 Dobbins) Meanwhile the Shinshū, which eventually enrolled about third of the entire population, developed a loose category of special exemplars who came to be known idiomatically as *myōkōnin* and who can be examined through the comparative religious and literary lenses of sacred biography (Item #27 Bathgate) In spite of Shin's relative tight official rhetoric, however, at the fringes its standard authority was challenged by secretive versions of Shinran's ideas which revealed the influence of the larger tantric Pure Land atmosphere which persisted despite being regarded as illegitimate by the Honganji. (Item #28 Chilson)

And diversity in the Pure Land imaginary in Japan actually increased during the Tokugawa period. Chinese Buddhism on the continent had long been characterized by co-existent practices of Chan (meditation) and Pure Land chanting ("devotional") routines. When this kind of program was brought to Japan by the late-arriving Ōbaku Zen school, it was criticized by the native Rinzai and Sōtō lines. (Item #29 Baskind) Or, far divergent from any normal practice, a figure like Shuichi Munō could emerge, formally a member of a Jōdōshu organization, but given to an atypical range of extreme austerities in diet, chanting, proselytization and sexuality. (Item #30 Groner)

8 Meiji and Modernity: Political Resettlement and Realignment, Moments of Intellectual Hybridization, Emigration, Collaboration, Postwar Progressivism, Lingering Conservatism

In the wake of the Meiji Restoration Japan underwent a huge, complex wave of political, economic and social changes to which all the Buddhist schools including the Pure Land ones had to react and adapt. Factors included a new governmental centralization, the rise to power of anti-Buddhist modernist Shintō ideologues, and the politicized invention of a conceptual category "religion" (*shūkyō*) which had not previously existed in Japan. These demanded that Buddhists find positions that suited the new configurations of power, especially decisions on new kinds of institutional activity (especially education) and collaboration with government. Additionally, Buddhist schools became aware, more or less acutely, of the fresh globalized intellectual fields dominated by "the West" which included Westernized Buddhological studies and general European philosophical traditions along with Christianity. This flood of modern concerns, far removed from the Heian, Kamakura or even Tokugawa periods, overturns any attempt to stereotype or caricature the stability of the Pure Land traditions. Intellectuals in the two large branches of Shinshū, Nishi (West) and Ōtani (East), into which Shin had been divided since the seventeenth century due to leadership conflict, reacted somewhat differently. The Ōtani side was conclusively changed by the thought of innovator Kiyozawa Manshi (1863–1903), who developed a kind of partial hybridization of Pure Land and Western language, arguably marking a new stage of diversity in Pure Land semantics under the label of "spirituality" (*seishinshugi*). (Item #31 Blum) On the Nishi side, the potential for accepting a new global imaginary for Mahāyāna Buddhism was tested by the scholar Murakami Senshō (1851–1929), with the eventual conclusion that the mainstream Shin institution could

INTRODUCTION 13

not accept that its teaching was fully identified with other Buddhist visions. (Item #32 Ward) Otherwise, from circa 1905 up to 1945, all Shin institutions (like other religions in Japan) engaged in heavy collaboration with the Japanese regime. (Item #33 Rogers)

Later twentieth-century scholarship in Japan developed a category known as Modern Buddhism which conceptually tended to fold the various traditions together. However, Pure Land remained distinguishable to a considerable extent, and in its relatively minimalist personal interiority, the most active version of "traditional" (i.e. non-New-Religion) Buddhism for the largest single bloc of the Japanese population has remained Shinshū.

Shinran's ideas, if not the Honganji headquarters institutions, have continued to have an influence on progressive thought, especially among postwar efforts to compensate for the era of collusion with the pre-World War II Japanese empire. (Item #34 Schepers)[3]

By the early twenty-first century, the Shin institutions retained a large membership but amidst a shrinking population and socioeconomic processes of community disintegration which had been underway since the 1950s. To some extent in common with other traditional lines of Buddhism, the leadership was occupied by an internal sense of crisis, a bad public image connected to the funeral business, embedded conflicts over austere versus folkish visions, and the challenges of new existential discourses, all of which produced a wide range of responses ranging from conservatism to accommodation to renewal. (Item #35 Borup) It was in that very recent context that close anthropological observation of modern Pure Land life finally arrived on the scene, with studies such as the role of ministerial family life in maintaining tradition. (Item #36 Starling) Insiders have voiced the complex ways Shin thinkers continue to struggle with ongoing losses in orientation to their tradition ("secularization") and with how to adapt the inherited material to changing needs. (Item #37 Dake)

At the elite levels, modern Pure Land thinkers by the beginning of the twenty-first century had found ways to negotiate key concerns like "gift," hope, and personal transformation (always against a background Mahāyāna theory of knowledge) but many remained bedeviled by the historically unavoidable attachment to the mythopoesis of Amida and the Pure Land as rendered by

---

3   And although no sample can be included here, yet another layer of "Pure Land" semantics was added in the twentieth century by certain leftist-oriented thinkers who assimilated the term to a "utopian" critical stance. See Melissa Anne-Marie Curley, *Pure Land, Real World: Modern Buddhism, Japanese Leftists, and the Utopian Imagination* (Honolulu: University of Hawai'i Press, 2017).

Shinran. Contemporary followers may take these terms as "symbolic," not substantively literal, but the tension between these options goes far back in time, perhaps to the founder himself, and thus interpretation continues to be twisty, diverse, and influenced by religious studies ideas originating in the West (Item #38 Tanaka) In a related manner, historians have struggled with the tension between an objective Shinran of the historians and the apologetic urge to exaggerate his modern qualities. (Item #39 Dobbins)

Finally a nod needs to be given to Pure Land as a piece of Japanese Buddhism that along with Zen has had a significant international reach (especially formerly at the mid-twentieth century mark), but in its instance due to Japanese migration to the Western Hemisphere. (Item #40 Ama) This movement can be described as acculturation, but it has also created a historically unprecedented context in which are manifested newly emergent problems, concerns and meanings. In the American environment, disputes about the proper role of meditation have encouraged a reevaluation of historical ideas and practices ("contemplation," "devotion," "ritual," "nembutsu") while potentially re-emphasizing Shinran's radicalism. (Item #41 Grumbach)[4]

At the risk of repetition, it might be stressed again that the sophistication of what has taken place in Pure Land Buddhism in Japan—while specific in philosophical fundamentals and historical details, and attuned to Japanese conditions alone and thus not paralleled in any other country—should in its complexity be seen as approaching par with the adaptive histories of Near Eastern monotheisms. It has been a layered theater of great activity, in the long view just the latest manifestation of old processes of trying to make long-inherited imaginaries work for human beings in constantly altering circumstances. In any case, this Pure Land has been a far cry from what might be initially suggested to the naïve who encounter phrases like "salvation through Amida's Paradise" in an introductory textbook.

---

4 And while again no sample can be included here, in North America, particularly due to World War II internments of Japanese persons, a unique additional layer was added to "Pure Land" semantics involving the politics of citizenship and ethnic identity. See Duncan Ryūken Williams, *American Sutra: A Story of Faith and Freedom in the Second World War* (Cambridge: Belknap Press of Harvard University Press, 2019).

PART 1

Useful Overarching Perspectives

∵

Buddhism as a Religion of Hope: Observations on the "Logic" of a Doctrine and Its Foundational Myth

Luis O. Gómez

> The gift, to be true, must be the flowing of the giver unto me, correspondent to my flowing unto him.
>
> R. W. EMERSON[1]

⁘

This paper is written from a perspective that may strike some readers as unusual. It was originally conceived as a public talk that began as an exercise in the interpretation of a religious narrative ("the myth of Dharmākara") but soon turned into an exercise in theological speculation.[2] Thus, by following my own thoughts I fell upon an exercise of the imagination that illustrated for me the close tie that exists between translating words and ideas and imagining sacred worlds.

As translation, the original lecture and the present paper are an attempt to understand a family of Buddhist beliefs that seems to baffle some interpreters of Buddhism. Although this family is often designated as "Pure Land Buddhism" or "the Pure Land tradition," it encompasses much more than what is regarded as "Pure Land" in East Asia and the West. I will retain the expression "Pure Land Buddhism," "Pure Land" for short, only because it is more convenient than a fully descriptive label. Expressed more accurately, the referent for these phrases would have to read something along the following lines: Pure Land Buddhism is a family of beliefs and practices associated with that genre of Buddhist texts that describes the purified buddha-fields, their constitution

---

Source: Gómez, Luis O., "Buddhism as a Religion of Hope: Observations on the 'Logic' of a Doctrine and Its Foundational Myth," in *Eastern Buddhist* 32(1) (2000): 1–21.

---

1 Ralph Waldo Emerson, "Gifts," in *Essays, Second series* (Boston and New York: Houghton, Mifflin and Company, 1975: 163. The first edition, 1844). One must take exception to the views expressed by Emerson further down the same page regarding the gift of "the Buddhist man" (163–64).

2 The talk was given in April 1983 at the Shin Buddhist Comprehensive Research Institute of Otani University in Kyoto.

and lay-out, and the conditions under which a human being can hope to reach such buddha-fields.

This family of beliefs has been represented in various ways throughout the history of Buddhism. Although the scholarly literature of the modern age has tended to conflate "Pure Land," "Amidism," and "Shinshū belief," they are not synonymous (and the second is problematic at best). My use of a broad term and my loose use of "Pure Land" to refer to this diverse family of beliefs is meant to signal its common ground in a mythology that links the vows of Buddhas and Bodhisattvas, their saving grace and power, and the purification of buddha-fields. This is the common ground for a constellation of beliefs that includes a wide variety of Amitābha-Amitāyus beliefs and practices, similar systems focusing on other Buddhas (e.g., Maitreya and Bhaiṣajyaguru), as well as lesser known, mostly literary witnesses to similar beliefs. By referring in this essay mostly to the mythology of the *Larger Sukhavativyüha*, I do not wish to imply that there are no important differences among various members of this larger family of Buddhist beliefs.

Ironically, our understanding of Pure Land Buddhism has been hampered by the putative proximity or similarity of its beliefs and practices to Western notions of divinity, paradise, and salvation. And, with the first person pronoun in the phrase "our understanding" I refer to both Western and East Asian interpreters. The Western observer tends to dismiss Pure Land Buddhism as not quite "Buddhism," and too much like "Christianity." Japanese Pure Land Buddhists spend much energy trying to distance their theological discourse from that of their Christian brethren.

But even a sympathetic reading of Pure Land Buddhism must face some difficulties in the conception of Pure Land faith. One can recognize and address sympathetically both its parallels and its fundamental differences with respect to systems of belief that may be called "theistic" (and these would have to include much more than just Christianity). Yet one is left with some puzzlement. It is not that Pure Land Buddhism is less (or more for that matter) consistent than other systems of religious belief, theistic, non-theistic, or of other types. Rather, my point is that certain problematic or baffling points of doctrine are seldom examined in part because so much energy is spent in distancing Pure Land from Buddhism, as well as from Christianity.[3]

---

3 Simplistic identifications with forms of Christian belief have not helped. Alexandro Valignano, a Jesuit visitor to Japan in 1579, claimed that Japanese Pure Land Buddhists "hold precisely the doctrine which the devil, father of both, taught to Luther" (*Re-visioning "Kamakura" Buddhism*, ed. by Richard Payne [Honolulu: University of Hawai'i Press, 1998], 101). The idea goes back to a letter (1571) of Francisco Cabrai, according to Florenz ("Die Japaner," in *Lehrbuch der Religions-Geschicht*, ed. by P. D. Chantepie de la Saussaye [Tübingen:

Regardless of its possible connections or similarities to other systems of belief, Buddhist or non-Buddhist, a series of problematic polarities coalesce in the Pure Land system of belief.[4] These include the following: (1) the coexistence of notions of merit with concepts of grace, (2) belief in the inevitability of suffering next to an expectation of redemption (or, rather, to be more accurate, assurance of salvation), and (3) ascetic ideals of liberation coupled with an avowed confidence in the existence of a power that can and will rescue the suffering person. Additionally, at the level of imagery, ideals that presume a denial of, or an escape from, worldly aims are placed next to or expressed by way of images of bliss and comfort that are less than ascetic.[5]

Mohr, 1925], vol. 1, 398). Formal parallels were recognized in a more generous vein by the Swiss theologian Karl Barth (1886–1968). In a long footnote in vol. 1, part 2 of his *Kirchliche Dogmatik* (3rd ed. Zollikon-Zürich: Evangelischer Verlag a.g., 1945: 372–77; English version *Church Dogmatics*, ed. by G. W. Bromiley and T. F. Torrance [New York: Charles Scribner's Sons. Vol. 1, 2, 1956], 340–44), he claimed that Pure Land Buddhism was the only parallel to Reform theology outside Christianity—most likely because he was not cognizant of Hindu and Muslim parallels. His opening remarks are worth quoting, because they show how complex and subtle was the mind of this theologian even at a juncture where his apologetic agenda is transparent: "We can regard it as a wholly providential disposition that as far as I can see the most adequate and comprehensive and illuminating heathen parallel to Christianity, a religious development in the Far East, is parallel not to Roman or Greek Catholicism, but to Reformed Christianity, thus confronting Christianity with the question of its truth even as the logical religion of grace (*konsequente Gnadenreligion*)." [The word "heathen" is in quotation marks in the German edition, but not in the English.] Barth appears to confuse Francisco Cabrai with his more famous namesake, Francis Xavier (loc. cit.); Barth does not cite his sources. I could not find a similar notion in the writings of Francis Xavier (Francisco Javier, *Cartas y escritos de San Francisco Javier*. Unica publicación castellana completa según la edición crítica de *Monumenta historica Soc. Jesu*, 1944–1945. Anotada por el padre Félix Zubillaga, S.I. 2nd ed. [Madrid: Biblioteca de Autores Cristianos, 1968]).

4   I use the phrase "system of belief" loosely, and as shorthand for "a constellation of families of belief and practice." I do not mean to imply that these beliefs or practices formed part of or derived from a complete or closed theological system (I am not sure such systems can exist in the strict sense of the phrase). Needless to say, at several points in the history of Pure Land Buddhist beliefs, attempts have been made to systematically consolidate belief or to close the system.

5   Here, as in the title of the paper, I use "foundational myth" to indicate the narratives and tropes that the tradition sees as its foundational event. There is no implication that I regard these narratives, or the texts in which we find them today, as the true or ultimate origin of the tradition. Furthermore, as I shall explain in more detail below, I use the word "myth" as a loose term for those aspects of belief and doctrine that are constituted by narratives or imaginal depictions of sacred events. I call these myths whether they are seen as "foundational" (that is, as the first or pivotal events that form the groundwork for the tradition's conviction that it carries the truth) or as "ideal" (that is, as descriptions of the way things will be or should be).

My effort at understanding these dichotomies is, at best, preliminary and schematic. A baffling belief, an apparently contradictory set of beliefs, or an apparently irrational belief does not yield meaning readily, and usually calls for a variety of analytical strategies. In this paper I will outline what I believe is one possible strategy, one that stands critically outside the tradition, yet attempts to understand what makes the tradition meaningful from within. This I call the clarification of the "inner logic" of the belief system.[6]

This interpretation is in part motivated by a strong interest in communication across cultures—partly for professional reasons, partly for reasons of life experience. In the context of such experiences and explorations I have adopted a hypothesis about the relationship of theology to culture that seems to me the most reasonable despite the difficulties inherent to any attempt to test it. This hypothesis postulates a hierarchy of meaning (not necessarily of value) between culture and theology. I propose that the complexities of communication, translation, and interpretation and the problems that attend these processes are superordinate on problems of "theological" interpretation, understood both as exegesis and scholarly clarification.

This working hypothesis is shaped to a great extent by a conception of doctrine (including cases where doctrine is coextensive with text) as both cultural artifact and human engagement (the two notions are not mutually exclusive). This conception can be applied to Pure Land belief systems in the following schematic way. A belief in the power of a Buddha's solemn promise entails a commitment that engages a person's behavior (and potentially the imaginal objects upon which they place their trust and hope). But such engagement is possible because the beliefs (narratives, confessional statements, ritual acts) are part of a cultural world the reality of which is beyond question. That is to say, the cultural world of belief is, like a ritual object, a concrete artifact in human imagination. The artifact is only partly represented by the text (as book, performance or recitation). It is also present in the mental landscape and the discourse of believers. For an outsider to grasp the full implication and the subjective meaningfulness of the belief and the practice, this outsider must come to understand the logic of this imaginal world.

---

6 Here too I use the terms loosely: I am not talking of a formal logic or a syllogistic necessity; rather I refer to the way in which the tradition sees certain steps in the narrative itself, and subsequently in its interpretation, as somehow necessary or as somehow "making sense" as events or arguments that call for certain beliefs. This particular use of "logic" is accepted in modern English, and is illustrated in part by the following quotations from the definition of "logic" in the tenth edition of the *Merriam-Webster's Collegiate Dictionary* (1998): "interrelation or sequence of facts or events when seen as inevitable or predictable."

As a philologist, I am interested in texts and in trying to understand what texts mean in a particular historical context. In spite of my belief that the Buddhist tradition has much to commend itself, the relevance of Buddhism is no reason for erasing the historical and geographical differences that exist within the tradition and between this and other traditions. Moreover, and this may be more crucial, understanding cannot take place if one ignores the cultural gaps that separate believers among themselves and believers from non-believers. These are gaps that occur in actual time and space, as well as in the imaginal spaces of culture and habit.

I therefore consider the following a useful corollary to my main working hypothesis: Buddhist values and beliefs exist in cultural contexts that may be radically different from my own, and hence my inability to understand them may be rooted in deep cultural differences. This is only a hypothesis, and I am willing to discard it if the evidence points elsewhere. But it is a reasonable hypothesis that also entails the possibility of incommensurable worlds—that is, the possibility that my world and that of the believer simply cannot meet. Incommensurability can also take a stronger form. This stronger form is as follows: even if I were to adopt wholeheartedly one of these beliefs, immersing myself in the culture that produces, maintains, and holds it, abandoning all contact with my own culture, even then I would still be unable to penetrate fully the meaning of the doctrine.

For lack of space I cannot explore here my preferred view of incommensurability, which is the following. I believe I can never fully penetrate even the meanings of my own culture, let alone those of other cultures. But this impossibility in fact reveals the fallacy of imagining culture as fully realized or as a bounded, discreet and stable entity. Culture—and religion as a cultural phenomenon—is constantly recreated. In a manner of speaking, culture is recreation of meanings. Culture cannot be abstracted from the struggle of individuals and subgroups to make sense of a vast pool of preconceptions and symbols whose meanings not only exist in potency, but actually most likely simply do not exist until they are understood and turned into human behaviors. Thus, culture is always simultaneously emerging, diverging and converging, and no single individual or group can claim to grasp (possess or understand) the totality of the process.

I believe such cultural reflections must also shape the task of the theologian. I am assuming that the moment theologians feel the impulse to explain, clarify or rationalize doctrine, they are thereby recognizing the degree to which religion, as part of culture, is ephemeral and evasive. Similarly, the effort to understand theologically should be seen in some ways as a symptom of the barriers that stand between individuals and between cultures, as well as within an individual's multiple readings of the religious tradition upon which that individual lays a claim.

Needless to say, the theological enterprise is also hermeneutical, not only in that it attempts to understand a tradition as the intentions of an ancestral mind, or the intentions of other living individuals, authoritative or heretical. Theology also tries to make sense of a changing world, and hence part of the frustration of the theological enterprise is built into the virtually impossible task of preserving beliefs that claim relevance for all human circumstances at all times, but were produced by some human beings at a particular time.

Hence, at all levels of theological discourse one is faced with a constant need to respond—that is, not "reply," but respond—accounting for the tradition and the world by some sort of adaptation. In this sense communication with a tradition (and between cultures) shares some elements with communication between individuals within a given culture. Effective interpersonal communication at the level of social equals often requires that one person walk halfway to the other person even as the other person walks halfway towards the first person. When this type of interaction takes place, communication is transformation.

When this model of communication is applied to religion, even the work of the historian becomes one of persuasion—to say nothing of the work of the theologian. Persuasion need not be irenic or gentle, but the suasive function of interpretation is inherent to the process of understanding. And I would argue that this is true whether the speaker (writer) is claiming to use "critical" methods or is attempting to read his doctrinal or cultural meanings with a method claiming to be totally neutral (as the so-called phenomenological understandings were supposed to be). I would go even further and argue that in this sense any process of interpretation in religion is inevitably a process of theological persuasion.

In making sense of another, the interpreter is transformed—at the very least interpreters attempt to transform each other. If the object of interpretation is a tradition and the representatives of that tradition are trying to make themselves understood, they too will be transformed. And, I repeat and expand, transformation is not necessarily gentle or voluntary, and is seldom fully conscious.

The original audience for this paper included many persons who were not historians of Buddhism but Shinshū believers and theologians.[7] Hence I felt

---

7   The word "theology" is here shorthand for "committed systematic reflection on religious doctrine and practice." This means mat in my view "theology" is an adequate word to connote a peculiar use of human imagination and rational thought that is committed, religious, and

a special need to include these preliminary reflections on my particular approach to the interpretation of religious doctrines. This approach assumes certain notions that are not commonly used by committed interpreters of Buddhism. These include notions that derive from the general history of religions, and also concepts of religious language and symbol. In that sense, they may be notions that are purely scholarly, and not wholly intelligible to believers. I propose that such notions may be helpful to the committed believer, as well as to the professional scholar. I now leave this preliminary note and focus on the question of the interpretation of Pure Land Buddhism.

For a significant period in the history of the contemporary scholarly study of Buddhism, doctrine was privileged as the only key to understanding Buddhist belief and practice. Even when the importance of ritual and devotion was recognized, the philosophical framework of the literate tradition was assumed to be the only way to understand religious feeling, belief, and practice. This period in Buddhist scholarship is now finished among the specialists, but the effects of the earlier attitude linger on. Furthermore, believers have yet to begin appreciating the potential value of rethinking religion as something more than doctrine and belief.

Westerners tend to emphasize the critical and ascetic elements of Buddhism. For many Western observers, Pure Land is not consistent with this elite philosophical dimension of the tradition. Many perceive Pure Land as a "simplification" of Buddhism, or, at best, a concession to those unable to practice meditation. One purpose of this paper is to argue against that position.[8]

Now there are some good reasons for this Western understanding of Buddhism. I think it is undeniable that Buddhism produced several systems

---

systematic. It is committed because it is carried out by a person who feels and expresses a sense of fealty to the tradition that is the object of this sort of thought. It is systematic, because it seeks an ordering of doctrine and practice that will be cogent, comprehensive, and rationally elegant. It is to be distinguished from philosophy only by the degree of the thinker's explicit commitment to a particular doctrinal frame, and from confessional discourse by the degree of critical or rational reflection on the doctrinal system.

8   I made similar arguments many years ago, but within the context of a book review, and my apologia may have been misconstrued as a criticism ("Shinran's Faith and the Sacred Name of Amida," in *Monumenta Nipponica*, 38–1, Spring 1983: 73–84, which was followed by a rejoinder by the authors of the book reviewed, Ueda and Hirota, in *Monumenta Nipponica*, 38–4, Winter 1983: 413–17, and Gómez's surrejoinder: 418–27). My remarks were critical insofar as they questioned the way in which Mahāyāna doctrines have been frozen or fossilized on the basis of particular readings of selected Indian *śāstras*. This standardization of orthodoxy, which began in India itself, is only one set of readings of Buddhist practice and belief. It ignores the potential for growth and creativity suggested by the imagery of the sutras and by actual Buddhist belief and practice.

of critical philosophy. Buddhism, like other philosophies that developed at the same time, was a system or family of systems that questioned traditional beliefs. Such questioning, we believe, resonates with modern agnosticism. Whether this identification is anachronistic or not is not as crucial as the fact that we imagine classical Buddhism as a demythologized system of beliefs and practices. (There are of course other elements of Buddhism, but at this point I am concentrating on this aspect.) To conceive of Buddhism as only a philosophy, or as only a critical philosophy, is to misunderstand the theological functions of critical theology. But there is such a critical element, and I want to underline that first.

Paul Mus used to discuss the outline of the *Upaniṣads* in the following way. He understood the conception of the *ātman*, or the self, as an extended (or social) self, and the *Upaniṣads* were then seen as a critique of this notion of self. So the Brahmanic theory would be one in which the social self was emphasized, and the *Upaniṣads* were a critique of that notion, still conceived, of course, in mystical-religious terms. Mus argued, furthermore, that Buddhism was a religious and social manifestation of this same critique.[9] One could further develop these ideas by suggesting that, as a critique of the individual self, Buddhism could be understood as consisting of two movements or two parts. One movement is the deconstruction of the self. This is seen in meditations such as the meditation on the body, in which the meditator imagines breaking up the self or the body into parts. There is also the transformation of the self, or the development of the self. In this case, the meditator reviews, visualizes, or constructs all the qualities of a Buddha or of buddha-like thoughts.

But a problem arises the moment you try to transform the self, or create a new self. This is done by moral progress or moral growth, or simply by ritual representation. Either way, one assumes a certain notion of building up the self. There is of course a tension between the deconstructive and the constructive process. Also in the notion of construction by moral development we get the idea or the metaphor of moral acquisition. In this practice, we see a repetition of the notion of a social self. The social self is constructed by acquiring life and property. In the same way you construct a religious or moral self by acquiring moral property, and this notion of acquisition of a moral self is expressed in India by the notion of merit (*puṇya*). In the same way that in society you

---

9 This summary of my teacher's views follows class notes from my graduate student days, but some of these ideas may be found in his later writings, such as "The Problematic of the Self— West and East and the Maṇḍala Pattern," in Charles A. Moore, ed., *Philosophy and Culture East and West: East-West Philosophy in Practical Perspective* (Honolulu: University of Hawai'i Press, 1962), 594–610.

become rich if you work hard, in the spiritual realm if you work hard you will acquire spiritual wealth, i.e. merit. This metaphor is common among religions of salvation (or human perfectibility), but it is especially strong in India.

Traditions do not always make explicit the parallels between the accumulation of wealth and growth toward spiritual perfection as a sort of accumulation of "goods." In fact, in the classical literature of Buddhism, the connection is seldom made even metaphorically, although in practice the parallel and the cause-effect relationship is obvious. Furthermore, the connection between accumulation and expenditure, having and giving, which takes a special importance in so-called "gift economies," is central to a number of Buddhist religious metaphors but is maintained only in an implicit form (wealth in merit increases the more you share the merit). However, it is not necessary to posit or prove an overlap between religious and economic meanings to understand that the metaphor of "merit" is structurally similar to common images of acquiring, losing, and giving wealth. Additionally, the giving of merit follows the rules that apply to gifts generally: it has no ultimate value, yet, in being given, it acquires infinite value.[10]

This complex set of metaphors plays an implicit role in Buddhism at two levels: a rhetoric of the emptiness of merit (or, no merit is the best merit), and a rhetoric of the accumulation of infinite merit. The first of these two doctrinal or rhetorical constructs is expressed in common renderings of the so-called "Perfection of Wisdom" or "Mādhyamika" dialectic. In these systems, the religious ideal is placed beyond all notions of acquisition. It is not that Mādhyamika philosophy exists in a disembodied state.[11] Rather, the issue is the rhetoric of Perfection of Wisdom literature and Mādhyamika, both of which tend to undermine the notions of merit and possession of merit.

But, another way of making this critique is by changing the order of time, in other words, by trying to express the time that is required for spiritual progress in paradoxical terms. So you can say, for example, that it would require an infinite time to acquire the merit you need, and that is one way of denying or rejecting the quantifiable notion of virtue. This is the second rhetoric of merit.

---

10   On the gift as a form of exchange that is homologous with or determinant of religious symbol and ritual, see Gerardus van der Leeuw, *Religion in Essence and Manifestation: A Study in Phenomenology*, trans. by J. E. Turner (London: G. Allen & Unwin, Ltd., 1938): sections 13–2, 50–1, 70, and 76–2, which discuss the power of the king, sacrifice, covenant, and the love of God respectively in relation to gifts.

11   See Gómez, "Two Jars on Two Tables: Reflections on the Two Truths," in Jonathan Silk, ed., *Wisdom and Compassion: The Buddhist Studies Legacy of G. M. Nagao* (Honolulu: University of Hawai'i Press, forthcoming).

Thus, I propose, for the sake of simplicity, two models of Buddhist critiques of quantifiable virtue. One of them is the negative way, which we may call the model of "zero merit." This is a way of saying that the process of "acquiring virtue" or becoming perfect is never quite mathematical, that it strives toward a dimension that is not a true dimension at all. Another way of expressing a similar idea is by saying that merit is quantifiable but in measureless amounts, which we may call the rhetoric of "infinite," or "measureless merit." This is the same thing as saying that the sacred becomes, under certain conditions, immeasurable—it cannot be reduced to any other quantity and thus becomes non-quantifiable. These are, I believe, not theological claims (though they may be read as such).[12] Rather they are claims regarding the logic of a certain type of religious rhetoric. These two approaches express the two extremes or ends of all numbers, at least poetically, if not mathematically.

The zero merit position is close to Mādhyamika or similar systems. In Japan, the Zen tradition sometimes comes close to this. The infinity position is found in some sutras, and I think this is an important point in the Pure Land tradition of India. Infinite merit is measureless merit. It has a quantity, its value is not zero, but it is not quantifiable. The Bodhisattva's path is supposed to lead to infinite merit. And the way to attain infinite merit is by giving up all merit.

The logic of this doctrine is based on the assumption that the greatest merit comes from detachment. It follows then that detachment from merit is the greatest merit. At some uncertain point in the history of Buddhism, it became a widely accepted belief that merit could be dedicated (invested, if you will) to a particular purpose. For instance, one had the hypothetical option of dedicating one's merit toward the attainment of buddhahood or to rebirth in one of the celestial spheres. But one could also opt to dedicate merit (including the merit derived from the ritual of dedication itself) to the benefit of other persons (parents, children, all sentient beings).

This ideal or imaginal process, which we would associate in a secular context with the culture of gift-giving, is called technically *puṇya-pariṇāmanā* (*ekō* 廻向 in Japanese). The second member of this compound (*pariṇāmanā*) already suggests change, as the term means "bringing to maturity." Hence, to dedicate merit means making it fructify. When one dedicates or hands over merit to a purpose, especially for the benefit of another, merit brings its fruit. In fact the greatest of all merits derives from abandoning merit. This is of course

---

12   And, needless to say, the concepts lend themselves for a variety of theological polemics. For instance, Christian theologians, and Buddhist scholars from a Christian background or persuasion, would insist that immeasurable and infinite are not synonymous. But I am not persuaded that the classical Buddhists would have made such distinctions.

BUDDHISM AS A RELIGION OF HOPE

a paradox, but I think it a beautiful and powerful paradox. One may think that it is hypocritical to say I give up merit to gain merit. But that is putting the emphasis on the wrong place, because it is not "I give merit to gain merit" but rather "I give merit."

The doctrine of merit transference has pervaded, in one form or another, all of Buddhism. It is however more closely associated with Mahāyāna and the origins of Mahāyāna. If we agree that most of Mahāyāna directs itself against the notion of quantifiable merit, men the ideal of Mahāyāna is somehow beyond merit, whether you express it as zero or infinity. But still the believer sees himself as separate from the ideal. Consequently it becomes necessary to explain somehow the mechanism or process that leads to enlightenment. So you can either say the ideal is beyond, or if you want to erase (this difference) and have sudden enlightenment, then the ideal coincides with reality. If you are speaking from the zero point of view, you can use expressions like "enlightenment is here and now." In the modality of the rhetoric or the dialectics of enlightenment, perfection is internal and in-mediate (non-mediated). This sort of rhetoric can be applied to images of the buddha-fields as well. This is done, for instance, in the *Vimalakīrti-nirdeśa*'s peculiar treatment of the myth of Abhirati, Akṣobhya's purified field. In this modality of the rhetoric or the dialectics of enlightenment, perfection is internal and in-mediate (non-mediated): the Pure Land is within you, and *only* within you. In this context "perfection" appears to be emptied of all forms of virtue and merit.[13]

But if we speak from the infinite point of view, we can say we share infinite merit. This is, I would argue, the underlying assumption of the *Smaller* and the *Larger Sukhāvatīvyūha Sūtras*. The underlying metaphor in these texts contrasts sharply with the metaphor of zero merit. Both expressions are somehow equivalent, but the choice of metaphor is different and that is significant.

The metaphor of infinite merit, furthermore, lends itself naturally for a narrative conception, a process image, of the attainment of buddhahood. It also highlights the gap between the imperfect and the perfect, the time lapse between the state of being imperfect and the achievement of enlightenment.

If we speak in terms of hope, then we are speaking of a person who conceives of himself or herself as a non-ideal person. Hope is in the future because it is indirectly the expression of imperfection. But hope sometimes demands that we explain how the ideal will become reality. And one way to do this is to argue that "the perfect" facilitates or bestows perfection on "the imperfect."

---

13   I use the phrase "appears to be" advisedly, because I am not completely persuaded that this is literally true. This peculiar form of the "rhetoric of immediacy" is, at least in the *Vimalakīrti*, clearly embedded in a broader argument about perfectibility and virtue.

This can make perfect sense as an extension of the notion of transference of merit. Transference appears to be a way to avoid the difficulties inherent to a doctrine of grace in a tradition that accepts the saving power of a "divinity" that is at the same time a human ascetic, and certainly falls short of being an all-powerful creator god. The situation is much more complicated than that, but this is not the place to explore this.

The actual or practical parameters of Buddhist belief are hard to discern. However, the literate tradition assumes that the roots of Buddhist doctrine are in the achievements of a human individual. This person, the Buddha Śākyamuni, pursued his self-interest (awakening), but, paradoxically, did so in the interest of others. When a Buddha experiences emptiness, he has experienced self-liberation. But most Indian Buddhist theologians were in agreement that emptiness was not enough. The expression *śūnyatā-karuṇā-garbha* ("that which has at its corse both emptines and compassion") was perhaps coined as shorthand for the claim that awakening and liberation are in essence a fusion of the vision of emptiness and a compassionate heart. To experience emptiness as self-liberation is not enough. A Buddha will also have to manifest that experience in compassion (*karuṇā*). To conceive of a Buddha without compassion is to conceive of only half a Buddha. An equally standard formula defines the efforts of the Bodhisattva as a quest for self-interest and other-interest. The first is cultivation of self and liberation resulting from a clear vision of emptiness—a realization of liberating power through knowledge. The second is regard for others, concern for their suffering, and effort toward the alleviation of that suffering.

The two ideals coalesce in a number of ways, but arguably the most important point of contact in the present context is the correspondence between liberation as "freedom from," realization as detachment, and saintly virtue as generous giving. To be free is, in one important sense, to be detached, to let go of everything, but to be fully compassionate is also to let go, to give away. As stated succinctly in Śāntideva's *Bodhicaryāvatāra* (III. 10–11):[14]

> 10. All bodies, property and merit that I have acquired in the past, the ones I have now, and the ones that I may acquire in the future, I surrender them all with indifference for the benefit of all living beings.

---

14   P. L. Vaidya, ed., *Bodhicaryāvatāra of Śāntideva*, Buddhist Sanskrit Texts, no. 12 (Darbhanga: The Mithila Institute of Post-Graduate Studies and Research in Sanskrit Learning, 1960), 39–40. The English translation is mine. For complete translation of this text, see Kate Crosby and Andrew Skilton trans., *The Bodhicaryāvatāra* (Oxford: Oxford University Press, 1996).

11. Nirvana means renunciation of all things, and my mind seeks this peace. If I must renounce all, it would be better to surrender it to all sentient beings.

Additionally, in terms of the metaphor of merit, we can also say that when one acquires infinite merit as the culmination of self-cultivation, one is able to share infinite merit as the culmination of concern for others. In terms of this pair of self and others, the metaphor of merit means that acquiring infinite merit is one's own salvation, and sharing infinite merit is rescuing others. Hence, merit transference is, at least theoretically, an expression of compassion. Even if merit may be seen as ultimately empty, its transference, motivated by compassion, is fruitful, effective, and beneficial.[15]

This brings us to two additional paradoxes, which are implicit in the sutras: if merit is measureless, it is already shared; if it is shared, it is measureless. Merit should be empty, and to be empty means to be shared. So that only shared merit is true merit or good merit. In this way the dialectic of emptiness and compassion is embodied in the ritual of transference, in the ethical implications of transference, and, above all, in the mythology of transference.

Now I would like to discuss briefly the myth of the Pure Land sutras, and how it connects with the notion of merit. In speaking about the myth, I will use the term in a slightly personal way. I am going to use certain terms that might be confusing. When I speak of metaphor or symbol, I mean something that stands for something else because of a certain similarity. However, "stands for" in the context of the literary and theological imagination often means "is the same as." If I connect symbols in a time sequence of descriptions and events, i.e., in a narrative, then I have myth. A myth is often like a tapestry. The way that the threads of a tapestry intertwine can be analyzed in two ways: (1) as static or structural, and (2) as dynamic. In the Pure Land sutras, we can speak of metaphors of grace and we can also speak of the logic of grace. In this context the "logic" is partly based on the doctrine of transference, but is also rooted in the narrative sequence of the myth. This means that "grace" is in this tradition both a ritual and a mythic category. This duality is embodied in the crucial term *prasāda* which means both the trusting disposition of the believer and the benevolent disposition of the Buddhas that grant salvation.

In the Pure Land sutras, the logic of grace is constructed with a narrative argument. The narrative is an argument of sorts. It is the story that makes

---

15 Speaking in comparative terms, "the gift" is empty of any value other than the transactional one. Giving away the gift is what turns it into a thing of value. Interestingly, in economics this is only really true of true monies.

possible, if not real, the connection between *prasāda* as trusting faith and *prasāda* as grace bestowing salvation. The conceptual and affective link is reinforced by the inner logic of the story. I will not spend time explaining the story of Dharmākara and Amitābha.[16] Rather, I will focus briefly on its "internal logic."

The logic of the myth is part of a system of beliefs that is not necessarily shared by persons outside the cultural world of the believer's presuppositions. Presuppositions refer to those ideas that would have been known and accepted by those who read or heard the sutras. These presuppositions are the following: (1) the Bodhisattva's vow; (2) the merit required to attain buddhahood, (3) the infinite merit (power, virtue) of a Buddha, and lastly, (4) belief in the existence of purified buddha-fields.

Each of these presuppositions needs a short explanation. First, (1) the notion of the Bodhisattva's vow was linked to notions about the power of words and the power of resolution. Second, (2) the merit upon which the attainment of buddhahood is based is incalculable. By the time the Bodhisattva pronounces the vow he is already more than just an ordinary human being, and the power of his resolution, as well as the incalculable length and difficulty of his practice, produce an even greater merit. Third, (3) it was a matter of course that Buddhas have infinite merit, that is, once they attain buddhahood, the effect of their past actions continues to be a source of sacred power. Fourth, (4) it was not enough to believe in the cosmology of the buddha-fields; for there to be a religion of Buddhism in this style, the believer had to hold the possibility that at least one buddha-field had been purified.

One can see in the sutras the following arguments that are based on these assumptions. First, there was the belief in what is called "an act of truth," and second the belief in the inherent truthfulness of the Bodhisattva as witness to his own virtue. The "act of truth" (*satya-kriya*) consisted of a statement in which a desired outcome or belief is caused or confirmed by a factual statement, without any implication or assumption that the two statements are related causally. For instance, one may say "As I am the son of my father, may my own son recover from this illness." This type of "moral" or "ritual" logic is found in cultures outside India as well. Related logical paradigms may be seen in prohibitive curses (e.g., "May the one who betrays me die an untimely death") and

---

16   This story can be found in Luis O. Gómez, trans., *The Land of Bliss: The Paradise of the Buddha of Measureless Light, Sanskrit and Chinese Versions of the Sukhāvatīvyūha Sūtras* (Honolulu: University of Hawai'i Press, 1996).

oaths (e.g., "May I die an untimely death, if I was the one who betrayed you," or "If I stole your horse, then I am not the son of my noble father").[17]

The order of such conditional statements varies. One could, for instance, declare "If I am the son of my father, then I am not the thief who stole your horse"—although a more idiomatic form in English would be, "As I am the son of my noble father, I have never touched your horse." Regardless of variants in the order (which may indeed express subtle nuances), they all have the following underlying logical structure: I state X. If X is true, then Y necessarily follows. Now, X is true, hence Y is true. The thematic or objective connection between X and Y is ultimately secondary or unimportant. The important connection is between the veracity of the first statement (which is usually undeniable) and the reality expressed by the proposition Y.

Additionally, the laws of this logic have been pushed one step further, especially in religious discourse: the quasi-deductive statements of the acts of truth do not distinguish clearly between the establishment of truth and the generation of reality. A concrete example of this use of the act of truth is Lokānanda's act of truth in Candragomin's version of the legend.[18] In an act of selfless generosity, Lokānanda has given away his wish-fulfilling crest-jewel, but, since this jewel was an inborn integral part of his body, he has had it cut out from his own skull and is on the verge of dying. Then he makes his act of truth, which may be paraphrased as follows: "If it is a fact that I have never regretted giving away the jewel, then let a new crest-jewel grow back."[19] Needless to say, a new jewel appears and the wound is miraculously healed.

The evident disjunction between content and power is seen in a well-known passage from *Milindapañha* studied by Eugene W. Burlingame.[20] The passage serves as a commentary on another classical story of a miracle wrought by an act of truth, the legend of King Śibi (Sivi), and the *Milindapañha* discusses

---

17   The connection between the secular and the sacred oath (the two are not easily distinguished) is discussed by van der Leeuw, *Religion in Essence and Manifestation*, section 59.2. See also Friedrich Heiler, *Erscheinungsformen und Wesen der Religion* (Stuttgart: W. Kohlhammer, 1961), 306 ff.

18   See Michel Hahn, trans., *Joy for the World: A Buddhist Play* (Berkeley, CA: Dharma Publishing, 1974).

19   Ibid., stanza 40.

20   V. Trenckner, ed., *The Milindapañho: Being Dialogues between King Milinda and the Buddhist Sage Nāgasena* (London: Williams and Norgate, 1880), 121–22. Eugene W. Burlingame, "The Act of Truth (*saccakiriya*): A Hindu Spell and its Employment as a Psychic Motif in Hindu Fiction," *Journal of the Royal Asiatic Society* (1917), 439–41. The story is also used by Heinrich Zimmer to illustrate Indian concepts of truth. See *Philosophies of India* (New York: Bollingen Foundation, 1951; Repr. Princeton, NJ: Princeton University Press, 1969, 1971), 160–69. Zimmer connects this ancient belief to Gandhi's notion of *satyagraha*.

the nature of the act of truth (*saccakiriya* in Pāli). It presents the following example.[21] King Aśoka once asked if anyone could make the waters of the Ganges flow against the current. The courtesan Bandhumatī said she could. She declared solemnly that she could make the waters of the Ganges turn back by an act of truth. And she did. Her act of truth was simple enough: she had never denied being a courtesan.

The vows of Bodhisattvas can take a form similar to that of the act of truth. Conceived as a subtype of the act of truth, the vow is not only the solemn and powerful declaration of a supremely virtuous person. It can also take a different structural and logical form, becoming a conditional statement in which the apodosis is factual or inevitable, and the protasis is a desired effect. In other words, the normal ontological order of the conditional has been inverted. Instead of saying "I will return if it does not rain," (or, as an act of truth, "if it is true that I will return, men it will not rain"), one would say "If it should rain, then I am not true to my word that I shall return." In a mythic or sacred context, this takes the formal characteristics of the following ideal or abstract statement: "if my liberation is not perfect, I will not achieve liberation." Given the fact that the speaker is a perfect being, whose eventual (or past) achievement of perfection is a given, then the fact that his liberation is perfect is established. Furthermore, since the speaker is known to be true to his word, then the truth of the second clause guarantees the fact of the desired outcome expressed in the first clause.

The Bodhisattva's vow is more than a simple act of truth, because the effect and the statement are identical, and because the vow is a solemn vow uttered and expressed by a truthful being—in other words, a being who always says the truth unquestionably—and the vow is spoken with the most selfless and virtuous intent. The speaker is also a living being who has already an exceptional degree of merit, who is by the vow itself renouncing or shaping all past, present, and future merit, and who will become an omniscient person. Moreover, the vow itself produces merit.

The way in which these elements connect is the following. The Bodhisattva says, "May this happen, or else this will not happen." To us, this seems like a contradiction, but at a certain level of myth and rhetoric it is a very convincing argument, because the Bodhisattva is saying, "if X then Y," but expressed in the following way: "if not-Y then not-X; but X is going to happen, therefore Y must happen." A Bodhisattva is a truthful being, he makes a vow to buddhahood, so we know he will be a Buddha; in other words, if you are a believer, these things follow one from the other.

---

21   Trenckner, *The Milindapañho*, 121–22.

BUDDHISM AS A RELIGION OF HOPE

But even more than that, the person who is listening to the sutra knows that the sutra is referring to the past, but that it is somehow a timeless or perfective past. Specifically, in the *Larger Sukhāvatīvyūha*, that mythological past is a time in which Dharmākara has already become a Buddha. Therefore, it is not only that we should expect him to become a Buddha, but that he is actually a Buddha. So he says, to paraphrase, "If living beings in my purified field are not in such a condition, then I will not become a Buddha." But he is a Buddha; therefore, his purified field must already be as he describes it.

This is one way to express the mystery or the metaphor of grace. Since this is closely connected to merit, in this case content and the power of the act of truth are closely related. Speaker, vow, virtue, and fruit are in fact much more closely intertwined with truth and the power of the word. But they are also closely connected to the accomplishments and virtues of Buddhas and Bodhisattvas.

One can think of this mystery in simple psychological terms as the puzzling effect of receiving something that one does not deserve, and never having to pay back the gift. This is a rare event if one calculates the total sum of exchanges in an individual human being's life.[22] However, when individual events, rather than a total sum, are considered, people often believe that they do receive, or that others do receive things that they neither deserve nor need to repay. This is the spectrum destiny-fortune-grace.

In Buddhist terms, this psychological phenomenon can be glossed as follows. Grace is both receiving and sharing infinite merit, and infinite merit has been shared since beginningless time.[23] In other words, the moment you define merit as being beyond quantification, it is beyond time and beyond possession. Now this has interesting implications in terms of experience and meaning. First, the connection between merit and grace can be seen, as I said before, as a critique of the notion of quantifiable merit. It also gives a new meaning to the vow, and a new importance to the Name of the Buddha. The sacred Name is as much an embodiment of buddhahood as the body of a Buddha. It is a word

---

22 The parallel to the logic of gift exchanges in the secular context is obvious, and further confirmed by the etymological and semantic connections of the word "grace" to some Western expressions of gratitude: Spanish *gracias*, Italian *gratzie* (which, derived from Latin *grātus*, go back to the idea that the gift is meant to please the recipient—Compare Sanskrit *anugrhīto'smi*). French *merci* highlights the presumed or normative affective state behind the gift (pity or compassion); whereas English "thank" suggests the normative state of mind (thoughtfulness, hence other-regard).

23 For similar notions in Japanese Buddhism outside Pure Land traditions, see Dōgen's essays "Effort" (*Gyōji* 行持) and "Worship" (*Kuyō-shobutsu* 供養諸仏). These essays are found in Terada Tōru 寺田透 and Mizuno Yaoko 水野弥穂子, eds., *Dōgen* 道元, 2 vols. (Tokyo: Iwanami Shoten, 1970–72), vol. 1, 165–221, and vol. 2, 382–413, respectively.

that expresses the essence of buddhahood and a sound that manifests its presence. More important, a Word becomes the sacred presence in the same way that the logic of the myth, by seeming to defy common logic, brings together futurity and actuality. The name of the Buddha brings together futurity, birth in the Pure Land, and actuality, the presence of grace. Needless to say, it also integrates the past, because this Name is the Vow.

Because the Name contains the essence and the presence of the Buddha, it embodies the Vow as living practice, and it also embodies the name of all Buddhas so that we can speak of an actualized vow, and we can also speak of the Vow as a moving force and guide in the path. This expresses, in the Indian tradition at least, the two aspects of hope: faith and effort. Hope can lead me to have faith, which in this context is more trust than confessional belief. But it can also lead me to make effort. Because I am confident of the outcome, I apply myself to the causes of the fruit I desire. Both elements I think are seen in Indian Buddhism very clearly, so that the notion that Indian Buddhism is a religion without faith or hope is I think very simplistic. However, Indian Buddhism does not see faith and effort as being as much in tension as Japanese Buddhism tends to do. In the same way, the tension between grace and merit, at least in Mahāyāna, is not as strong as it would seem to be in Japan. But this is not the same thing as denying a continuity of tradition, derivation, and metaphor. One of the implications of what I have just said is that Pure Land Buddhism is consistent with mainstream Mahāyāna. The idea of a traditional link between Mahāyāna and the Japanese Pure Land tradition was first inspired in me in an all too brief conversation with Professor Yamaguchi Susumu in 1969, and later when I read his arguments in *Daijō toshite no Jōdo* (Pure Land as Mahāyāna).[24] He saw the fundamental link in the formula "emptiness is form, and form is emptiness." Of course, the connection between this doctrinal dictum and Pure Land generally had been suggested long before, in the writings of T'an-luan. But Professor Yamaguchi made the connection to Japanese Pure Land and tried to see the link as a necessary one. That is, Pure Land doctrine was seen as a logical outcome of the nature of the synonymity or equation (*sokuze*) "form is emptiness, emptiness is form."

I am inclined to think that, historically, faith in the purified fields and the vows of the Bodhisattva were primary. That is, such faith did not derive from an abstract formulation or vision of the meaning of emptiness—most likely it even preceded historically the formation of the great systems of Mahāyāna philosophy. But, regardless of one's views as to the priority of this abstract

---

24   Yamaguchi Susumu 山口益, *Daijō toshite no jōdo* 大乗としての浄土 (Tokyo: Risōsha, 1963).

BUDDHISM AS A RELIGION OF HOPE

notion over the so-called "simple" faith of the Buddhism of hope, the concept of the identity of form and emptiness may be construed as a pertinent theological commentary on faith.[25] Even if it is only an abstract reformulation, it is an appropriate one, insofar as the kind of faith we find in these traditions is a faith that converts the emptiness of the holy into the fullness of the sacred power of salvation. It is an abstract and, admittedly, intellectualized formulation, a secondary rationalization, if you will. But it is also an apposite summary for the idea that merit is ultimately empty, and hence pliable, flexible, so that it is fluid, transferable. Merit is empty because it cannot be possessed, because it is ephemeral, and hence it is best realized when we give it away. Who better to embody this fact than the persons who have the most merit and give it away without hesitation: namely, the Bodhisattvas.

I have therefore suggested here mat the idea of faith in the Pure Land—as hope of rebirth in the Pure Land—follows from the metaphor of merit itself. In other words, the notion of merit leads, in some paradoxical way, to the notion of grace. Then finally, in a strange but not surprising way, Pure Land appears as another example of the critique of merit, an expression of the same notion of "non-duality" and the emptiness of form that Westerners see as so central to Mahāyāna Buddhism. In this sense, Pure Land hope is also an assertion equivalent to the formula "emptiness is form." But it is not derived from this formula (either philosophically or historically), but from a parallel development that I rather characterize as mythical—that is, from the way certain symbolic and narrative processes were interpreted in practices of faith and hope.

---

25 A critique of the notion of "Pure Land faith" as simplified concession to popular belief has been questioned by historians, but awaits a theological critique. Because this notion (and, I would argue, misconception) has been used apologetically to much advantage in the past, even Pure Land Buddhists themselves are reluctant to examine it critically. Barth, in the passage quoted above (*Die kirchliche Dogmatik*, 375; English version, 342) shows the flip side of this apologetic, arguing for the superiority of a doctrine of truth (meaning, naturally, his own theological position) over one of "concession." Needless to say, I would not defend the sectarian preferences that Barth derives, willy-nilly, from his otherwise illuminating reflections.

Pure Land Buddhism as an Alternative Mārga

Mark L. Blum

1 Main Issues in Consideration of a Pure Land Mārga*

The soteriological message of Pure Land thought has typically been presented in modern scholarship by utilizing a paradigm built on such theories as the three stages of the Dharma, the Buddha's vows of compassion, and the immense popularity of the Pure Land movement among the masses.[1] But, by ignoring the context of the sudden versus gradual debate in China pervasive at the time of the Pure Land movement's ascendancy, as well as other relevant soteriological issues such as nonretrogression and the mārga implications of samādhi experience, such presentations generally fail to lay out a proper hermeneutic required for modern understanding of the Pure Land Buddhist experience. It appears, rather, to have been the stress on faith in figures such as Shinran that has attracted many Western scholars to the study of Pure Land history and thought. Much of this research can be traced to the active scholarship of individuals associated with one of the branches of Shinran's school, the Jōdo Shinshū. Their work in Western languages has tended to focus on either the issue of man's religious standing vis-à-vis the salvific vows of Amitābha Buddha or the experiences in Shinran's life that led him to his own realization.[2] Yet, however subitist the soteriological message of Pure Land Buddhist thought

---

Source: Blum, Mark L., "Pure Land Buddhism as an Alternative Mārga," in *Eastern Buddhist* 27(1) (1994): 30–77.

---

* The author wishes to thank Dr. G. M. Nagao for his careful reading of the manuscript and suggestions for improving it.

1 W. T. de Bary, ed., *The Buddhist Tradition* (New York: Modern Library, 1969), pp. 198–99; see also p. 316.

2 A case in point is the posthumous translation of Shinran's *magnum opus*, the *Kyōgyōshinshō* 教行信證 prepared by D. T. Suzuki and edited by the staff at the Eastern Buddhist Society. For many years this was the only reliable book in English on Pure Land thought and its notes were used as a reference work. It may only be an accident of history, but in his translation Suzuki was only able to finish the first four of what are actually six fascicles of the original. Since it provides the basic source material for the issues of faith, practice, and the grace of the Buddha, many considered this invaluable translation to be complete. In fact, what was inadvertently omitted in the final chapters was Shinran's exegesis on the multifaceted problem of *mārga*. Fortunately, this lacuna has been filled by the new translation of this text from the Shin Buddhism Translation Series in Kyoto.

appears in figures even as radical as Shinran, it is nonetheless doctrinally grounded in the Indian gradualist concepts of mārga from which it emanated.

This discussion seeks to explore the major recurring themes in what is, in fact, an often complex and obscure relationship between these two notions of mārga. In the process I hope to shed some light on the manner in which the Buddhist tradition attempted to rationalize some of the inevitable doctrinal inconsistencies that accompanied the rise of this Chinese subitist alternative to the more gradualist assumptions of the Indian mārga schemata.

The notion of a path to liberation is basic to all Buddhist doctrine. Usually known under the rubric of the Sanskrit term *mārga*, the concept of path has generally reflected two aspects of practice: 1) *performative*: the delineation of required praxis (i.e., the exhortation of work to be done); 2) *attributive*: the relative value placed on particular spiritual attainments (i.e., the recognition of work that has been done).

How one is to reach the goal of nirvāṇa, the ultimate goal in all Buddhism, is the key reference point in any mārga discussion. The noble eightfold path, perhaps the earliest mārga message, may also be the best example of a purely performative mārga. Here eight different dimensions of an individual's life are discussed and the appropriate Buddhist guidelines explained for each. The other well-known early Buddhist mārga notion is the list of four stages of spirituality—stream-winner, once-returner, nonreturner, and arhat. In this scheme, there is an attempt to hermeneutically split the four stages into performative praxis and attributive attainments, thus we find a conscious attempt to clarify both dimensions of mārga by a dualistic division into "approach" (*pratipannaka*) and "fruit" (*phala*). In Chinese this is known as *ssu-hsiang ssu-kuo* 四向四果. This distinction expresses an awareness of both the performative and attributive phases of the path quite early in the tradition.

As the religion grew through individual experience and its interpretation in terms of established doctrine, the concept of mārga also expanded into myriad forms. It is quite beyond the intentions of this brief essay to identify the core mārga schemata of Buddhism, but it is worth mentioning some of the common mārga notions found in the Mahāyāna, some of which originate much earlier. One of these early comprehensive descriptions that remained resonant within the Mahāyāna is that of the so-called three learnings: morality (*śīla* 戒), meditation (*samādhi* 定), and wisdom (*prajñā* 慧). The eightfold path was often interpreted in terms of these three categories, but this tripartite conception proved useful in later Buddhist descriptions of praxis where the eightfold path no longer functioned as mārga referent. The Mahāyāna doctrinal system in its complexity added many new notions of the path, refining the discussion and adding the new element of choice. Mahāyāna sūtras refer to

Buddhist adepts with an assumption these individuals had chosen which type of path to follow. Thus the Mahūyūna initially outlined four basic paths: that of the ordinary person and/or deity (*pṛthagjana*), that of the "listener" (*śrāvaka*), that of the "solitary buddha" (*pratyeka-buddha*), and the path for those "attached to enlightenment" (*bodhisattva*). Although the category of "listener" represents followers of the pre-Mahāyāna teachings and was often belittled as an inferior path that led to an inferior goal, the *Saddharmapuṇḍarīka sūtra* and the *Ta chih-tu lun* recognize the listeners' abilities and together with the solitary buddhas they are encouraged to practice the so-called thirty-seven aids to enlightenment (*bodhipakṣa*) (三十七道品)."[3] This is actually a list of various practices, including the noble eightfold path, and appears to reflect a basic Mahāyāna expansion of earlier notions of mārga. Bodhisattvas also practice the thirty-seven *bodhipakṣa* but in addition are supposed to practice the six (later ten) so-called "perfections" (*pāramitā*).

---

3 Other Chinese translations include *San-shih-ch'i chüeh-fa* 三十七覚分 and *Sanshih-ch'i fen-fa* 三十七分法. Most of the basic mārga issues defined in the Abhidharma texts in both Pali and Sanskrit continue to play an important role in the Mahāyāna as well. One such tradition divides practice into four sets of mārga. According to the *Abhidharmakośabhāṣya*, these are defined as: (1) *prayoga-mārga* 加行道, preparation practice for the destruction of mental afflictions (*kleśas*); (2) *ānantarya-mārga* 無間道, actual cutting off of individual mental afflictions; (3) *vimukti-mārga* 解脱道, the path of liberation resulting from the confirmation of truth seen after the removal of the afflictions; and (4) *viśeṣa-mārga* 勝進道, the path of further progress, indicating continued practices directed toward the removal of more stubborn afflictions.

With the Mahāyāna a number of mārga categories are also added which are neither prescriptive nor descriptive, and can only be described as idealistic. One such scheme is the basic description of practice under the heading of "with and without *āsrava*" 有漏無漏. *Āsrava* are outflows of mental impurities or intoxicants, sometimes translated as fluxes (cf. Collett Cox, "Attainment through Abandonment," in *Paths to Liberation*, p. 67) and glossed by Edgerton (quoting Johnston) as "the influences which attach a man to saṃsāra" (p. 111b). The path of one who still has these impure outflows (*sāsrava-mārgā*) is also called the worldly path (*laukika-mārga*). In Abhidharma literature, kleśas can be cut off by someone in *sāsrava* status, although the *Yogācārabhūmi-mārga* denies this. There is also an *anāsrava*. Thus, in the pre-Mahāyāna analysis, *anāsrava* status meant a stage where the more subtle *kleśas* are removed, like the *viśeṣa-mārga* above. One who has reached the *anāsrava* status is said to be beyond learning, known as the *aśaikṣa-mārga* (the "path beyond instruction"), which is also used as a synonym for the stage of Arhat. This issue is confusing precisely because the term is used in both performative and attributive sense: performatively speaking, the *anāsrava-mārga* includes *darśana-mārga* and *aśaikṣa-mārga*.

These are just some of the schemes offered in Indian Buddhist doctrine. For a useful list of basic mārga schemes, see the introduction to Robert E. Buswell, Jr. and Robert M. Gimello, eds., *Paths for Liberation: The Marga and Its Transformations in Buddhist Thought* (Honolulu: University of Hawaii Press, 1992), pp. 7–9 (unfortunately without any source references!) and the following essays.

PURE LAND BUDDHISM AS AN ALTERNATIVE MĀRGA

If we look at the issues in the seven different lists that make up the thirty-seven *bodhipakṣa*, we find outlined some performative practices (the four foundations of mindfulness, the four exertions, the noble eightfold path), and others appear instead to express attributive attainments (the five powers, the four supernatural powers, the seven limbs of awakening). It should be noted that many qualities associated with mārga attainment can be both performative and attributive. In this *bodhipakṣa* list of lists, for example, the "five powers" (*pañca-bala*) and the "five faculties" (*pañca-indriya*) is in fact the same: faith, energy, attention, samādhi and wisdom; but the former list embodies an attributive implication which the latter does not. Thus acquiring these powers is not a final goal, as these now empowered faculties must be used to push the seeker further toward his goal. While this and other lists may seem to present an incongruous blend of different messages, in fact the combination of both performative and attributive dimensions of the path is not uncommon in Buddhism. Another example can be seen in the word *bodhisattva*. Denoting a being "attached to enlightenment,"[4] the word can represent both someone who is committed to the path but is at its early stages, i.e., a person aspiring to bodhi, as well as a fully accomplished person, standing one short step before Buddhahood.

It should also be mentioned that in contrast to the traditional Buddhist emphasis on meditative experience as the fundamental arbiter of religious value, with the rise of the Mahāyāna certain nonempirical sources of authority emerged that competed with or even superseded individual experience. One such source is the cult of the book. By exhorting their own unique platform for the experience of truth, Mahāyāna sūtras such as the *Saddharmapuṇḍarīka*, *Prajñāpāramitā*, *Laṅkāvatāra*, *Saṃdhinirmocana*, *Mahāparinirvāṇa*, etc., created loci of spiritual authority that became standards by which each practitioner was to judge his own religious experience.

The emergence of a lineage of teachers also served to define the limits of acceptable religious understanding. The impact of lineages is particularly strong in Tibet, where lineage mandalas display important personages equal to the authority of the Buddha and an entire subdivision of literature is devoted to this concern.[5] The lineage charts of the Chinese Buddhist schools as written in the Sung dynasty are also well known for establishing the authority of contemporary teachers and became the basis for sectarian orthodoxy in Japan as well.

---

4 From K. R. Norman, "Buddhism and Sanskririsation," lecture presented at Kyoto University, May 17, 1994.

5 See "Thob-yig or gSan-yigs" in *Tibetan Historical Literature* by A. I. Vostrikov, translated by Harish Chandra (Calcutta: Indian studies, 1970) pp. 199–204.

Within the Ch'an school, the so-called spiritual encounter with one's master, in both verbal and nonverbal expression, also became a well-respected measure of mārga proficiency; in extreme cases it was the only measure of attainment.

In the case of Pure Land Buddhism, we also see both performative and attributive descriptions of the path. The notion of the six or ten perfections of the Mahāyāna path, while not entirely abandoned, has disappeared as the focus of performative norms. This is replaced by an elevation of a number of devotional, ritualistic and meditational practices falling under the rubric of *nien-fo/nembutsu* 念佛 (*buddhaanusmṛti*), most of which cannot be found in Indian mārga schemes. The issue of faith, which can be found in the early stages of the path as defined by the *Hua-yen* (*Avataṃsaka*) and *P'usa ying-lo pen yeh* sūtras,[6] indeed functions in both performative and attributive aspects. What distinguishes mid-thirteenth-century Japanese Pure Land Buddhism is that faith has completely lost its performative dimension and is redefined as the ultimate soteriological attainment possible in this life. It is from this point of view that scholars needed to present a convincing argument to their contemporaries. This is the fuel driving Kamakura Pure Land exegetics.

Despite the often encountered assumption that the salvific myth surrounding the Buddha Amitābha/Amitāyus reflects a mature Mahāyāna statement, a quick look at the history of sūtra translation in China reveals that Amitābha-centered texts comprise some of the earliest material in the Mahāyāna corpus. Although there appears to be some borrowing of material within these early works, if we accept the dates recorded for Tao-an's lost catalog (as quoted in Sêng-yu's *Ch'u san tsang chi chi* 出三藏記集), according to the *Han-lu* Lokakṣema translated the larger *Sukhāvatīvyūha sūtra* and the *Akṣobhya-tathāgatasyavyūha sūtra* between 147 and 186 during the Later Han, and two translations of the *Pratyutpannabuddha-saṃmukhāvasthita-samādhi sūtra* (a.k.a. the *Bhadrapāla sūtra*) were made as well. Most of this work was completed a full century before the first translation of the *Saddharmapuṇḍarīka sūtra* was completed by Chih-ch'ien in 286.[7] While we cannot infer that an earlier date of translation in China necessarily means an earlier date of composition in India, and the lack of corroborating textual references to these texts and practices in Indian sources is problematic, the early transmission of texts mixing samādhi and devotional practices does imply the prevalence of soteriological movements

---

6 菩薩瓔珞本業經 J. *Bosatsu yōraku hongō-kyō*, T. 20.1010.

7 The same Chih-ch'ien's translation of the *Sukhāvatīvyūha sūtra*, also dated as 286, was already the third in China. He also translated a number of sūtras in the third century which contain elements that are thematically based on faith in the Pure Land: 菩薩生地經、慧印三昧經、無量門微密持經, etc.

PURE LAND BUDDHISM AS AN ALTERNATIVE MĀRGA   41

surrounding mythical Buddhas quite early in the Mahāyāna movement. There is the general consensus that the cult of Amitābha Buddha and his realm called Sukhāvatī probably arose during the first century AD in India and there is even evidence of Sukhāvatī functioning as an otherworldly ideal in texts unrelated to the Amitābha cult as early as the second century; that is, from evidence available, predating Nāgārjuna (~150–250 CE).[8]

But unlike Mādhyamika or Yogācāra, we know of no mention of a "school" of study and practice centered around the Pure Lands of Akṣobhya, Amitābha/ Amitāyus, Bhaiṣajyaguru and other Buddhas in either India or Central Asia.[9] The emergence of a Pure Land path or "gate" (*men/mon* 門) in Chinese writings coincides with the so-called *p'an-chiao* 判教, or evaluation of the teachings, debate that ensued in late sixth-century China. I believe the term *men* assumes some conceptualization of mārga, or path, and is thus to be distinguished from "school" (*tsung/shū* 宗), which rather implies a lineage of doctrines, practices or teachers. Among the writings of so many brilliant Buddhist thinkers of this golden age, the works of figures like Chih-i 智顗 (538–597) and Fa-tsang 法藏 (643–712) are notable for also bringing their interpretive and systematizing genius to bear upon sūtras and doctrines that we now associate with the so-called Pure Land tradition. Although not normally included in the standard list of the Pure Land patriarchs,[10] the commentarial efforts of these men, particularly those of Chih-i, have proved extremely influential throughout the development of the Pure Land movement. Indeed the notions of mārga that developed within all the major schools of Chinese Buddhism also undoubtedly affected writers considering a Pure Land path.

At this point it might be helpful to outline just what modern scholars mean by phrases such as "Pure Land tradition" or "Pure Land thought." Perhaps the most salient feature of this branch of Mahāyāna is the important role played

---

8   Fujita Kōtatsu 藤田宏達, *Genshi Jōdokyō shisō no kenkyū* 原始浄土教思想の研究 (Tokyo: Iwanami, 1968), concludes that the sūtra materials can begin as early as 100 CE; cf. p. 224. G. Schopen, in "Sukhāvatī as a generalized religious goal in Sanskrit Mahāyāna sūtra literature," *Indo-Iranian Journal*, 19.3–4 (August, September 1977), p. 204, following Régamey, also concludes the second century as the lower limit for the *Samādhirāja-sūtra* as well as "for the period during which rebirth in *Sukhāvatī* became a generalized religious goal open to the Mahāyāna community as a whole."

9   Schopen suggests this may be due to a "process of generalization and dissociation from Amitābha" (p. 204), and this is an important point to remember when trying to outline the hermeneutical context for the widely-practiced cult in East Asia.

10   Hōnen's list of five patriarchs in his *Jōdo goso den* 浄土五祖傳 (*Hōnen shōnin zenshū* 857) excludes both Chih-i and Fa-tsang. Even Gyōnen's extended list of nine patriarchs does not include either of them; see his discussion of Pure Land patriarchs in his *Jōdo hōmon genrushō* 浄土法門源流章 (T. 84.195a18–c21).

by Amitābha Buddha as omniscient teacher and source of spiritual compassion (*mahākaruṇā*). Doctrinally speaking, Pure Land thought is based on the pan-Buddhist concept that every Buddha has an impact on his environment by "purifying" (*pariśuddhi*) the space he inhabits, his *Buddha-kṣetra*, usually translated as "Buddha-field." Associated with the rise to prominence of the Mahāyāna movement is the concomitant growth in the number of Buddhas throughout the universe, each conceived of as dwelling in his own pure Buddha-field devoid of the distractions and defilements common to our own world. Just as the stūpas built to Śākyamuni Buddha attracted followers of the teaching because they became religious domains embodying the spirit of enlightenment, so, too, the mythologized regions wherein Buddhas dwelled became idealized realms of truth and beauty to which religious pilgrims aspired. Of these so-called "cosmic" Buddhas, none attracted so large a following as one known either by the name of Amitābha ("infinite light") or Amitāyus ("infinite life").

The "Pure Land" teachings refer only to the doctrines surrounding Amitābha Buddha, whose forty-eight bodhisattva vows contain the promise to make it possible for all beings to reach his Buddha-kṣetra and hear his elucidation of the Dharma if they decide to turn over their store of merit to achieving this end. In addition to his identity as provider of a universally accessible land of bliss, this Buddha also became the object of the popular Mahāyāna practice of recollection samādhi (*anusmṛti-samādhi*).[11] The precise relationship between these apparently disparate roles should be less obscure if seen in light of the relationship between the Pure Land mārga and the traditionalist mārga.[12]

The doctrines of Pure Land thought are often collectively referred to today under the rubric, "other-power." This term refers to the force of the Buddha's compassionate resolve to extend his hand from somewhere outside the practitioner's experience and by doing so lift him to higher spiritual attainments, specifically birth in the Buddha-kṣetra of Amitābha where one is promised swift progress to the highest enlightenment.[13] The concept of self and "other-power" in a Pure Land context was broached in China by T'an-luan 曇鸞 (476–542). Following T'anluan's usage, "self-power" (*tzž-li/jiriki* 自力) and "other-power" (*t'ali/tariki* 他力) gradually took on specific denotations in Buddhist literature, representing two divergent approaches to religious practice: self-power as the

---

11   Rendered into Sino-Japanese both as 念佛三味 *nien-fo san-mei, nembutsu zammai,* and 観佛三昧 *kuan-fo san-mei, kambutsu zammai.*

12   See Paul Harrison, "*Pratyutpanna-Buddhasammukhāvasthita samādhi sūtra," Journal of Indian Philosophy* 6 (1978).

13   Shinran reinterpreted the notion of Birth in the Buddha's Pure Land not as a means to unrestricted progress toward final enlightenment, but as the final enlightenment itself.

model of liberation by self-cultivation, other-power as the path to enlightenment openly dependent upon the compassionate assistance of Buddhas and bodhisattvas.

Though not explicitly stated as such in the classical texts of the Pure Land tradition in either China or Japan, it is nonetheless important for us today to recognize that the hermeneutical context of a term like "other-power" can only be understood properly when seen against the background of some notion of mārga. In effect, self-power and other-power are statements about two approaches to mārga. Given the variety of mārga schema existing in Buddhist doctrine in sixth- and seventh-century China, the creation of the notion of *a jiriki* mārga was indeed a simplification, yet it was one that helped establish the identity of the movement devoted to practices based on the great variety of scriptural sources for the Amitābha cult by affirming a raison d'être for the shibboleth *tariki*. Since the purpose here is to outline the identity of the Pure Land mārga, and since the term "self-power" only has meaning within the *jiriki/tariki* hermeneutic employed by the Pure Land tradition, I will refer to previous mārga schemes, particularly those originating in India, by the phrase "traditional mārga." Although the Pure Land path can certainly be described as unorthodox, it seems inappropriate to use the word orthodox to describe previous schemata of mārga simply because there were so many conceptions of the path that no one system appears to have ever sustained that degree of authority. Thus, though insufficient, I have selected the terms "traditional" and "alternate" to represent these two positions. "Alternate" mārga seems appropriate because the Pure Land path was dependent on Indian mārga assumptions for its validity, thus presuming the authority of other, more established and more traditional concepts of mārga.

Expressed as *jiriki* and *tariki*, these two paths in a Japanese context parochially imply mutual exclusivity today. Such an assumption, however, is largely the outcome of powerful sectarian forces operating in Japan since the eighteenth century and should not be taken as representative of how the overall Buddhist tradition attempted to understand their relationship. Seeing the hermeneutic of self-power/other-power in the context of mārga affords us an opportunity to clarify the very ground of their relationship, for questions of mārga represent the primary soteriological concerns of any Buddhist system.

One important theme embedded in mārga discussions in East Asia is the hermeneutic of "sudden" (*tun/ton* 頓) versus "gradual" (*chien/zen* 漸) teachings and practices. This method of assessing teachings and experience is pervasive in the scholastic writings of fifth- to seventh-century China, but should properly be seen as reflecting a problematic basic to all of Buddhism outside India. The debates at Sam-ye and Lhasa in Tibet focused on this as the central issue in the establishment of Buddhism in that land, the Pure Land exegetes of China also found the distinction compelling, and in Japan Hōnen 法然 (1133–1212) used the hermeneutic to clarify his thesis as well. The subitist/gradual assessment of teachings and experience is pervasive in the scholastic writings of fifth- to seventh-century China. The range of connotations of these adjectives is in fact quite broad, and recent work has begun to pinpoint their implications in particular contexts.[14] It is worth noting the difference in classical usage between sudden enlightenment (*tun-wu* 頓悟) and sudden doctrines or teachings (*tun-chiao* 頓教), the former being associated with the Ch'an master Shen-hui 神會 (684–758) and the latter perhaps best illustrated in the usage of Chih-i and Fa-tsang. The writings of Chih-i, particularly his *Tz'u-ti ch'an-men* 次第禪門 (T. 1916) and *Mo-ho chih-kuan* 摩訶止観 (T. 1911), proved quite influential and reflect a particularly creative expression of Buddhist teachings and practices in an orderly system after reassessing their relative merit vis-à-vis progression of the mārga. The *Mo-ho chih-kuan*, a more mature work, was widely quoted in China and Japan.[15]

The clearest statement among the Chinese Pure Land masters on the subject of *tun* (sudden) versus *chien* (gradual) is that of Shan-tao 善導 (613–681) in his commentary on the *Kuan wu-liang shou ching* 観無量寿經: "Question: Concerning this sūtra, in which of the two canons is it to be contained? In which of the two [types of] teachings is it to be included? Answer: This *Kuan*

---

14   It has been pointed out, for example, that *ton* may imply simultaneity rather than immediacy; cf. R. A. Stein, "Sudden Illumination or Simultaneous Comprehension: Remarks on Chinese and Tibetan Terminology," in *Sudden and Gradual: Approaches to Enlightenment in Chinese Thought* (Honolulu: University of Hawaii Press, 1987). See also G. Foulk's review of *Sudden and Gradual* in *Journal of the International Association of Buddhist Studies* 16–1 (1993), p. 135.

     We should also look at the political context of such writings. The logical inconsistency of many of the arguments only strengthens the smell of polemics. In the focus here merely on Pure Land writings, the exegetical, nay even polemical context, of the critical periods in which the "major" treatises were composed (sixth–seventh century China; twelfth–thirteenth century Japan) were rife with debate and controversy. Particularly in the case of Japan, where Hōnen and his disciples suffered political suppression of their movement, the societal and doctrinal environment must be considered in any evaluation of the literature.

15   Cf. John McRae, "Encounter Dialogue and Transformation in Ch'an," in *Paths to Liberation*, p. 343 ff., for details on the contents of these systems. John McRae's work has overcome centuries of sectarian entrenchment that exploited the pejorative label of gradual enlightenment hurled at the northern school of Ch'an by Shen-hui and his lineage to show the inappropriateness of this description; but how are we to understand any religious experience as a "gradual" event? The extant discussions in fifth-and sixth-century China between "sudden" and "gradual" soteriological positions have been excellently covered in P. Gregory, ed., *Sudden and Gradual*.

ching 観經 is included in the bodhisattva canon and the sudden teachings."[16] Here we see that by the second half of the seventh century in China, Pure Land sūtra doctrine was already defined in terms of the meta-doctrine of sudden and gradual. Hōnen adds to the sudden/gradual issues of teaching and enlightenment by addressing the evaluation of nembutsu in this way as well. He thus categorizes the *tariki nembutsu* 他力念佛 as "the sudden of the sudden (頓中頓)." In his commentary on the *Wu-liang shou ching*, Hōnen uses this phrase as a gloss on a passage from the *An-lo chi* 安樂集 by Taoch'o 道綽 (562–645) commenting on the same sūtra:

> Dhyāna master Tao-ch'o explains the sūtra's phrase, *"Cutting off the possibility of rebirth in the five tainted realms"* (T. 12.274b22–23), by saying: "If by cultivating this cessation, one first cuts off his mistaken opinions, and leaves behind the causes ... by separating oneself from the causes [leading to birth] as man or deva, the results of such causes are stopped. These are all gradual methods of removal and are not called "cutting off." If one achieves Birth in Amida's Pure Land, the five paths [of possible births] are abandoned at once, and this is called "cutting off." [Thus] "cutting off the five tainted realms" is to cut this karmic fruition. *"The tainted realms are naturally closed"* (T. 12.274b23) means closing off these causes.
>
> [Hōnen comments thusly:] "Tendai and Shingon are both called 'sudden teachings,' but since they are based on the principle of cutting off mistaken opinions, they are still gradual teachings. Because this [Pure Land] teaching is devoted to enabling ordinary people who have not yet cut off such errors to directly transcend the long night of transmigration in the triple-world, it is the sudden of the sudden (頓中頓) teachings."[17]

Well-trained in what had become an entrenched hermeneutic tradition affords Hōnen a rhetorical method of distinguishing this particular experience as unique among other religious experiences of immediacy. By raising *nembutsu* to a plane of higher soteriological value, Hōnen has also changed the topic from the evaluation of teachings and the practices they extol to the evaluation of *nembutsu* itself. Here the phrase *tariki nembutsu* designates more than a chosen practice and refers to an experience of awakening itself. After

---

16 T. 37.247a20. The two canons here refers to the śrāvaka and bodhisattva canons; the two types of teachings are the sudden and gradual.

17 In his *Daikyōshaku* 大經釋 (*Kurodani Shōnin gotōroku kandaiichi* 黒谷上人語燈録巻第一, *Jōdokyō zensho* 浄土教全書 9.314b12–315a2). The *An-lo chi* text can be found in *Jōdoshū zensho* 1.704a8 ff.

all, engaging in any practice, even *nembutsu*, involves an act of will and thus reflects a *jiriki* position. But by clarifying this as *tariki nembutsu*, Hōnen is instead referring to the sudden realization of the truth of the doctrine of Amida Buddha's grace. This is necessarily a *tariki* event; thus it is both *subitist* and *tariki*. The passage below from the writings of Seikaku 聖覺 (1167–1235), one of Hōnen's disciples, indicates a typical thirteenth-century Pure Land *p'an-chiao*:

> Insofar as the faculties [of men] are sharp or dull, there are teachings that are gradual or sudden. Insofar as their capacities are broad or narrow, their practices can be difficult or easy. It should be understood that all gates for saints [= *tariki* path] are of the gradual teachings and are difficult practices. The single school/lineage (*shū* 宗) of the Pure Land, is a sudden teaching and an easy practice. The Shingon and *śamathāvipaśyannā* [Tendai] practices are difficult to cultivate for those with a mind like a monkey's; the teachings of Sanron and Hossō easily bewilder those with eyes like cows and sheep.[18]

The fact that the label of gradual (漸) in a Pure Land context is always used pejoratively in Japan means that in equating the self-power/other-power dichotomy with a gradualist/subitist one, Seikaku obviously violates the self-designated sudden doctrines and practices of these traditional Chinese Buddhist schools, including his own Tendai sect. On the other hand, we also find definite gradualist aspects in the soteriological reflections of most Pure Land thinkers, as, for example, the patience to postpone final enlightenment until the next life when born in the Pure Land, or waiting for the experience of *ōjō* 往生 (Birth) to happen on one's deathbed.

When referring to the traditional mārga, Kamakura Pure Land exegetes generally rely on the soteriological scheme delineated in the *Hua-yen ching* or *P'u-sa ying-lo pen yeh ching*. Although believed to be apocryphal today, the *Ying-lo ching*, with its mārga scheme of a fifty-two-stage bodhisattva path to Buddhahood, seems to have been accepted as the standard referent and thus will be the point of reference in the discussion below. These fifty-two steps are organized into five main subheadings of ten, plus an additional two final stages. These may be translated as: 1) the ten stages of faith (*shih hsin* 十信); 2) the ten stages of abiding (*shih chu* 十住); 3) the ten stages of practice (*shih hsing* 十行); 4) the ten stages of merit transfer, or *pariṇāmanā* (*shih huihsiang* 十廻向); 5) the ten bhūmis (*shih ti* 十地); 6) veritable enlightenment (*teng chüeh*

---

18 *Seikaku Hōin hyōbyaku mon* 聖覺法印表白文, in *Teihon Shinran shōnin zenshū* (Kyoto: Hōzōkan, 1980), Vol. 6, p. 217.

等覺); and 7) sublime enlightenment (*miao chüeh* 妙覺). The Pure Land commentarial tradition came to regard everything below the ten bhūmis as indicative of *pṛthagjana* (J. *bombu* 凡夫) status, i.e., the locale of ordinary beings. Beings at the ten stages of faith may also be referred to as "putative bodhisattvas" (*ming-tzu p'usa/myōji bosatsu* 名字菩薩) because they are so low in their attainment they may be bodhisattvas in name only.

Within this outline, there are two aspects of the traditional bodhisattva path that are particularly relevant to Pure Land reformulations of Mahāyāna soteriology. One is the position on the mārga of the so-called "ordinary beings," and the other is the notion that some rankings in the higher stages of the mārga cannot regress to a lower spiritual level. As mentioned above, the first forty stages of the mārga were considered to designate those who were still regarded as "ordinary" as opposed to the "saints" (*ārya*) located within the ten bhūmis. Progressing from an ordinary stage to that of a saint brought with it the question of backsliding from this exalted position, and nonbacksliding is thus a commonly promised feature concomitant with many attainments in practice. In addition to the promise of nonretrogression, this quality was explained as also meaning that completion of the mārga, however conceived, was not too far off in the future. In this way, the idea of attaining a particular stage in one's praxis that had been defined as nonbacksliding came to assume enormous spiritual consequences, evidenced by such terms as *anjin* 安心 (pacified mind) in Mahāyāna Buddhism—unfortunately this also led to disagreement among the sūtras as to precisely which stage in the mārga holds this promise. But this disparity is generally confined to one of the ten stages of the bhūmis, thus precluding "ordinary beings" as defined in both the *Ying-lo ching* and *Hua-yen ching*.

Well aware of this restriction, Pure Land exegetes, most notably Shan-tao, nevertheless argued forcefully that the Pure Land mārga indeed offered nonbacksliding status to ordinary beings. This is an absolutely crucial point in the study of Pure Land doctrine that has received scant attention thus far. And it is vital to our understanding of the historical development of Pure Land Buddhism that we realize the soteriological significance of this claim and its direct contribution to the growth of the Pure Land movement in East Asia. The other side to this very *religious* of claims is that such an unorthodox idea inevitably created controversy among the Buddhist communities of China, Korea and Japan.

Considering the relative unimportance placed on faith in the standard mārga schema, where it is relegated to the early stages of attainment in which seekers are described as bodhisattvas in name only, the Pure Land alternative mārga appears to be turning the usual set of Buddhist soteriological priorities upside down. "Alternative mārga" may not be the most appropriate term for this discussion because the Pure Land path does not really attempt to substitute an entirely new soteriology for any of the traditional bodhisattva paths. It is thus important to keep in mind that while the Pure Land mārga does demand an alternative prioritization of practices and goals to those found in the traditional path, it does not deny the ultimate religious values embodied in the original Mahāyāna conception of the path and the ultimate Buddhist goal of nirvāṇa.

As a result of this relationship wherein the Pure Land path is limited in its soteriological concerns by the more common and traditional *jiriki* paths, the content and significance of bodhi itself does not become an issue but the importance placed on its rapid spiritual attainment in the Pure Land conception of mārga does lead to a reassessment of how bodhi should be best approached.[19] The emphasis in Pure Land literature is everywhere on the ease, the immediate access, the very *obtainability* of the goal of birth in the Pure Land. Pure Land Buddhist writers frequently speak of "leaping crosswise" (J. *ōchō* 橫超)[20] for expressing precisely the radical promise of progressing from the ten stages of faith, the first ten of the fifty-two steps of the mārga, directly up to a nonbacksliding position somewhere within the ten bhūmis, i.e., stages 41–50. This has been glossed also as "turning to the side" (J. *tenbō* 轉傍), which means turning away from and thus abandoning the usual procedure of trudging along the path in a straightforward fashion, ascending step by step. Instead, by facing the Buddha directly and gaining his intercession, one "leaps" to a stage close to that of the Buddha's own attainment. For Shan-tao, the originator of this phrase, this sideways leap meant experiencing *bodhi-citta*, which he equated with *darśana-mārga*.

Following Shan-tao, the Pure Land position is thus to reformulate the bodhisattva path by postponing at least the sections called the path of insight (*darśana-mārga*) and the path of meditation (*bhāvanā-mārga*) (viz., the stages of the ten bhūmis) until after one has realized what is conceptualized as either a rebirth physically or a regeneration spiritually in the Sukhāvatī of Amitābha Buddha. This reshuffling of the order of this process is alluded to in Hōnen's *Ōjōdaiyōshō* 往生大要抄:

---

19   The *bodhi-citta* concept was, however, more problematic. Hōnen mentions in his *Senchakushū* the four kinds of *bodhi-citta* of Tendai, the three kinds of *bodhi-citta* in Shingon, etc.

20   This phrase can be traced to the *Hsüan-i fen* 玄義分 section of Shan-tao's commentary to the *Kuan wu-liang-shou ching* (T. 1753), where he writes of the "leap crosswise that cuts off the four streams."

PURE LAND BUDDHISM AS AN ALTERNATIVE MĀRGA

Next we will [discuss] the Pure Land Gate. First one [must be in a position to] loathe and abandon this Sanā world. He is [then] quickly born in the Sukhāvatī Pure Land and in that land practices the Buddha-mārga. For that reason it is imperative that one attain this Birth (ōjō) by immediately cultivating the desire that leads to the Pure Land.[21]

Hōnen reflects here the standard Pure Land mārga imperative of first reaching the proximate goal of birth in the Pure Land before accomplishing the ultimate goal of completing the path to Buddhahood. However, this in turn necessitates yet another mārga—namely, that for attaining birth in the Pure Land. Shinran 親鸞 (1173–1262) and his followers, however, appear to understand this attainment of Birth both as the attainment of *bodhi-citta* as well as the attainment of *bodhi* itself. This ambiguity in the tradition has led to significant controversy down to the present day over the interpretation of the implications of the term Birth (ōjō) among the different branches of the Jōdo Shinshū school."[22]

2   The Development of a Pure Land Path in Chinese Buddhism

The notion that there indeed exists a separate Pure Land path, however loosely defined, as something inherent in directing one's praxis toward reaching Amitābha's Pure Land should be seen as a process evolving over roughly three hundred years which begins with the translated works of Nāgārjuna and Vasubandhu and is brought to maturity in the writings of T'an-luan, Tao-ch'o and Shan-tao. The two key areas in which Pure Land thought has sought to extrapolate the adept's new mārga status are the experience of birth in the Pure

---

21   *Hōnen Shōnin zenshū* (Kyoto: Heirakuji Shoten, 1956), p. 49. This is one of Hōnen's commentaries to Genshin's *Ōjōyōshū*.

22   Even D. T. Suzuki's writings on Shinshū reflect this doctrinal contradiction. In endnote 325 to his translation of Shinran's *Kyōgyōshinshō*, he explains the term *ōchō* by stating, "it indicates the way in which the true faith in *nembutsu* is imparted from the other-power, resulting in the severing of illusion and the attainment of Buddhahood in the Pure Land. Based on this idea, Shinran analyzed *bodhi-citta* in this way" (p. 304). But elsewhere in the same work Suzuki shows his assumption that, "Ultimately, Pure Land is equivalent to Nirvāṇa or Enlightenment." Taken together, these statements imply that the experience of Birth in the Pure Land includes the destruction of the *kleśas* and the attainment of Nirvāṇa. This ignores, however, Shinran's line in the *Shōshinge* 正信偈 in which he quotes T'an-luan: "One attains Nirvāṇa without destroying the *kleśas*." This is an important theme in Shinshū mysticism; see, for example, Kakunyo 覺如 in his *Kaijashō* 改邪鈔 (*Shinshū shōgyō zensho*, vol. 3, p. 85, line 14), where he lists it alongside other such attainments as nonbacksliding and joining the group of those rightly assured.

Land and the attainment of faith in the fact that this event is destined to occur in one's future.

One of the earliest non-sūtra [commentary, śāstra, etc.] sources to play a major role in the development of a Pure Land path in China is an Indian text regarded by the Pure Land tradition as its first major authoritative treatise. This is the *Shih chu p'ip'o sha lun* 十住毘婆沙論 (T. 1521), which survives as a partial commentary to the *Daśabhūmika sūtra*, and was attributed to Nāgārjuna and translated by Kumārajīva (344–413) early in the fifth century.[23] We find here the first reference to an alternative mārga conceived as being in direct contrast with the traditional mārga, both now distinguished under the rubric, "path of easy practices/path of difficult practice":

> Question: If the various Buddhas have [also] expounded a means to quick attainment of a nonbacksliding (*avinivartanīya*) stage by *a path of easy practice*, I beseech you to explain this to me as well.

> Answer: The Buddha's teaching has immeasurable approaches. Just like the paths of the world, some are difficult and some are easy. Some demand diligent practice and vigorous pursuit (*vīrya*). To travel the roads of the earth on foot is painful; to travel the water by boat is easy. Some lead quickly to the stage of nonbacksliding with an easier practice based on the skillful means of faith....[24]
>
> If a Bodhisattva wants to be able to gain the nonbacksliding stage in this body and then attain the highest enlightenment (*anuttarasamyak-sambodhi*), he should keep in mind (*nien* 念) the Buddhas of the ten directions and chant their holy names (*ming-hao* 名號).[25]

I wish to draw particular attention to the fact that the major role played by this text in the evolution of Pure Land soteriology lies primarily in introducing not only the conception of a path of easy practice but also the legitimization of that path by pegging it to the doctrine of nonbacksliding. This is a theme to be repeated throughout the history of Pure Land thought, where Nāgārjuna's commentary served as a primary referent. This is one example of how Pure

---

23   It is an unresolved debate at this point in history as to whether or not the author of this text is the same Nāgārjuna of the Mādhyamika school. Since that dispute revolves around different opinions on the same topics as found in the *Ta chih-tu lun*, which is itself of controversial origins, we will not pursue such discussion at this time.

24   T. 26.41a13–14 and 41b2–6.

25   T. 26.41b15–17.

PURE LAND BUDDHISM AS AN ALTERNATIVE MĀRGA 51

Land thinkers utilize a seminal concept from the traditional mārga to support the authority of their radical views, which are in fact subverting that mārga.

There were, of course, inherent problems concerning how the universality of the Pure Land path could be squared with this claim; in other words, how is every individual, regardless of the amount of his religious training, to be brought to the same plane as a bodhisattva immediately destined for Buddhahood? One of the most confusing aspects of this issue is the fact that this nonbacksliding status is promised sometimes before and sometimes after birth in the Pure Land. We can even find both meanings within the same sūtra, such as the *Fo-shuo A-mi-t'o ching* 佛説阿彌陀經. (T. 366).[26]

After consideration of this path of easy practice and its dependence on the pivotal role of Amitābha Buddha, T'an-luan further clarified the Pure Land mārga by giving it the terse designation "other-power" (*t'a-li/tariki* 他力). The *locus classicus* for the concepts of *jiriki/tariki* is thus found in T'an-luan's *Commentary on (Vasubandhu's) Treatise on Birth (in the Pure Land)*, the *Wu-liang shou ching yu-p'o-t'i-she yüansheng chieh chu*, commonly known as the *Ching-t'u lun-chu* 浄土論註 (T. 1819):

> Giving examples, I shall explain the characteristics 相 of *jiriki* and *tariki*. It is just like the case of someone who accepts and maintains the precepts because he fears he may fall into the three tainted realms. And because he accepts and maintains the precepts he is [thus] able to practice dhyāna and samādhi. Because of his dhyāna he therefore cultivates the supernatural powers (*abhijñā*). Because of his abhijñā, he can move around freely in the four continents. These are called (the working of) self-power (*jiriki*).
>
> On the other hand, there are those who are as if inferior, who may be able to climb up onto a donkey but cannot climb up into the sky. If they are able to join the retinue of a cakravartin, however, they will reach the sky and be able to move freely among the four continents without impediment. This is thus called other-power (*tariki*).... Alas, how foolish the students of this later age are! However, if you hear that you may *climb*

---

26 To wit, "Śāriputra, the sentient beings born in the Land of Ultimate Bliss are all nonbacksliding. Among them there are many who will become a Buddha in one more lifetime (*eka-jāti pratibaddha*)" (T. 12.347b4). "Śāriputra, there are sentient beings who have either already hoped, who or now hoping, and who will hope to be born in the land of Amitābha Buddha. All of these people attain nonbacksliding from *anuttarasamyaksaṃbodhi*, and they have either already been born in that land, they are now being born there, or they will be born there" (T. 12.348a13).

up onto the other-power (*tariki*) [of the Buddha], you should arouse the mind of faith (*shinjin*). Never abide in your own partiality.[27]

Apparently aware of the need to clarify the soteriological implications of the *tariki* path even before he expounds it, in the very beginning of his essay T'an-luan chooses to emphasize its links to the promise of nonbacksliding. Glossing Nāgārjuna's phrasing, he explains:

The *path of easy practice* is ... maintained by the force of the Buddha's [will such that] one thus enters "the group of those rightly established" (*cheng ting chü/shōjōjū* 正如房定聚)[28] in the Mahāyāna. Being rightly established is none other than nonbacksliding.... This *Upadeśa on the Wu-liang shou ching* (i.e., this *Ching-t'u lun ch'u*) is the ultimate extension of the Mahāyāna: a boat driven by the wind of nonbacksliding.[29]

Later scholars writing on Pure Land doctrine in East Asia made great use of T'an-luan's hermeneutic glossing of the attainment of "the group of those rightly established" as indicative of nonbacksliding status. Even Shinran, who stands out as one of the few Pure Land thinkers who asserts one can reach the highest bodhi in this life by means of the Pure Land path,[30] filled his writings with frequent references to the attainments of such goals as nonbacksliding, *anutpattikadharma-kṣānti*, and joining "the group of the rightly established" as proof the Pure Land path was in no way inferior to the traditional path.

The elaboration of what I am calling the alternative Pure Land mārga existing alongside the traditional mārga schemata is given probably its clearest explication in China by Tao-ch'o in his *An-lo chi*. Living approximately one hundred years after T'an-luan, Tao-ch'o is thought to have combined the "difficult/ easy path" distinction of the *Daśabhumika śāstra* commentary with T'an-luan's "self-power/other-power" construct into what he termed the Path for Sages (*sheng-tao men/shōdōmon* 聖道門) and the Pure Land Path (*ching-t'u men/*

---

27 T. 40.844a21–27.

28 The other usage of 正定 as *samyak samādhi* notwithstanding, T'an-luan elsewhere glosses it as *avaivartika* (T. 40.826b9). In this instance we should take 定 as *niyata* or *niyāma*. Paramārtha's translation of the *Abhidharmakośa bhāṣya* renders *samyaktvaniyato-rāśiḥ* as 正定聚.

29 T. 40.826b7.

30 This point is still hotly debated among the different branches of Shinshū, the sect he founded, with the Ōtani or Eastern Honganji taking the opinion I have expressed above and the Ryūkoku or Western Honganji doctrine maintaining the experience of Birth and the subsequent completion of the mārga, though simultaneous, occur after death.

jōdo-mon 浄土門). Since the phrase *sheng-tao* was the common translation for *ārya-marga*, an early term denoting simply "the Buddhist path," Tao-ch'o at once creates an entirely new interpretative framework with his dichotomy. By adding the word *men* to *ārya-mārga*, *the* Buddhist path became *a* Buddhist path, one whose length and difficulty was only reinforced by the overlay of the pre-Buddhist implications of the Chinese word *sheng*—an accomplished sage.[31] Drawing from sources recently translated into Chinese elaborating the *mo-fa/mappō* 末法 concept—that Buddhism had entered an age of decline or degeneration in which enlightenment was no longer possible— Tao-ch'o suggests a *p'an-chiao* of sorts that leads not to one particular text as ultimately authoritative but rather to the Pure Land mārga itself as the apex of his hermeneutical scheme. Also known as a scholar on the *Nirvāṇa sūtra*, Tao-ch'o is just one of many religious figures in East Asia whose study of Tathāgatagarbha doctrines brought them to an appreciation of the Pure Land path. In Tathāgatagarbha thought, not only is there a Buddha-essence in all sentient beings, but all sentient beings are said to be contained within or "embraced" (*shê/shō* 攝) by the Buddha as well. This doctrine led to the inference that conscious contact with a Buddha was not at all impossible, and brought into proximity Amitābha and his Pure Land. Tao-ch'o's *An-lo chi* speaks from this perspective, incorporating within it a sense of urgency arising out of the *mo-fa* doctrine.[32]

31 The word *ārya* in phrases like *ārya-aṣṭaṅga-mārga*, "the Noble Eightfold Path," probably meant something like "ideal" or "excellent" (= the path of excellence) or simply "Buddhist" and functioned primarily to exalt the Buddhist path as something worth pursuing. However, the common use of the Chinese *sheng* 聖 for *ārya* implied something more rare, even exclusive. *Sheng* denoted someone who has obtained sagely status after long years of cultivation, someone said to be accomplished in all fields. Thus used as an epithet for emperors, *sheng* functioned to glorify their special, even shamanistic powers, which were thought to have accrued from their unusually vast knowledge.

32 This is how Tao-ch'o explained the two paths: "One may also ask: '[Since] all sentient beings possess Buddha-nature, we should have had meetings with many Buddhas since kalpas long past. What is then the cause of why we have instead been revolving in saṃsāra [and continue to do so] up to the present moment, unable to emerge from this burning house?'"

Answer: "According to the holy teachings of the Mahāyāna, it is truly because you are unable to master either of the two excellent teachings for ridding yourself of saṃsāra. That is why you cannot escape from the burning house. What are the two?} The first is called the Path for Sages; the second is called Birth in the Pure Land. The first kind, the Path for Sages, is difficult to realize in this age. One reason is that it has been a long time since the Great Sage [Śākyamuni] left [this world]. A second reason is that the doctrine is profound but the comprehension [of people at the present time] is slight. Therefore the *Ta-chi yüeh tsang ching* 大集月藏經 says: 'During the final stage of my Dharma (*mo-fa*), hundreds of millions of people may endeavor to practice by cultivating the [traditional]

As the Pure Land movement developed, Tao-ch'o's carefully constructed apologetic, so heavily based on sūtra quotations, provided scholars within the Pure Land tradition with a useful and convincing argument for affirming the Pure Land position. Pertinent to our discussion here, as a work of central authority it became *de rigueur* to cite the *An-lo chi* as the authoritative statement of the Pure Land path as an alternative mārga fully commensurate with traditional mārga schemata.

3   Basic Themes of the Pure Land Path

Beginning as early as Nāgārjuna's commentary, we can now perceive a litany of four basic themes that appear pervasively in Pure Land treatises written throughout China, Korea and Japan: 1) The traditional path takes an extremely long time to complete, is fraught with difficulties and is beyond the abilities of most people, particularly in this historical milieu. 2) There is another, alternative path outlined by the Buddhas which is easier to travel and which will bring quicker results—specifically, reaching the nonbacksliding stage of a bodhisattva. 3) The key to this alternative path is some type of mental concentration on one or more Buddhas and recitation of the Buddha's name. 4) This is the latter stage of the Buddha's teachings (*mo-fa/mappō*) and therefore traditional *jiriki* practices no longer have the same efficacy. The Pure Land path is quicker, easier and therefore the only real choice.

Discussion of the Pure Land tradition as an alternative mārga must address all four of these points, and contemporary misunderstanding of the Pure Land message often stems from less than full appreciation of the fact that Pure Land doctrine depends on all four legs of this thematic structure. At the same time, the writings of all the so-called Pure Land patriarchs (T'an-luan, Tao-ch'o, Shan-tao, Chia-ts'ai, Genshin, Hōnen, Shinran, etc.) reaffirm the position that this alternative path is soteriologically dependent on the traditional bodhisattva mārga. That is, any discussion of Pure Land doctrine without the presupposition of the *ārya-mārga* severs it from the ground that gave it birth, removing its hermeneutical context. While one must never lose sight of the fact that such a radical counter-path only has meaning insofar as it embodies partial or total rejection of the approach, methods and assumptions of the authoritative

---

path, but there will not be a single person who attains it. In the final stage of the Dharma, the world will show itself to be an evil place filled with the five pollutions (*pañca kaśayāḥ*). There will be only the one gate leading to the Pure Land and it is the path you should follow'" (T. 47.13c2ff).

orthodox path, the final goals of both positions remain the same. If the Pure Land mārga went so far as to reject the goals of the traditional mārga, then its very Buddhist identity at that point could be called into question. Indeed, these are precisely the questions raised with regard to some of the so-called new religions in postwar Japan that are heavily Buddhist-based, such as Agon-shū and Sōka Gakkai. Much like the Vajrayāna, the Pure Land yāna is a statement about methods rather than goals; the teachings of the *ārya-mārga* are not denied, simply assumed to be unavailable existentially.

This mārga relationship can be seen, for example, in the structure of the sūtra that played perhaps the most pivotal role in the Pure Land tradition: *Fo-shuo Wu-liang-shou ching* 佛説無量壽經, translated by Saṅghavarman in 252.[33] In its discussion of the Buddha Amitābha/Amitāyus and his Pure Land, this text is best known for the forty-eight vows (*praṇidhāna*) of the Buddha, which center on the explication of his paradise of Sukhāvatī and his promise of welcoming all beings who aspire to attain it. But there is more to be learned from its story. In the first fascicle of the sūtra we are given the story of Dharmākara Bodhisattva's elucidation of his famous forty-eight vows, his struggle over many kalpas to complete the Buddha-mārga, and his success in doing so when he becomes the Buddha Amitāyus. In the second fascicle we have the efficacy of his vows of compassion confirmed by a reiteration of how easy it is to gain access to Sukhāvatī. My point here is that the sūtra's narrative structure presupposes important elements of doctrinal authority that are based on the traditional mārga concept. To wit, both the power of Amitābha as a Tathāgata as well as the force of his vows to set up a magico-realistic Pure Land and invite everyone to join him there are only meaningful given the truth value of the traditional mārga, for it is in the context of the traditional mārga that a bodhisattva becomes a Buddha and the significance of his vows, both general and specific, is realized. This entire event has its authority further confirmed by the fact that the story's narrator is Śākyamuni Buddha, whose own religious career is described in terms of the same bodhisattva mārga attainment.

Vowing to bring imperfect sentient beings into a perfect environment to help them reach their spiritual goals presupposes an inherently corrupt world filled with deluded, confused individuals. But however attractive the Sukhāvatī may be by contrast, it is not a heaven. It has been created expressly for mārga practice precisely because conditions in this Sanā world inhibit the spiritual progress of so many. This point is easily understood from reading through the

---

33 *The Larger Sūtra of Eternal Life*, a.k.a. the *Larger Sukhāvatīvyūha Sūtra* or simply the *Larger Sūtra*. The translation completed by Saṅghavarman in 252, is the standard text of the East Asian tradition.

vows themselves, where we find promises such as "if men and devas in my realm do not reside among the group of the rightly established who inevitably attain Nirvāṇa, may I not attain full enlightenment" (Vow 11)[34] or "if men and devas in my realm cannot attain [the *abhijñā* of] knowing the thoughts of others (*para-citta-jñāna*) to the point where they are aware of the thoughts of sentient beings in other Buddha realms one hundred thousand hundred million *nayutas* in number, may I not attain full enlightenment."[35] Thus the soteriological fundament of the larger *Sukhāvatīvyūha sūtra* rests squarely on attainments defined by the traditional mārga, and it is the unspoken acceptance of, or belief in, the reality of that mārga that raises this book from mere legend to salvific myth. By promising significant mārga stages after reaching the Pure Land, the presumption of postponing the completion of the path to a holy other time and place, the mārga itself has been somewhat mythologized.

The issue of the traditional path being arduous and beyond the reach of most people is not a doctrinal matter per se, at least within Indian Buddhism, although we may look to this as a possible cause of the doctrine of the three periods of the law. This element of the mārga experience represents something akin to a "transmission beyond the scriptures," stemming from a common feeling of existential crisis within individuals regarding their expectations and internal sense of achievement. Insofar as we have no historical confirmation that anyone has actually ascended from one stage to another in the order prescribed in any of the Buddhist mārga schemata, it is difficult to assess the general level of expectation toward the bodhisattva path within any particular Buddhist community. But it certainly should come as no surprise to read about individuals who felt a sense of frustration, if not despair, at what they saw as a lack of progress after years of dedicated practice. Particularly in East Asia, where the notion of progress on the mārga over many lifetimes never achieved the same *de facto* acceptance as it did on the Indian subcontinent, the temporal dimension of the mārga concept inevitably evolved into something new.

The emergence of the subitist movements in Sinitic Buddhism is the most obvious testimony to this fact. Add to this the eschatology of the *mo-fa/mappō* concept wherein true understanding of the Dharma by conventional means was interpreted to be beyond anyone's reach, and it should not be difficult to see how so many people were receptive to new definitions of mārga and

---

34 T. 12.268a11.

35 T. 12.268a3. It is not entirely clear how the phrase 下至 *geshi* should be read. If we take this as equivalent to 乃至 *naishi* it is thus a translation of *antaśas* in Sanskrit. However, *antaśas* is problematic. Possible translations are *so much as, at least, even, up to, including*, etc.

praxis that might be easier than the complex systems of both demanded in the Indian Buddhist tradition. It might also be helpful to remember that in the Pure Land religious equation the option of choosing the Sukhāvatī goal is couched in the most alluring language in the sūtras, with both Śākyamuni and Amitābha Buddhas urging their listeners to cast aside all doubt and proceed quickly in this direction. The appeal from the Dharma-side is thus equal to the intensity of aspiration from the sattva-side (which probably indicates their common origins). While the sūtras emphasize the unfailing compassion of the Buddha, the many interpretative treatises manifest a more emotional appeal. The best known and probably most dramatic example of the latter is the White Path allegory by Shan-tao, which depicts an individual standing at the beginning of a narrow path between two raging rivers of fire and water. With bandits pursuing from behind, the Buddha's calm voice urges him forward down the narrow, precarious path to the other side where peace and security await him.[36]

People become committed to religious paths from many different sources of motivations. The persistent appeal of Pure Land Buddhism in East Asia down to the present day presumes many adherents who accepted its premises and promises without dithering. But there have also been many for whom this alternative mārga became appealing only after a sense of frustration or even failure as mentioned above. The Chinese tradition developed an interesting concept to express the notion of an individual's spiritual capacity: the term *chi/ki* 機.[37] Having no apparent Sanskrit counterpart, *chi* is perhaps best known from that favorite phrase in *p'an chiao* discussions: *tui-chi shuo-fa/taiki seppō* 對機説法, "the Buddha's preaching is shaped to correspond to the ability of his audience to understand him."[38] This expression can often be found as a hermeneutic tool in East Asian writings to justify new slants on old teachings because it allowed the authority of the word of the Buddha (*buddhavacana*) to be molded by later commentators into doctrines that were seemingly never intended by the author(s) of any particular sūtra. Not surprisingly, Shan-tao uses it in his *Hsüan-i fen* 玄義分 section of his commentary to the *Kuan wu-liang shou ching.*[39] But the popularity of this term in the commentarial literature

---

36 Shan-tao's parable is contained within his commentary on the *Kuan wu-liang-shou ching.* The parable has been translated in full in Wm. de Bary, ed., *The Buddhist Tradition,* pp. 205–207.

37 See Ozawa's article, *Ki no go o megutte* 機の語をめぐって, in *Bukkyō daigaku Daigakuin kenkyū kiyō* 13 (1985), in which he argues that *chi* 機 can equal *vineya.*

38 In Tendai doctrine, this term is used to explain how the first four periods of teachings are only *upāya*, while the fifth period of the *Saddharmapuṇḍarīka* and *Nirvāṇa sūtras* is the direct truth.

39 T. 37.246b26; p. 3.16 of 浄土学選書 text.

also points to conscious attention being paid to the meaningful *differences* in the abilities and motivations of students of the Dharma. Given this orientation, it should come as no surprise, therefore, to see something close to personal confessions of inadequacy in the writings of the Pure Land masters, particularly in Japan.

While Shinran is better known outside Japan for such spiritual honesty, it was Hōnen, renowned as a scholar, teacher and Vinaya preceptor, who is said to have been the first to have the courage to come forth publicly with an admission of having confronted his own limitations. The religious movement that followed him began when he started preaching dependence on the Vows of the Buddha after having had a spiritual transformation wherein he found liberation in his ignorance. By the end of his life, Hōnen's impact on society was so vast it reached a level probably unsurpassed by any other religious individual in Japanese history.[40] As his fame as a teacher grew, Hōnen's self-awareness of his own lack of enlightenment seemed to grow as well. Hōnen's Pure Land message was not simply that the Pure Land mārga was more genuine than the traditional mārga because it was truly universal in application. He also clarified the need to first commit to the traditional mārga—only then could one appreciate the meaning of failure in praxis as an expression of the existential truth of knowing the limitations of one's own capacity. In other words, the adept must set out to conquer the bodhisattva mārga and push himself/herself with maximum effort in order to confront his/her spiritual limits. It is precisely this confrontation with what we may call "the meaning of nonattainment" that is the key to understanding the profound significance of the Buddha's message of prajñā-infused compassion. Thus one is required to ascend the path only to be able to descend it. For Hōnen, this realization meant that despite differences in our spiritual capacities, we are all nonetheless ordinary beings: any individual attainment is dwarfed by the stature of the Buddha's willpower. Hōnen's mārga thus may be classified as a kind of *pṛthagjana-mārga*, a path for ordinary people, where ordinary means admitting one will never become a sage or a saint, though he himself was anything but ordinary. The reason for

---

40   Of course there have been many influential spiritual leaders throughout the history of Japanese Buddhism, but Hōnen stands unique as someone who generated such an overwhelming response that in addition to lists of hundreds of his disciples, we also have records of the divided loyalties he created among many at court when his banishment was considered. Critiques of him appear in the writings of all the *other* major Buddhist schools (Hossō, Kegon, Shingon, Tendai, Zen, Nichiren, Ji). Gyōnen's *Genrushō*, which will be discussed briefly below, illustrates that a great many of Hōnen's students came from other schools; indeed this may have been the origin of much of the criticism lodged against him.

PURE LAND BUDDHISM AS AN ALTERNATIVE MĀRGA

the overwhelming response to Hōnen's message seems to lie not only in its promise of instant access to liberation at a time of great social upheaval, but also in the charismatic but genuine humility of its chief spokesman.

4   The Role of Samādhi in Pure Land Soteriology

The issue of which practices were considered proper for the attainment of the proximate goal of birth in the Pure Land is also an important one, for it played a major role in carving out the identity of the Pure Land movement. Although the recitation of the Buddha's name in the phrase *Nan-wu a-mi-t'o fo/Namu amida butsu* is the centerpiece of practice in the East Asian Pure Land tradition, it does not exhaust the range of that practice. Despite its reputation to the contrary, Hōnen's *Senchakushū* (*Collection* [*of Passages*] *on the Selection* [*of Nembutsu*]) includes a number of standard Tendai practices, reflecting a broad-minded view of practice. For example, although he argues for the unique significance of the recitation nembutsu practice, Hōnen also cites the authority of Vasubandhu's *Ching-t'u lun* for the scheme of the five kinds of *nen* (mindfulness) practice, only one of which is recitation.[41]

Concerning the efficacy of recitation in general, it should also be noted that there is a long tradition in the Mahāyāna wherein many sūtras contain lists of names of buddhas and bodhisattvas to be held in the mind or chanted. Also overlooked is the broad range of practices under the rubric of *nembutsu*. Nembutsu practice could encompass a wide array of potential meanings, from a ritual enactment of the "holy name," to single recitation at the moment of religious transformation, to Hōnen's 70,000 recitations a day, to Vasubandhu's fivefold *nien* (*smṛti/anusmṛti*) praxis, to a whole set of samādhi practices, to Shinran's expression of gratitude, etc. Genshin's *Collection of Essentials on Birth in the Pure Land* (*Ōjōyōshū*) is essentially a nembutsu manual illustrating the full range of practices inherent in this term.

The origins of the Pure Land movement in East Asia can be traced to an early visionary meditative tradition in which the practice of *buddhânusmṛti-samādhi* (*nien-fo san-mei/nembutsu zammai* 念佛三昧) merged with the ritual invocation of the Buddha's name. One important aspect of Hōnen's mass following

---

41   Hisao Inagaki has translated these *wu nien-men* 五念門 (*go-nen mon*) as "the five practice-gates of mindfulness: worship; praising his virtue by invoking his name; aspiration for birth in the Pure Land; contemplation on Amida, the Pure Land and the bodhisattvas dwelling there; and *pariṇāmanā*, transferring merit to other sentient beings there in order to save from suffering." Cf. H. Inagaki, *A Dictionary of Japanese Buddhist Terms* (Kyoto: Nagata Bunshodo, 1984), p. 77.

that has not been mentioned outside Japanese studies is that his reputation was supported by the widely-held belief during his lifetime that he had achieved *nembutsu samādhi*.[42] Although dhyāna and prajñā have always been closely linked from early in the Buddhist tradition, in Mahāyāna we also find the assumption that the attainment of certain designated states of samādhi *de facto* gave the adept the attainment of certain stages of prajñā as well.[43] This notion then conveyed the implication that the experience of these samādhi states by themselves signified certain stages on the mārga. Nowhere is this view of the importance of samādhi experience more evident than in the writings of Chih-i, whose fourfold samādhi practice forms an important goal in his meditative system. At least one of these, the *ch'ang hsing san-mei/jōgyō zammai* 常行三昧, or "constantly moving samādhi," based on the *Pratyutpanna-samādhi sūtra*, was aimed at achieving a vision of Amitābha Buddha, which was interpreted as indicating nonbacksliding status.

Tao-ch'o's *An-lo chi* also stressed the value of reaching samādhi states that produce a vision of, or even an encounter with, a Buddha. His essay devotes a considerable amount of space to this discussion of what he termed either "visualization" samādhi (*kuan-fo san-mei/kambutsu zammai* 觀佛三昧) or what may be termed "recollection" or "mentation" samādhi (*nien-fo san-mei* 念佛三昧). These two terms share a relationship that is too complex to delineate here, but Tao-ch'o appears to use them interchangeably.[44] In his *An-lo chi*, Tao-ch'o quotes a number of texts, including the *Mahāparinirvāṇa sūtra, Hua-yen ching, Ta chih-tu lun* (**Mahāprajñāpāramitośupadeśa*), etc., to build a persuasive argument that experiencing this samādhi is a guaranteed means to the attainment

---

42   This is the subject of the *Sammai hottoku-ki* 三昧發得記 which is contained in *Hōnen Shōnin zenshū* pp. 863–67. Tradition holds this work to reflect a secret transmission from Hōnen to his disciple Genchi 源智 (1183–1238), which the latter made public only after Hōnen's death, but it is probably a thirteenth-or fourteenth-century compilation of stories about the master, collected perhaps by a student in Genchi's lineage.

43   At this point in the discussion it might be helpful to remember that there arose a tendency in Mahāyāna Buddhism to stress samādhi attainment as the apex of praxis. Funahashi Issai in *Bukkyō to shite no Jōdokyō* 佛教としての浄土教 (Kyoto: Hōzōkan, 1973), (pp. 66–67), believes there appears to have been a subtle shift in the relationship between prajñā and samādhi whereby their simultaneous cultivation is overshadowed by a later approach which implied that the achievement of certain states of samādhi itself was tantamount to realization of the fundamental truths of Buddhism. *Buddhānusmṛti-samādhi* is frequently mentioned in this context as providing the practitioner with the benefits of *anutpattikadharma-kṣānti* and reaching the first bhūmi. This attitude can be contrasted with earlier notions of mārga focusing on prajñā where having reached a designated stage on the path one then had the ability to pass in and out of a particular type of samādhi.

44   At least this is the opinion of Takagi Akiyoshi in his *Shichiso Kyōgi Gaisetsu* 七祖教義概説 (Kyoto: Nagata Bunshodo, 1968), p. 159.

PURE LAND BUDDHISM AS AN ALTERNATIVE MĀRGA 61

of birth in front of the Buddha in the Pure Land. But Tao-ch'o is only following the position held much earlier by Hui-yüan 慧遠 (334–416) who led his group of followers in buddhânusmṛti practice before an altar to Amitābha Buddha in hopes of realizing the same goal. Shan-tao also clarifies the central themes of the *Kuan wu-liang shou ching* to be both *kuan-fo san-mei* and *nien-fo san-mei* (T. 37.247a18). Much later, Hōnen worked to establish a distinction between these two types of samādhi, as he needed to isolate the nembutsu-samādhi in order to build his theory that nembutsu was the Buddha's chosen practice for the Pure Land path.

Although the practices of samādhi and ritual recitation may result in different cognitive experiences, they merge religiously in the promise of the Buddha Amitābha to visit the practitioner at the end of his life to lead him to the Pure Land. It is unclear in the sūtras if this refers to the last moments of consciousness in this life or an experience after one has crossed over the boundary into the next, but many ancient biographies are replete with stories of portentous signs such as flowers falling from the sky, the presence of sweet aromas or purple clouds, etc., to indicate to those left behind that the hoped-for religious encounter did indeed occur.[45] This blending of the two forms of practice associated Amitābha Buddha was enhanced when early Pure Land exegetes took advantage of the ambiguity inherent in the term *nien* 念. As a term of translation, *nien* was used to represent *smṛti* (memory), *anusmṛti* (recollection), and *manasikāra* (attention); that is, the mental concentration of holding something in one's consciousness, and at times even stood for *citta*, or mind/thinking itself. As a Chinese term, however, *nien* also had a secondary meaning of recitation, probably the result of semantic borrowing from a similar glyph pronounced *nien* or *tien* 唸, which, adding the mouth radical, means "to hum."

It is also important to point out that the soteriological significance of experiencing a visual confrontation with a Buddha is not a phenomenon limited to, or defined by, the so-called Pure Land tradition. Taoch'o's reliance on the scriptural authority of the *Ta chih-tu lun, Huayen ching*, etc. for such samādhi states as mentioned above enabled him to go outside textual material based solely on the Amitābha cult in supporting his thesis.[46] For example, one of Tao-ch'o's quotes of the *Hua-yen ching* reads:

---

45 Such events spawned a genre of literature known as *wang-sheng chi/ōjōki* 往生記.

46 There are six sūtras whose translated titles began with the character *kuan* that appeared in Chinese translation in the fourth and fifth centuries (e.g., Taishō numbers 643, 649, etc.). It is assumed this genre was based on visualization meditation, and sought visionary parapsychological experiences. These are listed and explained in *The Sūtra of Contemplation on the Buddha of Immeasurable Life as Expounded by Śūkyamuni Buddha* (Kyoto: Ryukoku University, 1984), p. xvii.

What is the gate of *nien-fo san-mei?* Within the gate of this samādhi one is able to gaze at all the Buddhas as well as their retinues and the splendid, pure Buddha-kṣetra, enabling sentient beings to leave behind their conceptual errors (*tien-tao* 顛倒; *viparyāsa*). *Nien-fo san-mei* is a subtle realm in which one sees the realm of freedom of all the Buddhas and attains to an error-free state (*pu tien-tao*) over numerous kalpas. *Nien-fo san-mei* is able to bring forth all Buddha-kṣetras without their destruction [wherein] one sees all the Buddhas everywhere and one attains this error-free state over the triple-world.[47]

But the *locus classicus* for buddhânusmṛti-samādhi practice remained the *Pratyutpanna-samādhi sūtra* throughout the Pure Land tradition. It is a curious fact that, judging from the writings of the Pure Land patriarchs, later developments in the conception of a Pure Land mārga designed for people who could admit their inability to succeed on the traditional path did not obviate interest in samādhi practice. Perhaps most striking of all is that we have a monograph specifically on the subject of visionary samādhi, the *Kuan-nien fa men* 觀念法門,[48] a meditation manual of sorts, written by, of all people, Shan-tao. Shantao is, of course, best known for his unorthodox interpretation of the *Kuan wu-liang shou ching*, wherein he states that its sixteen different meditations on the forms of the Buddha and his Pure Land are only an introduction to the Buddha's real intention in the sūtra, which is the encouragement of recitation nembutsu practice. Modern discussions of how he became the most influential philosopher of continental origins in Kamakura Pure Land thought have tended to remain fixated on this latter point and its further promotion by Hōnen. As mentioned above, he also defined the central themes of that scripture as *kuan-fo* and *nienfo* samādhi. His writings on samādhi practice, however, particularly his attempts at harmonizing the samādhi teachings of *Pratyutpanna-samādhi sūtra* and the *Kuan wu-liang shou ching* are frequently quoted in Kamakura texts. Here Shan-tao identifies his taxonomy of the *Amitābha buddhânusmṛti-samādhi*: "The teaching of the visualization of the Buddha samādhi (*kuan-fo san-mei*) is based on the *Kuan ching*, the teaching of the recollection of the Buddha samādhi (*nien-fo sanmei*) is based on the *Pratyutpanna-samādhi sūtra*."

---

47   T. 47.15b15–20. This is not a direct quote from the *Hua-yen ching*, but rather a collection of phrases from a section in chapter 46 of the Buddhabhadra translation, see *T* 9.690a15–b4.

48   T. 1959.47.22. Full title: *Kuan-nien a mi t'o fo hsiang hai san-mei kung-te fa-men* 觀念阿彌陀佛祖海三昧功德法門.

Our understanding of Shan-tao's perspective on practice must therefore take into consideration his commitment to samādhi practice in addition to his advocacy of recitation. Some have found these two aspects of Shan-tao irreconcilable and concluded that his samādhi writings predate his *Kuan ching* commentary, where his affirmation of recitation nembutsu expresses his "final statement." But this interpretation assumes the two doctrinal statements are mutually exclusive, a position reflective of Japanese sectarian concerns but not demonstrable. Does it not make more sense to seek the rapprochement of these two positions within the thought of Shan-tao as a whole? A better way to view Shantao is from the perspective of the mārga problematic. That is, his acceptance of the value system of the traditional mārga is reflected in his concern with samādhi and his implicit recognition of the mārga significance of samādhi practice. His advocacy of recitation nembutsu is thus not a rejection of the value of samādhi but instead manifests his search for a means by which ordinary beings can attain it. Whether it be recitation practice (称名) or visualization practice (観佛), the *tariki* aspect is similarly reflected in the intercession of the Buddha's vow of compassion toward the practitioner: to help any being to attain buddhânusmṛti-samādhi.

In the *Ta chih-tu lun*, there is one discussion of *nien-fo san-mei* which offers a similar perspective to that of Shan-tao:

> In addition, by profound concentration on the Buddha, one is joined with the Buddha throughout. By cultivating [the practice of] *nien-fo san-mei* 念佛三昧 time after time [lit., age after age], one thus does not lose one's *bodhi-citta*. Never separated from the Buddha's vows [of compassion], one therefore desires to be born in the Buddha's world. Having planted the karmic seed of encountering a Buddha, this relationship is one whose continuation will never be cut off, up to the point of reaching unsurpassed perfect enlightenment. [In this sense] one is never separated from seeing the Buddha.[49]

Here we have a definite link between the attainment of buddhânusmṛti-samādhi, the desire for the proximate goal of birth in the Pure Land, and the attainment of the ultimate goal of final enlightenment. The formula given here thus combines nembutsu visualization samādhi with desire for birth in the Pure Land, while the phrases "not separate from the Buddha" and "not separate from the Buddha's vows" affirm the reality of the promised aid of the Buddha as well. The "encounter with the Buddha and the effect of His deeds"

---

49   T. 25:333b24–28.

expound the spiritual importance to the individual of contact with the omniscience (*sarvajñā*) of a Buddha while also affirming the active participation of Amitābha in the practitioner's particular experience.

Although buddhânusmṛti-samādhi could be applied to any Buddha, in East Asia it was generally linked to Amitābha, as is found in the *Pratyutpanna-samādhi sūtra*. As an orthodox Mādhyamika text, the *Ta chih-tu lun* illustrates a synthetic conception of Amitābha Buddha's two roles as the savior of ordinary beings and the object of samādhi practice. The adept is thus instructed to combine samādhi practice with aspiration for the interim goal of birth in the Pure Land in order to reach his ultimate goal along the mārga. Particularly in the phrase, "because one practices well this nembutsu samādhi, he is not separated from the Buddha's vows," the *Ta chih-tu lun* confirms the interpretation offered above regarding Shan-tao's interest in samādhi practice: namely, buddhānusmṛti-samādhi based on nembutsu practice was understood as encouraged and assisted by the Buddha himself. Thus nembutsu samādhi is extolled as a means of ensuring or confirming the relationship with Amitābha's Primal Vows. We should therefore understand the importance of a "deathbed vision" of the Buddha as the quintessential sign of salvation to be based in the high soteriological value placed on the buddhānusmṛti-samādhi experience. From this point of view it is easy to see why the achievement of this visionary state during meditation under healthy conditions was thought indicative of the ultimate empirical confirmation that birth in the Pure Land and subsequent ascension to final enlightenment were part of one's future.

In terms of mārga, this experience of encountering a Buddha is also significant because it was said to be indicative of nonbacksliding status. In the *Wu-liang shou ching*, the Nineteenth Vow promises an appearance of the Buddha before the dying believer, and the Forty-seventh and Eleventh Vows (by the traditionally accepted interpretations of T'an-luan, Chia-ts'ai and others) signify the nonbacksliding status of the inhabitants in the Pure Land.[50] Even in the *Shih-chu p'i-p'o-sha lun* it is stated that at the first bhūmi "there are sentient beings who will see the Buddha, which thereupon means they reside in the nonbacksliding stage [with regard to] *anuttarasamyak-sambodhi*"[51]

By the Kamakura period in Japan, the equivalence of buddhânusmṛti-samādhi with a nonbacksliding rank within the ten bhūmis had become orthodox. In

---

50   Chia-ts'ai 迦才 (ca. 627) in his *Ching-t'u lun* 浄土論 (T. 47.19b3) outlines four types of nonbacksliding. The first three are identical to those outlined by Chi-ts'ang 吉藏 (549–623) in his *Fa hua yi shu* 法華義疏 (T. 34.1721); Chia-ts'ai adds nonbacksliding from the Pure Land.

51   T. 26.32c.

PURE LAND BUDDHISM AS AN ALTERNATIVE MĀRGA 65

both his *Senchakushū* and *Amidakyōshaku*, Hōnen makes the soteriological value of buddhânusmṛti-samādhi quite explicit, perhaps reflecting concern about ambiguities prevalent in the minds of his audience. In a section discussing who should and should not be considered within the lineage of the Pure Land patriarchs, Hōnen offers a system of judgement based on one factor only, the attainment of samādhi:

> Question: There are many patriarchs [in our tradition], such as Chia-ts'ai of Hung-fa ssu and Tz'u-min san-tsang 慈愍三藏; are you not relying on them but solely on Shan-tao 善導?

> Answer: Among all of these teachers, although they take the Pure Land [teaching] as their center point, they have not attained samādhi. Venerable Shan-tao is a person who has attained samādhi. With regard to the path, there is [thus] already proof [of his success].[52]

And when then asked why he has chosen Shan-tao first instead of Shan-tao's teacher, Tao-ch'o, Hōnen replied:

> Tao-ch'o, although he was Shan-tao's teacher, had not yet [reached the state wherein] samādhi had arisen. Therefore we do not know if he attained Birth in the Pure Land.

In this passage we see that Hōnen has taken the position that without the experience of samādhi, understood to be buddhānusmṛti-samādhi, even an individual's birth in the Pure Land could not be confirmed. This is yet another example of how the Pure Land mārga, despite its best intentions to represent the goal of universal salvation, simply was unable to cut itself loose from its moorings to Chinese notions of orthodox Mahāyāna mārga. Hōnen, arguably the most significant figure in defining the Japanese conception of the Pure Land mārga, vilified and persecuted for proposing that it is possible to reach the Pure Land without the bodhi-citta experience, nevertheless determined that the ultimate measure of an individual's chances for liberation is his achievements in meditation.

---

52   *Hōrten shōnin zenshū* pp. 157.15 (*Amidakyō shaku* 阿彌陀經釋). Also in the *Senchakushu:* "Question: 'The masters of Kegon, Tendai, Zen, Sanron, and Hossō schools have composed treatises on the Pure Land tradition. Why is it you do not rely on these teachers, but only stand on the one master Shan-tao?' Answer: 'All those teachers, although they have composed ..., do not take the Pure Land as their main focus.'" The next line is identical to the *Amidakyō shaku* text above.

In orthodox Pure Land doctrine, nonbacksliding status is interpreted as resulting from not only the attainment of buddhānusmṛti-samādhi, the accomplishment of joining the group of those who are rightly established,[53] but also experiencing one of the forms of *anutpattikadharma-kṣānti*, or "acquiescence to the nonproduction of all dharmas" (*mushōbōnin* 無正法忍).

Outside of Pure Land dogmatics, *anutpattikadharma-kṣānti* is a term used with a variety of mārga implications throughout the Buddhist tradition. However, it is clearly linked with nonbacksliding status in Pali literature,[54] in the Prajñāpāramitā literature,[55] and in the *Ta chih-tu lun*.[56] The latter also confirms the attainment of Buddha-vision samādhi (*pratyutpanna-samādhi*) as signifying a nonbacksliding bhūmi.[57] Even within the purview of sūtras focused on Amitābha Buddha, it is written that this is attained in some instances before and in others after one's Birth in the Pure Land. The *A mi t'o fo ching*, for example, mentions this attainment by beings both prior to reaching the Pure Land as well as by beings residing in the Pure Land.[58]

Rigorous discernment of the precise nature of *anutpattikadharmakṣānti*, particularly its mārga implications, is not easy. *Kṣānti* itself is an important virtue throughout the Buddhist tradition, with a variety of psychological implications. Sometimes translated as "patience," "forbearance," or "acceptance," *kṣānti* originally referred to a state of mind wherein insight into the truth results in the meditator's being unperturbed by either external threats or internal suffering. There are lists in various places throughout the literature of two, three, four, five, six and even ten types of *kṣānti*.

It is common to see a threefold *kṣānti* set in Chinese Buddhist literature, but even this grouping can reflect two distinct sets of meaning. One parallels the early definition given above and is based in the *kṣānti-pūramitā*. This state is said to result from understanding of the nonarising and nondisappearing of dharmas, creating a special patience toward 1) external sources of anxiety, 2) internal sources of anxiety, and 3) the world in general. Another threefold scheme, and the one relevant to Pure Land doctrine, is in reference to a state of acceptance linked to, but just prior to *jñāna*, spiritual knowledge.

The presentation of *anutpattikadharma-kṣānti* in the *Mahāyānasūtrālaṃkāra* also appears to have been quite influential on the Mahāyāna tradition. Here the threefold list presented above is glossed as patience (*marṣaṇa* and

---

53 See note 27 above. See also Inagaki, p. 317.

54 Cf. Funahashi Issai, *Bukkyō toshite no Jōdokyō*, pp. 96–108.

55 See *Mahāprajñāpāramitā sūtra* 大般若經 (T. 7.264b26–27).

56 T. 25.263c6.

57 T. 25.86c3.

58 T. 12.348a.

adhivāsana) and spiritual knowledge (jñāna), with this usage of jñāna explained as dharma-nidhyāna (reflection on the nature of dharmas). This can be traced to the Pali Canon, where we find the phrases dhamma-nijjhāna-kkhanti (M.i 140) and diṭṭhi-nijjhānakkhanti (S.ii 115, M.ii 170, 218, 234, etc.). The Mahāyānasūtrālaṃkāra statement notwithstanding, Vasubandhu decided in the Abhidharmakośabhāṣya that kṣānti should be taken as a form of dṛṣṭi rather than a form of jñāna.[59]

Edgerton renders anutpattikadharma-kṣānti as "intellectual receptivity" (p. 27). His explanation of the basic Mahāyāna sense of the three forms of kṣānti also corresponds well to the usual Chinese usage: 1) acceptance of the oral teachings of the Buddha (ghoṣānuga-kṣānti 意響忍), 2) feeling intellectually comfortable with the Dharma (ānulomikakṣānti 柔順忍), 3) direct insight into the truth that dharmas do not originate from anywhere or from anything (anutpattikadharma-kṣānti 無正法忍).[60]

The Wu-liang shou ching confirms the attainment of these same three kṣānti as listed by Edgerton. But it also specifically links this attainment to other mārga goals: "The trees of this sacred ground ... when even a slight wind blows, it raises the immeasurably beautiful sound of the Dharma which spreads throughout the entire kingdom. Those who hear this sound will obtain the profound dharma-kṣānti, reside in a nonbacksliding state, and [eventually] attain the Buddha-mārga."[61] In addition to confirming the link between kṣānti attainment and nonbacksliding status, here we also see both attributive mārga qualities linked specifically to final attainment of Buddhahood. This linking of the first two achievements with "the completion of the Buddha-mārga" thus confirms the felt need of the authors of this early Pure Land sūtra to clarify the significance of religious attainment of birth in the Pure Land in terms of the traditional conception of the path. The term "profound dharma-kṣānti" here can be understood as anutpattikadharma-kṣānti because elsewhere in the sūtra a distinction is made between the achievement of the "two kṣānti"

---

59 For this discussion, see Sakurabe Hajime, Bukkyōgo no kenkyū 佛教語の研究 (Kyoto: Hōzōkan, 1975), pp. 58–59. The gloss for kṣānti in the Kośa itself is saṃtīraṇa (judgement). Yaśomitra's gloss on saṃtīraṇa is upanidhyāna, meaning "consideration" or "observation." In the Pali Abhidhamma, santīraṇa is the last stage of investigation of an object, a kind of discriminating observation before the object is recognized (voṭṭhapanna).

60 Edgerton also illustrates that, as a result of insight into the nonarising of dharmas, anutpattikadharma-kṣānti is usually linked with anirodhadharma-kṣānti, the "acceptance of the nondisappearance of dharmas"; see Edgerton, pp. 55–56.

61 T. 12.271a2–9.

by those whose faculties are dull and the *anutpattikadharma-kṣānti* by those whose faculties are sharp.[62]

In its discrimination of nine different grades of being in the Pure Land, the *Kuan ching* manifests a usage of *anutpattikadharma-kṣanti* that is also clearly attributive of mārga attainment. Here the particular spiritual achievements of those who reach the Pure Land are described in detail for each stage—the highest stage being where one will not only be able to perceive the physical attributes of the Buddha and bodhisattvas present (*Buddha-anusmṛti*) but, mirroring the *Wu-liang shou ching*, will "immediately awaken to *anutpattikadharma-kṣānti*" upon hearing the sound of the Dharma in the jeweled trees.[63] In the case of those rated one step below this highest rank, however, although it is assured they will attain to a nonbacksliding status, they will need one small kalpa before their samādhi practice will yield the obtainment of *anutpattikadharma-kṣānti*.[64]

It was the *Kuan ching* that inspired the composition of commentaries by major figures in late sixth-century and early seventh-century Buddhism, such as Chih-i, Hui-yüan and Shan-tao, which had the biggest impact on the important T'ang period development of Pure Land doctrine. Shan-tao's interpretation of the implications of this term as expounded in his commentary, the *Fo-shuo Kuan wu-liang shou ching shu* (T. 1753) had particular resonance in Japan after Hōnen laid so much stress on it. Quite different from what one sees in the Indian tradition, Shan-tao refers to what appears to be a new tripartite scheme of *anutpattikadharma-kṣānti*: joy (*hsi-jen* 喜忍), realization (*wu-jen* 悟忍), and faith (*hsin-jen* 信忍).

The *Kuan ching* itself discusses the process of Birth in the Pure Land in terms of nine grades of spiritual ability without identifying them in terms of their relative positions on the bodhisattva mārga. In glossing the meaning of the accomplishments of the top three categories of people described in the sūtra, Shan-tao discusses the prevalent interpretation in China regarding *anutpattikadharma-kṣānti*:

> Let us take up the issue of how the various teachers have first explained the three kinds of people of the upper group. Those of the highest rank of the highest grade are bodhisattvas from the fourth bhūmi up to the seventh

---

62 T. 12.273b29–c1.

63 T. 12.344b25–345a2.

64 T. 12.345a19–21. See the chart illustrating the five usages of the term *anutpattikadharma-kṣānti* in *The Sūtra of Contemplation on the Buddha of Immeasurable Life as Expounded by Śākyamuni Buddha*, p. 126.

PURE LAND BUDDHISM AS AN ALTERNATIVE MĀRGA   69

bhūmi. The reason we are able to know this is that upon reaching that [Pure Land], they immediately attain *anutpattikadharma-kṣānti*. Those of the middle rank of the highest grade are bodhisattvas from the first bhūmi up to the fourth bhūmi. The reason we are able to know this is that upon reaching that [Pure Land], they attain *anutpattikadharma-kṣānti* after the elapse of one small kalpa. Those of the lowest rank of the highest grade are bodhisattvas of lineage (i.e., the ten stages of settlement, *shih chu* 十住) up to the first bhūmi. The reason we are able to know this is that upon reaching that [Pure Land], they commence their entrance into the first bhūmi after the elapse of three small kalpas. These three grades of people are all born into ranks [in the Pure Land] as Mahāyāna sages.[65]

Although Shan-tao then critiques this reasoning, his inclusion of it in his treatise affords us a look at what is at least his own understanding of the standard view of his contemporaries in the seventh century. In the context of this discussion, the linking of *anutpattikadharma-kṣānti* with certain specific stages on the ten-bhūmi path is most interesting, particularly with respect to the amount of time it takes (e.g., three small kalpas) to reach this insight after reaching the Pure Land. Shan-tao's own interpretation is, of course, somewhat different. He first reminds his readers of the significant fact that the Buddha comes to greet anyone on their deathbed if so requested, regardless of their spiritual capacity. He then offers the opinion that this means all nine grades of beings must be considered *pṛthagjana*.

After the sermon is finished, it is written that the interlocutor of the sūtra,

> Queen Vaidehī and five hundred attendant-women, having heard the Buddha's exposition, suddenly saw the broad form of Sukhāvatī and achieved a vision of the Buddha's body and his two bodhisattvas (in attendance), experienced a welling up of joy in a way they felt was unprecedented, and suddenly attained to a great enlightenment, acquiring *anutpattikadharma-kṣānti*. The five hundred attendant-women put forth the *bodhi-citta* of unsurpassed enlightenment as well as the desire to be born in that land. The World Honored One then predicted that all would [attain] Birth (*ōjō*) and after their birth in that land would attain *pratyutpanna-buddha-sammukhâvasthita-samādhi* ...[66]

---

65   T. 37.247c22.
66   T. 12.345a27.

Though clearly two separate psychological events, attaining a vision of a Buddha and attaining *anutpattikadharma-kṣānti* happen as consecutive experiences for the actors in the sūtra drama during the epiphany of their comprehension, implying that they are indicative of the same state of mind, if not the same stage on the mārga. Since elsewhere the sūtra promises the attainment of this *kṣānti* only "one small kalpa" after reaching a stage of nonbacksliding, it was naturally interpreted that the Queen had attained a nonbacksliding status as well.

Thus Shan-tao's assertion that the Queen does not represent an advanced stage bodhisattva but rather has only *pṛthagjana* status seems to imply a contradiction: how can someone who is only capable of understanding things through their form achieve the highest *kṣānti* whose content is of the nonarising (i.e., formlessness) of dharmas? Is not such a distinction of spiritual ability the reason why the *Kuan ching* divides the world into nine grades of beings? Shan-tao sees things in a different way:

> If you look at the meaning of the passages in the *Kuan ching* concerning good behavior with a focused mind and the different levels of the three grades of beings, [this illustrates] these are all ordinary people with the five defilements living after the Buddha has left this world. It is simply the result of different encounters that they are different, causing them to be discriminated into nine categories. What are these? The three ranks of people of the highest grade are ordinary people who have encountered the Mahāyāna. The three ranks of people in the middle grade are ordinary people who have encountered Hīnayāna [teachings]. The three ranks of people of the lowest grade are ordinary people who have encountered evil.[67]

Shan-tao has thus switched the paradigm for interpreting the sūtra in which distinctions in the type of meditation the adept can perform no longer determine how one is born into the Pure Land but rather the presence or absence of the appropriate occasion for spiritual advancement is affirmed as the determinate factor. In other words, the distinctions this and other sūtras make regarding how one enters Sukhāvatī is not based on one's inherent capacity (*gotra*) but the opportunities made available to the individual. Therefore, the identification of Vaidehī as an ordinary person who nonetheless experiences mārga attainments such as the enlightenment of *anutpattikadharma-kṣānti* normally reserved for people located somewhere within the ten bhūmis is central to

---

67   T. 35.249a29–b3.

the entire soteriological framework of the Pure Land path. The axis of this approach as an alternative mārga is thus the self-consciousness of oneself as not of saintly status and yet capable of saintly achievements given a fortunate encounter with the right teacher or teachings.

5   Conclusion: the Pure Land Path within the Larger Context of Buddhism

The purpose of this essay has been to situate properly the Pure Land Buddhist tradition within the soteriological framework of the Mahāyāna Buddhist mārga. In that the ultimate goal of the so-called Pure Land path is none other than the same final enlightenment of *anuttarasamyaksambodhi* similar religious issues pertain as would likely be found in any form of Mahāyāna Buddhism: *bodhi-citta*, moral cultivation, appropriate praxis, samādhi attainment, the realization of what the tradition designates as spiritual understanding, and nonbacksliding from these achievements until the final goal is achieved. What I have tried to show is that a reading of the experiences possible after one has reached Sukhāvatī in the *Sukhāvatīvyūha sūtra* should leave no doubt in the reader that any emphasis on the proximate goal of Birth in Buddha Amitābha's Sukhāvatī did nothing to obviate the primary goal of completing the ten bhūmis, the bhāvanā-mārga, the fifty-two stages, or however the Mahāyāna path is defined. But despite efforts by influential scholars such as T'an-luan, Shan-tao and Hōnen to declare the Pure Land version of this mārga as "the subitist of the subitist," the fact remained that two of the three major sūtras in the Pure Land tradition discriminate the manner in which one is born into Sukhāvatī into different grades or classes of people. This is the undeniable element of particularism found at the very core of the most authoritative scriptures that inevitably creates tension with the crucial message of universalism so vital to the school's identity.

To understand the evolution of Pure Land Buddhist doctrinal system properly, it is therefore essential to appreciate the fact that the universalism of its appeal did not remove its soteriological grounding in the traditional mārga and its concomitant recognition of individual differences in spirituality. At least by the Kamakura period in Japan, there was a clearly conceived alternative mārga available to Pure Land exegetes. After accepting (existentially or otherwise) the conclusion that one cannot reach traditional mārga goals and turning instead to the task of achieving the goal of Birth in the Pure Land, the key signposts along that path were nonetheless samādhi attainment, particularly buddhānusmṛti-samādhi; *kṣānti* attainment, namely, *anutpattikadharma-kṣānti*; and the promise of reaching a nonbacksliding status; and finally the concept that we are all ordinary beings. Without necessarily resolving these tensions, the assumption of this approach to bodhi nonetheless played an important role in the spread of the various Pure Land lineages in China and Japan. However, by trying to assert that ordinary beings, not advanced bodhisattvas, were capable of attaining these difficult practices, the important thinkers in the Pure Land movement were, in a word, trying to do the impossible. Perhaps we should look upon the figure of Hōnen as the quintessential paradoxical Pure Land figure: having experienced a vision of the Buddha in samādhi and carefully kept the monastic precepts, he is the prototype if not the archetype of someone who claims "ordinary being" status and yet experiences all the attainments associated with a nonbackslider destined for the Pure Land. But to recognize Hōnen as a successful Tendai monk weakens the sectarian consciousness, so in keeping with the *tariki* point of view, modern scholars often state that Hōnen's samādhi attainments were not the result of reaching any specified goal on his part, but occurred "naturally."

Psychologically, the Pure Land soteriological conception adds a third category to the more usual bipolar valence of Buddhism usually defined as knowledge and purification. This is faith, which perhaps may be defined in a Pure Land context as 1) a sincere acceptance of the working efficacy of the pledges to help made by the Buddhas and bodhisattvas (*praṇidhāna*) as elucidated in the sūtras, and 2) the personal realization that one cannot attain bodhi by oneself in this lifetime. There is always an inevitable tension in any subitist approach between immediacy of purpose on the one hand and the value of cultivated meditative insight and the accumulation of wholesome karmic roots on the other. Faith as the basis for a subitist school shakes up this formula somewhat by stubbornly insisting any soteriological discussion must accommodate the problem of *chi/ki*, the spiritual potential of the individual. The Pure Land position based on the lineage of T'an-luan, Tao-ch'o, Shan-tao and Hōnen is that the appropriate attitude for an individual to take, the one most spiritually fruitful, is that he or she is only an ordinary being, capable of only limited progression on the mārga by his or her own efforts. This is the core assumption of the Pure Land mārga, and all discussions of this "other" mārga come back to the fact that it is a mārga designed for ordinary people. When thus confronted with the Pure Land mārga as an alternative, the individual is forced to take stock of himself and somehow affirm that he is indeed more than "ordinary" in order to reject it completely. At the same time, even within the Pure Land soteriological conception, the traditional focal points of knowledge and purification continue to play a vital role. A figure such as Gyōnen 凝然 (1250–1321) is a good example of what we might call the mature Japanese harmonization of the conflict between the two approaches that first appears in Kamakura Buddhism. Gyōnen's phenomenal literary output and social recognition as one of the eminent monks of his time (he was one of the few national teachers, *kokushi* 國師, so designated during his lifetime) cannot be questioned. As a scholar of Hua-yen and the Vinaya literary traditions he embodied the values placed upon knowledge and purification that one would expect from someone of his stature within the *jiriki* path. At the same time, however, his Pure Land writings show he felt a great deal of resonance with Hōnen's teachings, which, among other things, manifests Gyōnen's personal admissions of humility regarding his own spiritual abilities.

Without any clear-cut resolution in China regarding this conflict between the demands of faith and the competing forces of knowledge and purification, the Pure Land doctrinal tradition was transmitted to Japan. This is just one example of how the Japanese and Koreans absorbed intact from their Chinese mentors the internal contradictions within the continental Buddhist traditions. Concomitant with and somewhat dependent on the sudden versus gradual debate and indeed the entire *p'an-chiao* evaluation of sūtras, doctrines, and their chronology were the various mārga schemata worked out in the commentarial traditions in India and China. In seeking an acceptable vehicle for their personal insight into Pure Land thought, Hōnen and his students seemed to have found the Chinese development of a Pure Land mārga concept to be insufficient. Instead they chose the hermeneutic tool of *p'an-chiao* to subsume the traditional mārga under a new formula wherein the legacy of their learned doctrine could be kept intact but with the three central Pure Land sūtras now elevated to a higher authority such that traditional Mahāyāna teachings and practices were given a new soteriological valence. In so doing, Hōnen gave new clarity to the concept of an alternative mārga as instigated by Tao-ch'o, yet never gave up his identity as a Tendai monastic.[68] This is perhaps best illustrated in Hōnen's *Senchakushū* where his existential choice of accepting the primacy of the nembutsu practice never entirely excluded other practices but rather demoted them to secondary status. This shows us that *p'an-chiao* was a more fluid concept than mārga. In other words, the relative significance of certain concepts coupled with the relative efficacy of certain practices leading to their comprehension could be reorganized by Kamakura thinkers, but the goals of the traditional mārga itself were never really redefined. This may be due to the fact that even Chinese speculations on mārga were based on Indian models perceived to be authoritative, but the attribution of relative degrees

---

68 Hōnen died in his Tendai monastic robes with a traditional Tendai ceremony, except that he refused to have a string tied from his hand to the Buddhist statue before him.

of importance to specific doctrines and practices through a *p'an-chiao* type of classification was something inherently Chinese and therefore more contiguous with the Japanese exegetical tradition.

The experience of the Ch'an/Zen schools in Kamakura Japan suggests many comparisons with Pure Land Buddhism of the same period. In terms of mārga, Zen seems to suffer the same fate as Pure Land in its offer of a subitist goal that is more obtainable than the traditional goal of Buddhahood or nirvāṇa. Both, for example, are forced to hedge their new formulations of the path by equally affirming the traditional goal of attaining Buddhahood. In Zen the ultimate goal of Buddhahood and proximate goal of *satori* are collapsed into the same event. In the Pure Land mārga the ultimate goal remains, by virtue of postponement, distinguished from the proximate goal of birth in the Pure Land. Both schools thus appear to gain and lose in their protestant stances. Zen gains by offering accessibility to the ultimate goal by means of the enlightenment experience of *zazen* and, in doing so, effectively denies the constraints implicit in any of the Indian mārga schemata. It loses by cheapening that ultimate goal, for enlightened Zen masters, despite their "living Buddha" status, clearly do not possess many of the mental or physical qualities of a Buddha as described in the sūtras, a fact readily admitted by at least the Japanese Zen tradition. In the case of Pure Land, the gain is clearly the universality of a practice so simple anyone can perform it, even without a focused mind. The proximate goal of birth in the Pure Land, moreover, can be rationalized as occurring immediately after death, thus removing the need for empirical evidence of attaining any or all mārga goals. The ultimate goal is instead removed to another place and time, but the position of man vis-à-vis this final goal of Buddhahood can only be seen as having been pushed even more remote from him because of man's stark dependence on a previous achiever of that goal, i.e., a Buddha, to enable him to reach even his proximate goal. Thus while Pure Land sacrifices the mārga's ultimate goal by relocating it to a "holy other" realm and in doing so effectively defines it as unobtainable in this world, the Zen tradition similarly sacrifices the same ultimate goal by idealizing it out of our existence in its substitution of the lesser but possible experience of *satori*. In both cases, the ultimate goal is replaced by a more accessible proximate goal. A by-product of both these new approaches to the mārga, then, is the dramatic increase in the distance between the Buddha and ourselves.

The role of ritual in Zen and Pure Land practice also suggests some interesting parallels. If we can take *zazen* as having a chiefly ritualized function in Dōgen 道元 (1200–1253) in the sense that it is not a means to anything but a kind of mystical participation in the Buddha's own enlightenment experience, then it is not difficult to see recitation nembutsu working in the same way.

The consensus that nembutsu is the chosen practice for Pure Land followers does not imply that it is the actual cause for attaining birth in the Pure Land any more than sitting Zen actually causes enlightenment. Nembutsu in the Kamakura age has a definite ritual function in that one is called to perform it by the Buddha; and as the "true" or "proper" practice (*shōgyō* 正行), participation meant recognition and acceptance (*kṣānti*) of the Buddha's attitude toward sentient beings. Thus there is a faith in the truth of the teachings and a reenactment of that faith each time the nembutsu is uttered. Zazen seems to fulfill a very similar role for Dōgen: the student is asked to accept on faith the historical truth of the Buddha's experience of enlightenment, the genuine transmission of the truth through a centuries-old lineage of teachers, and his own practice of zazen is a reconfirmation of his faith in that truth with every sitting.

The utilitarian dimension to zazen as a specific means to attain enlightenment is, moreover, quite parallel to the use of samādhi in Pure Land thought. As I have tried to show above, commitment to the *tariki* path did not obviate the value of samādhi for those engaged in Pure Land practices. Not only did such meditative experiences serve to confirm one's Birth as assured, they also brought about a different kind of birth in the Pure Land. Though everyone can be born in the Pure Land, not everyone is born in the same place in the Pure Land or at the same stage on the mārga. This is why there are three grades (*Wu-liang shou ching*) or nine grades (*Kuan wu-liang shou ching*) of beings discussed in Pure Land sūtras, all of whom can achieve Birth in Amitābha's realm, but may achieve it differently. One can even be born on the outskirts (*henchi* 辺地) of the Pure Land, which the *Wu-liang shou ching* defines as referring to those who doubt the truth of the Buddha's wisdom but are born in the Pure Land nevertheless.[69] Not only are they born on the outskirts of the Pure Land, they are born into an unopened lotus flower where they cannot see the Buddha or hear the Buddha's preaching for five hundred years. In Gyōnen's *Jōdo hōmon genrushō*, we read that Ryūkan 隆寛 (1148–1227), one of Hōnen's disciples, believes this happens to those who have practiced with a *jiriki* attitude.[70] Gyōnen also discusses how different kinds of practice can result in different births in different Pure Lands, some presided over by a *saṃbhogakāya-kṣetra* of the Buddha, others expressing a *nirmāṇakāya-kṣetra* of the Buddha. Considering thus the possibility of different types of births in different Pure Lands, the experience of *ōjō* 往生 can encompass a broad variety of meanings, much as the experience of *satori* can.

---

69   T. 12.275c14.

70   T. 84.198a2–4.

What remains unclear is the relationship between *ōjō* and samādhi. While *ōjō* is frequently discussed with specific mārga references, nembutsu-samādhi is not, other than its nonbacksliding implication mentioned above. Shinran's denunciation of any reference to *jiriki* practice precludes him from commenting on the topic meaningfully. For Hōnen's disciple Kōsai 幸西 (1163–1247), for example, the terms *ōjō*, *samādhi* and *shinjin* 信心 (the attainment of faith) all appear to be used synonymously; namely, they denote one moment of life-changing religious experience when one's own mind is a mirror image of the Buddha's mind.[71] In this instant, one not only sees the Buddha, one becomes the Buddha. This is precisely the manifestation of the Buddha-nature within the kleśa-ridden mind of the ordinary human being. In the Pure Land tradition, it would never be said that having experienced such an event, the person was "enlightened" or had become a "living Buddha." Rather, the terminology is that he has achieved *anjin* 安心, or reached nembutsu-samādhi, or even that he has "attained immediate Birth" (*sokutoku-ōjō* 即得往生). The latter is found in the *Wu-liang shou ching*, where we also find this attainment as indicative of nonbacksliding, thus the mārga is never left behind.

Just as zazen is spoken of in Kamakura times as the "preferred practice," Zen is also said to be the true orthodox Buddhism. That is, all Buddhist goals can be achieved through Zen, all Buddhist teachings and practices flow from Zen, all seekers must ultimately find their liberation through the Zen path. Kamakura Pure Land thinkers express no less certainty in the significance of their own path. Most importantly, Amitābha Buddha is understood not as a new Buddha introduced in the *Sukhāvatīvyūha sūtra*, but as the primordial Buddha from whose lineage Śākyamuni himself emerged and his introduction by Śākyamuni in this sūtra is but another form of *upāya*. As Kōsai explains, the entire canon can be thus understood as various forms of *upāya* created to bring all sentient beings eventually to this path selected by the Buddha. Hence the notion that Zen is the foundation of all Buddhism because it reflects the Buddha-mind of enlightenment is exactly paralleled in Pure Land thought, where seeking the interim goal of birth in the Pure Land reflects the Buddha's true intention for everyone. In this sense, the importance of the role of *mo-fa/mappō* doctrine of the latter stage of the Dharma in Pure Land thought, while playing a crucial role in East Asia until the appearance of Hōnen, becomes largely irrelevant in Kamakura Pure Land doctrine. To wit, if the Pure Land path is the only true path to follow, it makes no difference what age we are in. The circumstances in this degenerate age only make that alternative mārga more accessible. One must then wonder if there is not the notion of an "alternative mārga" within the Zen tradition as well.

---

71   T. 84.196bl8–197c19.

PART 2

Early Presence in Japan

∴

The Development of *Mappō* Thought in Japan (1)

Michele Marra

1 Introduction: *Mappō* in India and China

The idea that the Buddhist Doctrine is subject to continuous decline and that human beings cannot escape such a law is a concept known in Japan as the Last Dharma Age (*mappō shisō* 末法思想). The cardinal points on which this idea was based developed into the following theories:

1. The theory of the Three Ages, according to which history is divided into three periods, reflecting the progressive deterioration of the Buddhist Doctrine. These three periods are the True Dharma Age (*saddharma*, Jpn. *shōbō* 正法), the Imitation Dharma Age (*saddharma-prativāpava*, Jpn. *zōbō* 像法), and the Last Dharma Age (*saddharma-vipralopa*, Jpn. *mappō* 末法). With the exception of the Last Dharma Age, which was thought to last ten thousand years, the first two ages were supposed to last the space of either five hundred or one thousand years after the date of Śākyamuni's demise. These periods were combined in different ways according to four theories, as schematized below.[1]

		1	2	3	4
Shōbō	500 years after Buddha's death	500	1,000	1,000
Zōbō	500 years after *shōbō*	1,000	500	1,000
Mappō	10,000 years after *zōbō*	10,000	10,000	10,000

Source: Marra, Michele, "The Development of Mappō Thought in Japan," in *Japanese Journal of Religious Studies* 15(1) (March 1988): 25–54.

1 The first theory is based on the *Daijōsanjūsangekyō* 大乗三聚懺悔経 (Sūtra of the three categories of Mahāyāna repentance, T. 24, 1091–1095) and the *Kengōkyō* 賢劫経 (Sūtra of the sages' kalpa, T. 14, 1–65). The second is based on the *Daijikkyō* 大集経 (Great collection sūtra, T. 13, 1–408) and the *Makamayakyō* 摩訶摩耶経 (Sūtra of great Māya, T. 12, 1005–1015). The third is based on the *Hikekyō* 悲華経 (Sūtra of the compassion flower, T. 3, 167–232).

2. The theory of the Five Periods, a further division showing the deterioration of human abilities, each period lasting 500 years.

   a. Period of Strong Enlightenment (*gedatsu* 解脱), the first 500 years following Buddha's death, when the True Dharma was still in effect and enlightenment was secure for everybody.

   b. Period of Strong Meditation (*zenjō* 禅定), corresponding to the beginning of the Imitation Dharma Age, when all monks were practicing deep meditation.

   c. Period of Strong Listening (*tamon* 多聞), which corresponds to the end of the Imitation Dharma Age, when many people were still listening to the sūtras and following the commandments.

   d. Period of Temple and Pagoda Building (*zōji* 造寺), at the beginning of the Last Dharma Age, when teachings and practices were already being neglected but temples and pagodas were still built.

   e. Period of Strong Conflicts (*tōsō* 闘争), the end of the Last Dharma Age, when the Buddhist teachings had been completely forgotten, and the monks neglected the precepts, being too busy in doctrinal fights which gave rise to pagan views (*Daihōdōdaijūgachizōkyō* 大方等大集月蔵経, T. 13, 298–381).

3. The theory of the Five Defilements (*kaśāya*), according to which the world is defiled by the impurities of kalpa (*kōjoku* 劫濁), views (*kenjoku* 見濁), evil passions (*bonnōjoku* 煩悩濁), the mind and body of sentient beings (*shujōjoku* 衆生濁), and the human lifespan (*myōjoku* 命濁). These five marks indicate the prevalence of wars and disasters, the dominance of false teachings, the strengthening of desires, the increase of mental and physical frailty, and the shortening of man's life span (see the *Amida Sūtra* 阿弥陀経, T. 12, 346–348). This last idea developed into the theory of the life span of people, according to which life expectancy varies according to the period in which people were living. The length of human life was supposed to fluctuate between 80,000 and ten years, diminishing with the increasing evil of the age.

The concept of the impurities of kalpa was a development of the Buddhist cosmological view known as the "theory of the rotation of the four kalpas," in which history was seen as developing through the passing of four huge spans of time (medium kalpas, *chūgō* 中劫): the kalpa of becoming (*jōgō* 成劫), *the* kalpa of existing (*jūgō* 住劫), the kalpa of destruction (*egō* 壊劫), and the kalpa

---

The fourth is based on the *Daihikyō* 大悲経 (Sūtra of great compassion, T. 12, 945–972) as quoted in Hui-kuan's *Shakujōdogungiron* 釈浄土群疑論 (Treatise explicating the multitude of doubts concerning the Pure Land, T. 47, 30–76).

THE DEVELOPMENT OF MAPPŌ THOUGHT IN JAPAN (I)

of emptiness (*kūgō* 空劫). Each of these periods was subsequently divided into twenty small kalpas (*shōgō* 小劫), each of which was characterized by increase in the first half, and decrease in the second half. At the beginning of the kalpa of becoming, mountains and rivers appear, and during its nineteenth small kalpas, celestial beings, hell, men and all sentient beings are born. The process of human activity unfolds during the kalpa of existing. During the kalpa of destruction everything is destined to chaos and ruin under the destructive power of fire and wind. At the end, only the void is left in the kalpa of emptiness, waiting for the time of regeneration to begin over again in an eternal process.[2]

These theories, well known to the Japanese of the medieval age, were the result of development and mixture of ideas brought by Buddhist scriptures from India and China. Although the *Āgamas* presented the belief in the inevitable decline of the Buddhist Doctrine, stating that the True Dharma Age will disappear giving place to the Imitation Dharma Age (*saddharma-patirūpaka*), a coherent formulation of the theory of the Three Ages never developed in India.[3] Nevertheless, the word "final age" (*sue no yo* 末の世), which does not appear in early texts (*sutta* and *vinaya*), made its appearance in Mahāyāna scriptures like the *Vajracchedikā Sūtra* (*The Diamond Sūtra*, T. 8, Nos. 235–237, pp. 748–762). Here we find Subhuti's question: "Will there be any beings in the future periods, in the last time, in the last epoch, in the last five hundred years, at the time of the collapse of the good doctrine, who, when these words of the Sūtra are being taught, will understand their truth?"[4] The number five hundred came from the anecdote telling that the True Dharma Age, which was expected to last one thousand years, was reduced to the limited span of five hundred years after the acceptance of women into the Buddhist order, a story which developed into the theory of the Five Periods, each of them lasting five hundred years (*Daihōdōdaijikkyō* 大方等大集経, *Great Collection Sūtra*, T. 13, 1–408).

The twelfth chapter of the *gachizōbun* 月蔵分 roll of the *Daijikkyō* presents the Buddha's words that, after his demise, the True Dharma Age will follow for

---

2 This follows Vasubandhu's theory as found in the *Abhidharmakośa* (T. 29, 1–126).

3 See, for example, the following passage from the *Saṃyutta-nikāya*: "When the True Dharma of the Tathāgata is about to become extinct, an Imitation Dharma will appear. When the Imitation Dharma appears in the world, the True Dharma will be eradicated. For example, a ship in the ocean, when loaded with too many treasures, sinks at once. The True Dharma of the Tathāgata is not like this, but it disappears gradually.... Evil sentient beings appear in the world and do evils at pleasure. Plotting all kinds of evil deeds, they actually do evil. They talk non-Dharma into Dharma, and Dharma into non-Dharma" (T. 2, 226c). Quoted in Ryukoku University Translation Center 1980, p. xiii.

4 The original Sanskrit reads: *anāgate'dhvani paścime kāle paścime samaye paścimāyām pañcaśatyāṃ saddharma-vipralopakāle vartamāne*. Quoted in Kumoi 1976, p. 330, and Conze 1958, p. 30.

five hundred years, and then the Buddhist Doctrine will start to decline. The Buddha talks about monks who, looking for fame and profit, do not hesitate to abandon good practices and throw away the Buddhist teachings, adorn their robes, and live by trade or agriculture like laymen. These monks like to quarrel, feel jealous towards those monks who follow the precepts, and indulge in negligence, thus accumulating vast evil karma which finally brings several calamities to a world already destined to dry up like a desert. Floods, typhoons, and famines bring people to exhaustion and to war in countries destroyed by earthquakes, pestilences, and fire, where wells, springs, and ponds dry up, and crops suffer the consequences of a total lack of rain.

The description given by the *Great Collection Sūtra*, whose goal was the protection of the true Doctrine, is very detailed. In fact, this description is followed by the formulation of magic formulas (*dhāraṇī*) made in order to eternally preserve the true Buddhist Doctrine. To deny the existence of the true Doctrine was a necessary premise in order to sustain this Doctrine since, as the basic Buddhist teaching says, everything is destined to change. This sūtra didn't have, as its main goal, the purpose to present an apocalyptic view of the world, as we can see from the fact that no mention of the Last Dharma Age (*mappō*) was made in the roll mentioned above. The author's goal was to show that the decline of the Buddhist Doctrine was only due to the increase in the breaking of the precepts and to the absence of virtue in people's behavior. The same sūtra presents the theory of the Five Periods which, combined with the concepts of True and Imitation Dharma Ages, makes us certain that the main features of *mappō* thought were already present in this scripture. Nevertheless, the *Great Collection Sūtra* did not introduce the theory of the Five Periods in order to stress the view of an uninterrupted historical decline, as we can see from Buddha's statement that, if we reach enlightenment through one of the practices still alive in the five periods, we are equal to those people who lived during the True Dharma Age. As in the case of the description of the world's catastrophes, the theory of the Five Periods was presented with the purpose of illustrating the necessity to preserve the Buddhist Doctrine. The sūtra's main idea was turned to the sad possibility that the Doctrine had to decline, without implying any inevitable historical destruction (see Kazue 1961, pp. 11–23).

The same critical attitude against the secularization of the Buddhist community during the Final Age, meant as the time immediately following Buddha's entering into *nirvāṇa*, was taken by the compiler of the *Daihōdōmusōkyō* 大方等無想経 (T. 12, 1077–1106).

In India, moreover, the theories of the Five Defilements, with particular regard to the idea of the life span of people and of the rotation of the four kalpas, were all fused together in the third chapter of the *Abhidharmakośa*

THE DEVELOPMENT OF MAPPŌ THOUGHT IN JAPAN (I) 83

(T. 29, 1–160) by Vasubandhu (ca. 420–500). Here we read that at the end of the kalpa of becoming (*vivarta-kalpa*), the lifespan of people is nearly eternal, but with the arrival of the kalpa of existing (*antaḥkalpa*) such life expectancy decreases until it reaches the short span of ten years. This process takes place during the first small kalpa of the medium kalpa of existing. In the following eighteen small kalpas life expectancy keeps increasing and decreasing from ten to 80,000 years, and the twentieth small kalpa witnesses only the process of increase in life. The Buddha appears only at the time when human life drops from 80,000 to one hundred years and not after that time, since, because of the worsening of the five defilements, it becomes difficult to teach the Doctrine to human beings (Poussin 1971, II, pp. 181–194). Many later Mahāyāna scriptures would argue that the Buddha appeared exactly because of the sinful nature of this world.

Although there is no doubt that the germs of *mappō* thought were already there in the Pali and Sanskrit scriptures, they still lacked a coherent systematization. Nobody went so far as to formulate a theory of the Three Ages, the main pillar of *mappō* thought, which was the result of the strong opposition met by Buddhism from the Chinese Emperors Wu 大武帝 (424–451) of the Northern Wei 北魏 (386–534) and Wu (561–577) of the Northern Chou 北周 (557–581) Dynasties. External factors allowed Chinese monks to express clearly what, until then, had been kept inside the heart of believers who inwardly felt the declining of the Buddhist Doctrine, but who still needed historical proof to confirm their beliefs. The Emperors Wu provided that proof, thus causing the diffusion through China *of mappō* thought at the time of the Sui 隋 (581–618) and T'ang 唐 (618–907) dynasties. In a sūtra carved on a stone north of Peking by monk Jing-wan 静琬 of the Sui dynasty we read: "The True and Imitation Dharma Ages lasted 1,500 years. Being now in 628, already seventy-five years have passed from the time we entered the Last Dharma Age. I carved this sūtra at the time of the persecution of Buddhism, during the Last Dharma Age, in order to spread Buddhist teachings" (Michihata 1976, p. 339).

The same consciousness of being already in the Final Age was presented in the *An lo chi* 安楽集 (Collection of essays on the western paradise, T. 47, 4–22) by Tao-ch'o 道綽 (562–645), a witness of the Northern Chou persecution who saw in the Pure Land the only escape available to ignorant people during the degenerate age of the Buddhist Doctrine. The theory of the Three Ages appeared clearly formulated in the *Li shih yüan wen* 立誓願文 (T. 46, 786–792) by the T'ien-t'ai monk Hui-ssu 慧思 (515–577) of Northern Chou, and in the works of monk Chi-tsang 吉蔵 (459–623) of the San-lun school. In China the theory of the Three Ages and the theory of the Five Defilements were mixed together in the attempt to show the degeneration of the times in which people were living, as it is stated in the *Fa yüan chu lin* 法苑珠林 (Forest of gems in the garden of the Law, T. 53, 269–1030) compiled by Taoshi 道世 of the early T'ang. These were years of Buddhist persecutions, a time when, as a consequence of the Buddhist suppression of 574, Buddhist temples, statues and sūtras were all objects of confiscation and destruction. This was fertile ground for the spreading of *mappō* thought and the search for salvation, through the activities of the sect of the Three Stages (Sanchieh-chiao 三階教) established by Hsin-hsing 信行 (540–594), and of the Pure Land school led by Tao-ch'o and Shan-tao 善導 (613–681). Both sects, although differing in their conclusions, shared the belief that a particular type of Buddhism was required by people of the Last Dharma Age, who were too ignorant to be able to find salvation by themselves. In his main work, the *San chieh fo fa* 三階仏法 (The doctrine of the Three Stages), Hsin-hsing stressed the fact that the old Buddhist sects (T'ien-t'ai, Hua-yen, San-lun, Ch'engshih) satisfied the needs of the people living in the first two ages, whereas in the Last Dharma Age people could be saved only by his own teaching, a universal Buddhism which overcame all the prejudices and particular views of the other sects and which, at the same time, incorporated the belief in all Buddhas and all doctrines. The same concern for the ignorant people living in an age devoid of doctrines led the Amidists to preach the cult of Amida and of the invocation of his name (*nenbutsu* 念仏) as the easiest way to reach salvation. In both sects we detect the search for a Buddhist doctrine suitable to a particular time, namely the Last Dharma Age. Tao-ch'o's *An lo chi* clearly states that the Buddhist Doctrine has no meaning if it is not fit to the time of the listeners to which it is addressed. Quoting the theories of the Three Ages and Five Periods, it says that one simple recitation of Amida's name washes the sins of 800,000 kalpas. The recitation of Amida's name was the way offered by the Jōdo school in order to escape *mappō*. The sect of the Three Stages disappeared soon (845), leaving the Pure Land school the true hero of *mappō* thought.[5]

2 *Mappō* in Japan—Kyōkai

In Japan the theory of the Three Ages was dealt in the *Sangyōgisho* 三経義疏, a commentary written by Shōtoku Taishi 聖徳太子 (573–621) on three sūtras, the *Shōmangyō* (Sūtra of Queen Śrīmālā 勝鬘経), the *Yuimakyō* (Vimalakīrti Sūtra 維摩経), and the *Lotus Sūtra*. Shōtoku Taishi accepted the theory of the True Dharma lasting five hundred years and of the Imitation Dharma lasting one

---

5 For details on the sect of the Three Stages see Yabuki 1927.

THE DEVELOPMENT OF MAPPŌ THOUGHT IN JAPAN (I)

thousand years. Following the tradition of the *Chou shu i chi* 周書異記 (Record of the extraordinary events of the Chou Dynasty), according to which Buddha would have died in 949 BC, he calculated that the Last Dharma Age had begun in 552, during the 13th year of Emperor Kinmei's reign (539–571). But he also presented the theory according to which the historical Buddha would have died in 609 BC, in which case *mappō* was believed to begin in 891. According to the first theory, Shōtoku Taishi was already living in the Last Dharma Age, a fact which must have amazed the same Shōtoku, who was witnessing the peak of prosperity enjoyed by Buddhism in Japan. This was a time when Buddhist Law and Imperial Law were one and the same, mutually supporting one another, with Buddhism a supporter of the *ritsuryō* system and Buddhist prayers a means to protect the country from disasters and to strengthen it. Should we accept the year 552 as the beginning of the Last Age in Japan, we might add that *mappō* coincided in that country with the introduction of Buddhism. According to the *Nihon shoki* 日本書紀 (Chronicles of Japan, 720), an image of Śākyamuni in gold and copper was sent in 552 by the Korean King Syöng-myöng 聖明王 of Paekche as a gift to emperor Kinmei, together with several flags and canopies, a number of volumes of sūtras, and an exhortation to embrace the new religion (Sakamoto 1965, 68, pp. 100–101; Aston 1980, 2, pp. 65–66). The year 552 was not a casual choice for the introduction of Buddhism to Japan, being the fifteen-hundredth year after Buddha's supposed demise in 949 BC.

When, at New Year's day of 743, the *Konkōmyōsaishōōkyō* 金光明最勝王経 (Skt. *Suvarṇaprabhāsa Sūtra*, Sūtra of the golden light, T. 16, 403–456) was read in the Konkōmyō-ji, the monk intoning the word *zōbō* (Imitation Doctrine) was filled with hope, since *zōbō* meant a period when the Buddhist Doctrine was going to be restored, thus reaching the glory enjoyed in the past age of the True Dharma. Such optimism can be explained only when we recall the fact that this sūtra was, along with the *Lotus Sūtra* and the *Ninnōkyō* 仁王経 (Sūtra of the benevolent kings, T. 8, 825–833), one of the three scriptures officially adopted for the protection of the country, thus excluding the possibility of giving *zōbō* the connotation of decline and degeneration.

The consciousness of a spiritual crisis which started the process of diffusion of *mappō* ideas was brought about a few years later by unofficial monks who operated outside the monastic institutions codified by the *yōrō* 養老 code (701), and who addressed themselves to common people. A good example is provided by Gyōgi 行基 (668–749), whose activity as itinerant preacher helped to change Japanese Buddhism, the audience of which until then had been limited to political leaders. A new sense of self-criticism was brought into the Japanese monastic order by the arrival of Chinese monks like Taohsüan 道宣 (Jpn. Dōsen, 596–667) and Chien-chen 鑑真 (Jpn. Ganjin, 687–763), who were instrumental in breaking the identification of Buddhist Law and Imperial Law, transforming Buddhism into a way of thinking and believing which every single human being must face personally (see Ishida 1976, pp. 359–360).

Such sensibility can be detected in the figure of the self-ordained monk Kyōkai 景戒 (757?–after 822), who must have been very well acquainted with the *Daijikkyō*, quoted several times in the *Nihon ryōiki* 日本霊異記 (Wondrous stories of karmic retribution of good and evil in Japan), a collection of Buddhist tales. As we have already seen, the *Daijikkyō*, while teaching the scheme of the Five Periods, stressed the neglect in which monks were keeping Buddhist teachings and precepts, being prey to envy, jealousy, and other mundane concerns. Kyōkai himself witnessed a similar reality in light of the edicts proclaimed by Emperors Kōnin 光仁 (r. 770–781) in 780 and Kanmu 桓武 (r. 781–806) at the end of the eighth century. These edicts had the purpose of removing the monks' interest in politics and plots, and restoring a community devoted to religious practices. The relationship between Empress Shōtoku 称徳 (r. 764–770) and monk Dōkyō 道鏡, with all its political implications, was only one, albeit the clearest example of the totally worldly nature of religion in that time. Moreover, Kyōkai must have been very much struck by the antagonism between different sects of the same Buddhist faith, and among jealous monks, as seen in the story of Chikō, an eminent monk of Gangō-ji belonging to the Sanron school. Chikō was summoned to hell by King Yāma because of the jealousy he felt when Gyōgi, a mere novice in Chikō's opinion and a man who had experienced the condemnation of the court because of activities outlawed by the codes of the time (*sōni-ryō*), was appointed to the high position of Great Chief Executive (*Daisōjō* 大僧正) (Koizumi 1984, pp. 123–129; Nakamura 1973, pp. 167–171). This story stands as a proof of Kyōkai's realization that he was already living in the fifth and last of the Five Periods, the Period of Strong Conflicts (*tōsō*), at the end of the Last Dharma Age.

Another reason which confirms Kyōkai's knowledge of the *Daijikkyō* can be found in the many passages throughout the *Nihon ryōiki* defending the figure of the monk and of all those who have undertaken the Buddhist way, even the self-ordained monks, the true beggars of the time who were so persecuted by Emperor Kanmu. The crimes perpetrated against monks and lay-brothers are those most severely punished in the *Nihon ryōiki*.[6] This may seem to be in contradiction to the criticism moved in the *Daijikkyō* against the corruption of the Buddhist community. The *gachizōbun* roll of the same *Daijikkyō*, however, states that in the Last Dharma Age, when no one of high capability is left alive in this human world, the common person who takes the tonsure

---

6 *Ninon ryōiki* (hereafter "NR") 2:1, 2:11, 2:18, 2:35, 3:14, 3:15, 3:24, 3:33.

THE DEVELOPMENT OF MAPPŌ THOUGHT IN JAPAN (I)   87

or simply undertakes Buddhist practices, whether one keeps the precepts or breaks them, must be considered a Buddha Treasure. This was because, by simply thinking of the Buddha, this person was doing something more meritorious than anybody else in that age. This idea, developed in *Mappō tōmyōki* 末法燈明記 (The candle of the Latter Dharma) and, later, in Shinran's works,[7] led Kyōkai to quote a passage from the *Jizō jūringyō* 地蔵十輪経 (T. 13, 721–776): "As an orchid, even if it has withered, excels other flowers, so monks, even if they violate precepts, excel non-Buddhists. To talk about a monk's faults such as whether he violates or keeps the precepts, whether he recognizes or does not recognize the precepts, or whether he has or has not faults is a graver sin than that of letting the bodies of innumerable Buddhas bleed" (NR 3:33; Koizumi, p. 286; Nakamura, pp. 268–269).

This quotation, included in a chapter devoted entirely to the defense of self-ordained monks, sounds like a matter of self-defense written by a Kyōkai who was trying to free from Kanmu's persecution all those peasants who had to abandon their work because of the enormous amount of taxes levied for building the great temples of Nara, and because of the compulsory conscription started in order to build an army against the northern Emishi, and who were thus forced to find their sustenance wandering as unofficial or self-ordained monks (*shidozō* 私度僧). However, beside very personal motivations, we cannot ignore the fact that such a defense could only be built on the premises that these monks were living in an age as corrupt as the one described in the *Daijikkyō*, thus showing that Kyōkai was quite aware of what had been written on *mappō* before his time.[8]

In the first part of the preface to the third volume which is known as *Maeda-bon itsubun* 前田本逸文 (Lacuna of the Maeda manuscript), a controversial passage believed spurious by some scholars, Kyōkai writes about the True Dharma Age lasting five hundred years, the Imitation Dharma Age one thousand years, and the Last Dharma Age destined to last 10,000 years. Moreover, he took 949 BC, the date of Śākyamuni's death, to be in total accord with the theories presented in the *Daijikkyō*, and AD 552 to be the year for the official introduction of Buddhism to Japan. The passage says: "The Inner Scriptures show how good and evil deeds are repaid, while the Outer Writings show how good and bad fortunes bring merit and demerit. If we study all the discourses *Śākyamuni* made during his lifetime, we learn that there are three periods: first, the period of the True Dharma (*shōbō*), which lasts five hundred

---

7   See the second part of this article in Vol. 15/4.
8   On the position of Kyōkai as a "pioneer of Japanese *mappō* thought" see Masuko 1969, pp. 35–58.

years; second, the period of the Imitation Dharma (*zōbō*), lasting one thousand years; and third, the period of the Degenerate Dharma (*mappō*), which continues for 10,000 years. By the fourth year of the hare, the sixth year of the Enryaku era (787), seventeen hundred and twenty-two years have elapsed since Buddha entered *nirvāṇa*. Accordingly, we live in the age of the Degenerate Dharma following the first two periods. Now, in Japan, by the sixth year of the Enryaku era, two hundred and thirty-six years have elapsed since the arrival of the Buddha, Dharma and Samgha" (Koizumi, pp. 207–208; Nakamura, p. 221).

Knowledge of the theory of the Three Ages doesn't necessarily lead to belief in the continuous and uninterrupted deterioration of the quality of human beings. When we examine the purpose or reason why Kyōkai compiled the stories of *Nihon ryōiki*, we realize that the author was aiming at a practical goal, to "lead people to good, and show them how to cleanse their feet of evil," as Kyōkai himself put it in the same preface (Koizumi, p. 210; Nakamura, p. 222). The same thing was said in the preface to the first volume where Kyōkai stressed the didactic nature of his work, in the attempt to make the reader to "put aside evil, live in righteousness and, without causing evil, practice good" (Koizumi, p. 25; Nakamura, p. 102). If Kyōkai believed in the possibility of teaching human beings, he couldn't accept the consequences hinted at in the theory of the Three Ages. He believed that a correct knowledge of the inexorable laws of karma could drive people along the right path in this life, and therefore he strove to show the sad consequences that ignorance of the Buddhist teachings could have in the present world. The basic idea underlying *Nihon ryōiki* was Kyōkai's belief in the possibility of earthly improvement. Even if many references to Amida's paradise, the western land of bliss, do appear in the book, they remain outside the author's main concern.[9]

Kyōkai's interest in the present world is well documented by the kind of description he gave of hell and of the other world, and by the role played by hell in more than fourteen stories.[10] The story of the assistant governor Hirokuni 広国 who, after his sudden death, was brought back to life so that he could tell of his experiences in the other world, gives the same details that we find in all the other descriptions of hell included in the *Nihon ryōiki*. Hirokuni was accompanied on his journey by two messengers who brought him to a river with a golden bridge. Crossing the bridge he found himself in a strange land known as "the land in the southern direction" (*tonan no kuni* 度南の国). After reaching the capital, he was escorted by eight armed officials to a golden palace, residence of King Yāma, who was sitting on a golden throne. There Hirokuni

---

9   References to the Pure Land are made in NR 1:22, 2:22, 3:30 and postscript.

10   NR 1:30, 2:5, 2:7, 2:16, 1:19, 2:24, 2:25, 3:9, 3:22, 3:23, 3:26, 3:35, 3:36, 3:37.

met his wife, whose body was pierced with iron nails and with an iron chain around her limbs, on account of the sin of envy and hate committed when the woman was driven out of the house by her husband. Yāma let Hirokuni go, warning him not to talk thoughtlessly about the land of the dead (*yomotsukuni* 黄泉). Hirokuni continued his journey following a southern direction where he met with his father, who was standing and holding a hot copper pillar. He had thirty-seven nails in his body and was beaten nine hundred times a day for having killed living beings, and for having collected high interests on loans in order to support his family. Moreover, Hirokuni's father confessed to having robbed others of their possessions, committing adultery with the wives of others, neglecting filial piety and reverence to his elders, and to having used abusive language to his debtors. He urged his son, therefore, to make a Buddha-image and to copy holy scriptures in order to atone for his sins. Hirokuni, back at the bridge, was about to cross it when he was stopped by the guards watching the gate, who reminded him of the prohibition of letting out anybody who had already stepped into hell. Thanks to the wondrous intervention of a human incarnation of the *Lotus Sūtra* that he had copied in his childhood, Hirokuni was finally able to return to this world (NR 1:30; Koizumi, pp. 86–93; Nakamura, pp. 143–146).

We can detect many heterogeneous elements in Hirokuni's description of hell, from a shamanistic concept of a bridge over which it is possible to pass from one cosmic region to another, thus establishing communication with the world above and the world below (Eliade 1972, p. 173), to a Buddhist interpretation of a vedic deity, Yāma, seen as a judge dispensing penalties and rewards, not to mention the Confucian behavior of Hirokuni, whose filial piety makes him repay his father's love by atoning for his sins. Beside all these influences which confirm the complex manner in which the pattern of Japanese civilization had already been woven by the time of the recording of the first written documents, we are presented in the ninth century with a kind of other world conceived as an open realm in constant communication with the living world, in the very tradition of Japanese indigenous thought. Hirokuni's hell is on this point very similar to *tokoyo* 常世, the land at the bottom of the ocean conceived by ancient Japanese as a spot in constant communication with this world, as the land of the spirits of the ancestors, where all the dead are going and from where all new lives are coming. We may think of the pages of the *Kojiki* 古事記 (Record of ancient things, 712) presenting the myth of Ōkuninushi, the land-creator and culture hero of Izumo mythology. He overcame his eighty evil brothers after having obtained the sword, bow, and divine *koto* which Susanoo, son of Izanagi, jealously kept in the underworld. *Ōkuninushi* succeeded in his attempt only after having surmounted Susanoo's tricks, and thanks to

Susanoo's daughter, Suseribime. He managed to escape safely from the underworld, together with Suseribime who had become his wife.[11]

At the same time, Hirokuni's hell, known as *yomotsukuni* (another reading for *yomi no kuni* 黄泉国, Land of the Yellow Springs), is the same underworld as the one visited by Izanagi, ancestor of the Sun-Goddess Amaterasu, in his failed attempt to rescue his wife Izanami, who was burnt to death while giving birth to the fire-deity (Nishimiya 1979, pp. 36–40; Philippi 1968, pp. 61–67). Hell, as described by Kyōkai, appears on the same level of the high plain of the gods (*takaamanohara* 高天原) and the world of human beings (*nakatsu no kuni* 中津国). With this scheme in mind, Kyōkai started to tell the story of monk Chikō's experiences in the underworld, replacing the high plain of the gods with Amida's Pure Land. In fact Chikō, before reaching hell in his journey, was taken by Yāma's messengers to the west (= the Western Paradise), where he saw a golden pavilion waiting for the birth of the bodhisattva Gyōgi. Only then, turning north, was he finally able to reach Yāma's kingdom, and later, after further travel to the north, he eventually reached the Abi hell (*abi jigoku* 阿鼻地獄), the worst of the eight hells in Buddhist cosmology. At last Chikō was able to come back to life (NR 2: 7; Koizumi, pp. 123–129; Nakamura, pp. 167–171). In spite of this confused description of the other world presented along the same lines as the Pure Land and dressed in very Buddhist clothes, it confirms the opinion that the underworld is in perpetual communication with this world and is located on the same level as this world. Perhaps it would be better to say that hell in the *Nihon ryōiki* is not something transcending this world, but only another dimension of this world. We do not get the impression that the inhabitants of such an underworld are definitely cut away from our existence. Dead people look as if they are hiding themselves, while their spirits still wander in this world and influence the present reality. They are like spiritual existences wearing a magic coat which makes them invisible (*kakuremino* 隠れ蓑). Here again we see reflected in the *Nihon ryōiki* the ancient belief in spirits (*mono no ke* 物怪) which had the power to take revenge or to bring all sorts of disaster to living people, and must therefore be pacified. As long as the spirit was believed to remain in the body and not yet gone back to its home land, a mortuary hut (*moya*) was built in order to keep the corpse unburied for a limited period. This practice, known as "temporary enshrinement" (*mogari*), is attested to in several poems of the *Man'yōshū* (756), and is reported by Kyōkai who used the device of this custom in order to stress the possibility that a spirit had to come back to life and, therefore, that it may need its body again. In fact, it would be

---

11   See Nishimiya 1979, pp. 62–65 and Philippi 1968, pp. 98–112. On the concept of *tokoyo* see Tanigawa 1983.

THE DEVELOPMENT OF MAPPŌ THOUGHT IN JAPAN (I)   91

a tragedy for a spirit to come back to life and find that one's body had already been cremated. This reportedly happened to Kinume of Utari, who was advised by King Yāma to take the body of another lady of Yāmada summoned to hell at the same time, since Kinume's body had already been transformed into ashes (NR 2:25; Koizumi, pp. 168–170; Nakamura, pp. 194–195).

That Kyōkai's hell is a copy of this world is also proved by the nature of Yāma and his messengers, whose behavior was modeled on weak human dispositions. We know that Kinume of Yāmada, in the story mentioned above, had been summoned to hell by King Yāma, and that she saw her life temporarily spared because of the generous hospitality she gave to Yāma's messenger who had come to take her to hell. Thanks to the delicious food received, the messenger suggested that she take to hell in her place the unlucky lady Kinume of Utari, whose only fault was that she shared the same name as the messenger's host (Nakamura, pp. 194–195). The same plot is proposed in the story of the three fiend messengers sent by King Yāma to take the life of Nara no Iwashima, who finally canceled his death on the account of a rich banquet given in their honor by their victim (NR 2:24; Koizumi, pp. 164–168; Nakamura, pp. 192–194). Yāma's compromising nature can be seen in his way of dealing with the matter of Kinume of Utari, who had been sent back to life by the king, being the wrong person, only to find her body already cremated. Not knowing what to do, Yāma suggested that the woman take the body of Kinume of Yamada who, eventually, was unable to escape her destiny (NR 2:25). The aesthetic side of King Yāma is well described in the story of Tokari no Ubai, who had been summoned to hell by the king only because he wanted to listen to the beautiful voice of a woman reciting holy scriptures (NR 2:19; Koizumi, pp. 154–156; Nakamura, pp. 186–187). He sides with the majority when asked to pronounce a difficult sentence toward a wealthy householder haunted by seven subhuman beings, the seven oxen he had killed in his religious services, and protected by ten million men, the living beings he had freed during his life (NR 2:5; Koizumi, pp. 117–121; Nakamura, 164–166). He looks like a magician when stroking Fujiwara no Hirotari's, marking him with a charm, so that he will never meet with disaster (NR 3:9; Koizumi, pp. 229–232; Nakamura, pp. 233–235).

Hell, with all its earthly elements, stands as a justification of everybody's destiny, as a simple warning of the law of karma which nobody can escape. For Kyōkai hell had no value in itself; it couldn't be separated from its function as the carrier of immediate rewards in this world. Hell was not the ultimate, sad abode to which sinners were destined, but the place where one's destiny in this world was decided. Therefore, for all those who were ignorant of the laws of karmic causation, the real hell with all its pains and tortures could only be this human life. This is clearly stated by Kyōkai at the end of the story of the wicked boy whose feet were burnt in a field aflame because he used to hunt, boil, and eat birds' eggs. The flames of hell had reached him on the hills of Izumi province, so that Kyōkai could conclude, "Now we are sure of the existence of hell in this world" (NR 2:10; Koizumi, pp. 133–135; Nakamura pp. 174–175). Kyōkai's concern was turned to the present world, as we can see from the abused expression "immediate reward" (*genpō* 現報) occurring throughout his work. A man had his body covered with scabs as the consequence for skinning a live rabbit without mercy (NR 1:16; Koizumi, pp. 63–64; Nakamura, p. 127). Miyasu died of hunger and cold for having pressed his aged mother to repay him for borrowed rice, since a penalty is imposed "not in the distant future, but in this life" (NR 1:23; Koizumi, pp. 74–76; Nakamura, pp. 135–136). Miroku appeared to a wealthy man who was thus able to fulfill his vow to copy one hundred scrolls of the *Yugaron*, so that the man "could attain deep faith and happiness here below in this land bound by suffering" (NR 3:8; Koizumi, pp. 227–228; Nakamura, pp. 232–233). The greedy Hiromushime was promised by King Yāma in a dream to become an ox, as an immediate penalty in this life (NR 3:26, Koizumi, pp. 268–271; Nakamura, pp. 257–259). Even the role played by Buddhist scriptures like the *Lotus Sūtra* and by bodhisattvas like Kannon are this-worldly oriented, inasmuch as they are sources of magical power able to bring to the change of one's destiny and to happiness in this life. The *Lotus Sūtra*, as a book containing mystical syllables (*dhāraṇī*), works as the magical revenger of its reciter against the criticism of laymen who got their mouths twisted for having ridiculed monks reciting this scripture.[12] Kannon brings wealth to believers in need[13] and restores the eyesight of a devoted blind man.[14] Their role is quite different from the one they play in a later collection, the *Hokkegenki* 法華験記 of the Heian era, where holy scriptures and bodhisattvas were prayed to in order to obtain a positive salvation in the other world, to be born in the Pure Land.

Kyōkai's concern with this world meant also faith in this world and on the capability that the Buddhist Doctrine still maintained in regulating the course of history. On this point, again, Kyōkai was indebted to the *Daijikkyō* which, beside describing the degeneration of the age and the corruption of monks and laymen, stressed the eternal presence of the true Dharma that could be kept with the help of *dhāraṇī*. Kyōkai believed that, even in the Last Dharma Age,

---

12   NR 1:19; Koizumi pp. 69–70; Nakamura, pp. 130–131. Also 2:18; Koizumi, pp. 152–153; Nakamura, p. 185. For other examples of the magic nature of the *Lotus Sūtra* see 1:8, 2:6, 2:15, 3:1, 3:9, 3:10, 3:13, 3:20.
13   NR 1:13, 2:34, 2:42, and 3:3.
14   NR 3:12; Koizumi, pp. 236–237; Nakamura, pp. 237–238. For other episodes concerning Kannon see NR 1:16, 1:17, 2:17, 2:36, 2:37, 3:7, 3:13, 3:14, 3:30.

THE DEVELOPMENT OF MAPPŌ THOUGHT IN JAPAN (I)   93

the eternal presence of the dharma-body (*hosshin* 法身, Skt. *dharmakāya*)—
absolute reality—could guarantee the prosperity of the Buddhist Doctrine and
the salvation of human beings. We can see this in the story of the six bronze
statues of Kannon stolen from a nunnery and found again in a pond thanks to a
heron—symbol of the incarnated Kannon—standing on them. This story ends
with a quotation from the *Nehangyō* (*Mahāparinirvāṇa Sūtra*) saying, "The
dharma-body always exists even after the death of Buddha" (NR 2:17; Koizumi,
pp. 150–152; Nakamura, pp. 184–185). The same belief in the eternity and un-
changeableness of the dharma-body even after the death of the historical
Buddha was shown by Kyōkai in the story of the groaning voice coming from
the head of a sixteen-foot image of Miroku, fallen to the ground and eaten by
a thousand ants (NR 3:28; Koizumi, pp. 275–277; Nakamura, pp. 261–262). This
indestructible, timeless Absolute which cannot deteriorate in any historical
period and which is, at the same time, the bearer and the object of enlightenment or Buddhahood, as embodiment of truth and wisdom (*ricchi hosshin*
理智法身), justifies the returning to its place of its own accord the head of a
Kannon statue which had fallen off for no apparent reason.[15]

This faith in the strength of the Buddhist teachings may also explain the
reason why Kyōkai chose the year AD 552, the first year of *mappō* according
to one theory, as the year of the introduction of Buddhism in Japan, thus following the tradition transmitted by the *Nihon shoki*. It seems that, by accepting the first year of *mappō* as the first year of Buddhism in Japan, Kyōkai was
trying to demonstrate that Japanese Buddhism was going to be the stron-
gest weapon in the fight against the age of degenerate dharma that in China
was showing signs of victory because of the weakening of Buddhism there.
Therefore, Kyōkai focused his harshest criticism against the slanderers of the
Buddhist Doctrine and all those who were not contributing to the protection
of Buddhism and of its community. According to him, the slanderers of the
Three Treasures—Buddha, his doctrine, and his community—were devoid
of Buddha-nature, and their murder was not going to bring damnation to the
killer. He agreed on the fact that among the five separate and distinct species
in which men were divided by the Hossō sect, the last one known as *ichisendai*
一闡提 (Skt. *icchantika*) was the true danger to the world and the carrier of
corruption and degeneration. All human beings with a little wisdom were responsible for avoiding becoming one of them. Kyōkai presented on this point
two quotations from the *Nehangyō*. The first runs: "I have a high regard for the
Mahāyāna teachings. I killed a Brahman who spoke ill of a Mahāyāna scripture.

---

15   "Indeed we know that the dharma-body of wisdom exists." NR 2:26; Koizumi, pp. 193–194;
      Nakamura, p. 120.

Consequently I will not fall into hell hereafter." And again: "Those of the *ichisendai* shall perish forever. If you kill even an ant, you will be accused of the sin of killing; you will not, however, be accused of the sin of killing if you kill the *ichisendai*" (NR 2:22; Koizumi, pp. 162–163; Nakamura, p. 191).

This only confirms our belief that Kyōkai, who knew quite well the debates on *mappō*, was still very confident in the power of the faith he had embraced. His acceptance of the theories of the Hossō school makes us feel the Kyōkai's age was still far from feeling the necessity of opening the way of salvation to all human beings. It was too early to give up in front of a mere theoretical knowledge which still needed time before changing into a psychological reality.

3   Other Concepts of *Mappō* in the Early Heian Period

Saichō 最澄 (767–822), the founder of Japanese Tendai, never stated that his age was already in *mappō*. In his *Kenkairon* 顕戒論 (A manifestation of the discipline, 820) he said that he was living at the end of the Imitation Dharma Age, while in his *Shugo kokkaishō* 守護国界章 (Defense of the country, 818) he stressed the fact that they were already very close to the Last Age, although both works were written after the year when *mappō* was thought to have begun. Anchō 案澄 (763–814) of Daian-ji believed that the True Dharma Age lasted five hundred years and the Imitation Dharma Age one thousand years, and accepted 949 BC as the year of Buddha's death, thus reflecting the common belief that *mappō* had already started in 552. However, he stated in the *Chūkanronsogi* 中間論疏記 written as late as 806, that he was living during the Imitation Dharma Age. The Japanese of the ninth century seemed unable to accept for Japan a reality conceived in China. They hid theoretical teachings beneath the vague term of "the final age" (*masse* 末世) and made great efforts to reject such a reality. This was true also for the monk Gen'ei 玄叡 (ca. 840) of the Sanron sect who, in his work *Daijōsanrondaigishō* 大乗三論大義鈔 (T. 70, 119–172), maintained that the True Doctrine lasted one thousand years, not five hundred, in order to postpone the first year of *mappō* from 552 to 1052. He claimed that there was no reason to be frightened by a reality which was still so far away.

The same belief was shared by the Hossō school. The *Hossōtōmyōki* 法相燈明記 (T. 71, 48–49) by Zan'an 慚安 (ca. 776–815), adopted the theory presented by Fei Tchang-fang 費長房 in the *Li tai san pao ki* 歴代三宝記 (T. 49, 22–128, ca. 597), according to which the historical Buddha would have died in 609 BC. He stated that from the time of the death of Buddha until 815, 1,430 years had passed, thus implying that seventy years of the Imitation Dharma Age were

THE DEVELOPMENT OF MAPPŌ THOUGHT IN JAPAN (I)   95

still left. This confirms the fact that *mappō* was seen by people of the ninth century as something to come in the future. Up to this time there was no doubt that the Buddhist Law could be restored to its old glory through cooperation with Imperial Law, and this belief was justified by the relative stability of the *ritsuryō* system. Moreover, the existence of different theories about the date of Śākyamuni's death and the length of the Three Ages led to confusion concerning when the Last Age should have started. An attempt was made by Annen 安然 (841–884) of the Tendai sect in his *Kyōjijō* 教時諍 (T. 75, 355–362) to find out which of these theories was the most reliable, and he was influential in establishing the year 949 BC as the date of Buddha's demise. This date was accepted with little variation by successive writers like the compiler of the collection of Buddhist legendary tales *Sambō ekotoba* 三宝絵詞 (984) and by Jakuren 静胤 in his *Tōnomine ryakki* 多武峰略記.

4   Genshin

In the tenth century *mappō* was felt to be the product of a deep inner crisis, not as a simple matter of dates, such as in Genshin's 源信 (942–1017) *Ōjōyōshū* 往生要集 (The essentials of salvation). Here no mention of any date was made with regard to the beginning of the Last Age, although the author clearly showed an awareness that he was already living in such a dreadful period. Annoyed by the doctrinal fights between rival monks on Mt. Hiei and by the secularization of the community of Enryaku-ji, Genshin resigned the high title and position of Provisional Lesser Vicar General (*Gonshō sōzu* 乾小僧都) in 1005, one year after his appointment, and secluded himself in a mountain retreat of the Yokawa area (Kazue 1961, pp. 75–80). This must have had something to do with Genshin's perception of his age as the Final Age of corruption and impurities, as he stated in the preface to his *Ōjōyōshū*. Exactly because of the limited human capabilities at the end period of the Buddhist Doctrine, Genshin says he started to compile quotations from important Buddhist scriptures in order to show common beings (*bonbu* 凡夫) a way out of the net of history. The solution given by Genshin was a Tendai interpretation of Jōdo beliefs, stressing teachings and practices necessary to be born in Amida's Pure Land, with a particular concern for the efficacy of both contemplative and invocational *nenbutsu*. *Ōjōyōshū*'s preface clearly shows that Genshin wrote his book with the idea of *mappō* in mind: "Teachings and practices in order to be born in the Pure Land are the most important things in this Final Age of defilements (*jokuse matsudai* 濁世末代). Who, either among monks or laymen, noblemen or commoners, is not going to follow this way? But many are the Buddhist teachings, esoteric and exoteric, which aren't necessarily the same. Many are the practical and the theoretical ways of meditation on Buddha and on his Pure Land. Wise people, excellent people, earnest in their devotion, won't find any difficulty to undertake these practices, but for a foolish being like myself, how is it possible to bear them? Therefore I assembled important passages from holy scriptures and Buddhist treatises elucidating the practice of *nenbutsu*. I think that, looking at these quotations, it will be easier to understand these teachings and less difficult to undertake such practices."[16]

Genshin's concern for ordinary beings of the Last Dharma Age points to his knowledge of the theory of the Three Ages which was not directly mentioned in *Ojōyōshū*, but to which Genshin referred when quoting from the Jōdo scripture *Muryōjukyō* 無量寿経 (Large Sūtra of immeasurable life, T. 12, 265–278) saying that "although this world of the Last Dharma Age is going to end and the Buddhist Doctrine is going to perish, this scripture will survive one hundred years [after the ten thousand years of *mappō*] in order to lead people to the Pure Land" (Hanayama, p. 219).

In Genshin's work we do not find the optimism shared by the writers of the ninth century and confirmed in Senkan's 千観 (918–983) *Jūgan hosshinki* 十願発心記 (Ten vows testimonial), according to which the Last Age was considered an attempt to restore the Imitation Dharma Age, in much the same way as the Imitation Dharma Age was trying to recapture the spiritual purity of the period of the True Doctrine. Genshin gave a detailed description of the ruin faced by both the Buddhist Law and the Imperial Law, stressing the continuous fights between the monks of Tōdai-ji and Kōfuku-ji, and describing the war, famine, and other natural calamities which were exhausting the country. All these events were put by Genshin in the dimension of *mappō*, which was considered for the first time in a conscious way as a fact of the present time. Genshin personally suffered the ruin of the *ritsuryō* system and the consequent conflict between Buddhist and Imperial Laws, which brought about the decline of his own school, the Tendai sect, now that it could not play its original role of protector of the country. Therefore, Genshin turned his attention to the power of the savior Amida.

Starting with basic Buddhist teachings, he gave in the first roll of his *Ojōyōshū* an extremely vivid, pictorial image of the consequences of human ignorance and misunderstanding of the Buddhist truth that life is impermanent (*mujō* 無常) and full of suffering (*ku* 苦). To consider such impermanence as authentic truth and reality binds men to this world of defilements (*edo* 穢土),

---

16   See Hanayama 1972, pp. 36–37. I am indebted for the English terminology to Andrews 1973.

THE DEVELOPMENT OF MAPPŌ THOUGHT IN JAPAN (I)

preventing them from finding a way out of the cycle of birth and death (*rinne* 輪廻), and forcing them to be born again in one of the six paths (*rokudō* 六道) of Buddhist cosmology. Therefore Genshin wrote his first roll to teach ordinary beings of the Last Age the need to "despise this defiled realm" (*onri edo* 厭離穢土). Each of the six realms, from the lowest (hell) to the highest (gods' realm), present such cruel and inexorable features that the reader cannot avoid believing that all human faults, even the smallest and most trivial, are destined to be punished, and that all human beings are shackled to one of these courses for the simple reason that they are a product of this illusory world. The worst destiny of human beings who do not believe in the law of karmic causation is birth in one of the eight terrible hells described by Genshin in very different terms from those used by Kyōkai. Genshin put all his strength in the attempt to cause fear and incredulity in the reader's mind. We can visualize the atrocious pains inflicted upon sinners when reading the beginning of the *Ōjōyōshū*, and while looking at the pictures of *Jigoku zōshi* 地獄草子 (Hell scroll), presumably compiled at the beginning of the Kamakura era on the basis of Genshin's description (Ienaga 1960, plates 1, 2, 3, 4).

Hate is the main characteristic of the Hell of Revival (*tōkatsu jigoku* 等活地獄), where sinners wound each other with iron claws until nothing remains of their bodies except bones. Fiends strike them with iron sticks from head to feet, until their bodies are reduced to a heap of sand. Unfortunately for the sinners, their pain is not over, since a fresh breeze brings them back to life again and their bodies are ready to suffer the same punishment. Time in the present world is infinitely shorter than in this hell, to which are destined those who commit the sin of killing living beings.

Murderers and robbers are destined to the Hell of the Black Whips (*kokujō jigoku* 黒縄地獄) where they must lie down on a flaming iron ground, and suffer the lashes of the fiends' iron whips. Their flesh is cut by axes, swords, and saws along the marks left by the whips, until the sinners' bodies are reduced to a thousand small pieces of flesh. On both sides of this hell there stands a huge iron mountain crowned on the top by many iron poles. On each connecting set of two poles is a chain under which is located a big boiling pot. Sinners must walk on all fours on the chains with heavy weights on their backs, until they inevitably fall into the pot, thus being immediately boiled. Four doors lead from the main hell to sixteen minor hells where those who committed suicide without paying attention to their duties find their punishment.

Immoral behavior causes people to be born in the Hell of Striking and Crushing (*shugō jigoku* 衆合地獄), where they are put between the moving walls of two iron mountains which, pushed by ox-headed and horse-headed fiends, crush the bodies of the unfortunate sinners while their blood flows all over the ground. Moreover, those destined to be born in this hell are put in big mortars and pounded with iron pestles. Tigers, wolves, crows, and other birds spread flesh and bones in every corner, while eagles with iron beaks pick up sinners from the ground and hang them on tall trees, making prey of their victims. This hell is characterized by the presence of a forest whose leaves are as sharp as swords, while on the top of each tree there is a beautiful girl inviting a sinner to climb the tree. When he reaches the top of the tree, thus being wounded by the leaves, the woman suddenly disappears, showing herself at the bottom of the tree from where she again invites her victim to descend. The same process repeats until the indefatigable suitor has his entire body cut to pieces by the leaves.

Murderers, robbers, immoral people, heavy drinkers, those who sold *saké* mixed with water, and liars are destined to the Hell of Wailing (*kyōkan jigoku* 叫喚地獄) and to that of Great Wailing (*daikyōkan jigoku*), where they are terrified by the shouts of monstrous fiends mixed with the laments of sinners. The liars cannot even scream since their mouths and tongues are stuck together with iron needles, as a consequence of their past sins.

The flames of the hells mentioned above are said to be like snow when compared to the flames of the Hell of Scorching Heat (*shōnetsu jigoku* 焦熱地獄) to which are destined those who didn't believe in the laws of karmic causation. Here sinners are stuck on iron skewers and roasted on the back and on the trunk. People who let themselves starve to death in order to reach paradise the quickest way are invited by a voice to look for a pond where many white lotuses are in bloom, so that they can appease their thirst and rest in the shadow of the trees. The credulous sinners start their search unaware of the fact that the road is full of holes spurting flames into which they finally fall. Brought back to life again, they keep on looking for the pond, driven by their terrible thirst, only to meet repeated failure. Those who doubted the truth that everything is impermanence are blown by a strong wind which makes their bodies rotate with such speed that they finally become a heap of sand.

The Hell of Great Scorching Heat (*daishōnetsu jigoku*) is waiting for all those who committed violence against nuns and pious women of sincere faith. Here the fiends are made of fire and with their enormously long arms seize the sinners by their throats, making them float in the sky. Moreover, they scare their prey by reminding them that they are burnt not by the flames of hell but by the flames of their sinful behavior. In this hell the fire is said to reach a height of four thousand kilometers, and to stretch out on an area of sixteen hundred square kilometers. The inhabitants of this hell fall from the top to the bottom of such a fire.

The lowest and the most cruel of all hells is called the Unremitting Hell (*abi jigoku* 阿鼻地獄), the abode of those guilty of the five crimes, of those who denied the principle of cause and effect, who cursed the Mahāyāna teachings, broke the precepts, improperly took alms from believers, and burnt Buddhist images and lodgings belonging to monks. This hell is dominated by a castle surrounded by seven walls, protected all around by a forest of swords and by four huge dogs made of copper, put in the four corners of the castle. The dogs' eyes are as bright as lightening, their teeth as sharp as swords, and their tongues are similar to iron thorns, while their pores emit flames producing a stinking smoke. Each of the fiends guarding the castle have sixty-four eyes which cast iron bullets against the prisoners kept inside. On the four doors of the castle lay eighty pots full of melted copper which flows all over the castle and its inhabitants. Pythons and other poisonous snakes cover the walls, and insects emit flames from their countless mouths, making the Unremitting Hell the hottest of all, where sinners' pains do not know a moment of rest. People here are made to climb extremely hot iron mountains and to swallow hot bullets which burn the victims' bowels. Those who have stolen food from monks are moved by such a violent hunger and thirst that they end up eating each other (Hanayama, pp. 38–91).

Such dramatic description is not limited to the sphere of hell. The realms of starving ghosts (*gaki* 餓鬼), beasts (*chikushō* 蓄生), raging spirits (*asura* 阿修羅) are painted in very similar colors which sometime get even darker than those of hell, considered the increasing realism used by Genshin in the description of realms drawing nearer and nearer to that of human beings (*jin* 人). On this point we can describe the sad destiny of those who didn't provide food to their husbands, wives, and children and that, therefore, as starving ghosts, must feed on remains vomited by others. Additional examples are those destined to appease their thirst by drinking the drops of water trickling from the feet of people crossing a river, or by using the water offered by sons holding memorial services for their dead parents, because of having sold diluted *saké*; or those jailers who committed the crime of stealing food from prisoners, so that now they have to be content with corpses' ashes (Hanayama, pp. 91–97).

Although all these examples present a world outside human experience, and still could be doubted by the most skeptical readers—they weren't by medieval Japanese—Genshin's description of the world of human beings is presented as the last, convincing proof that people must flee from their evil nature and abandon their wrong views. If the condition of the human being is the necessary starting point for final deliverance and enlightenment, a position even more favorable than the superior realm of the gods (*ten* 天), nevertheless, birth in human form cannot be desirable when the characteristics of a human being are considered. Quoting the *Nehangyō* 涅槃経 and the *Daihōshakkyō* 大宝積経 (T. 11, 1–686), Genshin analyzed human beings with their characteristics of impurity, pain, and impermanence. The human body is conceived as a rolling chain made of three hundred sixty bones which are assisted in their functions by nine hundred muscles, thirty-six thousand veins, nine hundred and ninety thousand pores, ninety-nine layers of skin, five liters of blood, the five viscera (lungs, heart, spleen, liver, kidneys), and the six bowels (stomach, bowels, etc.). All these details aim at showing the perishable nature of the human body destined soon to be rotten, and, according to the idea of spontaneous generation, to be eaten by millions of insects. Moreover, the body is the main source of pain since, behind its imperfect functioning which causes physical illness, it cannot easily stand the winter cold, the summer heat, and the torture of thirst and hunger. Finally, however long life continues, physical weakness leads to inevitable death which, Genshin says, cannot be avoided even by those sages thought to possess super-human powers (*sennin* 仙人) (Hanayama, pp. 101–120).

Considering the fact that even the gods tire of the bliss of their realm so that their struggle to abandon it becomes a source of great grief, the reasonable solution suggested by Genshin was the Buddhist teaching to cut the chains of the law of causation, to reject the idea of an impure self, and to realize human existence as the expression of an absolute, selfless void (*kū muga* 空無我). With these teachings in mind men can hope to free themselves from the net of cravings, to obtain a pure, unmovable enlightenment, and to long for a world outside the six realms, the Pure Land of Amida, which is described in detail in the second roll, "Longing for the Pure Land" (*gongu jōdo* 欣求浄土). Genshin suggested that the way to the Pure Land requires the fivefold practice of *nenbutsu*, including worship (*raihai* 礼拝) of Amida and of his land, praise (*sandan* 讃歎) meant as the practice of meditation on Amida's virtues and oral praise of them, vow (*sagan* 作願) to cut off all sorts of cravings, to master the Buddhist teachings, to obtain enlightenment, and to bring others to the same goal, thus showing perfect faith in Amida, meditation (*kanzatsu* 観察) on Buddha's marks and features, and merit dedication (*ekō* 廻向) conceived as the believer's effort to turn all karmic merits to bring himself and others to the Pure Land (Hanayama, pp. 239–247). The superior practice acknowledged by Genshin in order to reach Amida's land was contemplative *nenbutsu* based on meditation of Buddha's marks and features, and invocational *nenbutsu*, that is, calling upon Amida's name. The performance of *nenbutsu* practice can be helped by the right attitude of the believer, who must be deeply devout, keep the precepts, avoid pagan views, extinguish feelings of arrogance, anger, and jealousy, repent of past crimes, and resist evil spirits (pp. 363–468). The results achieved by *nenbutsu* can be more easily obtained when, together with this main practice, the believer respects common moral norms like filial piety, recitation of scriptures, defense of the Buddhist faith, and religious obedience (pp. 586–601).

As a reward of these constant practices, the believer can hope to be granted several benefits, such as the annulment of evil and the production of good karma, the protection of Buddhas and other spiritual beings, the possibility of being saved by Amida and to be born in his land, and the power to bring other people to faith, thus saving many evil beings (pp. 518–577).

Genshin realized that to follow all these practices was not an easy matter for ordinary beings (*bonbu*) of the Last Age, and raised several times in his book the question of how ordinary human beings could make the vows required to reach enlightenment (pp. 252–253), how could they practice the difficult kind of contemplation known as Buddha-mark contemplation (*bessō kan* 別相観), in which all the forty-two Buddha-marks had to be mentally seen in their most particular details (p. 346), how could they keep their weak minds constantly concentrated on *nenbutsu* practice (p. 395), and, finally, how could dull and evil beings reach the Pure Land? (pp. 621–622)

The Jōdo belief in Amida's eighteenth vow which proclaims his refusal to attain Supreme Enlightenment as long as all human beings are not saved, provided Genshin with the answer he sought. Amida assures salvation to all those willing to reach it. Mind (*kokoro* 心), attitude, and purpose are important, more than the performance of any single practice. For an ordinary being it is enough to long for the Pure Land while enjoying the pleasures or suffering the pains of this world, always keeping alive one's aspiration for birth there. From such desire faith, the necessary element on the way to enlightenment, will arise. With faith one must turn one's mind to Amida, since faith is at the bottom of the "three devotional hearts" (*sanshin* 三心) which one must possess in order to be born in the Pure Land, sincerity (*shijōshin* 至誠心), deep faith (*jinshin* 深心) which excludes any kind of doubt, and dedicating merit in aspiration for rebirth (*ekō hotsugan shin* 廻向発願心, pp. 365–366). Genshin stressed the fact that faith in Buddha's virtues is much more meritorious than either offerings or the building of temples and pagodas (p. 395). An ordinary being can be saved as far as his faith is deep, exclusive, and continuous, and as long as he practices *nenbutsu* (p. 625).

As far as *nenbutsu* was concerned, Genshin, in the Tendai tradition, recognized throughout the *Ōjōyōshū* the superiority of contemplative *nenbutsu*. But he had to address an audience living in the Final Age, as he wrote in his preface, and on this point he borrowed the Jōdo idea of different practices suitable to the different capacities of the practicers. Those without any capability, unable to figure out and meditate on the Dharma-body (*hosshin* 法身) of the Buddha should follow easier practices, thus replacing the complicated Buddha-mark contemplation and other types of contemplative *nenbutsu*[17] with the simple invocation of Amida's name. To concentrate one's mind on the recitation of the syllables of Amida's name is worth the extinction of a large amount of bad karma, and will enable the believer to see all the Buddhas of past, present, and future, as stated in the *Monjuhannyakyō* 文殊般若経. (T. 8, 726–731). Genshin stressed the importance of invocational *nenbutsu* for ordinary beings by quoting the interpretation of Shan-tao 善導 (613–681) of a passage of the scripture mentioned above: "The obstacle of evil in ordinary beings makes difficult the accomplishment of meditational *nenbutsu*. Therefore the Buddha, moved to pity, advised them to simply intone the syllables of his name" (Hanayama, p. 530). Although Genshin kept his belief in the superiority of contemplative *nenbutsu*, thus stating that "if even those converted to Buddha's faith who only practice invocational *nenbutsu* are freed of the cravings and sins of the past ten-thousand kalpas, so much more rewarding must be the practice of contemplative *nenbutsu* made with a pure mind" (p. 519), he nevertheless recognized the importance of invocational *nenbutsu* as a skillful means (*hōben* 方便) ideated in order to keep awake the faith of those people too weak to be earnest in their belief in Amida (p. 580).

In particular, he stressed the importance for ordinary beings of extreme *nenbutsu*, the recitation of Amida's name at the time of death. Ten repetitions of the holy name could bring the bearer of evil karma at least to the Land of Transformation (*ke no jōdo* 化の浄土), the imitation land of the true land, a temporary transformation of truth, if not to the Land of Recompense (*hō no jōdo* 報の浄土), the essentially formless and empty land (pp. 626–627). In addition, this extreme *nenbutsu* was the only resource in the hands of those sinners belonging to the lowest grade of the lowest rank (*gebon no geshō* 下品下生) of the nine grades of beings, who had committed the five capital offenses (*gogyaku* 五逆) and the ten evil deeds (*jūaku* 十悪),[18] in order to see reduced the heavy weight of karmic retribution (pp. 589–590). The only problem concerning extreme *nenbutsu* was that the ten invocations of Amida's name could

---

17   A general Buddha-contemplation (*sōsō kan* 総相観), or the phenomenal and noumenal aspects of Amida, and a simplified Buddha-contemplation (*zōryaku kan* 雑略観). On this point see Andrews, pp. 58–67.

18   The five capital offenses are patricide, matricide, slaying an *arhat*, bringing disharmony in the Buddhist community, shedding the blood of Buddha's body. The ten evil deeds are destroying life, theft, adultery, lying, talking nonsense, speaking evil of others, being double tongued, greed, anger, and irrationality.

THE DEVELOPMENT OF MAPPŌ THOUGHT IN JAPAN (I)

only be done by those used to such practice, those who had persevered in invocational *nenbutsu* during their lives so as to possess the correct attitude necessary to intone Amida's name at the very end of their existence.

Genshin, beside the theoretical explanation of the approach to extreme
nenbutsu and of its benefits, gave a practical example of how it should be treated and what a dying person should perform. At the hour of death, the sick
person should be transferred into an "impermanence hall" (*Mujō-in* 無常院), a
building compared by Genshin to a hospital, with a statue of Amida Buddha
enshrined inside, where the dying patient could recited the holy name.
Genshin was the first to import into Japan the idea of the "impermanence
hall." Quoting the *Ssu fên lü shan fan pu ch'üeh hsing shih ch'ao* 詩文律刪繁補
闕行事鈔 (Commentary on the *Vinaya in Four Parts*, T. 40, 1–156) by Tao-hsüan
道宣 (596–667), Genshin stated that the origin of such a building went back to
the Jetavana monastery (*Gion shōja* 祇園精舍) of Śrāvastī in India. The *Mujō-in*
contained a statue of Amida facing the western direction, behind which was
put the dying man. The statue had its right hand raised, while its left hand was
grasping five strings of five different colors hanging on the back of the statue.
The patient was required to catch the strings with his left hand, so to be led
to the Pure Land by Amida. Moreover, he was assisted by a kind of guardian
appointed with the duty of burning incense, scattering lotuses, keeping the
place clean, and, at the same time, continuously asking questions to the dying
person in order to check whether one was already in the presence of Amida or
of hell. The guardian had, in fact, the role of helping the dying person reach the
Pure Land by continuously reciting the *nenbutsu*, and by writing down the last
visions of the sick person. If one was seeing images of hell, one was urged by
the guardian to continue the practice of *nenbutsu*, until he was finally able to
visualize the coming of Amida.[19]

What Genshin couldn't say was what happens if the dying person is unable
to see Amida. This marks Genshin's limitation, due to his unsolved attempt
to compromise the Tendai idea of self-effort in merit accumulation and annulment of evil karma through the diligent observation of precepts, with the
Jōdo belief in Amida's benevolence and vow to bring all beings to his land. The
result was the formulation of a self-power (*jiriki* 自力) *nenbutsu* which could
not guarantee final salvation to those suffering of a too heavy evil karma, and
to those unable to long for birth in the Pure Land and to arouse the necessary
faith in Amida. Also, since this was a *nenbutsu* based on personal effort and not
on the exclusive benevolence of Amida, as we will see with Shinran, Genshin
could not even guarantee salvation to those who, like himself, spent all their

---

19   Hanayama, pp. 490–492. The role of the Mujō-in is discussed in Yamaori 1982, pp. 109–115.

life in search of enlightenment. This explains Genshin's recourse to magic upon the death of a member of the "Nenbutsu-samādhi Society of Twenty Five" (*Nijūgo sanmaie* 二十五三昧会). This society, founded by Yoshishige no Yasutane (d. 997) and Genshin himself, was composed of twenty-five people coming from a dissatisfied low and middle nobility, and from monks unfavorable to the secularization of Mt. Hiei, who gathered together for the purpose of practicing constant *nenbutsu* in order to reach Amida's land. *Ōjōyōshū* seems to have been composed as a *nenbutsu* manual for these people, who lived in very rudimentary huts, ate simple food, and gathered on the fifteenth of each month at Shuryōgon temple in Yokawa, in order to practice the uninterrupted *nenbutsu* all day and all the following night. This kind of practice, which included the reading of the *Lotus Sūtra* and other scriptures, was done for the purpose of imploring Amida so that no doubt would hinder their birth in the Pure Land at the time of their death. Genshin's *Yokawa Shuryōgon-in nijūgosanmai kishō* 横川首楞厳院二十五三昧起請 (The pledge of the nenbutsu-samādhi society of twenty-five gathering at the Shuryōgon Temple in Yokawa) informs us that, when one of the members of the society died, he was buried in a cemetery called "the paradise of tranquillity" (*anyōbyō* 安養廟). The bones were covered with earth and sand which had been previously treated with an incantation made according to a magic formula (*kōmyō shingon* 光明真言), so that, thanks to this earth endowed with magic powers, the evil karma of the dead was destroyed (Kawasaki 1983, pp. 349–350).

Genshin's *nenbutsu* was unable to overcome the resort to magic, since self-power *nenbutsu* could not offer any certain guarantee of birth in Amida's paradise. This can also explain the reason why Genshin, at the time of his death, longed for birth in the highest grade of the lowest rank (*gebon no jōshō* 下品上生) of Amida's land.[20] He knew, in fact, that as a being of the lowest grade of the lowest rank (*gebon no geshō* 下品下生), his chances to see Amida were close to nothing. Only Shinran could be so bold as to say that he was destined to the lowest rank, sure as he was that salvation was guaranteed to everybody.

Genshin's teachings were welcomed by both the common people and the nobility. The first found in Amida's paradise an easy way to escape the daily sufferings of this world, while the nobility saw in it an extension in the other world of their present blissful life, and a glorious model on which to base their worldly behavior. Genshin lived in a period which witnessed the transformation of a Buddhism conceived as the protector of the country into a religion of

---

20   We know this from the *Nijūgosanmai kechien kakochō* 二十五三昧結縁過去帳 (Death registry of the nenbutsu-samādhi society of twenty-five), a record of the last words of the members of the society. See Kawasaki 1983, p. 382.

private salvation. This transformation coincided with and was brought about by the increasing power of the Fujiwara family, which chose the Kōfuku-ji as its clan temple, while Hōjō-ji 法成寺, Seson-ji 世尊寺, and Byōdō-in 平等院 were the private temples respectively of Michinaga 道長 (966–1027), Koremasa 伊尹 (924–972), and Yorimichi 頼通 (992–1074). When Genshin was preaching as a way of salvation a type of *nenbutsu* based on the contemplation in the believer's mind of the splendid Amida Buddha and of his gorgeous paradise, he was providing the nobility with a religion of aesthetic appeal which could guarantee the eternity of the nobility's fortunes and glory. This aspect of Genshin's thought was absorbed into the literature of the Heian period more than the detailed analysis of hell and of the sad consequences brought by the arrival of the Last Dharma Age. We can see it in the description of Michinaga's death presented by the *Eiga monogatari* 栄花物語, where no reference to fear or desperation could make the reader feel like a victim of *mappō*. Michinaga dies in a most seraphic way, exhorted by the Mii Novice Narinobu to invoke the holy name. He keeps his eyes fixed on nine Amida images, concentrating his thoughts on Amida's features and attributes, listening to the harmonious recitation of holy scriptures, and thinking only of his future life. He finally dies while grasping the braids held by the Amida statues, with a Buddha-invocation on his lips. His birth in Amida's land is confirmed by Michinaga's daughter, the empress Ishi, who was informed in a dream of her father's salvation (Matsumura 1965, pp. 326–333; McCullough 1980, pp. 762–771).

Genshin's message was not immediately accepted by the Heian nobility. Their literature reveals more a sense of impermanence dictated by a belief in the law of karmic causation, and a sense of stiffness caused by the limits of a too closed society, like the one depicted in *Genji monogatari* 源氏物語, rather than a deep analysis of the problem of personal and universal destiny to which Genshin had already turned his attention.

While Genshin was ascribing the ruin of the times to the inevitable arrival of the Final Age, the nobleman Fujiwara no Sanesuke 実資 (957–1064) was identifying in his diary, the *Shōyūki* 小右記 the cause of the same ruin in the lost of political power from the hands of his own family. Fujiwara no Yukinari 行成 (971–1027) arrived at the point of denying Genshin's explanation of natural calamities in terms of *mappō*, showing in his diary, the *Gonki* 権記, the belief that evil could be destroyed if only bad actions were punished and virtuous ones were praised. Only with the approaching of the fatal year 1052, the year beyond which even from the theoretical point of view it was impossible to go on denying the beginning of the Last Age, *mappō* was taken by the nobility to be the scapegoat for all disasters. When Fujiwara no Sukefusa 資房 (1007–1057) was indicating in his *Shunki* 春記 that the ruin of the country was called upon by the authoritarian government of Michinaga's son, Yorimichi, he didn't stop his analysis on the political level, but went on searching the first cause of all evils in the metaphysical sphere, ascribing it to the arrival of the Final Reigns (*matsudai no yue* 末代の故). He saw what he took to be irrefutable proof in the fire which burnt the Hasedera temple in 1052 that the period of the Last Doctrine had finally come (Mezaki 1984, p. 43). Nevertheless, as we know from his diary, Sukefusa was not a religious man. His attention was still very much directed to the political and social meanings of the word "final reigns" (*matsudai*), which he used on several occasions in order to show his dissatisfaction towards the present social conditions, and his criticism against the government.

From the second half of the eleventh century the expression "final age" (*masse* 末世) occurs in many diaries, novels, and works of history, often bringing with it a connotation of fear and inevitability. The idea that disasters happen because of the ruin of the Buddhist Doctrine was a concept stressed in Fujiwara no Munetada's 宗忠 (1062–1141) diary, the *Chūyūki* 中右記. The item under the 30th day of the 3rd month of 1104 gives a detailed description of the violent nature of the monks at Enryaku-ji. But Munetada believed that even in such a dark age a revival of the Buddhist Doctrine was still possible. As a sign of the "strangeness of this Final Age," he recorded in the 28th day of the 10th month of 1096 the episode of a temple located in southern Kyoto, which was assaulted by robbers after a fire had occurred. The thieves, moved to repentance by warning dreams, brought back to the temple all the stolen objects. This act was explained by Munetada in terms of the power of the Buddhist spirit, active even in the most degenerate periods (Sasagawa 1934, 1, pp. 390–391). Such an explanation would have been impossible without Munetada's confidence and faith in an external power (*tariki* 他力) able to help human beings, whose self-efforts (*jiriki* 自力) were insufficient to stand the inexorability of the times. This faith was provided by the cult of Amida which owed its prosperity to the easy solution it offered to the problem of *mappō*. Neither was Amida the only Buddha to whom Munetada and his contemporaries turned. In fact, Amida guaranteed salvation only during the 10,000 years of the Final Age, after which no scripture was going to survive. Therefore, in such circumstances, faith in a new Buddha was felt necessary, and the cult of the bodhisattva Maitreya (Jpn. Miroku), the Buddha of the future, became popular. In this way the Japanese of the eleventh century guaranteed themselves an eternal salvation away from the net of *mappō*. But still they lacked the ability to follow the path undertaken by Genshin, to question their innermost feelings and to meditate on their guilty human nature. This tendency was to develop very soon, after the Gempei war (1186), the first great war in Japanese history.[21]

---

21   This article will be concluded in the December issue of this journal, Vol. 15/4.

Abbreviation

T. Takakusu Junjirō 高楠順次郎 and Watanabe Kaigyoku 渡辺海旭, eds., 1922–33
Taishō shinshū daizōkyō 大正新修大蔵経 [Newly revised Tripiṭaka of the Taishō
era]. Tokyo: Taishō Issaikyō.

References

Andrews, Allan A., 1973. *The Teachings for Rebirth. A Study of Genshin's Ōjōyōshū*. Tokyo:
Sophia University.

Aston, W. G., transl., 1980. *Nihongi. Chronicles of Japan from the Earliest Times to
A.D. 697*. 2 Vols. Tokyo: Tuttle (reprint).

Conze, Edward, 1958. *The Diamond Sūtra and the Heart Sūtra*. London: George Allen
& Unwin.

Eliade, Mircea, 1972. *Shamanism. Archaic Techniques of Ecstasy*. Princeton: Princeton
University Press.

Hanayama Shōyū 花山勝友, ed., 1972. *Genshin. Ōjōyōshū* 源信－往生要集 Tokyo:
Tokuma Shoten.

Ienaga Saburō 家永三郎, ed., 1960. *Jigoku zōshi* 地獄草子 [Hell scrolls]. In *Nippon ema-
kimono zenshū* 日本絵巻物全集 [Collection of Japanese scroll paintings] *Japanese
Scroll Paintings* 6. Tokyo: Kadokawa Shoten.

Ishida Mizumaro 石田瑞麿, 1976. *Nippon ni okeru mappō shisō* 日本における末法思想
[*Mappō shisō* in Japan]. In *Bukkyō shisō—aku* 仏教思想・悪 [Buddhist concepts—
evil], Bukkyō Shisō Kenkyūkai, ed. Kyoto: Heirakuji Shoten.

Kawasaki Tsuneyuki 川崎庸之, transl., 1983. *Genshin* 源信. *Nippon no meichō* 4. Tokyo:
Chūōkōronsha.

Kazue Kyōichi 数江教一, 1961. *Nippon no mappō shisō—Nippon chūsei shisōshi kenkyū*
日本の末法思想－日本中世思想史研究 [*Mappō shisō* in Japan—Studies on the
history of medieval Japanese thought]. Tokyo: Kōbundō.

Koizumi Osamu 小泉道, 1984. *Nihon ryōiki* 日本霊異記 [Wondrous tales of Japan].
Shinchō Nihon koten shūsei [Shinchō collection of classical Japanese literature] 67.
Tokyo: Shinchōsha.

Kumoi Shōzen 雲井昭善, 1976. Indo bukkyō no mappō shisō インド仏教の末法
思想 [Concepts of the Latter Dharma in Indian Buddhism]. In *Bukkyō shisō—aku*
[Buddhist concepts—evil], Bukkyo Shisō Kenkyūkai, ed. Kyoto: Heirakuji Shoten.

Masuko Kazuko 増古和子, 1969. *Nihon ryōiki* ni mini mappō 日本霊異記にみる末法
[*Mappō* in the *Nihon ryōiki*]. In *Bukkyō bungaku kenkyū* 仏教文学研究 [Studies on
Buddhist literature] 8, Bukkyō Bungaku Kenkyūkai, ed. Kyoto: Hōzōkan.

Matsumura Hiroji 松村博司 and Yamanaka Yutaka 山中裕, eds., 1965. *Eiga monogatari*
栄花物語. *Nihon koten bungaku taikei* 76. Tokyo: Iwanami Shoten.

McCullough, William H. and Helen Craig, transls., 1980. *A Tale of Flowering Fortunes. Annals of Japanese Aristocratic Life in the Heian Period*. Two volumes. Stanford: Stanford University Press.

Mezaki Tokue 目崎徳衛, 1984. Matsudai—mappō to Jōdo shinkō 末代・末法と浄土信仰 [Jōdo faith and the latter age]. In *Kōza nippon shisō, 4, jikan* 講座日本思想・4・時間 [Lectures on Japanese thought 4: Time], Sagara Tōru 相良享, Bitō Masahide 尾藤正英 and Akiyama Ken 秋山虔, eds. Tokyo: Tōkyō Daigaku Shuppankai.

Michihata Ryōshū 道端良秀, 1976. Chūgoku ni okeru mappō shisō 中国における末法思想 [*Mappō shisō* in China]. In *Bukkyō shisō—aku* [Buddhist concepts—evil], Bukkyō Shisō Kenkyūkai, ed. Kyoto: Heirakuji Shoten.

Nakamura, Kyoko Motomichi, 1973. *Miraculous Stories from the Japanese Buddhist Tradition. The Nihon Ryōiki of the Monk Kyōkai*. Cambridge: Harvard University Press.

Nishimiya Kazutami 西宮一民, ed., 1979. *Kojiki* 古事記 [Record of ancient things]. *Shinchō nihon koten shūsei* 27. Tokyo: Shinchōsha.

Philippi, Donald L., transl., 1968. *Kojiki*. Tokyo: Tokyo University Press.

Poussin, Louis de La Vallée, 1971. *L'Abhidharmakośa de Vasubandhu*. Tome II. Bruxelles: Institut Belge des Hautes Études Chinoises (first edition, 1914).

Ryukoku University Translation Center, ed., 1980. *Shōzōmatsu Wasan. Shinran's Hymns on the Last Age*. Kyoto: Ryukoku University Press.

Sakamoto Tarō 坂本太郎 et al., eds., 1965. *Nihon shoki* 日本書紀 [Chronicles of Japan]. *Nihon koten bungaku taikei* [Compendium of classical Japanese literature] 68. Tokyo: Iwanami Shoten.

Sasagawa Taneo 笹川種郎, 1934. *Shiryō taisei* 史料大成 [Collection of historical documents], Vol. 8. Tokyo: Naigaishoseki.

Tanigawa Ken'ichi 谷川健一, 1983. *Tokoyoron—Nihonjin no tamashii no yukue* 常世論・日本人の魂のゆくえ [*On tokoyo—The*, whereabouts of the spirits of the Japanese]. Tokyo: Heibonsha.

Yabuki Keiki 矢吹慶輝, 1927. *Sankaikyō no kenkyū* 三階教の研究 [Studies on the teachings of the Three Stages]. Tokyo: Iwanami Shoten.

Yamaori Tetsuo 山折哲雄, 1982. Jōdo no kansō—Genshin 浄土の観想—源信 [Contemplation of the Pure Land—Genshin]. In his *Jigoku to Jōdo* 地獄と浄土 [Hell and the Pure Land]. Tokyo: Shunjū Sensho.

The Development of *Mappō* Thought in Japan (II)

Michele Marra

1 The *Mappō Tōmyōki*[1]

Mappō ceased to be analyzed in its mere political implications and started to be felt and suffered as an existential problem on a larger scale after the appearance of a short treatise known as *Mappō tōmyōki* 末法燈明記 (The candle of the Latter Dharma) at the beginning of the Kamakura era.

Traditionally attributed to Saichō (767–822), the *Mappō tōmyōki* has been the object of lively debate among scholars, some of whom defend its authenticity, while others consider it a forgery by a Pure Land believer of the Heian period. Whatever the answer, we know that the first person to mention it in his writings was Hōnen 法然 (1133–1212), and that the major thinkers of the Kamakura period, including Eisai, Dōgen, Shinran, and Nichiren were greatly influenced by it.

The *Mappō tomyoki* is a defense of the monastic community against the criticism of people denouncing the decline of morality in monks and nuns' behavior, and of emperor Kanmu 桓武 (r. 781–806) who was trying to put an end to such behavior with regulations on the moral code of the Buddhist community of Nara. The author argues that the government, in its criticism, tends to forget that these monks are living in the Last Dharma Age (*mappō*) and that, therefore, they cannot apply to themselves rules which were made for and fitted to monks living in the ideal period of the True Doctrine. Since in the Last Age only verbal teachings survive, while practices are non-existent and enlightenment unreachable, precepts also have disappeared and, therefore, to maintain that monks are breaking precepts is meaningless. How can something which is non-existent be broken? For the same reason, precepts cannot be kept. The *Mappō tōmyōki* says on this point: "If there were Dharmas of precepts, there may be the breaking of the precepts, but since by now there are no Dharmas of precepts, what precepts are there to break? And since there is no breaking of the precepts, how much less is there the keeping of the precepts?" (Matsubara 1960 [hereafter "MT"], p. 180; Rhodes 1980, pp. 91–92).

Source: Marra, Michele, "The Development of Mappō Thought in Japan," in *Japanese Journal of Religious Studies* 15(4) (December 1988): 287–305.

---

1 The first part of this article appeared in Volume 15/1 of this journal.

Moreover, since a person keeping the precepts in the Last Age is as rare as finding a "tiger in the marketplace," we should see in the nominal monks of this age—nominal because they are monks in name only—the True Treasure of the world, the merit-field of the people. People were invited to worship them because they had reached the highest spiritual level achievable in the period of the Last Doctrine. By shaving their heads and putting on the Buddhist robes, these monks did something superior to the usual activities of common beings. By choosing the Buddhist way they indicate the path to *nirvāṇa* to various people. The *Mappō tōmyōki* implies that those monks who strive to keep the precepts, thus bowing to the requirements of the government, show a formal attitude towards Buddhism, forgetting the human meaning of their religion. They are, therefore, compared to locusts which destroy the country, and condemned according to a passage from the *Ninnōkyō* 仁王経 (Sūtra of the benevolent kings, T. 8, 824–845), "If any disciple of mine serves the government, he is not my disciple." These monks, following formal precepts not suitable to their age, are doers of false good since, if they had to follow the real precepts, they should abstain from "stepping on the king's land and drinking the king's water" (MT, p. 193; Rhodes, pp. 102–103). Therefore, the government was invited to stop its discrimination between monks who kept the precepts and monks who did not, in order to avoid the ruin of the country.

2   Shinran and the *Mappō Tōmyōki*

Besides its strictly political meaning, the *Mappō tōmyōki* was extremely influential on the thinkers of the Kamakura period in general, and on Shinran in particular, on three points:

1. In showing a deep consciousness of the fragile, foolish, unenlightened (*oroka*, *gu* 愚) nature of human beings living in the Last Age, which brought about the necessity to reflect upon oneself and experience a deep feeling of repentance.

    The *Mappō tōmyōki*, in this sense, pointed not only to the Buddhist community, but to laymen in general who tended to forget their true nature while despising the nominal monks. This feeling of malaise caused by the real understanding of oneself reached its apex with Shinran 親鸞 (1173–1262), who surnamed himself Gutoku Zenshin 愚禿善信, where "Gu" means "foolish" or "ignorant," and shows his realization of his true nature.

2. In its concern with the salvation of all human beings, not only of those few who strove to reach enlightenment through exterior practices, thus showing a tendency to be in complete accord with Mahāyāna teachings.

The *Mappō tōmyōki* does not encourage the practice of evil, but justifies it as an inevitable trend of the times, encouraging people to be conscious of this situation and to meditate upon it, and thus realize that mere formal acts cannot be considered good practices. Even though a monk commits evil practices, he is still able to reveal the hidden storehouse of all goodness and virtue to others, thus becoming a good master to sentient beings (MT, p. 188; Rhodes, p. 98). On this point the *Mappō tōmyōki* was still addressing a religious audience, and Shinran would develop this same concept by applying it to all human beings.

3. In showing the necessity of judging things according to the constant correlation of the three elements time (*ji* 時), teachings (*kyō* 教), and human capabilities (*ki* 機).

In its discussion of nominal monks, the *Mappō tōmyōki* stresses the fact that in a world devoid of the real Buddha Treasure, of *pratyekabuddha, arhat*, wise sages, people who have obtained *samādhi*, keepers of precepts, and monks who keep the precepts imperfectly, a nominal monk must be considered the supreme treasure, in the same way that nickel, iron, pewter, lead, or tin would be considered priceless treasures in a world devoid of gold, silver, and brass (MT, pp. 181–182, Rhodes, pp. 92–93). Every age has its own priceless treasure: the Last Dharma Age's priceless treasure is the nominal monk, whose limited capability must follow the teaching prescribed for the age in which he is living. A monk living in the Last Dharma Age cannot behave according to the precepts of the time of the True Doctrine, otherwise "the teachings and the capabilities will be opposed to each other, and the Doctrine and the people won't match" (MT, p. 191; Rhodes, p. 101).

The deep influence that *Mappō tōmyōki* had on the thought of Shinran is acknowledged by the fact that he quoted it almost entirely in the sixth roll of his *Ken jōdo shinjitsu kyōgyōshinshō monrui* 顕浄土真実教行信証文類 (Collection of passages expounding the true teaching, living, faith and realizing of the Pure Land) begun in 1224. The reading of such a treatise must have had a not small influence on his resolution at twenty-nine years of age to leave Mt. Hiei and abandon the official Tendai teachings in order to attend Hōnen's hermitage in Yoshimizu and embrace the Pure Land faith. In using the text of the *Mappō tōmyōki*, Shinran left aside all political implications, and addressed his attention to the absence of precepts during the Last Dharma Age, and to the impossibility of reaching enlightenment through training and practices. Following the teachings of the Jōdo patriarchs Tao-cho 道綽 (562–645) and Hōnen, teachings reinforced by the *Mappō tōmyōki*'s idea of the correlation of time, teachings, and human capabilities, Shinran stressed in his main work the unfitness of the teachings of traditional Buddhism, known as the Holy Path (*shōdō* 聖道), when applied to the present age. He showed how difficult it was to follow doctrines made for people living in the True Dharma age, whose understanding was much greater than that of the people living in the present time. Instead of these difficult practices (*nangyō* 難行), he suggested the necessity of following a way suitable to all people living in the Imitation, Last Dharma Ages, and after the Dharma-extinction, a way which made no distinction "between the noble and the humble, between the black-robed and the white-robed, between male and female, old and young, which did not question the amount of sinfulness; it did not weigh the duration of discipline one had gone through, nor had it anything to do with discipline or morality, with suddenness or gradualness, with the contemplative or practical states of mind, with the right views or the wrong views, with thought or no-thought, with living moments or the moment to die, with many thoughts or one thought" (Ienaga 1971, p. 133; Suzuki 1973, pp. 118–119).

The Pure Land Path (*jōdomon* 浄土門) gave him the answer to the problem, being a teaching which proclaimed itself to overcome the barriers of time, suitable as it was to the time of Śākyamuni's life, and of the True, Imitation, and Last Dharma Ages. It offered, in fact, a solution easy to grasp for people of all times. *Kyōgyōshinshō* says on this point: "Indeed we know that the various teachings of the Path of Sages are practicable only for the Buddha's time and the Right Dharma Age, not for the Imitation and the Last Dharma Ages and after the Dharma-extinction. The time for those teachings has already passed and they do not agree with the capacities of sentient beings, whereas the true teaching of the Pure Land compassionately guides the defiled and evil multitudes in the Imitation and Last Dharma Ages and after the Dharma-extinction, as well as those in the Buddha's time and the True Dharma Age" (Ienaga 1971, pp. 214–215; Ryukoku 1980, p. xv).

3　Shinran's *Hymns on the Last Age*

The Path of Sages aimed at reaching enlightenment through practices dictated by a self-effort (*jiriki* 自力) attitude in a time when practices were non-existent

THE DEVELOPMENT OF MAPPŌ THOUGHT IN JAPAN (II)   113

and there were no precepts to which human beings could conform their behavior. Only the absolute trust in an Other-Power (*tariki* 他力), Amida, could solve problems unsolvable by beings of the present time. Shinran came back to this theme at the end of his life, when in 1257 he wrote in his "Hymns on the Last Age" (*Shōzōmatsu wasan* 正像末和讃) a poem on the unsuitability of the teachings of the Path of Sages in the Last Dharma Age:

> The aspiration in the Path of Sages for enlightenment through self-power
> Is beyond our minds and words.
> For us, ignorant beings, always sinking in the ocean of saṃsāra,
> How is it possible to waken such an aspiration?[2]

The *Mappō tōmyōki* offered to Shinran the opportunity to justify the existence of the Pure Land school as the only way available to people living in an age devoid of precepts. This is also confirmed by Shinran's explanation of the reason why nominal monks are the Buddhist Treasure of the Last Age. As he says in *Kyōgyōshinshō*, at the end of the long quotation from *Mappō tōmyōki*, the nominal monks' importance is acknowledged on the ground that, as it is stated in the *Daihikyō* (Sūtra of great compassion 大悲経, T. 12, 945–973), "if they have called upon Buddha's name even only once, their merit will not be in vain" (Ienaga 1971, p. 225).

The practice of *nenbutsu* as a proof of the nominal monks' trusting in Amida's compassion justified in Shinran's eyes the worthy existence of those monks for whom *Mappō tōmyōki* had been written, and against whom traditional Buddhism had been so demanding. No matter if they were monks in name only, they had to be respected and revered in the same way as Śākyamuni's best disciples.

In the *Shōzōmatsu wasan* one hymn dedicated to such monks is:

> Although they are monks in name only and do not follow the precepts,
> This is the defiled world of the Last Dharma Age,
> So, equally with Śāriputra and Maudgalyayāna,
> We are encouraged to pay homage to and revere them.[3]

---

2 *Jiriki shōdō no bodaishin / Kokoro mo kotoba mo oyobarezu / Jōmotsu ruten no bongu wa / Ikude ha hokki seshimubeki.* From *Shōzōmatsu wasan*, ITŌ 1981, p. 148; *Shinran's Hymns on the Last Age* (16), p. 16. Henceforth in my notes *Shōzōmatsu wasan* refers to ITŌ 1981 and *Shinran's Hymns on the Last Age* to the English translation by the RYUKOKU UNIVERSITY TRANSLATION CENTER, 1980.

3 *Mukai myōji no biku naredo / Mappō jokuse no yo to narite / Sharihotsu Mokuren ni hitoshikute / Kuyō kugyō o susume shimu.* From *Shinran's Hymns on the Last Age* (106), p. 106.

But Shinran, in his attempt to show that salvation was available to everybody, went much further than the *Mappō tōmyōki*, pointing out that there was no reason to differentiate between monks and common beings, since we are all destined to be embraced by Amida's compassion. Common beings are the Buddhist Treasure, in the same way as nominal monks, since they share the same nature, live in the same period, and have the same opportunities to reach enlightenment. This way of thinking came to Shinran from his long period of absence from the capital (1207–1245), when he had the opportunity to travel extensively all around Japan, continuing, at the same time, his work of evangelism and the common life of husband and father. While lamenting being neither a monk nor a layman, he experienced all the difficulties of life, feeling more and more the necessity of finding a religious answer which could satisfy people living in this world. This explains Shinran's feeling of *mappō* as the present reality, where beings are necessarily evil. As a man of *mappō* living with other beings with whom he was sharing the same nature, Shinran, for the first time in the history of Japanese thought, realized that *mappō* was not something outside human beings, so he was able to say that "I cannot consider my existence apart from the existence of *mappō*." *Mappō* was equated by Shinran to the eternal cycle of birth and death, being nothing but existence, *saṃsāra*. To escape *mappō*, therefore, meant in Shinran's judgment to escape oneself, a thing impossible to do from the perspective of this world. For a man enduring the hardships of this life, sensible to the requests of people looking for concrete answers grounded in the present reality, the weakness of the traditional teachings of the Pure Land which had satisfied the necessities of the Heian nobility were exposed. If the problem of existence required a solution satisfactory to people living in this world, the traditional escapist approach to *mappō*—to abandon this defiled world in order to reach the Pure Land (*onri edo gongu jōdo* 厭離穢土欣求浄土) through training and practices—was of no avail. This was the solution followed by Genshin and his followers who had secluded themselves in mountain huts, and by several members of the nobility who looked for seclusion in their gorgeous palaces. Shinran, in the same Pure Land tradition and respectful of its main doctrines, tried to provide an answer more relevant to the present world, keeping the existence of human beings at the center of his thought. The answer came in the *Shōzōmatsu wasan*, a work concerned with the destiny of people living in the Last Dharma Age and with Shinran's own destiny. All previous ideas about *mappō*—the consciousness of decline in the Three Ages, Genshin's view of human sin, the Heian nobility's sense of social instability—are objects of deep reflection, revealing Shinran's search for meaning in the present life.

THE DEVELOPMENT OF MAPPŌ THOUGHT IN JAPAN (II)   115

The *Shōzōmatsu wasan* starts with the presentation of the Three Dharma Ages. We know from the *Kyōgyōshinshō* that Shinran adopted the year 949 BC as the date of Buddha's demise, and that he accepted the theory according to which the True Dharma Age lasted five hundred years and the Imitation Age one thousand years, thus saying that Gennin 1 (1224) of the Kamakura period was already the six hundred eighty-third year (mistake for six hundred seventy-third year) of the Last Dharma Age (Ienaga 1971, p. 217). Shinran tended to emphasize a single division of the three Dharma Ages, either at the middle of the Imitation Dharma Age, or between the True and Imitation Dharma Ages. In this second period all Buddhist scriptures except those of the Jōdo school were destined to lose their effectiveness.[4] Moreover, Shinran talked about the five defilements in this world, to each of which he dedicated a poem. He started by describing the impurity of kalpa (*kōjoku* 劫濁), the time when the life span of human beings was destined to fluctuate between eighty-thousand years and ten years, as a consequence of the worsening of the karma of sentient beings. This was an inevitable law dictated by the continuous passing of time and by the increasing defilements in the world. Shinran says on this point:

> When the tens of thousands of years' life span of sentient beings,
> Because of the gradual decay of their good karma,
> Was shortened to twenty-thousand years,
> The world was given the name "evil world of five defilements."[5]

Moreover, he talked about the impurity of the mind and body of sentient beings (*shujōjoku* 衆生濁), stressing the fact that human beings became smaller and smaller as a consequence of the increasing of defilements and viciousness in human beings. Here Shinran was influenced by the *Fo tsu t'ung chi* 仏祖統記 (T. 49, 129–476), by the Chinese monk Tshe p'an 志磐 of the T'ien-t'ai sect, where we read that length and height of human beings are proportional and vary according to the passing of time and the growth of defilements. When the length of human life increases to eighty-four thousand years, the height of human beings is eight *jō* (about twenty-five meters). However, since the life span shortens one year every hundred years, so the height decreases by one *sun* (about 3 cm.) every hundred years. Therefore when, at the top of defilement,

---

4   *Shōzōmatsu wasan* 235 (1), 236 (2), 237 (3); *Shinran's Hymns on the Last Age* (2), (3), (4).

5   *Shumanzai no ujō mo / Kahō yōyaku otoroete / Nimanzai ni itarite wa / Gojoku akusei no na o etari.* From *Shōzōmatsu wasan* 239 (5), p. 144; *Shinran's Hymns on the Last Age* (6), p. 6.

the life span is ten years, the height of men will be one *shaku* (about 30.5 cm.) (T. 49, 299a). Shinran's hymn says:

> When, with the passing of time, we reach the corrupted kalpa,
> The bodies of sentient beings grow smaller and smaller.
> Since the wickedness of the five defilements increases,
> They become like spiteful dragons and poisonous snakes.[6]

Such circumstances bring about the rise of ignorance (Jpn. *mumyō* 無明, Skt. *avidyā*), causing feelings of hatred in human hearts, as it is stated in the hymn on the impurity of evil passions (*bonnōjoku* 煩悩濁):

> Ignorance and passions grow thick
> Filling all corners like particles of dust.
> Love and hate rise up in human hearts
> Like mountain peaks and high ridges.[7]

Ignorance causes anger and heretical views, encouraging people to slander those practicing *nenbutsu*. While writing the following hymn on the impurity of views (*kenjoku* 見濁), Shinran must have thought of the persecution undergone by his master Hōnen and by Shinran himself, for having preached a nonmeditative type of *nenbutsu* in order to cut all signs of self-effort, and to use *nenbutsu* as the proof of complete trust in Amida. Therefore, in the slanderers of the followers of the *nenbutsu* of this hymn we can see the official monks of Nara and Mt. Hiei:

> The false views of sentient beings grow thicker and thicker
> Like dense forests of thorns and brambles.
> They slander the followers of the *nenbutsu*
> And by anger they try to destroy the faith.[8]

---

6   *Kōjoku no toki utsuru ni wa / Ujō yōyaku shinshō nari / Gojoku akuja masaru yue / Akuryū dokuja no gotoku nari.* From *Shōzōmatsu wasan* 240 (6), p. 145; *Shinran's Hymns on the Last Age* (7), p. 7.

7   *Mumyō bonnō shigeku nite / Jinju no gotoku henman su / Aizō ijun suru koto wa / Kōbu gakusan ni kotonarazu.* From *Shōzōmatsu wasan* 241 (7), p. 145; *Shinran's Hymns on the Last Age* (8), p. 8.

8   *Ujō no jaken shijō nite / Sōrin kokushi no gotoku nari / Nenbutsu no shinja o gihō shite / Hae shindoku sakari nari.* From *Shōzōmatsu wasan* 242 (8), p. 145; *Shinran's Hymns on the Last Age* (9), p. 9.

THE DEVELOPMENT OF MAPPŌ THOUGHT IN JAPAN (II)   117

By following wrong views men inflict harm upon themselves, not realizing how close to death they are and how brief is the life of their surroundings. In the hymn on the impurity of man's life (*myōjoku* 命濁) we read the sad destiny of human beings:

> Now that, because of its impurity, human life is so short,
> Man and his surrounding are destined to come to an end.
> Since they turn away from the true, liking only false views,
> They unreasonably inflict harm on each other.[9]

In such conditions human beings cannot even hope to escape their evil nature by themselves. All practices, all actions, even those thought to be the most meritorious, are false and futile for the simple reason that they spring out of a human mind which is always moved by selfish motivations. To believe in the possibility of breaking the chain of birth and death is an illusion bringing sad consequences, since nothing can be solved by self-effort. Evil is the main component of a human being, whose mind was compared by Shinran to the deceitfulness of serpents and scorpions.[10] Therefore, the main problem faced by Shinran was to explain how it was possible to escape from the chain of causation if the individual was defenseless as far as the accumulation of good karma was concerned. Shinran brought the Jōdo teachings to their extreme conclusions, giving to Amida an absolute power by which all human beings could be saved. Amida was presented by Shinran as the perfect bodhisattva who had temporarily renounced reaching supreme enlightenment in order to bring to salvation all sentient beings. His compassion was shown by the forty-eight vows, made when he was known as bodhisattva Hōzō, in which he promised that he would achieve his goal or else he would not accept enlightenment. Of these forty-eight vows presented in the *Muryōjukyō* 無量寿経 (The larger sūtra of eternal life), eight were mentioned by Shinran in his *Kyōgyōshinshō*, among which the eighteenth summarizes Amida's plans:

> If, upon my attaining Buddhahood, all beings in the ten quarters aspiring in all sincerity and faith to be born in my Country, pronouncing my name up to ten times, were not to be born there, then may I not attain the

---

9   *Myōjoku chūyō setsuna nite / Eshō nihō metsumōsu / Haishō hija o konomu yue / Ō ni ada o zo okoshikeru.* From *Shōzōmatsu wasan* 243 (9), p. 146; *Shinran's Hymns on the Last Age* (10), p. 10.

10 *Shōzōmatsu wasan* 317 (3), p. 172; *Shinran's Hymns on the Last Age* (96), p. 96.

Supreme Enlightenment. Excepted from this are those who have committed the five grave offenses and those who slander the True Dharma.

SUZUKI 1973, p. 338

Shinran's interpretation of this vow was quite different from that of previous Pure Land teachers who believed in the effort of the individual in order to reach the Pure Land. We may think of the Heian nobility intent on piling up continuous recitations of Amida's name, so to be accepted by Amida in his land. Determination to be born there was thought to be the necessary state of mind required for the practice of the *nenbutsu*. In Shinran's interpretation, faith (*shinjin* 信心) is not something which is to be cultivated by the practicer. It is Amida's sincere mind given to beings, flowing into them, in a time when a person had neither the ability nor the strength to arouse by himself a feeling of faith. Faith was considered by Shinran to be a total trust in Amida's vow which promises salvation to everybody. Shinran, in the preface to the third roll of his *Kyōgyōshinshō*, criticized all those laymen and monks of the Last Dharma Age for not believing that faith comes from Amida's will, for doubting Amida's compassion, and for trying to obtain a personal faith through meditation and practical discipline. They are called "ignorant of the true faith which is as solid as vajra" (Ienaga 1971, p. 71; Suzuki 1973, p. 85).

Nenbutsu had been interpreted by Shan-tao 善導 (613–681) and Genshin as the chief means of salvation for the coarse minds of ordinary people too weak to undertake practices of purification and meditation. Shinran considered *nenbutsu* not a way to achieve birth in Amida' Paradise, but a consequence of the impulse received by Amida, which is to say that the urge or inspiration to pronounce Amida's name comes as a gift from Amida. Therefore the continuous repetition of the name is of no avail, since salvation comes from Buddha, not from the individual's mind. The *Kyōgyōshinshō*, again in the third roll, states that "true faith inevitably provides the name, but the name does not assuredly provide the faith of the Vow Power" (Bloom 1965, p. 73). This is the clearest proof that faith, not *nenbutsu*, is at the center of the problem of salvation, and that birth into the Pure Land is caused by faith (in Shinran's meaning), not by *nenbutsu* or any other practice. The practice of *nenbutsu* was explained by Shinran as the height of Amida's activity as a compassionate bodhisattva, who doesn't hesitate to transfer his merits to others. From this perspective *nenbutsu* became a real gift offered by the turning-over of Amida's meritorious practice (*ekō-hotsuganshin* 廻向発願心), and not coming from the will of sentient beings, as a means of attaining birth in the Pure Land. This is stated in the following hymn of *Shōzōmatsu wasan*:

> Since pronouncing the Name with true faith
> Is what is transferred by Amida,
> It is called "non-transference from the side of the common beings."
> Therefore, we must distinguish it from reciting the *nenbutsu* through self-power.[11]

Faith is Amida's gift arisen and manifested when a person is aware of one's sinful state and of the availability of Buddha's compassion. It is the moment when salvation is guaranteed through a conversion called by Shinran "transverse transcendence" (*ōchō* 横超), a conversion coming directly from Amida. No contrivance is involved, and it allows people to cut off the five evil paths and pass over the sea of birth and death (Bloom 1965, pp. 58–59). The concept of faith as the complete rejection of self-centered actions was epoch-making in so far as it allowed human beings to accept themselves as they were, with their passions and evil nature. At the same time, it offered a means to escape the bondage of causation and karma through complete trust, the only way to enlightenment in the time of the Last Dharma. Karma worked independent of Amida who, through his power, could transcend it, breaking the bondage of birth and death to which human beings were enslaved. For a person arisen to faith, the world of karma is destined to end at one's death. This is because, according to Shinran, those who had obtained faith could reach in this life the stage of assurance of definitely attaining ultimate realization (*shōjōju* 正定聚), a stage traditionally accorded only to a bodhisattva of an advanced stage, who was sure to realize supreme enlightenment. Those in whom faith was arisen obtained in this world the result of what was called "profit in the present" (*genyaku* 現益), the stage of being "equal to perfect enlightenment" (*tōshōgaku* 等正覚), thus assuring them not only birth in the Pure Land but also attainment of Buddhahood (*jōbutsu* 成仏) at the time of their death. Therefore human beings had the potential to reach in this life a stage of enlightenment accorded by previous Jōdo teachings only to those already born in the Pure Land, and the assurance of becoming a Buddha immediately at the time of death, without having to go through a series of births in the Pure Land, as it was believed in Shinran's time. Therefore, for Shinran, birth in Amida's Paradise (*ōjō* 往生) occurred in this life, as soon as faith was obtained. Moreover, Shinran dispelled the fear of the possibility of losing the high stage obtained in this life

---

11   *Shinjitsu shinjin no shōmyō wa / Mida ekō no hō nareba / Fuekō to nazukete zo / Jiriki no shōnen kirawaruru.* From *Shōzōmatsu wasan* 272 (38), p. 155; *Shinran's Hymns on the Last Age* (39), p. 39.

by saying that when faith arises in us there was no way to lose it. This explains the reason why such a stage is also known as the stage of "non-retrogression" (*futaiten* 不退転). Common beings were guaranteed to attain in this world the same stage as the bodhisattva Maitreya, the Buddha of the future, thus being able to reach supreme enlightenment immediately after their present life. But, whereas people of faith obtained Buddhahood at the same time as their death, it took five billion six hundred seventy million years for Maitreya to become a Buddha. This is stated in the following hymn:

> Five billion six hundred seventy million years will pass
> Before the bodhisattva Maitreya becomes a Buddha.
> Those who have obtained true faith
> Will achieve enlightenment at this time.[12]

Shinran transformed the future-oriented interpretation of the Jōdo beliefs by the early patriarchs into a way of thinking which assured human beings that ultimate salvation was reachable in this life. The first patriarch of Jōdo in China, T'an-luan 曇鸞 (476–542), stressed the fact that the stage of non-retrogression and enlightenment could only be achieved after one's birth into the Pure Land, whose blessed nature would allow common mortals to perform the bodhisattva discipline. Shinran refuted this theory on the ground that one moment of faith in this life had the power to determine once and for all the destiny of the individual. By giving to the believer a spiritual status equal to that of a Buddha, Shinran rescued men from the fear of their sinful nature, cutting them off from the process of causation. Amida's vow was, according to Shinran, the only way available to common beings to escape the six evil forms of existence and the eight kinds of calamities—to be born in hell, in the animal world, in the world of hungry ghosts, in the Heaven of Longevity, in the continent Uttara-Kuru, to be born blind, deaf, and dumb, to be born secularly wise, and to be born before the birth or after the death of Śākyamuni. At the same time, as an immediate consequence of the attaining of faith, the believers, while living in this world, were assured enjoyment of the following ten benefits, as stated in the roll on faith in the *Kyōgyōshinshō*:

> They will be protected by spiritual powers.
> They will be provided with the highest merits.

---

12   *Gojūrokuoku shichi senman / Miroku Bosatsu wa toshi o hemu / Makoto no shinjin uru hito wa / Kono tabi satori o hirakubeshi.* From *Shōzōmatsu wasan* 259 (25), p. 151; *Shinran's Hymns on the Last Age* (26), p. 26. See also *Shōzōmatsu wasan* 260 (26).

THE DEVELOPMENT OF MAPPŌ THOUGHT IN JAPAN (II)

They will be able to convert evil into good.

They will be well thought of by Buddhas.

They will be praised by Buddhas.

They will always be in the protective light radiating from the light of Amida.

Their minds will be filled with feelings of joy.

They will know what it is to be grateful and how to requite favors.

They will be able to practice the great compassionate heart all the time.

They will attain to the group of the right Definite assurance (*nyūshōjōju no yaku* 入正定聚の益 Skt. *Samyaktvaniyata-rāśi*).

IENAGA 1971, p. 99; SUZUKI, pp. 126–127

The third benefit is of particular importance, since it touches on evil, one of the main themes in Shinran's thought. Starting from the axiom that human nature is necessarily evil and that nothing can be done about it, Shinran showed that, thanks to Amida's vow which transforms evil into good, human beings did not need to destroy or escape evil. This is because, while the believers' body was in the world of karma, their minds were already in the Pure Land of Amida. Shinran compared human minds, either good or evil, to various rivers flowing into the ocean and becoming one with it. Thanks to Amida's vow, good and evil were immediately turned into compassion, where no differentiation was allowed. The *Shōzōmatsu wasan* says on this point:

When the waters of the good and evil hearts of foolish beings
Enter into the ocean of Amida's Wisdom-Vow,
Then immediately
They turn into the heart of great compassion.[13]

Here the two notions of good and evil were both discarded on the ground that they were value judgments based on the relativity of human minds. Yuiembō, one of the immediate disciples of Shinran, recorded in his devotional tract *Tannishō* 歎異抄 (Passages deploring deviations of faith), that Shinran used to say that he didn't know anything about good and evil for the reason that his insight could never be "as penetrating as to fathom the depth of Amida's own mind as to the goodness and badness of things." Since common beings had no means to discriminate between good and evil, they were left only with the

---

13 *Mida chigan no kōkai ni / Bonbu zen'aku no shinsvi mo / Kinyū shinureba sunawachi ni / Daihishin to zo tenzunaru. Shōzōmatsu wasan* 273 (39), p. 156; *Shinran's Hymns on the Last Age* (40), p. 40.

choice to entrust themselves completely to Amida, and not worry about their evil nature. Although karma keeps on following its course, the devotee who had been shined on by Amida's light was freed of all burdens and crimes, since karma had lost all its effects on him. There was no reason, therefore, to grieve concerning past crimes, since the vow was a ship and a raft over the vast sea of *saṃsāra*, and the power of Amida's vow was inexhaustible, as the following hymn indicates:

> Since limitless is the power of Amida's Vow
> Our evil karma, however deep it may be, is not heavy.
> Since boundless is Buddha's wisdom
> He will never abandon even the most bewildered and lost being.[14]

Not only do human beings need not grieve over evil, but they should rejoice, knowing that it is only through their defilements that they can realize the presence of the other-power within themselves. Evil is the fundamental characteristic in the salvation of all beings, since it is because of evil human nature that Amida decided to save them. Moreover, evil is the cause which makes people realize that self-effort practices are fruitless, since they are the product of minds doubtful of Amida. Only those who cannot be sure of Amida's doing, thus not trusting him completely, struggle to reach salvation through personal practices. Therefore, the real crime acknowledged by Shinran was doubt, whose emotion leads one ultimately to faith. This explains Shinran's apparent paradox according to which if a good man is born in the Pure Land, a wicked man has many more chances to be born there.[15] This because a good man reciting *nenbutsu* and making copies of sūtras in order to reach enlightenment relies on his own power, forgetting the only way available to men of the Last Age, namely Amida's power. On the contrary, a sinful man, realizing his evil nature thanks to Amida's compassion, finally entrusts himself completely to the other power. We must read the following hymn from the *Jōdo kōsō wasan* 浄土高僧和讃 (Hymns on the Pure Land patriarchs, 1248) in this light:

> Karma hindrance is the substance of merit,
> It is like ice and water.

---

14   *Ganriki mugu ni mashimaseba / Zaigō jinjū mo omokarazu / Butchi muhen ni mashimaseba / Sanran hōitsu mo suterarezu.* From *Shōzōmatsu wasan* 270 (36), p. 155; *Shinran's Hymns on the Last Age* (37), p. 37. See also on the same topic *Shōzōmatsu wasan* 269 (35).

15   "Even a good man is born in the Pure Land, and how much more so with a wicked man!" Itō 1981, p. 15; Imadate 1973, p. 208.

THE DEVELOPMENT OF MAPPŌ THOUGHT IN JAPAN (II)

> The more ice, the more water,
> The more impediment, the more merit.[16]

Faith, therefore, was required by Shinran, but no deeds of morality, since faith makes the believer stand above morality where no sins nor karmic effects will affect him (*Tannishō* 7. Itō 1981, p. 19; Imadate 1973, p. 210). There are no deeds of morality that can surpass the *nenbutsu* when recited from the perspective of the true Jōdo believer, as an act of "no-deed" (*higyō* 非行) and "no-good" (*hizen* 非善) (*Tannishō* 8. Itō, p. 20; Imadate, p. 210), as an expression of gratitude for the benevolence of Amida, who accepts all beings with their sins. *Nenbutsu* is not a practice followed for the sake of filial piety (*Tannishō* 5. Itō, p. 17; Imadate, p. 209), or for any other practical reason which can impose our will on Amida's will.

In order to stress the depth of the crime committed by those who doubt Buddha's wisdom and strive to reach the Pure Land through self-effort, Shinran reserved two different places inside Amida's Paradise for "good" people and "evil" people. The second were destined to the Land of Recompense (*hōdo* 報土) where, as we have already seen, the believer immediately becomes a Buddha, and, thanks to the returning phase of merit-transference (*gensō ekō* 還相廻向), he can come back to this world for the sake of others. The first must endure birth in the Border Land (*henji* 辺地) of the Pure Land, where people must wait five hundred years before being able to see Amida and listen to his teachings. During these five hundred years, people born in the Border Land must repent of having doubted Amida's compassion. This land was also known as the Castle of Doubt (*gijō* 疑城); as the Realm of Sloth and Complacency (*keman* 懈慢), since negligent people are destined to be born in this land; as the Womb-Palace (*taigu* 胎宮), since here are kept those who cannot see Buddha, Dharma, and *saṅgha*, thus being likened to a baby who cannot see the light in his mother's womb; and as the Jail of the Seven Treasures (*shippō no goku* 七宝の獄). This land, in fact, looks like a jail where people are in golden chains, reminding them of the destiny of the princes of King Cakravartin who were bound with chains of gold and isolated by the king for their misdeeds. Since the people confined in this land had not entrusted themselves to Amida, they are still under the influence of karmic laws, waiting for their complete repentance, so as to be freed from the severe law of causation. Moreover, they cannot come back to this life in order to save other human beings, thus being unable to fulfill the greatest wish of those awakened

---

16   *Zaishō kudoku no tai to naru / Kōri to mizu no gotoku nite/ Kōri ōki ni mizu ōshi / Sawari ōki ni toku ōshi.* From *Jōdo hōsō wasan* 156 (20), ITŌ 1981, p. 114.

to enlightenment, i.e. to come again to this world and transfer (Buddha's) merits to others, in the same way as Amida has transferred his merits to us (ōsō ekō 往生廻向).

From the several poems on the Border Land appearing in *Shōzōmatsu wasan* we will take two examples:

Those who commit the crime of doubting the Buddha's wisdom
Are destined to stop in the Border Land, the realm of sloth and complacency.
Since the crime of doubting is grave,
Many years and kalpas have to be spent there.[17]

Since all those who do virtuous deeds through self-power
Doubt the inconceivability of the Buddha's wisdom,
Due to the laws of karma
They get born in the prison of the seven treasures.[18]

Shinran's condemnation of any sort of deeds made for selfish purposes was meant to justify a religious system, not to satisfy moral demands. People who interpreted Shinran's ideas as an ethical system misunderstood his abrogation of formal acts, thinking that the believer was allowed to be unconcerned about his behavior, and judged Shinran's thought a justification of crime and non-virtuous acts. Shinran made it quite clear in his letters addressed to disciples that to recite *nenbutsu* pretending to be taken into Amida's compassion, while committing things which should not be committed, was to be considered a serious hindrance on the way to enlightenment. Shinran showed his indignation at being accused of preaching a behavior unrelated to moral norms. "This is deplorable!" he exclaimed in a letter collected in *Mattōshō* 末燈鈔 (Lamp for the Latter Ages, 1333) by his great-grandson Jūkaku, stressing the fact that to be driven to evil by illusion and to do it on purpose were two completely different things.[19] To continue a life of evil after having been taken into Amida's compassion was unthinkable since, when faith was achieved, one should "come to abhor such a self and lament his continued existence in birth and death" (*Mattōshō* 20. Itō, p. 232; Ueda, p. 61). To the wrong view that, since Amida's

---

17   *Butchi giwaku no tsumi ni yori / Keman henji ni tomarunari / Giwaku no tsumi no fukaki yue / Nensai kōshu o furu to toku.* From *Shōzōmatsu wasan* 295 (3), p. 164; *Shinran's Hymns on the Last Age* (63), p. 63.

18   *Jiriki shozen no hito wa mina / Butchi no fushigi o utagaeba / Jigō jitoku no dōri nite / Shippō no goku ni zo irinikeru.* From *Shōzōmatsu wasan* 312 (22), p. 170; *Shinran's Hymns on the Last Age* (67), p. 67.

19   *Mattōshō* 16, in Itō, p. 220; see also Ueda 1978, p. 52.

vow was made for the salvation of evil-doers, evil deeds were to be intentionally committed to be born in the Pure Land, Shinran answered that one must not take poison only because the remedy may be near at hand.[20] Evil itself is not an obstacle to salvation, but to do evil in order to reach salvation meant to rely on one's effort, with a clear purpose in mind. But, first of all, it means to misunderstand Shinran's theological goal as an attempt to build a moral code for human beings. No code was possible for people of the Last Dharma Age, so much were they influenced by the *Mappō tōmyōki*'s idea of the disappearance of all precepts.

4 Conclusion

Usually decades, even centuries are needed before philosophical systems or simply ways of thinking spread and are accepted by large strata of the population, first of all the intellectuals. At the same time Shinran was proclaiming the necessity to counteract *mappō* within daily activities of this world, the poet Kamo no Chōmei 鴨長明 (1153–1216) was trying to flee worldly defilements by secluding himself in a hut on Mt. Hino, putting into practice Genshin's suggestion to "despise this defiled realm and to long for the pure Land" (*onri edo gongu jōdo*). Shinran, contrary to his own expectations and purpose, opened the way to the re-evaluation of this human world and of its values, as we can see from the approach that the Japanese of the fourteenth century took toward the problem of *mappō*. Urabe Kenkō 卜部兼好 (ca. 1280–ca. 1352) attempted to exorcize the fear of Final Age thought by emphasizing the faith that a changing society was starting to feel in its practical achievements, more than in the fear caused by inscrutable laws. The fourteenth century witnessed an increasing confidence in human potentialities, which brought the final rejection of the concept of *mappō*, seen as a historical justification and pretext of human evil. To put it in the words of the historian Kitabatake Chikafusa 北畠親房 (1293–1354), worldly conditions were destined to worsen not because of external factors incomprehensible to the human mind, but because of the "gradual nurturing of evil peoples' hearts,"[21] where we are led back again to the main thesis of the *Daijikkyō*, the starting point of all debates on *mappō*.[22]

---

20 *Tannishō* 13. Itō, p. 31; Imadate, p. 215. The same idea appears in *Mattōshō* 20, p. 231; Ueda, p. 61.

21 *Jinnō shōtōki*, in Iwasa 1965, p. 185 and Varley 1980, p. 261.

22 For further information on *mappō* thought in Japan in the 13th and 14th centuries see Marra 1984, pp. 313–350 and 1985, pp. 319–342.

Abbreviation

T. → Takakusu Junjirō 高楠順次郎 and Watanabe Kaigyoku 渡辺海旭, eds. Taishō shinshū daizōkyō 大正新修大蔵経 [Newly revised Tripiṭaka of the Taishō era]. Tokyo: Taishō Issaikyō, 1922–33.

References

Bloom, Alfred, 1965. *Shinran's Gospel of Pure Grace*. Tucson: The University of Arizona Press.

Ienaga Saburō 家永三郎 et al., eds., 1971. *Shinran* 親鸞. *Nihon shisō taikei* 日本思想大系 [Compendium of Japanese thought] 11. Tokyo: Iwanami Shoten.

Imadate, Tosui, transl., 1973. The *Tannishō* (Tract on deploring the heterodoxies). In *Collected Writings on Shin Buddhism* by Daisetz Teitarō Suzuki, ed. by the Eastern Buddhist Society. Kyoto: Shinshū Ōtani-ha.

Itō Hiroyuki 伊藤博之, ed., 1981. *Tannishō, Sanjō wasan* 歎異抄・三帖和讃. *Shinchō nihon koten shūsei* 新潮日本古典集成 [Shinchō collection of classical Japanese literature] 46. Tokyo: Shinchōsha.

Iwasa Masashi 岩佐 正 et al., eds., 1965. *Jinnō shōtōki. Masu kagami* 神皇正統記・増鏡. *Nihon koten bungaku taikei* 87. Tokyo: Iwanami Shoten.

Marra, Michele, 1984. Semi-recluses (*tonseisha*) and impermanence (*mujō*): Kamo no Chōmei and Urabe *Kenkō*. *Japanese Journal of Religious Studies* 11/4:313–350.

Marra, Michele, 1985. The conquest of *mappō*: Jien and Kitabatake Chikafusa, *Japanese Journal of Religious Studies* 12/4:319–342.

Matsubara Yūzen 松原祐善, 1960. *Mappō tōmyōki* 末法燈明記 [Candle of the Latter Dharma]. Kyoto: Ōtani Daigaku.

Rhodes, Robert F., transl., 1980. Saichō's *Mappō tōmyōki. The Candle of the Latter Dharma. Eastern Buddhist* New Series 13/1:79–103.

Ryukoku University Translation Center, eds., 1980. *Shōzōmatsu Wasan. Shinran's Hymns on the Last Age*. Kyoto: Ryukoku University Press.

Suzuki, Daisetz Teitarō, transl., 1973. *The Kyōgyōshinshō. The Collection of Passages Expounding the True Teaching, Living, Faith, and Realizing of the Pure Land*. Kyoto: Ōtani-ha.

Ueda, Yoshifumi, ed., 1978. *Letters of Shinran. Translation of Mattōshō*. Shin Buddhism Translation Series. Kyoto: Hongwanji International Center.

Varley, H. Paul, transl., 1980. *A Chronicle of Gods and Sovereigns. Jinnō Shōtōki of Kitabatake Chikafusa*. New York: Columbia University Press.

The Growth of Pure Land Buddhism in the Heian Period

Robert F. Rhodes

When Pure Land Buddhism was first introduced to Japan during the seventh century, it was conceived primarily as a new spiritual technology for ensuring a blissful afterlife for the deceased. The relationship between Pure Land Buddhism and funerary practices remained close throughout Japanese history and continues to be so to this day. However, as scholar-monks of the Nara period began to study its teachings in detail, they began to see Pure Land Buddhism as a form of spiritual cultivation for gaining liberation from the cycle of transmigration and attaining buddhahood. Although the study of Pure Land texts during the Nara period was centered in the great monasteries of Nara, by the middle of the Heian period, Enryakuji, the chief monastery of the Tendai school, became the leading center of Pure Land practice in Japan. At the same time, beginning in the mid-900s, the Pure Land faith became a widespread religious movement, winning the allegiance of both the nobility and ordinary people.

1 Ennin and the Beginning of Japanese Tendai Pure Land Buddhism

The Japanese Tendai school was founded by Saichō 最澄 (767–822) in the early years of the Heian period.[1] Saichō, whose ancestors were immigrants from China, was born in the province of Ōmi 近江 (present-day Shiga prefecture). After ordination, he established a hermitage (which later became the Enryakuji) on Mt. Hiei, located near his birthplace, to devote himself to religious practice. Saichō subsequently began to study the Works of Zhiyi, which had been brought to Japan by Jianzhen 鑑眞 (Ganjin in Japanese; 688–763). In 794, Emperor Kammu 桓武 moved the capital to the newly founded city of Heiankyō (now Kyoto). Coincidentally, Mt. Hiei was located to the northeast of

---

Source: Rhodes, Robert F., "The Growth of Pure Land Buddhism in the Heian Period." in Robert F. Rhodes, *Genshin's Ōjōyōshū and the Construction of Pure Land Discourse in Heian Japan.* Honolulu: University of Hawaii Press, 2017, pp. 51–76.

---

1 On Saichō, see Groner, *Saichō.*

the new capital, the direction most vulnerable to evil influences according to Chinese geomancy. As a result, Saichō quickly attracted the attention and patronage of the court, which sought to utilize this monk and his temple to ward off any dangerous influence that might threaten the capital. In 802, Saichō was granted permission to accompany the official embassy to China for the purpose of studying Tiantai Buddhism. Saichō set sail in 804 and returned to Japan in the fifth month of 806. During his stay, he visited Mt. Tiantai and other temples and obtained a number of Buddhist texts. While in China he also received esoteric Buddhist initiations and was granted the bodhisattva precepts. After his return, Saichō worked to establish the Tendai school as an independent Buddhist institution in Japan.

Although Saichō brought back a variety of Buddhist practices from China, he did not transmit the Pure Land teachings to Mt. Hiei. The person credited with introducing it to the Tendai school was Saichō's disciple Ennin (794–864), who became the school's third *zasu*, or chief abbot. According to the *Jikaku Daishiden* 慈覺大師傳 (The Biography of Jikaku Daishi [Ennin]), composed sometime in the early tenth century,[2] "In the first year of Ninju 仁壽 (851), Ennin transmitted to his disciples the nenbutsu *samādhi* that he introduced from Mt. Wutai 五臺山 and began to practice the constantly walking *samādhi*."[3] The same text also states that the continuous nenbutsu (*fudan nenbutsu*), the ritual of reciting the nenbutsu without interruption for a fixed period of time, was first conducted on Mt. Hiei on the eleventh day of the eighth month of 865, a year after Ennin's death, "in accordance with Ennin's fervent hope."[4] Although these events are not mentioned in an earlier (and much shorter) biography of Ennin found in the *Nihon sandai jitsuroku* 日本三代實録 (Veritable Records of the Three Generations [of Emperors] of Japan), a history of Japan compiled in 901, this may be because it focuses on Ennin's trip to China and his relationship to the court after his return to Japan and pays little attention to his activities within the Tendai monastic institution.[5]

---

2 It is uncertain when this biography was compiled, due to the fact that two postscripts are found at the end of the text. The first is dated 939, while the second begins with the words "Since the Great Master's (Ennin's) death, forty-nine years have passed" (ZGR 8–2: 698), suggesting that the biography was written in 913. On these postscripts, see Enshin Saitō, *Jikaku Daishiden: A Biography of Jikaku Daishi Ennin* (Tokyo: Sankibō busshorin, 1992), 18–19.

3 Saitō, *Jikaku Daishiden*, 58, slightly modified.

4 Ibid., 73.

5 In addition to these two biographies, there also exists a third early biography of Ennin, the *Hieizan Enryakuji shingon hokkeshū daisan hossu Jikaku Daishiden* 比叡山延暦寺眞言法 華宗第三法主慈覺大師傳 (Biography of Jikaku Daishi [Ennin], the Third Dharma Lord of the Shingon Lotus School of the Enryakuji on Mt. Hiei), an undated biography that was discovered in the library of the Sanzen'in 三千院, a Tendai temple near Kyoto, in 1907. This biography is usually referred to as the "Sanzen'in version of the *Jikaku Daishiden*" (*Sanzenin-bon*

As Sonoda Kōyū pointed out, the introduction of Pure Land Buddhism to the Japanese Tendai school was facilitated by the fact that Amida Buddha was the central image of the constantly walking *samādhi*.[6] In the passage above, Ennin is said to have begun this *samādhi* on Mt. Hiei in 851.[7] The constantly walking *samādhi*, it may be recalled, is one of four types of meditations described in the *Mohe zhiguan* and consists of circumambulating a statue of Amida Buddha for ninety days, constantly reciting this buddha's name. Although Saichō hoped to construct halls for the practice of all four *samādhis* described in the *Mohe zhiguan* on Mt. Hiei, he was apparently able to build only the hall for the practice of the Lotus *samādhi*, one of the two subcategories of the half-walking/half-sitting *samādhi*.[8] But after Ennin, halls for the practice

---

Jikaku Daishiden 三千院本慈覺大師傳). The relationship between these three biographies has been the subject of a lively debate, which is summarized in Saitō, *Jikaku Daishiden*, 18. Unfortunately, the Sanzen'in biography is incomplete and contains little information concerning Ennin's activities after his return from China.

6 Sonoda Kōyū, *Heian Bukkyō no kenkyū* (Kyoto: Hōzōkan, 1981), 163.

7 Nara Hiromoto has argued that Ennin actually began the constantly walking *samādhi* even earlier, sometime before 838 when he embarked on his journey to China. Nara based his argument on a short document called *Shuryōgon'in shoin azukari wo ategau nokoto* 首楞嚴院宛行諸院預事 (On Assigning the Administration of the Various Halls of the Shuryōgon'in), in which Ennin entrusted the administration of various halls in Yokawa, the center of his community of monks, to his disciples prior to his departure for China. In it, the Constantly Walking Samādhi Hall is assigned to Shinyo 眞興 (dates unknown). The fact that this hall existed at this time, Nara argued, shows that the constantly walking *samādhi* was being practiced in Yokawa even before Ennin left for China. However, this document is found only in the *Tendai kahyō* 天台霞標 (Tendai Signposts in the Mist), which was compiled in the Edo period (1600–1867), and, as Nara himself notes, its authenticity has been questioned by Sonoda Kōyū. See Nara Hiromoto, *Shoki Eizan jōdokyō no kenkyū* (Tokyo: Shunjūsha, 2002), 36–39.

8 Sonoda, *Heian Bukkyō no kenkyū*, 164. However, Nara Hiromoto has challenged this view, arguing that there is some indication that this *samādhi* was being practiced on Mt. Hiei during Saichō's lifetime. Nara's claim is based on the following points. First, in the *Sange gakushō shiki* 山家學生式 (Regulations for the Students of Mt. Hiei), Saichō set forth two courses of practice, *shikangō* 止觀業 (the practice of the four kinds of *samādhi*) and *shanagō* 遮那業 (esoteric practice), for monks on Mt. Hiei. Since the former includes the constantly walking *samādhi*, this shows that Saichō intended to have this practice conducted on Mt. Hiei. Second, Saichō mentions the halls for practicing the four kinds of *samādhi* in his *Kenkairon* 顯戒論 (Treatise Revealing the Precepts), showing that he recognized the need to practice the constantly walking *samādhi* on Mt. Hiei. Third, Enchin mentions that, on his deathbed, Saichā enjoined his disciples to be diligent in conducting the constantly walking *samādhi*. This suggests that this *samādhi* was being practiced in Saichō's time. Fourth, a document entitled *Konryū jūrokuin bettō sangōjō* 建立十六院別當三綱状 (Letter Establishing the Administrator and Monastic Officials of the Sixteen Halls) signed by Saichō gives Dōshō 道昭 as the administrator (*bettō* 別當) of the Pratyutpanna *Samādhi* Hall (Hanjyu zanmai'in 般舟三昧院). The fact that a document affixed with Saichō's signature mentions the hall for conducting the *pratyutpanna samādhi* (as noted above, another name for the constantly walking *samādhi*) indicates that this *samādhi* was being practiced in Saichō's time.

of the constantly walking *samādhi* were constructed by Tendai monks until eventually each of the "Three Pagodas" (Santō 三塔), or the three areas of the Enryakuji (Tōdō 東塔, Saitō 西塔, and Yokawa 横川), had its own Constantly Walking Samādhi Hall.[9]

However, Sonoda also argued that the constantly walking *samādhi* that Ennin began in 851 differed considerably from the traditional form of this practice described in the *Mohe zhiguan*. In his opinion, it was a type of nenbutsu ritual then popular in China known as the "five tones nenbutsu" (*wuhui nianfo* 五會念佛; *goe nenbutsu* in Japanese). The five tones nenbutsu is a form of nenbutsu set to music in which Amida's name is chanted using the ancient Chinese pentatonic scale.[10] It was begun by Fazhao 法照 (ca. 740–ca. 805), who resided for a time on Mt. Wutai, a sacred peak in north China famous for its apparition of Mañjuśrī, and founded a temple called the Zhulinsi 竹林寺 there.[11] In his *Jingtu wuhui nianfo songjing guanxingyi* 浄土五會念佛誦經觀行儀 (On the Method of Sutra Recitation and Meditation of the Pure Land Five Tones Nenbutsu), Fazhao describes a vision he had while practicing the *pratyutpanna samādhi* at Nanyue 南嶽, a sacred mountain in south China. In his vision, he saw himself transported to the Pure Land, where he was ordered by Amida Buddha to spread the five tones nenbutsu after his return to the world.[12] Fazhao's experience was also mentioned briefly in Annen's 安然 (841?–915?) *Kongōkai dathō taijuki* 金剛界大法對受記 (Record of Transmission of the Great Dharma of the Diamond Realm), which states that Fazhao "went to the Land of Supreme (Bliss) in his very body, heard the sound of the nenbutsu (coming from) the water, birds, trees, and forests (of the Pure Land), and transmitted it to China."[13] This description contains an allusion to passages in

---

These arguments are found in Nara, *Shoki Eizan jōdokyō*, 34–36. However, they are all based on circumstantial evidence and none of these points actually proves that the constantly walking *samādhi* was actually carried out during Saichō's lifetime.

9   The Constantly Walking Samādhi Hall was constructed by Ennin in the Tōdō (Eastern Pagoda) region of Mt. Hiei but was moved to another site in the same region by Ennin's disciple Sōō 相讚應 in 883. In the Saitō (Western Pagoda) and Yokawa regions, the Constantly Walking Samādhi Hall was constructed in 893 and 954, respectively. See Take Kakuchō, *Hieizan shodōshi no kenkyū* (Kyoto: Hōzōkan, 2008), 199–200.

10   On Fazhao's five tones nenbutsu, see Sonoda, *Heian Bukkyō no kenkyū*, 173–180.

11   On this monk, see Tsukamoto Zenryū, *Tō chūki no jōdokyō* (Kyoto: Hōzōkan 1975), 98–192. A brief biography is also found in Sonoda, *Heian Bukkyō no kenkyū*, 174–175.

12   T 85, 1253b–c.

13   T 75, 179b. Cited in Sonoda, Heian *Bukkyō no kenkyū*, 169. The Taishō Tripiṭaka edition of the *Kongōkai daihō taijuki* gives the name of this monk as Fadao 法道 instead of Fazhao. See T 75, 179b. Sonoda argues that Fadao is a mistake for Fazhao. See Sonoda, *Heian Bukkyō no kenkyū*, 169. However, there is some controversy over this point. See Ishida Mizumaro, *Jōdōkyō no tenkai* (Tokyo: Shunjūsha, 1976), 94–95, note 11.

the *Sutra of Immeasurable Life* that state that, in the Pure Land, the ripples in the streams and the breeze blowing through the trees produce wonderful sounds that are heard as preaching the Dharma.[14] As this shows, the five tones nenbutsu can be understood as a musical performance to recreate in this world the wonderful sound pervading the Pure Land. It may also be noted that the term "five tones" also derives from this sutra, which states that, when a clear breeze blows through the trees in the Pure Land, here spontaneously arises the five tones of the musical scale.[15]

The passage from the *Jikaku Daishiden* above—that Ennin transmitted the nenbutsu *samādhi* that he introduced from Mt. Wutai to his disciples— has been interpreted to mean that he learned the five tones nenbutsu on Mt. Wutai. In fact, this claim is made explicitly in Annen's *Kongōkai daihō taijuki*, which states immediately after the line quoted above, "Jikaku Daishi went to Mt. Wutai, studied this (i.e., Fazhao's) musical (nenbutsu), and transmitted it to Mt. Hiei."[16] As is well known, Ennin embarked for China in 838 to study esoteric Buddhism and remained on the continent for nine years, until 847. The *Nittō guhō junrei kōki* 入唐求法巡禮行記 (Record of a Pilgrimage to Tang China in Search for the Dharma), a detailed diary of Ennin's travels in China, records that he spent two months in 840 on Mt. Wutai and resided at the Zhulinsi for over two weeks. He even describes his visit to the Pratyutpanna Practice Hall (*panzhou daochang* 般舟道場) attached to the Zhulinsi where Fazhao performed the *pratyutpanna samādhi* and mentions that a statue of the latter monk was enshrined in this hall.[17] This raises the possibility that Ennin learned the five tones nenbutsu there. But although Ennin describes in detail several rituals he witnessed at this temple, he does not mention that he studied the five tones nenbutsu there. Nor does he record that he attended any performance of this musical nenbutsu while on Mt. Wutai. For these reasons, Sonoda argued that Ennin probably did not have the opportunity to witness and learn the five tones nenbutsu on Mt. Wutai.

Sonoda suggested that Ennin encountered the five tones nenbutsu ritual in Changan, China's capital, when this monk resided there from 840 to 845. According to Ennin's diary, in 846, the monk Jingshuang 鏡霜 of Zhangjingsi 章敬寺 was given an imperial order to "transmit Amida's Pure Land nenbutsu

---

14   Gómez, *Land of Bliss*, 180, 182.

15   Ibid., 180.

16   T 75, 179b.

17   For an English translation of the diary, see Edwin O. Reischauer, trans., *Ennin's Diary: The Record of a Pilgrimage to China in Search of the Law* (New York: Ronald Press, 1955). Ennin's experiences on Mt. Wutai are described on pp. 214–251. Ennin's visit to the Pratyutpanna Practice Hall is found on pp. 216–217.

teachings" at various temples in the capital.[18] Sonoda interprets this to mean that Jingshuang was ordered to lecture on the nenbutsu teachings. The first lecture took place between the twenty-third and twenty-fifth of the second month of that year at the Zishengsi 資聖寺, and other lectures, all lasting three days, were given at various other temples every month thereafter.[19] Since Jingshuang was one of Fazhao's major disciples, Sonoda argued that it is reasonable to assume that the former monk lectured on Fazhao's nenbutsu teaching. Moreover, Sonoda suggested that the five tones nenbutsu may have been held in conjunction with the lectures. Significantly, the Zishengsi, the temple at which the first lecture was given, was the very place where Ennin was staying. For these reasons, Sonoda speculated that Ennin encountered the five tones nenbutsu during Jingshuang's lectures at Zishengsi. However, since Ennin was busily studying the esoteric Great Diamond Realm Ritual under Ācārya Yuanzheng 元政 at this time, there are only scattered entries in his diary from this period, and none of them mentions Ennin witnessing the five tones nenbutsu. Hence, it is not possible to say with certainty that Ennin learned the five tones nenbutsu at this time.[20]

2 The Spread of the Nenbutsu Practice in Japan

The continuous nenbutsu ritual, begun in response to Ennin's dying instructions, became a yearly event on Mt. Hiei. This ceremony, featuring the musical recitation of the *Amida Sutra*, was popularly known as the "Nenbutsu of the Mountain" (*yama no nenbutsu* 山の念佛). Although there is very little information on how it was performed in its early years, by the mid-900s, it had become an elaborate ceremony. A description of this ceremony is found in the section entitled "Continuous Nenbutsu of Mt. Hiei" in the *Sanbōe* 三寶繪 (The Three Jewels) compiled in 984 by Minamoto no Tamenori 源爲憲 (941–1011) for Sonshi 尊子 (966–985), the consort of Emperor Enyū 圓融 (959–991).[21] The final fascicle of this three-fascicle collection describes a number of Buddhist ceremonies conducted in Japan in Tamenori's time. The continuous nenbutsu

---

18 Edwin O. Reischauer, *Ennin's Diary*, 300. See Sonoda, Heian *Bukkyō no kenkyū*, 171.

19 Edwin O. Reischauer, *Ennin's Diary*, 300.

20 Sonoda, *Heian Bukkyō no kenkyū*, 170–173.

21 An English translation of the *Sanbōe*, also known as the *Sanbō ekotoba* 三寶繪詞, is found in Edward Kamens, trans., *The Three Jewels: A Study and Translation of Minamoto Tamenori's Sanbōe* (Ann Arbor: Center for Japanese Studies, University of Michigan, 1988). The Japanese text of the *Sanbōe* is found in Mabuchi Kazuo, Koizumi Hiroshi, and Imano Tōru, eds., *Sanbōe, Chūkōsen* (Tokyo: Iwanami shoten, 1997), 1–226.

THE GROWTH OF PURE LAND BUDDHISM IN THE HEIAN PERIOD 133

of Mt. Hiei is one of two rituals described in the entries for the eighth month. Tamenori begins with the statement that "the nenbutsu was transmitted from China by Jikaku Daishi and practiced for the first time in the seventh year of the Jōgan 貞観 era (865).[22] Among the four types of *samādhis*, it is called the constantly walking *samādhi*."[23] The description of the ceremony then follows. "When the cool mid-autumn wind is blowing and the clear mid-month moon is shining, the meditation is begun at dawn, on the eleventh day of the eighth month, and it continues without interruption until the seventeenth. The two thousand monks of the monastery are divided into four watches. Their bodies constantly circle the buddha, and all the sins of the body are negated. Their mouths constantly chant the sūtra, and all the transgressions of speech disappear. Their minds constantly contemplate the buddha, and all confusion comes to an end."[24] As this account shows, by Tamenori's time, the continuous nenbutsu was a complex ritual conducted by numerous monks over a period of seven days, from the eleventh to the seventeenth day of the eighth month. The length of the ceremony was based, not on the *Mohe zhiguan*, which stipulates that this *samādhi* should be conducted for a period of ninety days, but on a passage of the *Amida Sutra*, which states that anyone who holds fast to Amida's name for up to seven days will be welcomed to the Pure Land at death. During the ceremony the participating monks walked around a statue of Amida Buddha, reciting the *Amida Sutra*, the nenutsu, and other laudatory verses while focusing their minds on this buddha. It may be remembered that the *Mohe zhiguan* described how to practice the constantly walking *samādhi* in terms of one's physical, vocal, and mental actions. It is clear that Tamenori's description of the actions of the monks in the passage above consciously harks back to the *Mohe zhiguan*.

In his description of the continuous nenbutsu ceremony, Tamenori also stressed that this ritual serves to annul the effects of evil actions committed in the past. This is based on several passages in the *Contemplation Sutra* that claim that the nenbutsu recitation annuls the effect of evil karma created in the past. This claim, as noted above, is found, for example, in the sutra's description of the people of the lowest level of the lowest grade of birth into the Pure Land, which states that each time they recite "*Namu Amidabutsu*," the effects of evil karma created over eighty billion *kalpas* of lifetimes is annulled. Similarly, in

---

22   As noted above, 865 is the year when, according to the *Jikaku Daishiden*, the continuous nenbutsu was first performed in keeping with Ennin's dying instruction.

23   Mabuchi, Koizumi, and Imano, *Sanbōe, Chūkōsen*, 206–207. For an alternate translation, see Kamens, *The Three Jewels*, 342.

24   Kamens, *The Three Jewels*, 342, slightly modified.

its account of the highest level of the lowest grade, the sutra says that the nen-butsu recitation eradicates effects of evil karma created over fifty billion *kalpas* of lifetimes. As this shows, one of the reasons why the nenbutsu recitation was considered an effective means of gaining birth in the Pure Land was because it was believed to destroy the evil karma binding people to the cycle of transmigration. In this context, it may be added that Tamenori's colleague Yoshishige no Yasutane (931–997) also emphasized the close relation between the power of the nenbutsu to erase the effects of evil karma and to induce birth in the Pure Land. In a prose poem (*fu* 賦) composed on the occasion of the Kangakue (Association for the Encouragement of Learning) held at the Zenrinji 禪林寺, he states, "Truly now, nothing takes precedence over the *Lotus Sutra* in making all sentient beings enter into the buddha's insight and wisdom. For this reason, I arouse the aspiration (for enlightenment), place the palms of my hands together in prayer, and (hear) the lecture on the verses (of the *Lotus Sutra*). Nothing surpasses (the recitation of the name of) Amida Buddha in eradicating innumerable obstructions (to enlightenment created by my past) transgressions and (in leading me) to birth in the Land of Supreme Bliss. Therefore I open my mouth, raise my voice, and recite his name."[25] The Kangakue will be discussed in greater detail below, but its main activities included lectures on the Lotus *Sutra*, poetry composition, and nenbutsu recitation. Here Yasutane takes up two of these activities and discusses their importance. Specifically, he declares that listening to the *Lotus Sutra* results in the attainment of the buddha's insight and wisdom, while the nenbutsu recitation eliminates the spiritual obstructions resulting from one's evil actions in the past, enabling one to reach the Pure Land. The close connection between the eradication of the effects of evil karma and birth in the Pure Land is a major theme in the writings on Pure Land Buddhism during this time and is also stressed in the *Ōjōyōshū*, as we shall see below.

Parallel to the growth of musical nenbutsu ceremonies, a growing number of people, including laymen and laywomen as well as monks and nuns, came to pray for birth in the Pure Land and to incorporate the nenbutsu into their religious practices. Among the monks of the Enryakuji, Ennin is generally credited with being the first to entrust his afterlife to Amida. The *Jikaku Daishiden* states that, as his final hour approached,

> Ennin requested his disciples to (help him) shave his head, to put on a
> pure robe, and to burn incense. Then he joined the palms of his hands

---

25   This prose poem is found in the *Honchō monzui* 本朝文粹. See Ōsone Shōsuke, Kinhara Tadashi, and Gotō Akio, eds., *Honchō monzui* (Tokyo: Iwanami shoten, 1992), 293.

THE GROWTH OF PURE LAND BUDDHISM IN THE HEIAN PERIOD 135

together toward the western direction and had Enchō 圓澄 recite, "I take refuge in and venerate Amida, who possesses the knowledge of all modes of existence (*Kimyōchōrai Midashugaku* 歸命頂禮彌陀種覺)." Also Ennin had his disciples recite the names of various buddhas and bodhisattvas a hundred times in the order of Mahāvairocana Buddha, Śākyamuni Buddha, Amida Buddha, the bodhisattva Samantabhadra, the bodhisattva Mañjuśrī, the bodhisattva Kannon, and the bodhisattva Maitreya.[26]

According to this passage, as his death approached, Ennin faced west (the direction of Amida's Pure Land) and had his disciple call on Amida Buddha. It is important to note that he requested that his disciples recite the names of other buddhas and bodhisattvas as well, indicating that exclusive reliance on Amida was not the norm during this period. Following the quotation above, the *Jikaku Daishiden* continues that Ennin and his disciples remained reciting Amida's name. Soon thereafter, Ennin passed away, forming a mudrā with his hands and reciting mantras.[27] This final point suggests that Ennin's deathbed practice consisted of an amalgamation of esoteric Buddhism and devotion to Amida. This may be considered only natural, both because Ennin was a noted esoteric master and because Amida Buddha not only is associated with Pure Land Buddhism but is also a major figure in the esoteric Buddhist pantheon.

Another early Heian figure who sought birth in the Pure Land was Ryūkai 隆海 (815–886) of the Sanron school based in Nara. A brief biography of this monk is found in the *Nihon sandai jitsuroku*.[28] Ryūkai, born into the Kiyoumi 清海 clan, was a son of a fisherman from the province of Settsu 攝津 (constituting the southern half of modern Osaka prefecture). However, his talents were soon recognized by Yakuen 藥圓 (dates unknown), the Lecturer (*kōshi* 講師) of Settsu, and Ryūkai became a Buddhist novice. Subsequently, Ryūkai studied Sanron philosophy under Gangyō 願曉 (dates unknown) of Gangōji 元興寺 in Nara, a disciple of the famous Gonsō 勤操 (754–827). Ryūkai also studied the Hossō teachings with Chūkei 仲繼 (?–843) of Yakushiji, also in Nara. After taking the complete precepts in 835, Ryūkai received Shingon transmission from Shinnyo 眞如 (dates unknown), the third son of Emperor Heizei, who is counted as one of Kūkai's (774–835) major disciples. In 869, Ryūkai was appointed

---

26 Saitō, *Jikaku Daishiden*, 71, slightly modified. Ennin's final hour is also described in the *Nihon ōjō gokurakuki*. There it is said that he died forming the *samādhi mudrā* and reciting the nenbutsu. See Inoue Mitsusada and Ōsone Shōsuke, eds., *Ōjōden, Hokke genki* (Tokyo: Iwanami shoten, 1974), 20.

27 Saitō, *Jikaku Daishiden*, 71.

28 KT 4: 614–615. A similar biography of Ryūkai is also found in the *Nihon ōjō gokurakuki*. See Inoue and Ōsone, *Ōjōden, Hokke genki*, 20–21.

Lecturer of Yamato province and in 874 served as lecturer in the prestigious Yuimae 維摩會 ritual of Kōfukuji. In 883, he was given the rank of precept master (*risshi* 律師).

The *Nihon sandai jitsuroku* recounts Ryūkai's final hours at some length. When Ryūkai sensed his end approaching, he declared to his disciples, "The time for my life to end has arrived. Let me undertake practices for gaining birth in the Pure Land."[29] He washed his hands, rinsed his mouth, faced west, and began to recite the nenbutsu. With every ten recitations, he intoned verses in praise of Amida. After three days, he began to peruse the *Sutra of Immeasurable Life* and recite passages from it as well. On the day of his death, Ryūkai ordered his disciples to sweep the floor and prepare a seat for him. Sitting on the seat, he passed away at night. The story ends with the following hagiographic flourish. The morning after Ryūkai's death, his disciples discovered that his hands had formed the *mudrā* of Amida Buddha. Even when Ryūkai was cremated, his hands, still forming this *mudrā*, remained unscathed. This final detail is suggestive, since it once again underscores the close relationship between esoteric Buddhism and Pure Land practice during this age.

On Mt. Hiei, many monks began to pray for birth in Amida's land following Ennin's example. Ennin's disciple Sōō 相應 (831–918) met his end "facing west, reciting the name of Amida Buddha."[30] Sōō was a noted esoteric master credited with beginning the *kaihōgyō* 回峰行 practice on Mt. Hiei.[31] Zōmyō 増命 (844–927), who studied the Tendai teachings under Ennin, esoteric Buddhism under Enchin 圓珍 (814–891; also known as Chishō Daishi 智證大師), and later became Tendai *zasu*, started the continuous nenbutsu in the Saitō section of Mt. Hiei and died reciting the nenbutsu.[32] The Tendai *zasu* Enshō 延昌 (880–946) is said to have recited the esoteric Sonshō *dhāraṇi* 尊勝陀羅尼, the *dhāraṇī* (esoteric Buddhist incantation) of the Buddhist deity Butchō sonshō 佛頂尊勝, a hundred times every night. In addition, it is said that "on the fifteenth of every month, he gathered monks to chant verses in praise of Amida and, in addition, debate the causes and conditions (for birth in) the Pure Land and the inner mysteries of the *Lotus* (*Sutra*)."[33] When he realized his death

---

29   KT 4: 615.

30   ZGR 5: 552a. The description of the practices of the monks found in this paragraph is taken from Hayami Tasuku, "On Problems Surrounding Kōya's Appearance," *Japanese Religions* 21, no. 1 (1996): 12–14.

31   The *kaihōgyō* refers to the practice of walking around Mt. Hiei for a period of a thousand days, praying at the various sacred sites along the route. In English, the monks that undertake this practice are popularly called "marathon monks."

32   Inoue and Ōsone, *Ōjōden, Hokke genki*, 21.

33   Ibid., 27.

THE GROWTH OF PURE LAND BUDDHISM IN THE HEIAN PERIOD 137

was approaching, Enshō ordered his disciples to conduct a three-week-long continuous nenbutsu ritual for him. He died soon thereafter. Significantly, Sōō, Zōmyō, and Enshō were all associated with Ennin in one way or another, leading Sonoda to argue that the Amida faith was transmitted mainly among the monks of this lineage.[34] This may also account for the fact that many early nenbutsu practitioners on Mt. Hiei were also students of esoteric Buddhism.

The stories of a number of other people who undertook Pure Land practice during this time are found in Yoshishige no Yasutane's *Nihon ōjō gokurakuki* 日本往生極樂記 (Record of [People] in Japan Who Gained Birth in the Land of Supreme Bliss; cited hereafter as the *Gokurakuki*). The *Gokurakuki* is a work of Pure Land hagiography recounting the lives of forty-two people, including monks, nuns, laymen, and laywomen, who were believed to have attained birth in Amida's realm.[35] It is not certain when this collection was finally completed, but it is certain that it was in existence in 985, since Genshin mentioned it in his *Ōjōyōshū*, which was completed in this year.[36] The *Gokurakuki* subsequently spawned a number of similar works, which came to be known collectively as the *ōjōden* 往生傳 (biographies of people who attained birth in the Pure Land). As I have argued elsewhere, the *Gokurakuki* is not a straightforward narrative of the lives of Pure Land devotees. Rather, it highlights the accounts of their final hours in order to provide a model for a "good death" (i.e., a way of dying that ensures birth in the Pure Land) to be imitated by later Pure Land believers. Moreover, the biographies frequently focus on auspicious signs and dreams to demonstrate that the deceased truly arrived in the Pure Land.[37] Despite such hagiographic elements, the *Gokurakuki* is an important source for understanding the kinds of practices undertaken by Pure Land believers during the ninth and tenth centuries.

The biographies recounted in the *Gokurakuki* reveal that the most important practice undertaken by Pure Land devotees was the nenbutsu. The Shingon monk Mukū 無空 (?–912?),[38] the Sanron monk Saigen 濟源 (885–960),[39] a

---

34   Sonoda, *Heian Bukkyō no kenkyū*, 165.

35   The text of the *Gokurakuki* is found in Inoue and Ōsone, *Ōjōden, Hokke genki*, 10–41.

36   In the "Benefits of the Nenbutsu" chapter of the *Ōjōyōshū*, it is stated, "In our country, too, there are many people, monastics and lay as well as men and women, who attained birth in the Pure Land. Details can be found in Mr. (Yoshi-) shige's Nihon ōjōki." (The *Nihon ōjōki* refers to the *Nihon ōjō gokurakuki*.) See T 84, 76b.

37   See Robert F. Rhodes, "*Ōjōyōshū, Nihon Ōjō Gokurakuki*, and the Construction of Pure Land Discourse in Heian Japan," *Japanese Journal of Religious Studies* 34, no. 2 (2007): 257–258.

38   Inoue and Ōsone, *Ōjōden, Hokke genki*, 22.

39   Ibid., 23.

nun who was the sister of Major Bishop (Daisōzu 大僧都) Kanchū 寛忠,[40] and the nun from Kamutsuhira 上平 village of Iidaka 飯高 district in Ise 伊勢 province[41] all made the nenbutsu their daily practice. The *Gokurakuki* also states that Kanchū's sister had a continuous nenbutsu performed for her on her deathbed.[42] However, the accounts in the *Gokurakuki* indicate that the nenbutsu was frequently conducted in conjunction with other practices. Kensan 兼算 (dates unknown) of the Bonshakuji 梵釋寺 combined the nenbutsu with devotion to Fudō Myōō 不動明王.[43] Jinjō 尋静 (dates unknown, but probably late ninth to early tenth centuries), a monk residing at the Shuryōgon'in 首楞 厳院, the central hall of Yokawa, read the *Diamond Prajñāpāramitā Sūtra* during the day and Practiced the nenbutsu at night.[44] In a similar vein, Shunso 春素 (dates unknown, but also probably late ninth to early tenth centuries) studied the *Mohe zhiguan* during the day and focused his mind on Amida Buddha at night.[45]

As these examples reveal, the number of people practicing the nenbutsu gradually increased from the ninth to tenth centuries. However, it is worth repeating that devotion to Amida Buddha was often combined with other practices, especially those of esoteric Buddhism. Since the time of Hōnen and his exclusive nenbutsu movement in the Kamakura period, the notion that one should rely exclusively on the nenbutsu in seeking birth in the Pure Land had become widespread. However, this was not the case in the Heian period. Heian monks lived in a complex spiritual universe, populated by a variety of buddhas, bodhisattvas, and other spiritual beings, all of whom could be called upon to assist one's spiritual journey. This pluralistic approach to salvation, which is taken for granted by all Buddhist practitioners of this age, can also be found in the *Ōjōyōshū*, inasmuch as it maintains both that Pure Land birth can be attained by practices other than the nenbutsu (although Genshin insists that the nenbutsu is the most appropriate practice for his age) and that a variety of practices must be used to supplement the nenbutsu if the latter is to be truly effective.

---

40   Ibid., 36.
41   Ibid.
42   Ibid.
43   Ibid., 26.
44   Ibid., 21.
45   Ibid.

THE GROWTH OF PURE LAND BUDDHISM IN THE HEIAN PERIOD 139

3   The Religious Situation in Mid-Heian Japan

The previous section outlined how Pure Land Buddhism gradually spread in Japan in the early Heian period. However, it was only in the middle of the tenth century that it became a widespread religious movement, embracing not only monks but large numbers of lay believers, including both nobles and commoners. The central figure behind its rapid growth during this age was Kūya (also called Kōya).[46] But before turning to this figure, it is necessary to discuss briefly the extremely unsettled religious situation of mid Heian Japan.

As Ishimoda Tadashi has argued, from the Engi 延喜 (901–923) to the Tenryaku 天暦 (947–957) periods, Japan experienced far-reaching social, political, and economic changes. These changes, including the breakdown of the Nara period *ritsuryō* 律令 system of centralized government, the increasing domination of the court by the Fujiwara family, the proliferation of tax-free estates (*shōen* 荘園), the emergence of an increasingly powerful warrior class, and the rapid and uncontrolled growth of the capital city, led to a thorough restructuring of Japanese society.[47] Symptomatic of this upheaval were the revolts of provincial warrior chieftains during the third decade of the tenth century. In 935, Taira no Masakado 平将門 (?–940), a leader of a warrior band in the Kantō region of eastern Japan, began attacking other warrior groups. After defeating government forces sent to pacify him, Masakado declared himself emperor in 940, but was finally killed in battle later in the year. At about the same time, in response to endemic piracy in the Inland Sea west of the capital, Fujiwara no Sumitomo 藤原純友 (?–941) was sent by the court to restore order to the region. Unexpectedly, Sumitomo himself became the head of a powerful band of pirates and, commanding a large fleet, plundered and terrorized the Inland Sea. The disturbance finally ended in 941 when Sumitomo was defeated by government forces.[48] Needless to say, these disturbances, especially Sumitomo's revolt that took place within striking distance of the capital,

---

46   This monk's name is usually read "Kūya." However, the characters making up his name can also be read as "Kōya." Hori Ichirō has argued that the latter pronunciation is the correct one and cites as evidence the fact that this monk's name is also written with the characters 弘也, 公也, and 公野, all of which are pronounced "Kōya." See Hori Ichirō, *Kūya* (Tokyo: Yoshikawa kōbunkan, 1963), 1. However, Ishii Yoshinaga has recently argued that "Kūya" should be the proper pronunciation. See Ishii Yoshinaga, *Amida hijiri Kūya* (Tokyo: Kōdansha, 2003), 42–44.

47   Ishimoda Tadashi, *Chūseiteki sekai no keisei* (Tokyo: Iwanami shoten, [1940] 1985), 340.

48   On these revolts, see Sir George Sansom, *A History of Japan to 1334* (Stanford CA: Stanford University Press, 1958), 145, 244–246.

terrified the nobility and caused them great anxiety.[49] These years also saw outbreaks of violence in the provinces of Dewa 出羽 (presently Yamagata and Akita prefectures) and Owari 尾張 and Mino 美濃 (both now parts of Aichi prefecture), while earthquakes, typhoons, floods, fires, and epidemics assailed the capital.[50]

The severe dislocations brought on by the great changes of this period profoundly affected the field of religion. The rise of cults centered on popular deities, the growth of the notion of religious pollution, and the spread of beliefs in portents and directional taboos all bear witness to the widespread spiritual turmoil of this age.[51] Significantly, several popular religious cults appeared abruptly in the capital during the early decades of the 900s, only to disappear just as quickly. In 938, pairs of male and female wooden deities called *funado no kami* 岐神, painted red and wearing crowns, appeared at intersections throughout the capital. These deities, displaying prominently carved genitals, were worshipped with offerings of *heihaku* 幣帛 (strips of cloth presented to the *kami*), incense, and flowers.[52] Shibata Minoru has argued that these figures were gods of the highway, entrusted with keeping evil influences at bay.[53] However, the fact that they were also called *goryō* 御靈, or malevolent disease-spreading spirits of the dead, led Takatori Masao to suggest that they were worshipped to ward off illness. In his view, they are best understood as a kind of *katashiro* 形代, human figures cut from paper used in purification rites, onto which the cause of disease was transferred and ritually neutralized.[54]

Another disquieting event was the appearance of the Shidarashin 志多良神 (Shidara deities) in 945. According to the *Honchō seiki* 本朝世紀, a history of Japan compiled in the late Heian period, in the seventh month of that year, a rumor spread that these deities were approaching the capital. Subsequently, three portable shrines (*mikoshi* 神輿) suddenly materialized in the province of Settsu, accompanied by several hundred people, dancing ecstatically to the sound of drums. These three portable shrines (at some point the number increased to six) were carried over a period of several days from Settsu to

---

49   The fact that a number of Buddhist rituals to quell the revolts were performed at the order of the court at this time reveals the extent of the anxiety experienced by the nobility. See Hayami, "Kōya's Appearance," 20–21.

50   Nabata Takashi, "Tendaishū to jōdokyō: Kūya o megutte," in *Nihon jōdokyōshi no kenkyū* ed. Fujishima hakase kanreki kinen ronshū kankōkai (Kyoto: Heirakuji shoten, 1969), 128.

51   Taira Masayuki, *Nihon chūsei no shakai to Bukkyō* (Tokyo: Hanawa shobō, 1992), 65–66.

52   The *funado no kami* are taken up in the entry for 9/2/Tengyō 天慶 1 (938) in the *Honchō seiki*. See KT 9: 12.

53   Shibata Minoru, *Chūsei shomin shinkō no kenkyū* (Tokyo: Kadokawa shoten, 1966), 106.

54   Takatori Masao, "Goryōe to Shidarashin," in *Kyoto no rekishi 1: Heian no shinkyō*, ed. Hayashiya Tatsusaburō (Tokyo: Gakugei shorin, 1970), 416.

THE GROWTH OF PURE LAND BUDDHISM IN THE HEIAN PERIOD 141

Iwashimizu Hachiman Shrine, located to the southwest of the capital. By this time, the throng trailing the portable shrines had grown to several thousand people. Unfortunately, the description of this event in the *Honchō seiki* ends at this point and there is no record of what happened next. Apparently, this sudden outburst of religious enthusiasm ended as quickly as it had begun, soon after the arrival of the Shidarashin to Iwashimizu Hachiman Shrine.[55]

However, it was the growth of the worship of the *goryō*, which became widespread not only in the capital but in the provinces as well, that best exemplifies the spiritual turmoil of the people of this age.[56] Basically, the *goryō* were vengeful spirits of people who met premature, unjust, or violent deaths. Due to their unreleased anger, these departed spirits returned to haunt those responsible for their suffering and to cause various troubles, including epidemics, droughts, famines, and disasters of all sorts. As Neil McMullin has noted, the most prominent *goryō*s of this age were the spirits of the nobility who died as a result of political intrigue.[57] Among them, the most well known was the spirit of Sugawara no Michizane 菅原道眞 (?–903).[58] During the early and mid-Heian periods, the Fujiwara clan systematically ousted one rival clan after another from positions of influence in the government in their quest for hegemony at court. In 901. Michizane, who had risen to the high post of Minister of the Right, was defeated in a power struggle with Fujiwara no Tokihira 藤原時平 (871–909) and banished to Dazaifu in Kyūshū, where he soon died.

A series of ominous events, all attributed to Michizane's revenge-seeking *goryō*, followed. In 923, when the crown prince (Tokihira's nephew) died, Michizane's spirit was blamed as the culprit. As a result, Michizane was pardoned and posthumously restored to his position at court. This, however, did not settle the matter. In 930, the imperial palace was struck by lightning, killing several prominent court officials. Emperor Daigo 醍醐, under whom Michizane was exiled to Dazaifu, was profoundly shaken by this event, became bedridden, and died a few months later. In 941, Dōken 道賢 (905?–985?), a monk who

---

55 The Shidarashin are described in the entries for 7/28 and 8/3 of Tengyō 8 (945) in the *Honchōseiki*. See KT 9: 109–111. The classic study on these deities is Shibata, *Chūsei shomin shinkō*. 98–104. See also Takatori, "Goryōe to Shidarashin," 419–424. Robert Borgen has suggested that these deities may be related to Sugawara no Michizane's *goryō*. See Robert Borgen, *Sugawara no Michizane and the Early Heian Court* (Cambridge, MA: Council on East Asian Studies, Harvard University, 1986), 319.

56 On the *goryō* cult, see Neil McMullin, "On Placating the Gods and Pacifying the Populace: The Case of the Gion *Goryō* Cult," *History of Religions* 27, no. 3 (1988): 270–293. A recent and readable study summarizing the extensive Japanese research on the *goryō* is Yamada Yūji, *Bokko suru onryō* (Tokyo: Yoshikawa kōbunkan, 2007).

57 McMullin, "On Placating the Gods," 272.

58 On Michizane, see Borgen, *Sugawara no Michizane*.

had been practicing austerities on Mt. Kinpu 金峯山, proclaimed that he had encountered Michizane in a dream. In it, Michizane declared that he was responsible for the lightning that struck the palace. In the same dream, Dōken saw Emperor Daigo and three of his ministers suffering in hell for the evils they had committed, including exiling Michizane. The next year, Tajihi no Ayako 多治比文子, a woman living in the capital, was possessed by Michizane's spirit, which declared its desire to be enshrined at Kitano at the western edge of the capital. In 947, the spirit again possessed a seven year-old son of a shrine priest in Ōmi province to deliver a similar message. Subsequently, the Kitano Shine was constructed to enshrine Michizane's spirit.[59]

Although Michizane's *goryō* was the most famous of such malevolent spirits, the *goryōe* 御靈會, or rituals to placate these dangerous spirits, had been held in the capital for close to a century. The earliest recorded *goryōe* was held in 863 at the Shinsen'en 神泉苑, a spacious park adjacent to the imperial palace. According to the *Nihon sandai jitsuroku*, this ceremony was held to pacify the spirits of six victims of political intrigue who were held responsible for an epidemic of influenza that had ravaged the country since the previous year. During the ceremony, the monk Etatsu 慧達 recited the *Suvarṇaprabhāsa Sūtra* and chanted the *Heart Sutra* six times.[60] Music and dance were performed to propitiate the spirits and the Shinsen'en was opened to the public so that everyone could participate and pray for the epidemic to cease. The *Nihon sandai jitsuroku* further states that such ceremonies, accompanied not only by music and dance but also by archery contests and sumō wrestling, were being conducted in both the capital region and the provinces and that they had become regular events by this time.[61]

As this account suggests, fear of disease was one of the main reasons behind the rapid spread of the *goryōe*. The population of the capital increased

---

59   On the complex process of Michizane's deification, see Borgen, *Sugawara no Michizane*, 308–325.

60   Along with the *Lotus Sutra* and the Benevolent *Kings Sutra*, the *Suvarṇaprabhāsa Sūtra* was counted as one of the "three nation-protecting sutras" and was frequently recited when disasters threatened the country. The popular Heart *Sutra* concludes with a *dhāraṇī* for delivering sentient beings to the "further shore" beyond the cycle of transmigration. It may be for this reason that it was considered an appropriate sutra to be chanted during the *goryōe*, whose purpose was to pacify the vengeful spirits by releasing them from the cycle of transmigration. The fact that this sutra was chanted six times may be related to the fact that six *goryōs* were being propitiated and also to the fact that Japanese Buddhists consider the world of transmigration to be divided into six realms.

61   *Nihon sandai jitsuroku*, entry for 5/20/Jōgan 5 (863). See KT 4: 112–113. This *goryōe* is discussed in Hayami, "Kōya's Appearance," 18.

THE GROWTH OF PURE LAND BUDDHISM IN THE HEIAN PERIOD

enormously from the ninth century,[62] and, due to the squalid living conditions that resulted, large-scale epidemics regularly swept through the city.[63] The *goryōs* were blamed for the epidemics, and the *goryōe* to pacify these violent spirits soon became an established feature of the religious landscape of Heian Japan. When a major epidemic swept through the capital in 994, a *goryōe* was held on Mt. Funaoka, a hill located to the north of Kyoto. On this occasion, monks gave lectures on the *Benevolent Kings Sutra*, while musicians were invited to perform. All who attended brought with them a *heihaku*, which they cast into the ocean at Naniwa (present-day Osaka) after the festival ended.[64] The famous *goryōe* of the Gion Shrine, popularly known as the Gion Festival, also dates around this time.[65]

4 Kūya and the Spread of Pure Land Buddhism

As noted in the previous section, the widespread social and political turmoil of the mid-tenth century, abetted by the constant threat of epidemics in the squalid urban setting and the fear of malevolent spirits it fostered, led many people of all classes in the capital to turn to new religious practices. Among them, Pure Land Buddhism, which held out the promise both of safely transporting the spirits of the dead to the Pure Land (where they would be rendered harmless) and of attaining for oneself a blissful afterlife free from all anxiety and suffering, was one of the most successful in responding to the spiritual yearnings of the age. Actively preached by Kūya, who arrived in the capital in 938 (coincidentally the year the *funado no kami* appeared), it was turned

---

62 McMullin states that the population of the capital increased five- to tenfold between the time of emperors Ninmyō 仁明 (reign 833–850) and Seiwa 清和 (reign 858–876). One reason for this great influx of people to the city was the serious poverty in the provinces. See McMullin, "On Placating the Gods," 287.

63 Ibid., 273.

64 This epidemic and *goryōe* are discussed in Takatori, "Goryōe to Shidarashin," 416.

65 According to the *Gionsha honenroku* 祇園社本縁録 (Record of the Origin of Gion Shrine), the Gion Festival was begun in 869 to quell an epidemic that occurred during this year. On this occasion, sixty-six halberds (*hoko* 鉾) symbolizing the sixty-six provinces of Japan were carried in a procession to the Shinsen'en. However, since the year 869 predates the founding of the Gion Shrine (which is generally said to have occurred in 876), it is difficult to date the origin of the Gion Festival to 869. It is more plausible to date it to 970, following the *Nijūnisha chūshiki* 二十二社註式 (Annotated Liturgy the Twenty-two Shrines) written by Yoshida Kanetomo 吉田兼倶 (1435–1511) in 1469, which states that it began in this year. See the entry for "Gion Matsuri" in Kokushi daijiten hensan iinkai, ed., *Kokushi daijiten* (Tokyo: Yoshik awa kobunkan, 1983), 4: 20.

144 RHODES

to by members of the nobility as well as the common people to satisfy their religious needs.[66]

There are two major sources of information about Kūya, the *Kūyarui* 空也誄 (Eulogy for Kūya) by Minamoto no Tamenori[67] and Kūya's biography included in Yoshishige no Yasutane's *Gokurakuki* (Kūya's biography in this collection will be cited below as the *Gokurakuki* biography). The former is believed to have been composed soon after Kūya died, probably for a memorial service held either on the forty-ninth day after he passed away or on the first anniversary of his death.[68] It consists of two parts, a preface and the eulogy itself. The eulogy, written in verse and celebrating Kūya's deeds, is rather short, just thirty-four lines of four characters each. It is preceded by a lengthy prose preface recounting Kūya's life. This preface is the most important source of information concerning this monk. Unfortunately, despite its importance, there are several limitations to the *Kūyarui*. For example, it contains little concrete information concerning Kūya's life before his arrival in the capital. Moreover, much of the account of his activities in the capital is taken up with the miracles that he is said to have performed. Since Tamenori interviewed Kūya's disciples in writing the eulogy, it is possible that tales of this monk's supernatural powers were circulating among his followers by this time.[69] These stories are important since they show that Kūya was popularly perceived as a miracle worker, but it is unfortunate that Tamenori did not include more about Kūya's religious activities

---

66 There are a number of studies on this monk. An excellent study in English is Clark Chilson, "Eulogizing Kūya as More than a Nenbutsu Practitioner: A Study and Translation of the *Kūyarui*," *Japanese Journal of Religious Studies* 34, no. 2 (2007): 305–327. Other important works include Hori Ichirō, *Kūya*; Hayami, "Kōya's Appearance"; Ishii Yoshinaga, *Kūya shōnin nokenkyū* (Kyoto: Hōzōkan, 2002); Ishii Yoshinaga, *Amida hijiri Kūya*; and Itō Yuishin, ed., *Jōdo no seija Kūya* (Tokyo: Yoshikawa kōbunkan, 2005).

67 The *Kūyarui* is found in the *Zoku gunsho ruijū*. See ZGR 8–2: 743–746. This is based on a manuscript dated 1125 preserved in the library of the Shinpukuji 真福寺 in Nagoya. A photograph of this text is found in Kokubungaku kenkyū shiryōkan, ed., *Shinpukuji zenpon sōkan 6, Denki genkishū* (Kyoto: Rinsen shoten 2004), 283–311. This text is corrupt in many places, but it can be reconstructed by consulting the *Rokuharamitsuji engi* 六波羅蜜寺縁起 (Origin of the Rokuharamitsu Temple), which quotes the *Kūyarui*. The reconstructed text is found in Ishii Yoshinaga, *Kūya shōnin no kenkyū*, 133–149. An English translation is found in Chilson, "Eulogizing Kūya," 318–324.

68 The first theory is found in Ishii Yoshinaga, *Kūya shōnin no kenkyū*, 41, while the latter is found in Hirabayashi Moritoku, *Hijiri to setsuwa no shiteki kenkyū* (Tokyo: Yoshikawa kōbunkan, 1981), 148. Since people are believed to be reborn forty-nine days after they died, a memorial service is held on this day.

69 Itō Yuishin, *Jōdo no seija Kūya*, 19. Tamenori states in the *Kūyarui* that he talked to Kūya's disciples and collected various materials before writing the eulogy. See Chilson, "Eulogizing Kūya," 323.

THE GROWTH OF PURE LAND BUDDHISM IN THE HEIAN PERIOD 145

and thought. The *Gokurakuki* biography was written slightly later. As noted above, the *Gokurakuki* had been finished by 985 and this would date Kūya's biography in this collection to a time just a little over a decade after his death. Compared to the *Kūyarui*, the *Gokurakuki* biography is considerably shorter. Although this biography contains some interesting material not found in the *Kūyarui*, the two biographies are generally similar in content.

Both biographies begin with the statement that Kūya never divulged the names of his parents, but the *Kūyarui* adds, "Some knowledgeable people say that he was a scion of the imperial family."[70] The *Kūyarui* states that when he was "over twenty years old, he entered the provincial temple in Owari 尾張 and took the tonsure. Kūya was the acolyte (*shami* 沙彌) name he gave himself."[71] The biography continues that he traveled around the country in his youth, visiting "famous mountains and holy grottos."[72] During his travels, he helped improve highways and dug wells where needed. Moreover, whenever he encountered corpses that had been cast away in the countryside, he gathered them together, poured oil on them, and cremated them while reciting the nenbutsu.

At one point during his peregrination, Kūya resided in a temple called Mineaidera 峯合寺 in Harima 播磨 province (now Hyōgo prefecture) for several years to study the Buddhist scriptures. Whenever he encountered a passage he could not comprehend, a "golden man" appeared to him in a dream to explain its meaning to him. Later he secluded himself at Yushima 湯島, an island on the border of Awa 阿波 and Tosa 土佐 provinces (present-day Tokushima and Kōchi prefectures) in the island of Shikoku. Yushima was home to a miracle-working statue of Kannon, and Kūya undertook austerities to gain a vision of this bodhisattva. Unable at first to gain the vision he sought, Kūya ceased eating cereals and vowed to remain motionless for seven days, forgoing sleep and burning incense on his arm. On the final day of his austerities, Kūya beheld the statue of Kannon emitting a luminous halo. At some point after this experience, he traveled to Mutsu 陸奥 (presently Fukushima, Miyagi, Iwate, and Aomori prefectures) and Dewa provinces in north Japan to preach the Buddhist dharma to the people there.

The year 938 marks a major turning point in Kūya's career. In this year, Kūya abandoned his itinerant life and settled in the capital to proselytize the Pure Land teaching. The revolts of Taira no Masakado and Fujiwara no Sumitomo were then raging in the provinces, while epidemics, fires, floods,

---

70   Chilson, "Eulogizing Kūya," 318.
71   Ibid., slightly modified.
72   Ibid.

and earthquakes were assailing the city.[73] It was during such unsettled times that Kūya resolved to dedicate himself to spreading the nenbutsu teachings in the capital. The sobriquets he gained during this time reveal the kind of life he led here. According to the *Kūyarui*, "In the first year of Tengyō 天慶 (938), Kūya returned to the capital. In the market-place, he began to discreetly beg for food. Whenever he received anything, he would use it for Buddhist services or give it to the poor and sick. He was thus called 'holy man of the marketplace' (*ichi no hijiri* 市聖). He constantly recited without pause '*Namu Amidabutsu*' and the people called him 'Amida holy man' (*Amida hijiri* 阿彌陀聖)."[74] In the capital, Kūya continued the various social welfare projects that he had conducted during his travels. For example, the *Kūyarui* notes that he dug wells in the city that were known thereafter as "Amida wells" (*Amidai* 阿彌陀井).[75] The same year that he arrived in the capital, Kūya constructed a *sotoba* 率塔婆, or stūpa, hung with bells and adorned with a Buddhist statue, outside the prison gate in the eastern part of the capital (*tōto shūmon* 東都囚門), Kūya's aim in constructing the stūpa was to provide consolation and hope to the prisoners inside the prison. The *Kūyarui* underscores his success in ministering to prisoners, noting, "A few prisoners shed tears, saying, 'We have unexpectedly seen the face of the buddha and heard the Dharma. Such a wonderful thing has released us from our pain.'"[76]

In 944, Kūya created hanging scrolls depicting the thirty-three manifestations of Kannon along with paintings of Amida's Pure Land and Mt. Poṭalaka, Kannon's Pure Land. The fact that he was able to complete this project suggests that he had gained the support of wealthy noble patrons by this time. Four years later, in 948, Kūya received the full precepts at the Kaidan'in 戒壇院 (Precept Hall) in Enryakuji at the urging of Tendai *zasu* Enshō, thereby becoming a monk of the Tendai school. But although he was granted the name Kōshō 光勝 on this occasion, Kūya continued to use his old name.

In 951, Kūya embarked on another ambitious undertaking: the creation of a ten feet tall statue of Kannon, along with smaller statues of Brahma, Indra, and the Four Heavenly Kings. During the previous few years, Japan had been visited by severe typhoons, droughts, and epidemics, leading the government to host numerous Buddhist ceremonies to pray for the deliverance of the country from calamities. Kūya's desire to create these statues was probably not

---

73 Ishii Yoshinaga, *Amida hijiri Kūya*, 21.

74 Chilson, "Eulogizing Kūya," 319, slightly modified.

75 The *Gokurakuki* biography does not mention that Kūya dug wells in the city. However, it notes that he dug wells during his travels and states that these wells were known as "Amida wells." See Inoue and Ōsone, *Ōjōden, Hokke genki*, 28.

76 Chilson, "Eulogizing Kūya," 319–320, slightly modified.

THE GROWTH OF PURE LAND BUDDHISM IN THE HEIAN PERIOD   147

unrelated to these disasters, especially the severe epidemic of 947. In his mind, the nenbutsu still retained its function as magical incantations for delivering the dead to the Pure Land.[77] The *Kūyarui* notes that, at the time Tamenori wrote the eulogy, these statues were enshrined in the Saikōji 西光寺, the present Rokuharamitsuji 六波羅蜜寺, where Kūya died.[78] The fact that the temple was located at the eastern edge of the capital suggests that Kūya had moved his center of activity from the city market to this area by this time.[79] The location of this hall is significant, since it was adjacent to Toribeno 鳥邊野, an area set aside for the disposal of the dead. Throughout Heian Japan, the dead were generally neither buried nor cremated, but were left to decay naturally on the ground, often even in the middle of the city.[80] According to the well-known entry in the *Shoku Nihon kōki* 續日本後記 (Continued Later Chronicles of Japan), a history of Japan completed in 869, when an epidemic struck the capital in 841, fifty-five hundred skeletons were collected together and cremated.[81] A similar scene may have confronted the people of Kyoto during the pestilence of 947. Thus the statues of Kannon and other deities were enshrined close to the dead whom they were meant to comfort and pacify.

In 963, Kūya staged the crowning event of his career, a grand service to commemorate the completion of his project to copy the entire 600-fascicle *Mahāprajñāpāramitā Sūtra* in gold ink. Kūya had begun the project in 950 but was unable to complete it until this year. In order to procure the materials needed to copy the *Mahāprajñāpāramitā Sūtra*, Kūya solicited funds widely among the populace, some of whom responded, according to the vow Kūya read during the ceremony, by donating "half a coin" or "a grain of cereal" from their meager earnings.[82] Even if the sum was small, these donations had the important religious function of helping to create an indelible karmic bond (*kechien* 結縁) between the donor and the Buddhist Dharma, serving to ensure the salvation of the former. To hold the service, Kūya also received contributions from the court, revealing how widely his fame had spread by this time.[83]

---

77   Itō Yuishin, *Jōdo no seija Kūya*, 37.

78   Chilson, "Eulogizing Kūya," 320.

79   Ishii Yoshinaga, *Amida hijiri Kūya*, 154–155.

80   For a fascinating account of the disposal of the dead in medieval Japan, see Katsuda Itaru, *Shisha tachi no chūsei* (Tokyo: Yoshikawa kōbunkan, 2003).

81   Hayami, "Kōya's Appearance," 19.

82   This vow is included in the *Honchō monzui*. See Ōsone, Kinhara, and Gotō, *Honchō monzui*, 359. The entire vow is found in Ōsone, Kinhara, and Gotō, *Honchō monzui*, 359–360, and Ishii Yoshinaga, *Amida hijiri Kūya*, 234–240. A detailed analysis of the vow is found in Obara Hitoshi, *Bunjin kizoku no keifu* (Tokyo: Yoshikawa kōbunkan, 1987), 80–93.

83   Ishii Yoshinaga, *Amida hijiri Kūya*, 147–148.

The service, held on the twenty-third day of the eighth month, took place southeast of the capital, in a temporary hall built along the bank of the Kamo River. Intriguingly, this service coincided with an incident known as the Sectarian Debate of the Ōwa Era (Ōwa no shūron 應和宗論; this incident will be cited below as the Ōwa Debate). This debate, orchestrated by the Tendai monk Ryōgen as a means to advance his position within the Enryakuji, will be discussed in detail below.

Kūya's service was attended by numerous people, including the Minister of the Left (Sadaijin 左大臣) Fujiwara no Saneyori 藤原實頼 (900–970) and other nobles. According to the vow read by Kūya on this occasion (composed by Miyoshi no Michimune 三善道統 [dates unknown]), six hundred monks were invited to the service and the newly copied sutra was ritually "read" in the *tendoku* 轉讀 style.[84] Dance and music were performed and boats with dragon-shaped prows glided up and down the nearby Kamo River. The ceremony lasted into the night when, bathed in the light of numerous lanterns, the assembled people took the bodhisattva precepts and recited the nenbutsu in the hope of achieving birth in the Pure Land.[85]

In the vow, Kūya proclaimed that he began the sutra copying project in order to pray for the attainment of buddhahood by all beings bound to the six realms of transmigration.[86] However, it has been argued that, like the creation of Buddhist statues in 951, a major purpose of this ceremony was to pray for the welfare of the many people who had died in the various epidemics and disasters that had plagued Japan over the years. This is suggested by the following words of the vow. "In mountains, rivers, bushes, and marshes, is there any place where corpses of (beings bound to the cycle of) birth-and-death are not to be found? ... May bones, both old and new, in the wilderness, and spirits, both earlier and later, of Dongdai 東岱 ... all achieve sublime enlightenment."[87] As Tachibana Kyōdō pointed out, since the early Heian period, the *Prajñāpāramitā Sūtras*, and the *Mahāprajñāpāramitā Sūtra* in particular, had been employed in rituals to quell epidemics and were recited to pacify the spirits of the dead. Also by this time, these sutras had become associated with the *goryō* cult, as

---

84 This is a way of reading a sutra by chanting just a few lines from each fascicle and skipping the rest. It is used in rituals where it is necessary to chant extremely long sutras such as the 600-fascicle *Mahāprajñāpāramitā Sūtra*.

85 Ōsone, Kinhara, and Gotō, *Honchō monzui*, 359–360, and Ishii Yoshinaga, *Amida hijiri Kūya*, 236–237.

86 Ōsone, Kinhara, and Gotō, *Honchō monzui*, 359, and Ishii Yoshinaga, *Amida hijiri Kūya*, 235.

87 Ōsone, Kinhara, and Gotō, *Honchō monzui*, 359–360, and Ishii Yoshinaga, *Amida hijiri Kūya*, 234–238. Dongdai refers to Mt. Tai (Taishan 泰山) in China, which is believed to be the abode of the spirits of heaven and earth.

shown by the fact that the *Heart Sutra*, the shortest of the *Prajñāpāramitā Sūtras*, was recited at the Shinsen'en *goryōe* in 863.[88] Hence, it is no coincidence that Kūya chose to copy the *Mahāprajñāpāramitā Sūtra* in order to quell the anger and anguish of the spirits of the dead that were believed to haunt this world, unable to escape from the cycle of transmigration and venting their frustration by causing epidemics.

It may be mentioned here that Kūya's biographies contain a number of memorable anecdotes purporting to show that he was endowed with extraordinary spiritual powers. They include stories of how he successfully helped a spirit of a fox (which had transformed itself into a woman) gain salvation and how he saved a frog that had been swallowed by a snake by reciting a magical incantation. Another interesting episode concerns Kūya's influential follower Fujiwara no Morouji 藤原師氏 (913–970), the fourth son of Fujiwara no Tadahira. When Morouji died, Kūya wrote a petition addressed to Yama, the king of hell, entreating Yama to regard Morouji with compassion. Similarly, the *Gokurakuki* biography gives an idealized description of his final hour. According to this passage, on the day of his death, Kūya related to his disciples that he had a vision of Amida and his attendant bodhisattvas coming to lead him to the Pure Land. The passage continues that, when he died, music was heard in the sky and a wonderful fragrance filled the room.[89]

After working to spread the Pure Land teachings in the capital for over three decades, Kūya died in 972. In the final lines of the *Gokurakuki* biography, Yasutane provided the following assessment of Kūya's activities. "Before the Tengyō era (938–947) it was rare for a person to practice the nenbutsu *samādhi* in the Buddhist practice halls (*dōjō* 道場) and villages. Moreover, many common men and foolish women (*shōnan gunnyo* 小男愚女) shunned it as taboo (*imi* 忌). After the *shōnin* 上人 (saint; i.e., Kūya) came, he himself chanted ("*Namu Amidabutsu*") and taught others to chant it. Subsequently, everyone in the world practiced the nenbutsu."[90] Although this is certainly an exaggeration, deriving from the author's reverential attitude toward his subject, there

---

88 Tachibana Kyōdō, "Waga kuni ni okeru onryō shinkō to *Daihannyakyō* no kankei ni tsuite," *Bukkyō shigaku* 11, no. 1 (1963): 4–5. It must be noted that during the Nara period, the *Mahāprajñāpāramitā Sūtra* was also frequently recited, copied, and venerated to gain various spiritual and material benefits in this life, such as longevity, the eradication of evil karma, and relief from natural calamities. On the ritual uses of the *Mahāprajñāpāramitā Sūtra* in Japan, see M. W. de Visser, *Ancient Buddhism in Japan* (Leiden: E. J. Brill; Paris: Paul Geuthner, 1935), 2: 489–519.

89 Chilson, "Eulogizing Kūya," 323.

90 Inoue and Ōsone, *Ōjōden, Hokke genki*, 29.

is no question that Kūya's activities were crucial in spreading the Pure Land teachings among the residents of the capital.

5 Interpretations of Kūya's Religion

Kūya's nenbutsu spread rapidly among the people of the capital, gaining broad support among both ordinary people and the nobility. There is no question that Kūya had a decisive impact on the growth of the Pure Land teachings in Japan. However, scholars have differed on how to interpret the nature of Kūya's religion.[91] One influential line of thought, exemplified by scholars like Hori Ichirō, has depicted Kūya as a typical *hijiri* 聖 (holy man), whom they regard as an important type of Buddhist figure in Japanese religious history.[92] As noted above, Kūya was called both "holy man of the marketplace" and "Amida holy man." The *hijiri* is frequently described as living an itinerant life, remaining unaffiliated with any particular temple or school. *Hijiris* often undertook austerities in the mountains and other holy sites and were credited with possessing supernatural powers deriving from their practices. Besides being adept in performing miracles, they often engaged in projects to improve the life of the common people, such as building roads, bridges, and irrigation canals. The prototypical *hijiri*, Gyōki 行基 (668–749) of the Nara period, is celebrated as a compassionate bodhisattva who "dug ponds for reservoirs and built Irrigation dikes"[93] to the great benefit of the people of the countryside.[94]

Defined in this way, Kūya fits the pattern of a *hijiri* quite well. Not only was he popularly called "*hijiri* of the marketplace" and "*Amida hijiri*," but he was also a privately ordained monk who remained unaffiliated with any Buddhist school or institution until he joined the Tendai order in 948. During his travels, he not only practiced austerities but also undertook various public works projects, and it is worth nothing that his social activism did not end after he took up residence in the capital.

---

91 For a succinct overview of the various interpretations of Kūya's religion, see Obara, *Bunjin kizoku no keifu*, 75–77.

92 This is a major theme that underlies Hori Ichirō, *Kūya*.

93 Janet R. Goodwin, *Alms and Vagabonds: Buddhist Temples and Popular Patronage in Medieval Japan* (Honolulu: University of Hawai'i Press, 1994), 30. This passage originally appears in the *Hokke genki*. For the original Japanese, see Inoue and Ōsone, *Ōjōden, Hokke genki*, 51–52.

94 On Gyōki, see Jonathan Morris Augustine, *Buddhist Hagiography in Early Japan: Images of Compassion in the Gyōki Tradition* (London: RoutledgeCurzon, 2005).

However, Christoph Kleine has forcefully argued that the term "*hijiri*" was used in a much more restricted sense in texts written during the Heian period. Through an extensive study of these texts, including historical works, collections of *setsuwa* (Buddhist tales) like the *Nihon ryōiki*, and works in the *ōjōden* genre, Kleine concluded that the term "*hijiri*" was used to refer specifically to ascetic practitioners who shunned contact with the world and undertook rigorous asceticism in sacred mountains.[95] They were generally not "evangelical" in the sense that they worked to spread the Buddhist teachings among the people. Moreover, they hardly ever engaged in magical healing or exorcism, rarely conducted rites to placate the spirits of the dead, and almost never worked to spread their teachings among the populace.[96] Thus, Kleine argued that Kūya does not fit the typical Heian period image of a *hijiri* very well. Kūya probably came to be called a *hijiri* because he undertook austerities and gained a reputation as an ascetic in the years before he took up residence in the capital.[97]

Thus, Kūya was not a typical *hijiri* in that he used the power gained through austerities for thaumaturgic purposes. But it was his thaumaturgy that was perceived by his contemporaries as the characteristic—perhaps the most characteristic—element of his religious practice. Indeed, as noted above, Kūya's extraordinary ability to perform miracles was featured prominently in both the *Kūyarui* and the *Gokurakuki* biography. This aspect of Kūya's religion has been highlighted by Hayami Tasuku, who argued that Kūya is best understood as one of many miracle-working monks who appeared in the Heian period and that Kūya's nenbutsu is best described as "thaumaturges' nenbutsu" (*kenja no nenbutsu* 験者の念佛), that is to say, nenbutsu performed by such miracle-working monks for the purpose of delivering the spirits of the dead to the Pure Land.[98] As Hayami pointed out, from the late 800s to the mid-900s, there appeared a number of monks who had become proficient in performing miracles through their asceticism and mastery of esoteric rituals. He argues that during the early Heian period, esoteric rituals were primarily conducted by the court to pray for the safety and well-being of the state. However, beginning from the late ninth century, the nobility increasingly came to hold private esoteric rites to cure illnesses, to conduct exorcisms, and to pray for the prosperity and welfare of their own clans. The primary reason for the increase in private esoteric rituals was the changing political situation of the time. During

---

95 Christoph Kleine, "Hermits and Ascetics in Ancient Japan: The Concept of *Hijiri* Reconsidered," *Japanese Religions* 22, no. 2 (1997): 39–40.

96 Kleine, "Hermits and Ascetics," 32–33.

97 Ibid., 31.

98 Hayami, "Kōya's Appearance," 15.

this period, the struggle for supremacy among the noble families at court intensified, and under such circumstances, the nobility regularly employed esoteric rituals as a powerful spiritual weapon to achieve their political goals.[99]

Significantly, a number of these esoteric monks, including Ennin, Sōō. Zōmyō, and Enshō mentioned above, were concurrently nenbutsu practitioners.[100] According to Hayami, these monks were widely believed to have the power to deliver the dead to the Pure Land by reciting the nenbutsu and were frequently invited to funerals by the nobility to ensure the postmortem welfare of the deceased. For example, he refers to a passage in the *Rihōōki* 吏部王記, the diary of Shigeakira Shinnō 重明親王, which states that when Emperor Daigo died, "nenbutsu monks from various temples set up curtains on both sides of the road (leading up to the grave) at eighty-six places and recited the nenbutsu while ringing bells."[101] The passage continues that Shingon monks from Daigoji 醍醐寺 and Kanshūji 勧修寺 conducted the nenbutsu for three days at the deceased emperor's grave.[102] Although Kūya's biographies do not specifically mention that he undertook esoteric practices, Hayami maintains that Kūya must be regarded as one such monk who, through his austerities, gained the power to deliver the dead to the Pure Land through the nenbutsu.

Since Kūya is described as cremating corpses while reciting the nenbutsu during his travels throughout Japan, it cannot be denied that his use of the nenbutsu recitation to send the dead to the Pure Land was an important component of his religious practice. Many of the activities he undertook after his arrival in the capital, such as the *Mahāprajñāpāramitā Sūtra* ceremony of 963, were also intended to benefit the spirits of the departed. In using the nenbutsu as a powerful ritual invocation to pacify the spirits of the dead and deliver them to the Pure Land, he was continuing a tradition already found in the earliest period of Pure Land Buddhism in Japan. But, although Hayami's theory is highly suggestive, it is not sufficient to characterize Kūya's nenbutsu simply as a ritual tool to provide for the welfare of the dead. Although there is no denying that it is undoubtedly an important aspect of Kūya's religion, it must be remembered that he also taught the people to recite the nenbutsu for their own salvation. By preaching the way to attain birth in Amida's land through the nenbutsu, Kūya provided the people of the capital with a salvific path suited to the spiritual needs of the age, thereby contributing greatly to the spread of Pure Land Buddhism.

---

99   Hayami Tasuku, *Heian kizoku shakai to Bukkyō* (Tokyo: Yoshikawa kōbunkan, 1975), 33–38.

100   For examples, see Hayami, "Kōya's Appearance," 12–14.

101   DS, pt. 1, vol. 6: 361.

102   This passage is discussed in Hayami, "Kōya's Appearance," 14.

THE GROWTH OF PURE LAND BUDDHISM IN THE HEIAN PERIOD 153

Finally, two related points need to be addressed concerning the nature of Kūya's religion. First, as Clark Chilson has perceptively observed, although Kūya is invariably depicted as a nenbutsu practitioner in modern scholarship, there is surprisingly little mention of this practice in his biographies. Although they state that he recited the nenbutsu without interruption and that he cremated the dead while chanting Amida's name, that is about all.[103] Rather, the things highlighted in his biographies are his austerities, his compassionate acts for others (including public works projects like building roads and digging wells), and his miraculous deeds. Second, it also needs to be mentioned that Kūya, like many of his contemporaries, was not exclusively devoted to Amida. His biographies reveal that he was a faithful believer of other Buddhist deities as well, most notably the bodhisattva Kannon. Not only did Kūya commission a hanging scroll of Kannon's manifestations in 944, but this was followed in 951 by the creation of a ten feet tall statue of this bodhisattva, which became the central image of his temple. Given that Kannon is considered the epitome of compassion in Buddhism, it was perhaps natural for Kūya, with his commitment to working for the spiritual and material welfare of all people, to hold this bodhisattva in high regard.[104] For these reasons, it may be concluded that, although the Pure Land faith was central to Kūya's religion, he possessed a complex religion that defies simple characterization. His activities remind us once again that, even though Kūya was indeed a key figure in the spread of Pure Land Buddhism, exclusive reliance on Amida Buddha and the recitation of his name was not a part of the Pure Land faith he espoused.

6 Yoshishige no Yasutane and the Kangakue

The growing influence of Pure Land teachings had a major impact on the spiritual life of the nobility. Perhaps the most famous court noble attracted to

---

103 Chilson, "Eulogizing Kūya," 314. The *Gokurakuki* biography notes that a blacksmith was saved from having money robbed from him when he recited the nenbutsu as Kūya instructed. See Inoue and Ōsone, *Ōjōden, Hokke genki*, 28. However, this story is not found in the Kūyarui.

104 Futaba Kenkō has especially emphasized the importance of the bodhisattva ideal for Kūya. According to Futaba, a major characteristic of Kūya's religious life was his strong commitment to following the path of the bodhisattva, i.e. his commitment to seek buddhahood by working for the material and spiritual welfare of all living beings. See Futaba Kenkō, "Kūya jōdokyō ni tsuite: Senkan to no kyōtsūsei wo tsūjite," in *Nihon jōdokyōshi no kenkyū*, ed. Fujishima hakase kanreki kinen ronshū kankōkai (Kyoto: Heirakuji shoten, 1969), 186.

Pure Land Buddhism at this time was Yoshishige no Yasutane.[105] Yasutane was a highly respected literati who rose to the office of Major Secretary (*dainaiki* 大内記), responsible for the composition of imperial edicts, in the court of Emperor Kazan 花山. However, he became increasingly dissatisfied with court life and finally took the tonsure in 986, adopting Jakushin 寂心 for his religious name.

Yasutane is famous as the author of the *Chiteiki* 池亭記 (Record of the Pond Pavilion), written in 982, which is said to have been the model for the well-known *Hōjōki* 方丈記 by Kamo no Chōmei 鴨長明 (1153–1216).[106] Besides the *Chiteiki*, Yasutane also wrote the *Gokurakuki* mentioned earlier, as well as the *Jūrokusōsan* 十六相讃 (Verses in Praise of the Sixteen Aspects), a short work on the sixteen kinds of contemplations found in the *Contemplation Sutra*.[107] As will be noted below, when Genshin sent the *Ōjōyōshū* to China in 988, he sent along these two works as well, indicating how highly Genshin thought of them.

Apparently, Yasutane had been drawn to Pure Land Buddhism since his youth. In the preface to the *Gokurakuki*, he declares, "Since my youth, I have remained mindful of Amida Buddha, and after I turned forty, my resolution became increasingly passionate. With my lips I recite the name (of Amida) and in my mind I contemplate (this buddha's) marks and secondary marks (*kō* 好).[108] Whether walking, standing, sitting, or lying down, I do not forget (to practice the nenbutsu) even for an instant, and I practice it always, even when hurrying or stumbling."[109] According to this passage, Yasutane had practiced the nenbutsu since his youth but became increasingly committed to the Pure Land faith after he turned forty in 971.

---

105   On Yasutane, see Gotō Akio, "Yoshishige no Yasutane," in *Iwanami kōza Nihon bungaku to Bukkyō 1: Ningen*, ed. Imano Tatsuru, Satake Akihiro, and Ueda Shizuteru (Tokyo: Iwanami shoten, 1993), 195–213.

106   The *Chiteiki* is translated in Burton Watson, trans., *Japanese Literature in Chinese* (New York: Columbia University Press, 1975), 1: 57–64. A thorough study of the *Chiteiki* is found in Ōsone Shōsuke, "*Chiteiki* ron," in *Nihon kanbungakushi ronkō*, ed. Yamagishi Tokuhei (Tokyo: Iwanami shoten, 1974), 215–252.

107   On the *Jūrokusōsan*, see Satō Tetsuei, *Eizan jōdokyō no kenkyū* (Kyoto: Hyakkaen, 1979), 1: 88–103. The text of this work is found in Satō, *Eizan jōdokyō*, 2: 70–75.

108   In addition to the thirty-two marks, buddhas are also said to possess eighty secondary marks. For a list of these secondary marks, see Hurvitz, "Chih-i," 356–360.

109   Inoue and Ōsone, *Ōjōden. Hokke genki*, 11. The words "hurrying and stumbling" derive from the *Analects*, which states, "The gentleman never deserts benevolence, not even for as long as it takes to eat a meal. If he hurries and stumbles, one may be sure that it is in benevolence that he does so." See D. C. Lau, trans., *The Analects* (Harmondsworth: Penguin Books, 1979), 72.

THE GROWTH OF PURE LAND BUDDHISM IN THE HEIAN PERIOD   155

Already in his early thirties, Yasutane had taken the lead in organizing the Kangakue, which incorporated the nenbutsu into its activities. This fellowship, founded in 964, consisted of twenty students from the national university (Daigakuryō 大學寮) and twenty monks from Mt. Hiei.[110] According to a short description of the fellowship found in Tamenori's *Sanbōe*, it was formed to "give encouragement to one another in our studies of the way of the Dharma and the way of literature."[111] It met twice a year, on the fifteenth of the third and ninth months. The members gathered together on the evening of the fourteenth. On the morning of the fifteenth, a lecture was given on the *Lotus Sutra*, followed by a debate on the sutra's doctrines. In the evening, the members (both monks and laymen) chanted the nenbutsu and subsequently composed poetry until dawn on topics taken from the *Lotus Sutra*.[112] The initial meetings took place in Sakamoto at the eastern foot of Mt. Hiei. But despite the fact that It was held for a number of years, the society never found a permanent home and was obliged to meet at various temples in the environs of Kyoto. The Kangakue continued until about 986, when its leader, Yasutane, took the tonsure.[113]

The character of the Kangakue has been the object of a lively scholarly debate. As noted above, lectures on the *Lotus Sutra* (followed by a debate on its doctrines), nenbutsu recitation, and poetry composition were the main activities of the fellowship. In an influential theory, Inoue Mitsusada argued that the nenbutsu was the most important of the three elements and characterized

---

110   Basic information about the Kangakue is found in Momo Hiroyuki, *Jōdai gakusei no kenkyū* (Tokyo: Meguro shoten, 1947), 360–380. An important study, especially valuable for its summary of previous Japanese scholarship on this association, is Obara, *Bunjin kizoku no keifu*, 46–113.

111   Kamens, The Three Jewels, 295, slightly modified.

112   According to an influential theory set forth by the Chinese poet Bo Jiyi 白居易 (772–846), literary activities such as the composition of poetry were considered to function as a form of Buddhist practice. In Bo Jiyi's view, many Buddhists viewed the composition of poetry negatively. They characterized poetry as "crazed words and idle talk" (*kyōgen kigo* 狂言綺語), and poets were considered guilty of engaging in "idle talk" (*kigo* 綺語), one of the ten evil actions enumerated in Buddhism. However, Bo Jiyi argued that poetry may also serve as a way to praise the buddhas, making it a legitimate path to the attainment of buddhahood. It was undoubtedly under the influence of Bo Jiyi's thought (which was widely accepted by the literati of the Heian period) that the composition of poetry on Buddhist topics was considered to have religious significance and was adopted as a part of the Kangakue's activities. The notion of "crazed words and idle talk" is explored in Shirato Waka, "Kyōgen kigo ni tsuite," *Bukkyōgaku seminā* 9 (1969): 25–34. On its use by Bo Jiyi and Yasutane, see Yanai Shigeru, "Kyōgen kigokan ni tsuite: Haku Rakuten kara Yasutane e no kussetsu," *Kokugo to kokubungaku* 39, no. 4 (1962): 23–34.

113   The Kangakue was revived around 1004 and continued, with one more interruption, for a number of years. See Momo, *Jōdai gakusei no kenkyū*, 366–372.

the Kangakue as a kind of "nenbutsu fellowship."[114] However, Inoue's theory has been questioned by several scholars. Hori Daiji, for example, considered the lectures on the *Lotus Sutra* to be the focal activity of the Kangakue,[115] while Nara Hiromoto described it as a literary salon, in which the composition of poetry was considered most important by its members.[116]

A different perspective on the character of this association was offered by Sonoda Kōyū. Focusing on the fact that this association consisted of an equal number of clerics and laymen, Sonoda proposed that the Kangakue should be characterized as a fellowship in which lay Buddhists could meet and forge karmic bonds with monks. By forging such bonds with virtuous monks, it was believed that lay members could share in the monks' stock of merit and attain enlightenment in the future. Sonoda noted that services for establishing such karmic ties with monks were frequently held during this period. It was no accident, he argued, that the initiative for organizing the Kangakue came from the side of the students, since it helped satisfy the lay members' desire to strengthen their ties with Buddhist monks and to partake vicariously in the latters' store of merits.[117]

Higashidate Shōken has proposed another cogent interpretation of the Kangakue. Higashidate pointed out that the Kangakue was a multifaceted confraternity that incorporated a number of elements into its activities. According to this view, the lectures on the *Lotus Sutra*, nenbutsu recitation, and poetry composition were all important features of this association. However, through a close study of the then recently discovered *Kangakueki* 勸學會記 (Record of the Association for the Encouragement of Learning),[118] Higashidate argued that the structure of the Kangakue meetings closely resembled the liturgy of the various Hokke kōe 法華講會 (Buddhist ceremonies centered on lectures on the *Lotus Sutra*) that were frequently performed at that time. On the basis of this comparison, he concluded that the Kangakue was a type of Hokke kōe whose central elements were the lectures and debates on the *Lotus Sutra*.[119] Moreover, expanding on Sonoda's view that the Kangakue provided a

---

114 Inoue, Nihon *jōdokyō seiritsushi*, 92.

115 Hori Daiji, "Nijūgo zanmaie no seiritsu ni kansuru shomondai," *Kyoto joshi daigaku jinbun ronsō* 9 (1964): 158.

116 Nara, *Shoki Eizan jōdokyō*, 122.

117 Sonoda Kōyū, "Yoshishige no Yasutane to sono shūhen," in *Genshin*, ed. Ōsumi Kazuo and Hayami Tasuku (Tokyo: Yoshikawa kōbunkan, 1983), 239.

118 On the *Kangakueki*, see Gotō Akio, "*Kangakueki* ni tsuite," *Kokugo to kokubungaku* 63, no. 6 (1986): 13–25.

119 Higashidate Shōken, "Kangakue no seikaku ni kansuru ichi kōsatsu," *Shinshū kenkyū* 38 (1984): 17–18.

THE GROWTH OF PURE LAND BUDDHISM IN THE HEIAN PERIOD 157

setting where the participants could establish karmic bonds with Buddhism, Higashidate maintained that the *Lotus* lectures held by this organization served to introduce its members to prominent monks of the age.[120] Finally, and perhaps most importantly, Higashidate focused on Tamenori's statement that the fellowship was organized to "give encouragement to one another in our studies of the way of the Dharma and the way of literature." Based on this passage, Higashidate argued that the Kangakue was viewed by its members primarily as a type of learning center where its lay members could study Buddhist doctrines by listening to the lectures and debates on the *Lotus Sutra*, while its clerical members could study poetry composition with the help of the lay members.[121]

In any case, the Kangakue was the first organization that incorporated the nenbutsu into its ritual activities. This indicates that the members of the Kangakue considered the nenbutsu to be an important feature of their association. But what role did this practice have in the activities of the Kangakue as a whole? In Higashidate's view, the Kangakue took the innovative step of incorporating the nenbutsu recitation into its activities because it was believed to be an effective means for eradicating evil karma and hastening the attainment of buddhahood (the goal of Buddhist practice set forth in the Lotus Sutra) by allowing one to be born in the Pure Land. In this context, it may be remembered that Yasutane, in his prose poem composed during a Kangakue meeting held at the Zenrinji mentioned above, emphasized that the nenbutsu recitation is a potent method for eradicating evil karma and gaining birth in the Pure Land, where one can effectively undertake practices for attaining buddhahood.

In this connection, it is important to recall Sonoda's point concerning the format of the Kangakue. As stated above, the Kangakue was organized so that a lecture on the *Lotus Sutra* was held during the day, while the nenbutsu and poetry composition were conducted at night. According to Sonoda, this follows a pattern common to many Buddhist rituals in the early Heian period, in which lectures on sutras during the day were combined with rites of repentance at night. (The nenbutsu recitation can be seen as a form of repentance ritual since, as we have seen, it was widely believed to have the power to eradicate evil karma.) For example, in 849, a daytime lecture on the *Suvarṇaprabhāsa Sūtra* at court was followed by a rite of repentance at night. Similarly, in 833, the *Diamond Sutra* was "read" in the *tendoku* style and a repentance ritual addressed to Yakushi (Yakushi keka 藥師悔過) was held on the same night.[122]

---

120 Higashidate, "Kangakue no seikaku," 18.
121 Ibid., 22.
122 Sonoda, "Yoshishige no Yasutane," 239–240.

A similar pattern can be discerned in Kūya's *Mahāprajñāpāramitā Sūtra* ceremony of 963 described above, in which a daytime *tendoku* reading of this sutra was coupled with the recitation of the nenbutsu at night. Finally, the *Gokurakuki* contains the example of two monks, the brothers Zenjō 禪静 and Enei 延睿, who combined the daytime recitation of the *Lotus Sutra* with nightly nenbutsu practice in order to pray for their deceased mother.[123] Yasutane, too, in the Zenrinji prose poem mentioned above, juxtaposed the *Lotus Sutra* with the nenbutsu. It is significant that this daytime Lotus/night-time nenbutsu pattern was also incorporated into the Nijūgo zanmaie, a nenbutsu association with which Genshin was associated.

To conclude, it may be stated that, Inoue's influential theory notwithstanding, the Kangakue was not simply a nenbutsu fellowship. Instead, as Higashidate has argued, it was modeled on the various Hokke kōe that were current at the time. However, this is not to say that Yasutane and other members were not deeply attracted to Pure Land Buddhism.

This is shown by the fact that the Kangakue was the first lay-oriented Buddhist association incorporating the nenbutsu into its activities. Moreover the over, the interest in Pure Land Buddhism felt by many members of this association was no doubt intensified by their contact with Kūya. As Obara Hitoshi has noted, the members of the Kangakue (which included both Yasutane and Tamenori) were deeply influenced by Kūya, whom they perceived to be "the messenger from the *tathāgata*" (*nyoraishi* 如夾使).[124] In fact, Obara raised the possibility that Kūya's *Mahāprajñāpāramitā Sūtra* ceremony of 963 serves as a major stimulus for the creation of the Kangakue.[125] Hence, the Pure Land faith was an indispensable element of this fellowship. For these reasons, it is possible to conclude that the Kangakue played a significant role in focusing the attention of the nobility on the Pure Land teachings.

---

123   Inoue and Ōsone, *Ōjōden, Hokke genki*, 31.

124   This notion is found in a preface to a poem written by Yoshishige no Yasutane on the occasion of a flower-offering ritual held at the Rokuharamitsuji. The preface is found in the *Honchō monzui*. See Ōsone, Kinhara, and Gotō, *Honchō monzui*, 292. The notion that Kūya is the messenger of the *tathāgata* is discussed in Obara, *Bunjin kizoku no keifu*, 99–102.

125   Obara, *Bunjin kizoku no keifu*, 104.

Ōjōyōshū, Nihon Ōjō Gokuraku-ki, and the Construction of Pure Land Discourse in Heian Japan

Robert F. Rhodes

In *Actual Minds, Possible Worlds,* the psychologist Jerome Bruner distinguishes two distinct modes of thought, the paradigmatic (or logico-scientific) and the narrative, both of which he argues are equally important in ordering experience and constructing reality. The paradigmatic mode is descriptive and explanatory, and "employs categorization or conceptualization and the operations by which categories are established, instantiated, idealized, and related to one another to form a system" (Bruner 1986, 12). Bruner gives logic, mathematics, and the modern scientific method as representative examples of this mode of thought. On the other hand, the narrative mode employs storytelling as a way of organizing our experience in the world. Bruner concludes that the two modes are complementary and that "efforts to reduce one mode to the other or ignore one at the expense of the other inevitably fail to capture the rich diversity of thought" (Bruner 1986, 11).

The distinction that Bruner makes above highlights the increasing attention given to the narrative construction of meaning in a wide range of disciplines, including literary studies, history, philosophy, theology, ethics, and psychology.[1] If, as Stephen Crites (1971, 291) has argued, "the formal quality of experience through time is inherently narrative," then attempts to describe such experience through time must also be undertaken in the narrative mode. Following this line of thought, philosophers like Alasdair MacIntyre (1984) and Paul Ricoeur (1992) have stressed the importance of storytelling in constructing personal identity and in shaping how we relate to the world around us (that is, ethics). A similar point is also made by the theologian Michael Goldberg.

> By allowing a particular story to direct our attention to the world in some specific way, we let it direct our activity in the world in a certain manner.

Source: Rhodes, Robert F, "Ōjōyōshū, Nihon Ōjō Gokuraku-ki, and the Construction of Pure Land Discourse in Heian Japan," in *Japanese Journal of Religious Studies* 34(2) (2007): 249–270.

---

1 There is extensive literature on narrative. For a useful survey of how narrative has been taken into the various disciples, see Polkinghorne 1988. Hinchman and Hinchman 2001 contains a number of important studies on narrative and its place in the human sciences.

© KONINKLIJKE BRILL NV, LEIDEN, 2020 | DOI:10.1163/9789004401501_008

> As the story shapes our understanding of reality, it simultaneously qualifies the way we relate to reality.... By articulating a certain vision of the world, narratives provide us with a way of articulating what we are doing in the world.
>
> GOLDBERG 1991, 176–77

In other words, narratives both shape our perception of reality and provide guidelines or normative patterns to explain how we should behave in light of that reality.

One example of the way in which this new focus on narrative has manifested itself in the field of religious studies is the revival of interest in "sacred biographies" (which includes, but is not limited to, works belonging to the long disparaged genre of hagiography). In the introduction to a collection of essays entitled *The Biographical Process: Studies in the History and Psychology of Religion*, the editors suggest that sacred biographies "involve an intricate interweaving of the 'mythic' and 'historical' elements" (Reynolds and Capps 1976, 1). The term "mythic" here derives from Mircea Eliade, who used it to refer to a sacred story or, in his words, "true representation of reality" or "an account of what happened and how things are."[2] Hence sacred biographies are fundamentally accounts of the ways in which the sacred (or, to use Eliade's terminology, the mythic) is manifested in the life of a particular historic individual. Moreover, Eliade also suggests that myth provides the pattern for human behavior (Reynolds and Capp 1976, 2). In other words, these biographies, inasmuch as they describe how the mythic is made manifest in the life of a specific person, also establish a pattern of ideal religious behavior that later believers can follow. Sacred biographies, then, have a dual function, descriptive and prescriptive, in that they simultaneously describe how the sacred is manifested in a particular person's life and enjoin the readers/listeners of the biographies to fashion their lives in conformity with the vision of an ideal spiritual life depicted in them. To rephrase a formula used by Clifford Geertz to define religion in his celebrated essay, "Religion as a Cultural System" (Geertz 1973, 93), sacred biographies provide both a "model of" an exemplary religious life as well as a "model for" pursuing and actualizing such life.[3]

It is not my purpose here to argue for the importance of narratives in ordering human experience. Instead, taking my hint from Bruner's comments

---

2 This definition of myth is found in Cave 1993, 67.

3 For this formulation, I am indebted to Yōtaro Miyamoto's paper, "*Ōjōden* and *Taishiden*: An aspect of the development of sacred biography in Japan," presented at the XIXth World Congress of the International Association for the History of Religions (IAHR) held in Tokyo in March 2005.

above, I simply want to point out that texts in both the paradigmatic and the narrative modes played crucial roles in laying the foundation of Japanese Pure Land Buddhism. As is well known, Pure Land Buddhism became firmly established in Japan during the middle of the Heian Period (794–1185). A crucial text in this development is the *Ōjōyōshū* 往生要集, completed by Genshin 源信 (942–1017) in 985. Although quite different from modern scientific or mathematical treatises, the *Ōjōyōshū* can be classified as a text composed in the paradigmatic mode inasmuch as it employs categorization and conceptualization to construct a comprehensive theoretical outline of Pure Land soteriology. At exactly the same time, however, Yoshishige no Yasutane 慶滋保胤 (931–997) composed another influential Pure Land text, one which, unlike the *Ōjōyōshū*, was written in the narrative mode. This was the *Nihon Ōjō Gokuraku-ki* 日本往生極楽記 [Biographies of people who attained birth in the Pure Land; hereafter *Gokuraku-ki*], a collection of forty-two brief biographies of people (including monks, nuns, laymen, and lay women) who were believed to have attained birth in Amida Buddha's Pure Land. This was the first of many works in the genre called *ōjōden* 往生伝 (biographies of people who attained birth in the Pure Land) that were composed in Japan. Instead of constructing a "grand theory" about the Pure Land, the *Gokuraku-ki* attempts to "prove" that the Pure Land really exists by presenting stories of people who, through certain signs, could be "verified" as having gone to Amida's realm at death. However, the stories in the *Gokuraku-ki* not only attempt to persuade us to accept the reality of the Pure Land, but they also provide us with models with which to fashion ourselves into devout Pure Land believers. Hence, the narratives contained in this collection, no less than the systematic theoretical outline of Pure Land doctrine, cosmology, and practice in the *Ōjōyōshū*, helped legitimate birth in Amida Buddha's Pure Land as a genuine and viable path to salvation in the minds of its readers.

1   The Construction of Pure Land Discourse in the Ōjōyōshū

Scholars generally agree that the first historically reliable reference to Pure Land Buddhism in Japan dates to 640 (Andrews 1989, 21). According to the *Nihon shoki*, in the fifth month of this year, the monk Eon 慧隠, who had returned a year earlier after a stay in China lasting over three decades, lectured on the *Sutra of Immeasurable Life* (*Muryōjukyō* 無量寿経) at court.[4] Although

---

4   Aston 1972, pt. 2: 169–70. Eon's dates are unknown. He left for China in 608 as a member of an embassy led by Ono no Imoko 小野妹子 and returned in 639. The *Nihon shoki* also states that Eon again lectured on the *Sutra of Immeasurable Life* at court in 652. See Washio 1903, 31.

Amida Buddha became an important object of devotion in the latter half of the Nara Period (710–794), it was only in the mid-900's that it became a truly popular religion, gaining the allegiance of both the nobility and the commoners. The major figure in this development was Kōya 空也 (also known as Kūya, 903–972), who proselytized in Kyoto from 938. Parallel to this development, Tendai monks also began to incorporate elements of the Pure Land teachings into their school. Prominent among them were Ryōgen 良源 (912–985), Zenyu 禅瑜 (913–990), and Senkan 千觀 (918–983), all of whom composed Pure Land liturgical texts and scholastic treatises.[5]

This interest in Pure Land teaching and practice among Tendai monks came to full flower with Genshin's *Ōjōyōshū*.[6] According to its colophon, Genshin began work on this text in the eleventh month of 984 and completed it in just six months, in the fourth month of the following year (т 84, 89b). The bulk of the *Ōjōyōshū* consists of quotations from *sutras* and treatises concerning various aspects of Pure Land teachings. The number of passages quoted in the *Ōjōyōshū* is enormous: nearly a thousand from over one hundred and sixty different texts. In view of the prodigious effort needed to research all of these texts, Hanayama Shinshō has suggested that it could not possibly have been written in six months (Hanayama 1976, *chūki* [notes] 5). However, as Hayami Tasuku notes, after completing the brief *Amida Butsu byakugō kan* 阿弥陀佛 白毫觀 [Contemplation of the tuft of white hair between the brows of Amida Buddha], his first Pure Land work, in 981, Genshin must have continued to collect notes on Pure Land Buddhism with the intention of composing a treatise on the topic in the future. Thus, Hayami concludes, although the actual writing of the *Ōjōyōshū* may have been finished in just six months, it was the fruit of several years of intensive research (Hayami 1988, 95–96).

2 The *Ōjōyōshū* and the Rhetoric of Easy Practice

Underlying the entire Pure Land system of the *Ōjōyōshū* is the rhetoric of "easy practice" based on the notion of the Latter Dharma (*mappō* 末法). Genshin, like many people of his age, was convinced that the world was fast approaching the age of the Latter Dharma.[7] The notion of the Latter Dharma is the

---

5 The standard study on the history of Japanese Pure Land Buddhism during this period is Inoue 1956, 1–155.

6 On the Pure Land system of the *Ōjōyōshū*, see Andrews 1973.

7 The literature on the Latter Dharma and the theories of the decline of Buddhism is fairly extensive. On the origins of the concept of the Latter Dharma and its development in India

central element of a deeply pessimistic Buddhist interpretation of history that holds that the spiritual conditions of the world inevitably decline after the Buddha's entry into nirvāṇa. This view of Buddhist history holds that the time after the Buddha's entry into nirvāṇa is divided into three ages: (1) the age of the True Dharma (*shōbō* 正法), (2) the age of the Semblance Dharma (*zōbō* 像法), and (3) the age of Latter Dharma. In its classical form, found, for example, in the *Ta-ch'eng fa-yüan i-lin-chang* 大乘法苑義林章 (T 45, 344b), a monumental compendium of Buddhist doctrines compiled by the Fa-hsiang 法相 (Japanese: Hossō) scholar-monk Chi 基 (also known as Kuei-chi 窺基, 632–682), during the age of the True Dharma, the Buddhist teachings, their practice, and the attainment of enlightenment can all be found in the world. However, in the succeeding age of the Semblance Dharma, the world becomes increasingly corrupt, the spiritual capacities of the people decline, and it becomes less suitable for putting the Buddha's Dharma into practice. In this age, although the Buddhist teachings and their practice exist, there is no one who can attain enlightenment. Finally, during the age of the Latter Dharma, the spiritual conditions of the world become so poor that only the Buddha's teachings remain, and neither the practice of the Buddhist path nor the attainment of enlightenment would be possible. In such an age, it was believed that the world would be in constant strife, with the monks continually fighting each other. Several different theories concerning the lengths of each age can be found in Buddhist texts, but the *Ta-ch'eng fa-yüan i-lin-chang* maintains that the True and Semblance Dharmas each lasted a thousand years, with the Latter Dharma beginning after two thousand years.

As the historian Ishimoda Shō noted in his classic study, *Chūseiteki sekai no keisei* [Creation of the medieval world], between the Engi 延喜 (901–923) and Tenryaku 天暦 (947–957) Periods, Japan underwent far-reaching social, political and economic changes. These changes, including the breakdown of the Nara Period *ritsuryō* 律令 system of centralized government, the increasing domination of the court by the Fujiwara family, the proliferation of tax-free estates (*shōen* 荘園), the rapid and uncontrolled growth of the capital, and the emergence of an increasingly powerful warrior class in the provinces led to a thorough restructuring of Japanese society (Ishimoda 1985, 340). In face of such widespread turmoil and unease, many people felt convinced that the world of the Latter Dharma was indeed at hand.

Genshin argues that, in the benighted age of the Latter Dharma when the spiritual conditions of the world has deteriorated to the point that it is extremely

---

and China, see Chappell 1980 and Nattier 1991. For the influence of the Latter Dharma theory on Japanese Buddhism, see Marra 1988 and Stone 1985.

difficult to gain liberation from the cycle of transmigration by practicing in the traditional Tendai path of practice, the only feasible method of gaining salvation is to seek birth in Amida Buddha's Pure Land in the next lifetime. Since the Pure Land provides an ideal environment for practicing the Buddhist path, once in that land, it is possible to gain enlightenment quickly and effortlessly. Although he does not deny the efficacy of the various Tendai exoteric and esoteric practices, this "easy path" of Pure Land practice is, in Genshin's view, the most appropriate form of Buddhist practice for people unfortunate enough to be living in the age in which the influence of the Latter Dharma is highly apparent. Genshin further maintains that the most appropriate practice for achieving birth in the Pure Land is the nenbutsu 念佛, literally "mindfulness on (Amida) Buddha." In his view, the nenbutsu refers to a variety of practices focused on Amida Buddha, from elaborate contemplative exercises in which the practitioner visualizes this Buddha and his land while in a state of samādhi (meditative absorption) such as those described in the *Contemplation Sutra*, down to the simple recitation of the phrase "Namu Amida Butsu."

3   The Pure Land Path in the *Ōjōyōshū*

Beginning from such premise, in the *Ōjōyōshū*, Genshin engages in detailed theoretical reflection on Pure Land practice, constructing a "map" of the spiritual universe from the Pure Land perspective in its early chapters and outlining the salvific path based on this cosmology in its remaining pages. In the first chapter, "Loathing the Defiled Realm" (*onri edo* 厭離穢土), he takes up the Six Paths (*rokudō* 六道) or the realms of transmigration, and describes in great detail the suffering encountered by the beings there. The Six Paths are: (1) the realm of hell, (2) the realm of hungry ghosts (*gaki* 餓鬼), (3) the realm of animals, (4) the realm of fighting spirits (*asura* 阿修羅), (5) the realm of humans, and (6) the realm of heavenly beings. It is in the first of these six sections that we find the most famous passages of the *Ōjōyōshū*, a graphic depiction of the various tortures meted out in hell. Taking up in turn each of the eight subterranean hells of Buddhist cosmology, Genshin describes how the beings there are continually tormented by being slashed, crushed, pierced, boiled, and burned by the demons, animals, and the natural phenomena of those realms. But the suffering experienced by these beings are not gratuitous; according to the laws of karma, the pain inflicted upon beings in hell are understood as just retribution of evil actions performed in the past.

However, it is not only the beings of hell that are subject to pain and anguish. Adopting the standard Buddhist position, Genshin argues that all modes of existence within the Six Paths are characterized by suffering. For example, Genshin describes human existence as marked by impurity, suffering, and impermanence, and concludes that life as a human being is highly unsatisfactory, an ordeal to be rejected promptly. Even existence as a heavenly being is fraught with suffering. This is because, even though heavenly beings may enjoy exquisite pleasure during their exceedingly long lives, they must eventually pass away and be reborn in another realm.

Hence, Genshin concludes, genuine peace of mind is impossible to obtain as long as one is attached to existence within the Six Paths. True happiness can only be obtained by transcending the Six Paths and attaining birth in the Pure Land of Amida Buddha. In the second chapter, "Longing for the Pure Land" (*gongu jōdo* 欣求浄土), Genshin lists ten pleasures enjoyed by beings in the Pure Land in order to urge his readers to seek birth there. Significantly, although Genshin does not deny the various sensual and material pleasures of the Pure Land (for example, he explains that the Pure Land is most pleasing to look at), he stresses those aspects of the Pure Land that nurtures one's faith and insight into the Buddhist Dharma.

In this way, in the first two chapters of the *Ōjōyōshū*, Genshin contrasts the suffering of existence within the Six Paths with the blissful conditions of Amida Buddha's Pure Land. Its purpose is to demonstrate that one should not cling to this wretched world of transmigration, and to convince the readers that salvation is possible only by obtaining birth in the Pure Land. Hence, after a brief third chapter arguing for the superiority of seeking birth in Amida Buddha's Pure Land vis-à-vis those of other Buddhas and Maitreya (the future Buddha), Genshin turns to an analysis of the nenbutsu, which he claims is the central practice for attaining birth in Amida's realm. The major portion of the *Ōjōyōshū* (chapters four to ten) are devoted to a detailed and systematic analysis of the nenbutsu and the proper ways to practice it. The most important section here is the fourth chapter, "Proper Practice of the Nenbutsu" (*shōshū nenbutsu* 正修念佛) in which Genshin explains the correct way to practice the nenbutsu. Reflecting the emphasis traditionally placed on meditation in the Tendai sect, Genshin defines the nenbutsu primarily as the practice of visualizing, while abiding in a state of samādhi, the figure of Amida Buddha (or more specifically, Amida's marks [*sō* 相] or distinguishing features that, according to Buddhist iconography, adorn the bodies of all Buddhas). However, for those who are incapable of undertaking such complex practice, Genshin recommends simpler forms of Amida visualization, including the practice of visualizing Amida's *ūrṇākeśa* (*byakugō* 白毫), the tuft of white hair between the eyebrows, and the salvific light emanating from it. Finally, for those people who feel incapable of undertaking even this simplified form of visualization, Genshin recommends the recitative nenbutsu, or the recitation of "Namu Amida Butsu," citing the *Contemplation Sutra*, which declares that even thoroughly evil people can gain birth in the Pure Land just by calling out the name of Amida Buddha ten times on their deathbeds. In this way, Genshin holds the meditative nenbutsu to be the superior form of nenbutsu, but also recognizes the recitative nenbutsu as a legitimate means for achieving birth in the Pure Land.

To repeat, Genshin's central concern in the *Ōjōyōshū* was to present a systematic theoretical outline of Pure Land practice in such a way that all people could readily accept. To this end, he first set forth a Pure Land cosmology, focusing on the suffering of beings bound to the cycle of transmigration and the pleasures awaiting beings born in the Pure Land. Then, after setting forth this spiritual "map" of the universe, Genshin outlines the path of practice leading to birth in the Pure Land. Genshin's vision, set forth with exacting philosophical rigor, apparently proved quite convincing to his contemporaries. The *Ōjōyōshū* quickly became one of the most influential religious texts of his age.

4   The Narrative Construction of the Pure Land in the *Gokuraku-ki*

Although it has not received as much attention as the *Ōjōyōshū*, the *Gokuraku-ki* played an equally important role in authenticating the Pure Land faith in the minds of the many people in mid-Heian Japan. The author of this work of Buddhist hagiography was Yoshishige no Yasutane, a noted literati who served as Major Secretary (*dainaiki* 大内記) in the court of Emperor Kazan 花山. His *Chiteiki* 地亭記 [Record of the Pond Pavilion], written in 982, is said to have been the model for Kamo no Chōmei's 鴨長明 (1153–1216) well-known *Hōjōki* 方丈記 [Ten-foot square hut].[8] In his early thirties, Yasutane took an active part in the creation of the Kangaku-e 勧學会 (Association for the encouragement of learning), an association founded in 964, consisting of twenty students from the university and twenty monks of the Enryakuji. The members of this association met twice a year, on the fifteenth of the third and ninth months, at various temples around Kyoto to compose poetry on topics taken from the *Lotus Sutra* and to practice the nenbutsu. However, Yasutane became increasingly dissatisfied with lay life, and finally became a monk in 986, adopting Jakushin 寂心 for his religious name.[9]

---

8   The *Chitei-ki* is translated in Watson 1975, 1, 57–64. A thorough study of the *Chitei-ki* is found in Ōsone 1974.

9   A short biography of Yasutane is found in Gotō 1993. For an important collection of essays on Yasutane, see Hirabayashi 2001.

In the preface of the *Gokuraku-ki*, Yasutane states that he had conducted the nenbutsu since his youth, but became especially zealous in its practice after he turned forty. Henceforth, he claims,

> With my mouth, I recited the name (of Amida Buddha), and in my mind, I contemplated his major and minor marks. Whether walking, standing, sitting, or lying down, not for an instant did I forget (to practice the nenbutsu); even when surprised or stumbling, I continued (the nenbutsu).
>
> INOUE AND ŌSONE 1974, 11

Such yearning for the Pure Land was undoubtedly decisive in persuading him to become a monk late in life.

A draft of the *Gokuraku-ki* was completed a little before Yasutane took the tonsure, sometime between 983 and 985.[10] However, the *Gokuraku-ki* as we now have it was revised and augmented at least twice afterwards. According to a note appended after the second biography in the collection, that of the celebrated Nara-Period monk Gyōgi 行基, Yasutane completed the *Gokuraku-ki* and its preface while he was still a layman and even had it mounted as a scroll. However, after he took the tonsure, he learned about five or six more people who attained birth in the Pure Land and requested the Great Palace Secretary King (*chūsho daiō* 中書大王) to compose their biographies for inclusion in the collection.[11] Subsequently, the Great Palace Secretary King had a dream instructing him to add the biographies of Prince Shōtoku (Shōtoku Taishi 聖徳太子) and Gyōgi to the *Gokuraku-ki*. Since the Great Palace Secretary King was ill at that time, Yasutane wrote the biographies of these two figures himself and placed them at the beginning of the text (Inoue and Ōsone 1974, 19). It may be added here that these two biographies are by far the longest in the *Gokuraku-ki*.

It has already been mentioned that narratives are both descriptive and prescriptive, that is, they serve both to provide a description of sacred reality and to indicate how we should behave in light of that reality. Yasutane had both aims in mind when he composed the *Gokuraku-ki*. In the preface to this collection, he states,

---

10   The earliest possible date for the *Gokuraku-ki* is 983, since it mentions the death of Senkan that took place in this year. The latest date is 985, since it is mentioned in the *Ōjōyōshū*, which was completed in this year. See Inoue and Ōsone 1974, 712.

11   *Chūsho daiō* refers to the post of Nakamugyo 中務卿. He has previously been identified with Kaneakira Shinnō 兼明親王 (914–987), but Hirabayashi Moritoku has recently argued that it must refer to Tomohira Shinnō 具平親王 (964–1009). See Hirabayashi 2001, 99.

168 RHODES

> However, the wisdom of sentient beings is slight and cannot reach the Sage's (that is, the Buddha's) purport. Unless I note down (descriptions of) people who actually attained birth (in the Pure Land), it is impossible to influence their minds (to seek the Pure Land).
>
> INOUE and ŌSONE 1974, 11

In other words, although many Buddhist texts refer to the Pure Land, most people find it hard to accept that such a realm really exists. For this reason, Yasutane felt compelled to gather stories about people whose actions or deathbed experiences demonstrate that they attained birth in the Pure Land. Through these examples, he hoped to confirm the reality of the Pure Land and to testify that birth in the Pure Land provides a practical and effective path to salvation. In the preface, he mentions that records of such people, including *Ch'ing-t'u lun* 浄土論 [Pure Land treatise] by Chia-ts'ai 迦才 and *Wang-sheng hsi-fang ching-t'u jui-yin-ch'uan* 往生西方浄土瑞應伝 [Miraculous biographies of (people who) attained birth in the Pure Land in the western direction, cited hereafter as *Jui-ying ch'uan*], have already been written in China, but he felt the need to compose a collection of Japanese people who attained birth in the Pure Land in order to demonstrate that the Pure Land is accessible to the people of this country, too. As this suggests, Yasutane's aim in compiling the *Gokuraku-ki* was not only descriptive but prescriptive as well, inasmuch as his ultimate aim was to make his readers arouse the desire to seek the Pure Land.

5 The Structure of the *Gokuraku-ki*

As noted above, the *Gokuraku-ki* contains the biographies of forty-two people who, Yasutane maintains, attained birth in the Pure Land. They were all chosen because their final hours were accompanied by miracles (*isō ōjō* 異相往生) confirming their entry into Amida's world. In the preface, Yasutane states that he not only perused national histories and biographies of noted monks, but also interviewed several elderly people in his search for such examples (Inoue and Ōsone 1974, 11). Beginning with Prince Shōtoku, the text continues with entries, in this order, for twenty-eight monks (including two *shami*[12]), three nuns, four laymen, and six lay women. This follows the order found in the *Ching-t'u lun* and *Jui-ying ch'uan*, which Yasutane alludes to in the preface (Inoue and Ōsone 1974, 715). The actual number of people treated in the text is slightly higher,

---

12 A man who has shaved his head and become a monk but continues to live as a householder, often with a wife and children.

since several biographies describe the birth of more than one person into the Pure Land.[13] Although there are exceptions, the monks are generally listed in chronological order. Court rank seems to have been an important criterion in determining the order in which laymen were taken up in the text. Moreover in the cases of both lay men and women, those living in the capital appear before those residing in the provinces (Inoue and Ōsone 1974, 715). Significantly, none of the nuns or lay women is referred to by her clerical or given name. The nuns are identified by their lineage or more well-known relative, while the lay women are identified simply by their husbands, lineage, or place of residence. While many of the people in the *Gokuraku-ki*, such as Prince Shōtoku, Gyōgi, Ennin 圓仁 (794–864), Kōya, and Senkan, are well-known figures in Japanese Buddhist history, the majority are ordinary clerics and lay people who are not mentioned in any other records from this time (meaning that the *Gokuraku-ki* is the first place in which many of them appear). A significant number were Yasutane's contemporaries (Inoue and Ōsone 1974, 717).

The following are two typical biographies found in the collection. The first is that of the Tendai monk Jinjō 尋静 (dates unknown, but probably late ninth to early tenth centuries).

> Jinjō of Ryōgon-in 楞厳院 of Enryakuji 延暦寺 (who served as one of the) Ten Meditation Masters, was by nature free of stinginess. Whenever a person came for a visit, he would first serve food and drink. For ten-odd years, he never went beyond the temple gate. He read the *Diamond Prajñāpāramitā Sutra* during the day and remained mindful of Amida Buddha at night. All of the various good roots he cultivated were in the hopes of (gaining birth in) the Land of Supreme Bliss. In the first month, when he was over seventy years old, he took to bed with illness. He ordered his disciple to practice the nenbutsu samādhi during the three watches of the day (dawn, mid-day, dusk). During the early part of the second month, he related to his disciple and others, "I saw a dream. In a large halo of light, several tens of monks, bearing a palanquin and singing songs, came from the west and stood in the sky. I thought, 'They came to welcome me to the Land of Supreme Bliss.'" After five or six days,

---

13   A passage at the end of the *Gokuraku-ki* mentions that it contains descriptions of the birth of forty-five people into the Pure Land, including two bodhisattvas (Prince Shōtoku and Gyōgi), twenty-six monks, three *shami* (self-ordained monks), three nuns, four laymen, and seven lay women. See Inoue and Ōsone 1974, 41. However, this passage is missing in several editions of this text, suggesting that it was a later interpolation. See Inoue and Ōsone 1974, 41; note on *shijūgo nin* 四十五人).

he bathed and, without touching any food or drink for three days, single-mindedly practiced the nenbutsu. He also ordered his disciple, "You, monk! Don't offer me any water and don't ask me any questions. They will distract me from my contemplation [*kannen* 觀念]. Then, facing west and hands pressed together in prayer, he passed away.

INOUE and ŌSONE 1974, 26–27

The second is that of a nun, whose name, like those of all other nuns and lay women in the collection, remains unidentified.

Nun so-and-so was the granddaughter of Emperor Kōkō 光孝天皇. She married young and had three children, but they died in successive years. Before long, her husband also died. Widowed, she perceived the impermanence of all worldly things and took the tonsure to become a nun. She refused to eat more than once a day. After a few years, she suddenly began to feel pain in her back, and was unable to stand. The doctor said, "You are physically tired. Unless you eat meat, you will be unable to cure this illness." Having no attachment to her body or life, the nun (refused to do as the doctor ordered and simply) remained all the more mindful of Amida. The pain caused by the illness then naturally ceased. The nun was by nature gentle and her heart was filled with compassion. Although mosquitoes and horseflies bit her, she made it a point not to shoo them away. When she was fifty-odd years old, she suddenly was stricken with a minor illness. There was music in the sky. It surprised the people of nearby villages, who thought it strange. The nun said, "The Buddha has come to receive me. I am about to leave." After saying this, she passed away.

INOUE and ŌSONE 1974, 35–36

Although chosen at random, these biographies should suffice to indicate the overall character of the tales in the collection.

It may not be out of place here to mention that one important way in which Yasutane attempted to convince the readers of the veracity of the stories in the *Gokuraku-ki* was to give precise details about the people in question. Yasutane meticulously provides the monastic and court ranks of many of the figures in the collection, and, in cases where the subject lived outside the capital, includes exact information about the district and province in which they resided. Moreover, as Kobayashi Yasuji has noted, when the biographies in the *Gokuraku-ki* are compared with the texts that presumably served as their sources, it becomes apparent that Yasutane rarely embellished his accounts. Although some embellishment can be found in Kōya's biography, the amount

ŌJŌYŌSHŪ AND PURE LAND DISCOURSE IN HEIAN JAPAN

is small (Kobayashi 1968, 108). In these ways, Yasutane attempts to provide veri-similitude to the biographies, helping to counter the possible arguments by skeptics that these stories are nothing more than pious fantasy.

Even a cursory reading of the *Gokuraku-ki* reveals that there is a general pattern to these biographies. They normally begin by giving the individual's name, rank and (quite frequently) place of residence, then recount the practices they undertook during their lives, and finally describe their deathbed practices and the miracles that occurred at this time.[14] However, there are several stories in the collection that diverge significantly from this pattern. One example is the story of the monk Kōdō 廣道 (dates unknown), into which is imbedded a second story of how a woman living near his temple gained birth in the Pure Land.

> The monk Kōdō of the Dainichiji 大日寺 was from the Tachibana 橘 clan. For several decades, he exclusively sought (birth in) the Pure Land and refused to concern himself with worldly matters. There was a poor woman living next to the temple. She had two boys and they became Tendai monks. The elder was called Zenjō 禅静 and the younger was called En'ei 延睿. (When) their mother died, the two monks, with a single mind, read the *Lotus Sutra* during the day and remained mindful of Amida Buddha at night, praying only for their compassionate mother's birth in the Land of Supreme Bliss. At that time, Kōdō had (the following) dream. Innumerable music could be heard (from the area) between the Gokuraku 極楽 and Jōgan 貞觀 Temples. Surprised, he looked in that direction and (saw) three carts adorned with jewels, surrounded by several thousand monks holding incense burners. They proceeded directly to the

---

14 A more detailed list of eight elements that regularly appear in these biographies is given in Kobayashi 1968, 109. In the order of their appearance in the biographies, they are as follows:

(1) The status of person in question (that is, whether he or she is a monk or nun or lay person). If a monk, his rank or position.

(2) Place of birth or residence. Family background or circumstances surrounding birth.

(3) Personality and stories about childhood.

(4) Circumstances surrounding the taking of the tonsure, practices undertaken while alive, and miracles that occurred during his or her lifetime.

(5) Year of death or age at the time of death.

(6) Prophesies concerning death and birth in the Pure Land.

(7) Practices undertaken at time of death and/or miracles that occurred at the time of death.

(8) Miracles that occurred after death and signs confirming the person's birth in the Pure Land.

It must be noted, however, that none of the biographies contain all eight elements.

deceased woman's house. Leading out the woman, they clothed her in heavenly robes. When they were about to get on (the carts) and return together, two monks read an edict (to Kōdō): "You have been kind to the mother. For this reason, you will be led to the Pure Land by Amida and his retinue." In the same dream, there were signs of Kōdō's birth in the Pure Land. Kōdō passed away within a few years. On this day, music filled the sky. Both clerics and lay people stopped to listen to the music. Many of them rejoiced and aroused the aspiration for enlightenment.

INOUE and ŌSONE 1974, 31

Although the main figure of this story is the monk Kōdō, the tale of how the poor woman reached the Pure Land through the prayers of her sons is also a significant element in this account.

Another example is that of Chikō 智光 (709–Hōki 寶亀 Era [770–80]), a monk of the Nara Period, who is said to have visited the Pure Land in his dream. Virtually all of this biography is taken up with this dramatic story, already found in the *Nihon ryōiki* 日本霊異記 [Miraculous tales of Japan] by the early Heian monk Kyōkai (Nakamura 1973, 167–71). In this famous tale, Chikō went to the Pure Land, where he met his old companion Raikō 頼光 and was granted an audience with Amida Buddha, who instructs him on the way to achieve birth in that land by contemplating the land's features. Upon awakening from the dream, Chikō commissioned the famous Chikō Mandala, a pictorial representation of the Pure Land. The biography ends by noting that Chikō contemplated this picture throughout his life and finally attained birth in the Pure Land (Inoue and Ōsone 1974, 24–25). Significantly, this story does not contain any other references to Chikō's practices, nor does it provide any details about his deathbed practice. Chronologically, it is placed out of order, after several monks of the early Heian Period. Yasutane probably included this story, not because he believed Chikō's life provided an exemplary model of Pure Land birth, but because the well-known story of his visit to the Pure Land helps confirms the existence of Amida's Pure Land.

Another story that does not follow the standard pattern concerns the Shingon monk Mukū 無空 (?–912?), the second abbot of Kōyasan 高野山. This monk is famous for his role in the struggle between Kōyasan and Tōji 東寺, another major Shingon center, over the possession of the thirty volumes of text brought to Japan by Kūkai.[15] Yasutane, however, alludes neither to this monk's

---

15   After Kūkai's death, a struggle arose between Kōyasan and Tōji over which temple would possess the thirty volumes of text which Kūkai brought back from China and presented to the Japanese court. At this time, it was in the possession of Mukū at Kōyasan, but when

turbulent life nor his deathbed practice, but focuses primarily on Mukū's appearance in the dreams of Fujiwara no Nakahira 藤原仲平.

> Precept Master (Risshi 律師) Mukū made the nenbutsu his everyday practice. He was always lacking food and clothing. He said to himself, "Since I am poor, after I die I am sure I will cause trouble to my disciples who survive me." Secretly, he placed ten thousand in cash in the attic of his hermitage, hoping it would pay for his burial. (Subsequently) the Precept Master took to bed with illness, and suddenly passed away without having told anyone of the cash. The Loquat Minister of the Left (Fujiwara no Nakahira) was an old friend of the Precept Master. The Minister had a dream, in which the Precept Master came to him wearing dirty clothes and having a haggard appearance. In their conversation, (Mukū) said, "Because I have some money hidden away, I have unexpectedly become a snake. I beg you use that money to copy the *Lotus Sutra*." The Minister went to (Mukū's) old hermitage, and recovered the ten thousand cash. Among the money was a small snake, which took flight when it saw people. The minister immediately made a thousand copies of the *Lotus Sutra* and held a ceremony. At a later date, (the minister) had a dream, in which the Precept Master, wearing bright clean clothes and face full of joy, approached him carrying an incense burner. He said to the Minister said, "Thanks to your kindness, I have been able to escape from the path of heretics. I will leave now for the Land of Supreme Bliss." Having finished saying so, he flew off to the west.
>
> INOUE and ŌSONE 1974, 22

Interestingly, it is argued that Mukū was able to attain birth in the Pure Land through the merit generated from copying the *Lotus Sutra*. As I will show below, during this age, it was believed that birth in the Pure Land could be attained by undertaking a wide variety of practices, and not just devotion to Amida Buddha, the Buddha presiding over the Pure Land. But in any case, the point to notice here is that the focus of this story is not on Mukū's life or practice but on demonstrating that birth in the Pure Land is really possible, even for someone who has been reborn as a snake through his unwholesome actions in the past.

Kanken 観賢 of the Tōji, armed with an imperial decree, demanded that Mukū return it to Tōji, Mukū hid it away (Inoue and Ōsone 1974, 400, note on "Mukū Risshi").

6 Signs of Birth in the Pure Land

As mentioned above, Yasutane's aim in writing the *Gokuraku-ki* was to convince his readers to aspire for the Pure Land by adducing examples of people whose exemplary deaths confirm that they truly achieved birth in that land. It is for this reason that the majority of the stories focus on extraordinary signs that accompanied the subject's death. Many of the biographies describe how pleasant music and wonderful fragrance filled the room as the person in question passed away. When Ennin, the third patriarch of the Tendai school, was on his deathbed, a fellow monk heard music coming from the Tōin 唐院, Ennin's cloister. When the monk entered the Tōin and asked about the music, the monks in the hall replied that they had not heard anything (Inoue and Ōsone 1974, 20). When the nobleman Takashina no Mabito 高階眞人 passed away, a fragrant smell filled the room and music was heard in the sky (Inoue and Ōsone 1974, 37). Likewise, when the Tendai monk Zōmyō 増命 (844–927) was on his deathbed, he was suddenly bathed in golden light, purple clouds appeared, music was heard in the sky and a wonderful fragrance filled the room (Inoue and Ōsone 1974, 21).

Music also accompanied the deaths of several nuns and lay women. A certain Fujiwara lady practiced the nenbutsu diligently throughout her life. As she grew old, she reported that she could hear music, which she was convinced was a sign of her coming birth in the Pure Land. Year by year, the music became more distinct, and when as she was dying, she informed the others that it could be heard from above the roof of the house (Inoue and Ōsone 1974, 40). Similarly, music was heard in the sky when both the monk Hyōchin 平珍 (dates unknown) and the nun who was Emperor Kōkō's granddaughter passed away (Inoue and Ōsone 1974, 32 and 36).

Though less frequent than sublime music or fragrance, other extraordinary events are also recounted the *Gokuraku-ki*. When a devout woman of Sakata 坂田 district of Ōmi 近江 province died, her body was covered by purple clouds, an auspicious sign (Inoue and Ōsone 1974, 40). When Jin'yū 尋祐 (dates unknown) passed away, a brilliant light was seen at the at the top of the mountain on which his temple, Matsuoji 松尾寺, was located. It was so bright that the people of the village below thought that a fire had broken out in the temple (Inoue and Ōsone 1974, 35). On a more grotesque note, it is said that Takashina's body did not putrefy for several days after he died in spite of the hot weather (Inoue and Ōsone 1974, 37), and that Precept Master Ryūkai's 隆海 (815–886) right hand, which had miraculously formed the *mūdra* of Amida Buddha when he died, remained unscathed even after he was cremated (Inoue and Ōsone

1974, 20–1). Both of these events were interpreted as marvelous portents signaling the deceased person's entry into the Pure Land.

A rather different story of an inexplicable event at death is found in the biography of Yakuren 薬蓮, who physically disappeared when he died. The story goes as follows.

> Yakuren, who lived at Nyohōji 如法寺 in Nakatsu 中津 Village of Takai 高井 District in Shinano 信濃 Province, recited the *Amida Sutra* throughout his life. He had two children, a boy and a girl. One day, he announced to his children that he would depart for the Pure Land the next morning, and asked them to wash his clothes and help him bathe. The children did as requested. At night, donning his clean clothes, Yakuren entered a hall that enshrined a Buddha and ordered his children to keep the doors shut until the next morning. After he entered the hall, exquisite music was heard from the hall all night. When the doors were opened the next day, both Yakuren and the sutra that he had carried into the hall had disappeared, leaving no trace.
>
> INOUE and ŌSONE 1974, 34–35

Yasutane was apparently deeply fascinated by monks with thaumaturgic powers and the *Gokuraku-ki* includes stories of several monks, including Zōmyō and Kōya, performing miracles through their extraordinary spiritual powers while they were alive. However, Yakusen is the only person described as disappearing into thin air at death.

Many people taken up in the *Gokuraku-ki* are depicted as predicting the hour of their death or as having had visions of Amida Buddha and his retinue coming to lead him or her away to the Pure Land. The *Gokuraku-ki* gives the following story about a nun, the elder sister of Major Bishop (*daisōzu* 大僧都) Kanchū 寛忠 (906–977). When Kanchū visited his aged sister, she requested,

> "The day after tomorrow, I will go to the Land of Supreme Bliss. Until then, I ask you to perform the Continuous Nenbutsu [*fudan nenbutsu* 不断念佛]." With a number of monks, the Bishop performed the nenbutsu samādhi for three days and nights. (Thereupon, the nun) again spoke with the Major Bishop, saying, "A palanquin adorned with jewels has flown here, and it is now right before my eyes. However, the Buddha and bodhisattvas have gone back, because this place is polluted." Her words were accompanied by tears. The Bishop had (the monks) recited a sutra set to melody several times. The next day, the nun said, "The holy assembly (that is, Amida Buddha and bodhisattvas) have come once again. The

hour of my birth in the Pure Land has arrived." Sitting upright and leaning on an armrest, she (recited the) nenbutsu and passed away.

INOUE and ŌSONE 1974, 36

The monk Shunso 春素 (dates unknown) also dreamed on his deathbed that Amida's messengers came to him to take him to the Pure Land (Inoue and Ōsone 1974, 27). Kōya, too, related to his disciples that Amida had come to welcome him to the Pure Land when he was about to expire (Inoue and Ōsone 1974, 29). In a similar vein, when he died, Shinkaku 眞覺 (dates unknown) had a dream in which white birds with long tails flew off to the west while singing "Let's go, let's go" to him (Inoue and Ōsone 1974, 34).

Another interesting deathbed dream predicting birth in the Pure Land concerns Genkai 玄海 (dates unknown), a monk who resided at Komatsudera 小松寺 in Niita 新田 District in Mutsu Province in the northern extremity of Japan. Every day he read the *Lotus Sutra* and every night he recited the *Daibutchō shingon* 大佛頂眞言 seven times. At one time he fell into a coma. While unconscious, he dreamed that he had sprouted wings and that he had flown to a land adorned with the seven treasures. When he looked at himself, he realized that his left wing consisted of the *Daibutchō shingon* and his right consisted of the eight fascicles of the *Lotus Sutra*. In that land, he encountered a monk, who informed him that he was in a region at the outskirts (*henji* 邊地) of the Pure Land. The monk further instructed Genkai to return to the world, telling him that he would be taken to the Pure Land three days hence. With this, Genkai revived. He continued reciting Shingon texts with even more fervor and passed away three years later (Inoue and Ōsone 1974, 33–34).

Slightly different is a story of a dream-like vision told about the monk Myōshō 明靖 (dates unknown), a scion of the Fujiwara family. When he fell ill, he suddenly saw the fires of hell burning in front of his eyes. Realizing that nothing but the nenbutsu can save him from being cast into hell, he had monks sitting by his pillow recite the name of Amida Buddha. Thereupon the fire subsided (Inoue and Ōsone 1974, 30).

The above are all dreams seen by the dying themselves, but the *Gokuraku-ki* frequently relates a different type of dream, one seen by the acquaintances of the deceased person, signaling that the latter went off to the Pure Land after death. After Shinrai 眞頼 (dates unknown) of Ishiyamaji 石山寺 died, his fellow monk Shinju 眞珠 (dates unknown) had a dream in which several tens of thousands of monks and young boys greeted the dying Shinrai and led him away. Although it is not made explicit, the reader is led to assume that they led Shinrai to Amida's realm (Inoue and Ōsone 1974, 26–27). More explicit is the dream concerning Senkan, a Tendai monk who actively proselytized the

Pure Land faith in the mid-900's. According to his biography, the daughter of Fujiwara no Atsutada 藤原敦忠 was a devout follower of this monk. When he was alive, Senkan promised her that, if he actually attained birth in the Pure Land, he would appear in her dream to inform her of his success. Soon after his death, the woman saw a dream in which Senkan sailed off to the west on a lotus blossom boat, reciting verses in praise of Amida Buddha (Inoue and Ōsone 1974, 29–30).

7 Practices for Birth in the Pure Land

In the section above, I have discussed a number of miraculous events experienced by the dying person (or their associates) recounted in the *Gokuraku-ki* to substantiate that the deceased reached the Pure Land. However, as stated above, narratives are prescriptive as well as descriptive, suggesting that these biographies are also to be read as ideals or models for Pure Land devotees to emulate. How, then, did Yasutane think that one can attain birth in the Pure Land? Unfortunately, he is not very clear on this point. Perhaps he was too pre-occupied with demonstrating that there are people even in Japan who successfully entered the Pure Land, that he fails to specify what types of practices lead to birth there. Or perhaps it reflects the common assumption of his age (which is also apparent in Genshin) that birth in the Pure Land can be obtained by undertaking a wide variety of Buddhist practices. However, in the biographies, Yasutane regularly notes the practices undertaken by the people in question, so it is possible to gain some understanding of how he believed birth the Pure Land was made possible.

The biographies suggest that deathbed practices were of special importance in ensuring one's birth in the Pure Land. Perhaps it is only natural that the practice mentioned most often in this context is the nenbutsu.[16] Ennin and Zōmyō, among others, died practicing the nenbutsu (Inoue and Ōsone 1974, 20 and 21), while Enshō 延昌 (880–964), Shinrai, and the nun who was the sister of Major Bishop Kanchū had the Continuous Nenbutsu performed for them on their deathbeds (Inoue and Ōsone 1974, 27, 30, and 36). However, other practices are also mentioned. Myōyū 明祐 (878–961), a monk of the Tōdaiji 東大寺, died surrounded by his disciples reciting the *Amida Sutra*. When the Precept

---

16   The nenbutsu (literally, "mindfulness of the Buddha") could refer to the recitation of the name of Amida Buddha as well as to the practice of contemplating the features of the Buddha after attaining a focused state of mind through recitation. The distinction is frequently unclear in the *Gokuraku-ki*.

Master Ryūkai realized his end was near, he bathed every day, practiced the nenbutsu, and, in addition, recited passages from the *Sutra of Immeasurable Life* as well as the verses in praise Amida Buddha composed by Nāgārjuna (Inoue and Ōsone 1974, 20).

The *Gokuraku-ki* also frequently refers to the everyday practices undertaken by the monks, nuns, and lay people. Once again, a number of them are said to have made the nenbutsu their daily practice. They include monks like Saigen 済源 (885–960) of the Sanron school, Mukū, as well as the nun who was the sister of Major Bishop Kanchū, and the nun from Kamutsuhira 上平 Village, Iidaka 飯高 District, Ise 伊勢 Province (Inoue and Ōsone 1974, 36). However, the nenbutsu was frequently not practiced alone but was combined with other practices. Kensan 兼算 (dates unknown) of the Bonshakuji 梵釈寺 is said to have combined the nenbutsu with devotion to Fudō Myōō 不動明王 (Inoue and Ōsone 1974, 26). Jinjō of Ryōgon'in is (as noted above) described as reading the *Diamond Prajñāpāramitā Sutra* during the day and practicing the nenbutsu at night. Similarly Shunso is said to have studied the *Mo ho chih kuan* 摩訶止観 (Great contemplation and insight), the basic text of Tendai meditation, during the day and focused his mind on Amida Buddha at night. In addition to practicing the nenbutsu, Myōshō is said to have been well versed in esoteric Buddhism (Inoue and Ōsone 1974, 30). Throughout his life, Yakuren is said to have recited the *Amida Sutra* along with the nenbutsu (Inoue and Ōsone 1974, 34–35).

In this way, Yasutane suggests that a number of practices can lead to birth in the Pure Land. However, a striking feature of all the people included in the *Gokuraku-ki* is their exemplary character.[17] Yasutane often inserts passages describing the subjects' personality into his narratives, but in all such cases, the people are described as being kind and virtuous. Kensan, for example, is said to have been without anger, Jinjō as generous and providing food and drink to all who visited him, Jin'yū as compassionate, and a nun who was the granddaughter of Emperor Kōkō as gentle and compassionate. Zensha 善謝 (724–804) is said to have shunned secular fame and secluded himself in Mount Bonfuku 梵福寺. The only possible exception is Jōi 成意 (dates unknown), a Tendai monk who was free of all attachments and consequently shocked his disciples by eating after noon in defiance of the precepts. However, in this case, too, the emphasis is on his lack of attachment, not on the unwholesome consequences of the failure to keep the precepts. Later works in the *ōjōden* genre frequently include stories of how even incorrigibly evil people were able to attain birth

---

17   This has been stressed by Sekiguchi 1968, 89–90.

in the Pure Land by calling on the Amida Buddha.[18] These stories focus on the power of Amida's all-encompassing compassion in saving evil beings, but no such stories are found in the *Gokuraku-ki*. Apparently Yasutane assumed that birth in the Pure Land is closely related to a moral life. The absence of stories about the birth of evil people into the Pure Land is all the more surprising because Yasutane himself mentions, in the preface to the *Gokuraku-ki*, that his desire to compose this collection was strengthened by reading stories in the *Jui-ying-ch'uan* about people who "slaughtered cattle and sold chicken" for their livelihood and yet attained birth by practicing the nenbutsu (Inoue and Ōsone 1974, 11).

As I have repeatedly mentioned above, narratives in the *Gokuraku-ki* have a dual function. On the one hand, they are "models of" an ideal life devoted to the quest for birth in Amida's Pure Land. By focusing on their deathbed miracles, these biographies all prove that these figures were all able to attain birth in the Pure Land. Since the biographies refer to real people and real events, these stories confront us with the most compelling evidence that birth in the Pure Land is truly a viable path to salvation. But at the same time, these narratives also provide "models for" pursuing a life dedicated to the attainment of birth in the Pure Land. By following these examples, we, too, urges Yasutane, can go to the Pure Land after we expire. Hence, it can be said that narratives like the *Gokuraku-ki* was just as important in the formation of Japanese Pure Land Buddhism as theoretical treatises on Pure Land doctrine like the *Ōjōyōshū*.

References

Abbreviation

T *Taishō shinshū daizōkyō* 大正新修大蔵経. 85 vols. Takakusu Junjirō 高楠順次郎 and Watanabe Kaigyoku 渡辺海旭 eds. Tokyo: Taishō Issaikyō Kankōkai, 1924–1932.

Secondary Sources

Andrews, Allan A., 1973. *The Teachings Essential for Rebirth: A Study of Genshin's Ōjōyōshū*. Tokyo: Sophia University.

Andrews, Allan A., 1989. Genshin's "Essentials of Pure Land Rebirth" and the transmission of Buddhism to Japan. Part I. The first and second phases of transmission of

---

18   According to Sekiguchi, the earliest story of birth in the Pure Land by an evil person is that of Minamoto no Yoriyoshi 源頼義 found in the *Zoku honchō ōjōden* 續本朝往生傳. Sekiguchi 1968, 90.

Pure Land Buddhism to Japan: The Nara Period and the early Heian Period. *The Pacific World* 5: 20–32.

Aston, W. G., 1972. *Nihongi: Chronicles of Japan from the Earliest Times to A.D. 697.* Reprint. Tokyo: Charles E. Tuttle.

Bruner, Jerome, 1986. *Actual Minds, Possible Worlds.* Cambridge, MA: Harvard University Press.

Cave, David, 1993. *Mircea Eliade's Vision for a New Humanism.* Oxford: Oxford University Press.

Chappell, David W., 1980. Early forebodings of the death of Buddhism. *Numen* 27: 122–54.

Crites, Stephen, 1971. The narrative quality of experience. *Journal of the American Academy of Religion* 39: 291–311.

Geertz, Clifford, 1973. *The Interpretation of Cultures.* New York: Basic Books.

Goldberg, Michael, 1991. *Theology and Narrative: A Critical Introduction.* Philadelphia: Trinity Press International.

Gotō Akio 後藤昭雄, 1993. Yoshishige no Yasutane 慶滋保胤. In *Iwanami Kōza Nihon Bungaku to Bukkyō* 岩波講座日本文学と仏教. vol. 1. eds. Mizuno Kōgen 水野弘元 et al., 195–213. Tokyo: Iwanami Shoten.

Hanayama Shinshō 花山信勝, 1976. *Genpon kōtei kanwa taishō Ōjōyōshū* 原本校訂漢和対照往生要集. Reprint. Tokyo: Sankibō.

Hayami Tasuku 速水侑, 1988. *Genshin* 源信. Tokyo: Yoshikawa Kōbunkan.

Hinchman, Lewis P., and Sandra K. Hinchman, 2001. *Memory, Identity, and Community: The Idea of Narrative in the Human Sciences.* Albany: State University of New York Press.

Hirabayashi Moritoku 平林盛得, 2001. *Yoshishige no Yasutane to Jōdo shisō* 慶滋保胤と浄土思想. Tokyo: Yoshikawa Kōbunkan.

Inoue Mitsusada 井上光貞, 1956. *Nihon Jōdokyō seiritsushi no kenkyū* 日本浄土教成立史の研究. Tokyo: Yamakawa Shuppan.

Inoue Mitsusada and Ōsone Shōsuke 大曽根章介, eds., 1974. *Ōjōden, Hokke genki* 往生伝·法華験記. Tokyo: Iwanami Shoten.

Ishimoda Shō 石母田正, 1985. *Chūseiteki sekai no keisei* 中世的世界の形成. Reprint. Tokyo: Iwanami Shoten.

Kobayashi Yasuji 小林保治, 1968. Ōjō-den no kyōju to sono kōzō ni tsuite: *Nihon ōjō gokuraku-ki o chūshin ni* 往生伝の享受とその構造について―日本往生極楽記を中心に. In *Ōjō-den no kenkyū* 往生伝の研究, ed. Koten Isan no Kai 古典遺産の会, 94–117. Tokyo: Shindokushosha.

MacIntyre, Alasdair, 1984. *After Virtue.* Notre Dame, Indiana: University of Notre Dame Press.

Marra, Michele, 1988. The development of *mappō* thought in Japan. Parts 1 and 2. *Japanese Journal of Religious Studies* 15/1: 25–54; 15/4: 287–305.

Nakamura, Kyoko Motomichi, tr., 1973. *Miraculous Stories from the Japanese Buddhist Tradition: The Nihon Ryōiki of the Monk Kyōkai.* Cambridge: Harvard University Press.

Nattier, Jan, 1991. *Once Upon a Future Time: Studies in a Buddhist Prophecy of Decline.* Berkeley: Asian Humanities Press.

Ōsone Shōsuke 大曽根章介, 1974. *Chiteiki ron* 池亭記論. In *Nihon kanbungakushi ronkō* 日本漢文学史論考, ed. Yamagishi Tokuhei 山岸徳平, 215–52. Tokyo: Iwanami Shoten.

Polkinghorne, Donald E., 1988. *Narrative Knowing and the Human Sciences.* Albany: State University of New York Press.

Reynolds, Frank E., and Donald Capps, eds., 1976. *The Biographical Process: Studies in the History and Psychology of Religion.* The Hague: Mouton.

Ricoeur, Paul, 1992. *Oneself as Another.* Chicago: University of Chicago Press.

Sekiguchi Tadao 関口忠男, 1968. *Nihon Ōjō Gokuraku-ki no Jōdo ōjō shisō o megutte* 日本往生極楽記の浄土往生思想をめぐって. In *Ōjō-den no kenkyū* 往生伝の研究, ed. Koten Isan no Kai 古典遺産の会, 71–93. Tokyo: Shindokushosha.

Stone, Jacqueline I., 1985. Seeking enlightenment in the Last Age, Parts 1 and 2. *The Eastern Buddhist*, 18/1: 28–56, 18/2: 35–64.

Washio Junkyō 鷲尾順敬, 1903. *Nihon Bukke jinmei jiten* 日本仏家人名辞典. Tokyo: Kōyūkan.

Watson, Burton, tr., 1975. *Japanese Literature in Chinese.* 2 vols. New York: Columbia University Press.

With the Help of "Good Friends"
Deathbed Ritual Practices in Early Medieval Japan

Jacqueline I. Stone

> Child of the Buddha, do you realize that now is your last thought? This single reflection [on the Buddha] at death outweighs the karmic acts of a hundred years. If this instant should pass you by, rebirth [in *saṃsāra*] will be unavoidable. Now is precisely the time. Reflect on the Buddha single-mindedly, and you will surely be born on a seven-jewelled lotus pedestal in the pond of eight virtues in the subtle and wondrous Pure Land of Utmost Bliss in the west.
>
> GENSHIN[*]

∵

With such words as these, suggests the monk Genshin (942–1017), the dying should be exhorted to focus their minds on the Buddha Amida (Skt. Amitābha, Amitāyus), in order to escape the round of rebirth and instead achieve birth in the Pure Land (*ōjō*). Genshin's treatise *Ōjō yōshū* (Essentials of Pure Land birth), completed in 985, has already been introduced in Chapter 1 by Sarah Horton. In addition to its role in popularizing Pure Land devotion, it is famous for its detailed instructions—the first ever compiled in Japan—on Buddhist deathbed practice (*rinjū gyōgi*). The form of deathbed practice described in *Ōjō yōshū* soon gained popularity in monastic circles and spread to lay elites and also commoners.

Genshin's recommendations for deathbed practice marked the entry into Japanese Buddhist discourse of a concern with dying in a state of right-mindfulness and belief in the power of one's last thoughts, ritually focused, to

---

Source: Stone, Jacqueline I., "With the Help of 'Good Friends': Deathbed Ritual Practices in Early Medieval Japan," in Jacqueline I. Stone I and Mariko Tamba Walter (eds.), *Death and the Afterlife in Japanese Buddhism*, Honolulu: University of Hawaii Press, 2008, pp. 61–101.

[*] *Epigraph*: *Ōjō yōshū*, in *Genshin, Nihon shisō taikei* (hereafter NST) 6, ed. Ishida Mizumaro (Tokyo: Iwamani Shoten, 1970), 214; trans. from James C. Dobbins, "Genshin's Deathbed Nembutsu Ritual in Pure Land Buddhism," *Religions of Japan in Practice*, ed. George J. Tanabe, Jr. (Princeton: Princeton University Press, 1999), 174, slightly modified.

DEATHBED RITUAL PRACTICES

determine one's postmortem fate. In the logic of deathbed contemplation, the moment of death was constructed as a liminal realm, transcending ordinary moral calculus of sin and merit, when a lifetime of wrongdoing could potentially be reversed and even sinful men and women could achieve liberation. Horton's chapter has already suggested the immense hope conveyed by belief in this possibility of deathbed salvation. This hope was linked to broader arguments extending the possibility of birth in the Pure Land to "evil persons" (*akunin ōjō*) and gave promise of liberation even in an age widely thought to be degenerate and sinful. However, birth in the Pure Land was by no means a certain thing, and the discourse surrounding deathbed practices had its dark side, for the last moment was seen as pregnant, not only with immense salvific potential, but also with grave danger. If even a sinful individual who properly focused his mind on the Buddha at death might thereby reach the Pure Land, by the same token, it was thought that even a virtuous person, by a single distracted thought at the last moment, could negate the merit of a lifetime's devotion and fall into the evil realms. To die while unconscious, delirious, or wracked by pain thus came to be greatly feared, and the importance of ritual control over one's last moments was increasingly emphasized.[1] This essay will trace the development of written instructions for deathbed practice from Genshin's *Ōjō yōshū* on, focusing on the latter Heian (794–1185) and Kamakura (1185–1333) periods; their appropriation across sectarian lines and by an expanding range of social groups; their increasing emphasis on the difficulties of achieving right concentration at the last moment and consequent promotion of the role of the *zenchishiki* or "good friend," the person presiding over the deathbed ritual scene; and the eventual routinization of deathbed practices with their assimilation to the standardized funeral observances that began to emerge in late medieval and early modern times.

1   Deathbed Practices in *Ōjō yōshū* and the Samādhi Society of Twenty-Five

Genshin's instructions for deathbed practice in *Ōjō yōshū* consist of two parts. The first part draws on the work of Chinese predecessors to explain how the

---

1   On the moment of death as embodying both hope and anxiety, see Jacqueline I. Stone, "By the Power of One's Last Nenbutsu: Deathbed Practices in Early Medieval Japan," in *Approaching the Land of Bliss: Religious Praxis in the Cult of Amitābha*, ed. Richard K. Payne and Kenneth K. Tanaka (Honolulu: University of Hawai'i Press, 2004), 77–119.

dying should be cared for and encouraged in their final meditations.[2] Here Genshin quotes a passage from a "Chinese tradition" appearing in a Vinaya commentary by Daoxuan (596–667) in a section on "Attending to the Sick and Sending off the Dead," which purports to describe how the terminally ill were treated at the Jetavana monastery in India in Śākyamuni Buddha's time. According to its prescriptions, a dying person is to be removed to a "chapel of impermanence" (mujōin), so that the sight of his familiar surroundings and robe, bowl, and other possessions will not generate thoughts of attachment. A standing buddha image should be installed facing west; the sick person should be placed behind the image and made to grasp a five-colored pennant tied to the image's hand to help him generate thoughts of following the Buddha to his pure realm. Those in attendance are to burn incense, scatter flowers, and promptly remove any vomit or excrement.[3] Alternatively, Genshin cites the recommendation of Daoshi (d. 668?) that the buddha image should face east, and the sick person should be placed facing the image.[4] If no separate hall is available, Genshin says, one should simply have the sick person face west, burn incense, scatter flowers, and offer various encouragements. Or one may have the dying person face a fully adorned buddha image.

Genshin also cites the instructions for deathbed practice given by the Pure Land master Shandao (613–681), who advises that dying persons should be made to face west, visualize the coming of the Buddha Amida to escort them to the Pure Land, and continually recite Amida's name. If the dying see visions of Amida and his holy retinue, they should describe this, and those in attendance should write down what they report. If, on the other hand, they see images of painful punishment, their companions should chant the *nenbutsu* with them and help them to perform repentance so that their sins may be eradicated. Relatives and other visitors who have recently consumed meat, alcohol, or the five pungent roots should be refused access, lest the dying lose correct concentration, thus falling prey to demons who will cause them to fall into the evil

---

2 As Alan Cole has demonstrated, Genshin's sources were embedded in a larger, general body of Chinese Buddhist deathbed and funerary prescriptions that "was heavily dependent on Pure Land ideology and techniques of buddha-name recitation, even though it was not identified as Pure Land Buddhism" ("Upside Down/Right Side Up: A Revisionist History of Buddhist Funerals in China," *History of Religions* 35, no. 4 [1996]: 307–338 [329]).

3 *Sifenlü shanfan buque xingshi chao*, *T* no. 1804, 40:144a, cited in *Ōjō yōshū*, *NST* 6:206.

4 *Fayuan zhulin*, *T* no. 2122, 53:987a, cited in *Ōjō yōshū*, *NST* 6:206, though Genshin does not mention Daoshi by name. Daoshi's work contains a description of purported deathbed practices at the Jetavana monastery very similar to that quoted in Daoxuan's commentary. Daoxuan refers to his source as a "Chinese tradition" (*Zhongguo benzhuan*), while Daoshi terms his a "Diagram of the Jetavana monastery in the western region" (*Xiyu Zhihuansi tu*), but they appear to have worked from a single source.

DEATHBED RITUAL PRACTICES 185

paths.[5] Genshin also draws upon the words of Daochuo (562–645), who comments on the difficulty, in one's last moments, of sustaining ten reflections on Amida, deemed the minimum necessary to achieve *ōjō*:

> To have ten uninterrupted reflections in succession would not seem difficult. But most unenlightened individuals have a mind as untamed as a wild horse, a consciousness as restless as a monkey.... Once the winds of dissolution arise [at the moment of death], a hundred pains will gather in the body. If you have not trained prior to this time, how can you assume that you will be able to contemplate the Buddha on that occasion? Each person should thus make a pact in advance with three to five people of like conviction. Whenever the time of death approaches [for any of them], they should offer each other encouragement. They should chant the name of Amida for the dying person, desire that person's birth in the Pure Land, and continue chanting to induce [in him] the ten moments of reflection.[6]

The "ten moments of reflection" here refers, on one hand, to the famous eighteenth vow of Amida, which promises birth in his Pure Land to all who aspire to this goal with sincerity and call him to mind "even ten times";[7] it also refers to the *Contemplation Sūtra's* claims that even an evil person, if he encounters a good friend (*zenchishiki*) who instructs him at the hour of death so that he is able to sustain ten thoughts of Amida, shall, with each thought, erase the sins of eight billion kalpas and be born in Amida's Pure Land.[8] Exactly how these ten thoughts should be understood was a matter of considerable debate and was embedded in a larger controversy over the respective merits of the contemplative visualization of Amida or the chanting of his name. Genshin took "ten continuous *nenbutsu*" to mean reflecting upon Amida, aided by the invocation of his name in the formula "*Namu Amida butsu.*" While Genshin's approach to Pure Land practice focuses on visualization and contemplation, he also held that, under the liminal influence of approaching death, the chanted *nenbutsu* becomes vastly more powerful than it is at ordinary times.[9] After citing his Chinese predecessors, Genshin then proceeds to offer his own recommendations for encouragement to the dying. These comprise the second

---

5 *Guannian famen*, T no. 1959, 47:24b–c, cited in *Ōjō yōshū*, NST 6:207.
6 *Anle ji*, T no. 1958, 47:11b, cited in *Ōjō yōshū*, NST 6:208; trans. from Dobbins, "Genshin's Deathbed Nembutsu Ritual," 170, slightly modified.
7 *Wuliangshou jing*, T no. 360, 12:268a.
8 *Guan Wuliangshou jing*, T no. 365, 12:346a.
9 *Ōjō yōshū*, NST 6:296.

part of the *rinjū gyōgi* section of *Ōjō yōshū* and consist of ten exhortations, centering upon visualization of Amida's physical marks, his radiant light, and his descent, together with his holy retinue, to escort the practitioner to the Pure Land.

Genshin's interest in ritualized deathbed practice leading to birth in the Pure Land had Japanese as well as continental antecedents. For example, Senkan (919–984), a Tendai monk of the Onjōji line and an earlier Japanese Pure Land thinker, had expressed in a written prayer his hope that

> [a]t the time of death, may I be at ease in body and mind, receive Amida's welcoming descent, and achieve the highest level of birth on a lotus pedestal in the Pure Land. And how could I wish this for myself alone? May all beings throughout the dharma realm, in their last hours, having known the approach of death seven days in advance, distance their minds from perversions and dwell in right-mindfulness, encounter the teachings of a good friend, chant ten *nenbutsu*, and, freed from all bodily and mental pain, alike be born in Amida's Pure Land.[10]

In addition to prayers for a good death, such as Senkan's, we also find notices of individuals prior to Genshin's time dying in a ritualized fashion that expressed their aspirations for *ōjō*. Early tenth-century sources record, for example, that Emperor Seiwa (d. 880) had monks attend him at the end and chant the Diamond Wheel (*kongōrin*) dhāraṇī, while he himself sat upright, facing west with his hands forming the meditation mudrā (*jōin*).[11] The former minister of the right, Fujiwara no Yoshimi (d. 867), is said to have died "seated upright, facing west and forming the fundamental mudrā of the Buddha Amida," and the councilor Fujiwara no Yasunori (d. 895) is similarly said to have died with undisturbed mind, facing west and contemplating Amida Buddha.[12] The biography of the great Tendai master Ennin (Jikaku Daishi, d. 793–864) says that, at the time of his death, he washed his face and donned a clean robe, burnt incense, placed his palms together, and faced west; he also had his disciple Enchō chant, "I take refuge in and worship Amida of complete awaken-

---

10   *Jūgan hosshinki*, reproduced in Satō Tetsuei, *Eizan Jōdokyō no kenkyū* (Kyoto: Hyakkaen, 1979), Part II: *Shiryō*, 195. On Senkan, see Robert F. Rhodes, "Bodhisattva Practice and Pure Land Practice: Senkan and the Construction of Pure Land Discourse in Heian Japan," *Japanese Religions* 24, no. 1 (1999): 1–28.

11   *Sandai jitsuroku* (commissioned in 901), Genkei 4, 12/4, *Shintei zōho kokushi taikei* (hereafter *KT*), 66 vols., ed. Kuroita Katsumi (Tokyo: Yoshikawa Kōbunkan, 1929–1966), 4:486.

12   *Sandai jitsuroku*, Jōgan 9, 10/10, *KT* 4:223; "Fujiwara Yasunori den," in *Kodai seiji shakai shisō*, *NST* 8, ed. Yamagishi Tokuhei et al. (Tokyo: Iwanami Shoten, 1979), 72.

DEATHBED RITUAL PRACTICES　　　　　　　　　　　　　　　　　　　　　187

ing" (*kimyō chōrai Mida shukaku*) while other disciples recited the names of various buddhas and bodhisattvas.[13] While the biography certainly postdates Ennin, it would nonetheless appear to precede *Ōjō yōshū*. And Enshō (d. 959 or 963), chief abbot of Enryakuji, also mentioned in Horton's essay, is said to have died holding a cord tied to the hand of an image of the Buddha Amida, as Genshin had recommended.[14] Such notices suggest that embryonic forms of deathbed ritual practice were being practiced in Japan even before *Ōjō yōshū* was compiled. Genshin's text, then, did not initiate deathbed practice so much as it helped to systematize, elaborate, and promote a practice that had already begun to emerge.

As Horton has explained in Chapter 1, the deathbed practices described in *Ōjō yōshū* were first formally adopted by the Nijūgo zanmai-e or Samādhi Society of Twenty-five, a *nenbutsu* association based at the Yokawa retreat on Mt. Hiei, with which Genshin was closely associated. The Society's founding oath reads in part:

> We pledge together to be "good friends" to one another and, at life's last moment, to help one other contemplate the Buddha [Amida]. We hereby set the number of our Society at twenty-five. If one among us should fall ill, then by the power of the vow uniting us, without concern for whether the day be auspicious or not, we shall go to him and inquire after him and encourage [his deathbed contemplation]. And if he happens to achieve birth in [the Pure Land of] Utmost Bliss, then—whether by the power of his own vow or by relying on the Buddha's supernatural powers, whether in a dream or in waking reality—he shall so communicate this to the Society. Or, if he has fallen into the evil paths, he shall communicate this as well. Our society shall at regular times perform together with like mind those practices leading to the Pure Land. In particular, on the evening of

---

13　*Jikaku Daishi den*, in *Zoku Tendaishū zensho* (hereafter *ZTZ*), ed. Tendai Shūten Hensanjo (Tokyo: Shunjūsha, 1987–), *Shiden* 2:71–72. On the provenance of the text, see the accompanying *ZTZ Shiden* 2, *Kaidai*, 2–3, and Enshin Saitō, *Jikaku Daishi den: The Biography of Jikaku Daishi Ennin, Translation and Explanatory Notes* (Tokyo: Sankibō Busshorin, 1992), 16–19. Saitō estimates that this version of Ennin's biography was compiled "around 970."

14　*Nihon ōjō gokurakuki* 16, *Ōjōden, Hokke genki, Zoku Nihon bukkyō no shisō* (hereafter *ZNBS*) 1, ed. Inoue Mitsusada and Ōsone Shōsuke (rpt. of the 1974 *NST* 7; Tokyo: Iwanami Shoten, 1995), 27–28. *Gokurakuki* was compiled by Genshin's close associate Yoshishige no Yasutane (monastic name Jakushin, d. 1002) around 985, the year *Ōjō yōshū* was completed. Yasutane gives the date of Enshō's death as Tentoku 3 (959). However, both *Hokke genki* and *Fusō ryakki* give it as Ōwa 3 (963). It is not clear, of course, whether the detail of Enshō holding a cord tied to a buddha image is historically accurate or was added retrospectively.

the fifteenth day of each month, we shall cultivate the samādhi of mind-fulness of the Buddha (*nenbutsu zanmai*) and pray that we may be able to complete ten reflections [on Amida] in our last moments.[15]

Two extant sets of regulations for the Society stipulate that the members should devote the fifteenth of each month to *nenbutsu* practice with the aim of achieving birth in the Pure Land; recite the mantra of radiant light (*kōmyō shingon*) for empowering sand to be sprinkled on the corpses of deceased members; nurse any members of the society who fall sick, removing them to a separate chapel called the Ōjōin (hall for birth in the Pure Land), to be es-tablished for this purpose; and establish a gravesite for members and perform funerals, centering around *nenbutsu* practice.[16] The observances of the Nijūgo zanmai-e thus spanned a continuum from ordinary practice to funerary rites, within which practice at the moment of death played a pivotal role.

Deathbed protocols of the sort described in Genshin's *Ōjō yōshū* and prac-ticed by the Nijūgo zanmai-e represent the earliest formal articulation in Japan of much older, similar practices attested on the East Asian mainland; they also have resonances, if not direct historical connections, with the tra-ditional role of Buddhist monks and nuns in nursing the sick among them.[17]

---

15   *Ryōgon'in nijūgo zanmai konpon kesshū nijūgonin rensho hotsuganmon*, in *Nijūgo zan-mai shiki, Dai Nihon bukkyō zensho* (hereafter *DNBZ*), 100 vols. (Tokyo: Suzuki Gakujutsu Zaidan, 1970–1973), 49:31b. Though this text has been attributed to Genshin, his name does not appear on the list of founding members; thus this attribution may have been made retrospectively.

16   The two sets of regulations are an original set of eight regulations written in 986, attrib-uted to Yoshishige no Yasutane (*Kishō hachikajō*, *DNBZ* 49:28c–30b; *T* no. 2724, 84:878b–880b), and the 988 twelve-article *Yokawa Shuryōgon'in nijūgo zanmai kishō* (a.k.a. *Jūnikajō*), attributed to Genshin (*DNBZ* 49:27–30; *T* no. 2723, 84:876b–878b). The printed versions of these texts are all ultimately derived from a manuscript, possibly dating to the Kamakura period, held at the Chūshōin at Tōdaiji, but contain numerous discrepan-cies in titles, misprints, and other errors. These have been detailed in Koyama Masazumi, "Tōdaiji Chūshōin shozō 'Yokawa Shuryōgon'in nijūgo zanmai Eshin Yasutane rinjū gyōgi' no saikentō: Sōshobon no goshoku ni yoru mondaiten," *Bukkyōgaku kenkyū* 53 (1997): 56–95. Koyama also provides a critical edition of both sets of regulations.

      On the Nijūgo zanmai-e, see, for example, Richard Bowring, "Preparing for the Pure Land in Late Tenth-Century Japan," *Japanese Journal of Religious Studies* 25, nos. 3–4 (1998): 221–257; Robert F. Rhodes, "Seeking the Pure Land in Heian Japan: The Practices of the Monks of the Nijūgo Zanmai-e," *The Eastern Buddhist* 33, no. 1 (2000): 56–79; and Sarah Johanna Horton, "The Role of Genshin and Religious Associations in the mid-Heian Spread of Pure Land Buddhism (Japan)" (Ph.D. diss., Yale University, 2001).

17   On traditions of nursing in the monastery, see Paul Demiéville, "Byō," *Hōbōgirin: Dictionnaire Encyclopédique du Bouddhisme d'après les sources chinoises et japonaises* (Paris: Hōbōgirin, 1974), III:236–240 (translated by Mark Tatz as *Buddhism and Healing:*

DEATHBED RITUAL PRACTICES   189

Genshin's instructions in *Ōjō yōshū* in particular quickly became a model for conducting deathbed practices in Heian Japan. In a very early reference to the text, Genshin's disciple Kakuchō (d. 1034), who was active in the Nijūgo zanmai-e, recommends using its section on deathbed ritual to encourage and instruct practitioners during their final illness.[18] This *rinjū gyōgi* section of the *Ōjō yōshū* circulated in a somewhat modified, *kana* version as an independent text.[19] It also seems to have been read aloud on occasion to the dying. For example, when one member of the Society, Shōkin (a.k.a. Shōnen, d. 1015), fell ill, he reportedly "requested that worldly matters not be discussed in his presence but solely had the *rinjū gyōgi* section of the *Ōjō yōshū* read to him, learning its admonitions." On the night of his death, he again had his attendants read it to him, along with the "Fathoming the Lifespan of the Tathāgata" chapter of the *Lotus Sūtra*, and also had them chant the *nenbutsu*.[20] Within twenty years of the *Ōjō yōshū*'s appearance, hagiographies, literary sources, and court diaries begin to report individuals dying in accord with its prescriptions. The famous account of the death of the courtier Fujiwara no Michinaga depicted in *Eiga monogatari* is clearly based on *Ōjō yōshū*.[21] As Horton has noted in her chapter, *ōjōden* or biographical accounts of those said to have achieved birth in the Pure Land frequently describe the ritually correct death of devout persons who die in the posture of meditation, facing toward the west, or who hold cords tied to the hand of a buddha image. Similar references occur in diaries of the court nobility. Prince Sukehito (d. 1119) is said to have passed away chanting the *nenbutsu* while holding a five-colored cord attached to an image of Amida; Nishi no Okata (d. 1120), adoptive mother of the courtier Fujiwara no Munetada, also died with the colored cords in her hand.[22] Some later examples from literature include the former imperial consort Kenreimon'in, whose exemplary death is described at the end of *Tale of the Heike*, or the defeated commander Taira no Shigehira, in the same epic, who is allowed to hold a cord tied to the hand of a buddha image and chant ten *nenbutsu* before the executioner

---

     Demiéville's Article "Byō" from Hōbōgirin [Lanham, MD: University Press of America, 1985]; see esp. 31–35), and "Kangogaku," in Fukunaga Katsumi, *Bukkyō igaku jiten* (Tokyo: Yūzankaku, 1990), 292–298.

18   *Ōjō gokuraku mondō, DNBZ* 41:148b–c.

19   *Rinjū gyōgi, Eshin Sōzu zenshū*, ed. Hiezan Senshūin and Eizan Gakuin, 5 vols. (Sakamoto-mura, Shiga-ken: Hieizan Tosho Kankōjo, 1927–1928), 1:589–600.

20   See *Ryōgon'in nijūgo zanmai kakochō, ZTZ, Shiden* 2:285.

21   *Eiga monogatari* 18, ed. Matsumura Hiroji and Yamanaka Yutaka (Tokyo: Iwanami Shoten, 1965; rev. 1993), 2:326–328; *A Tale of Flowering Fortunes*, trans. William H. and Helen Craig McCullough (Stanford: Stanford University Press, 1980), 2:762–764.

22   *Chōshūki*, Gen'ei 2, 12/4, *Zōho shiryō taisei* (hereafter *ST*), ed. Zōho Shiryō Taisei Kankōkai, 45 vols. (Kyoto: Rinsen Shobō, 1965), 16:184; *Chūyūki*, Hōan 1, 9/19, *ST* 12:253.

lops off his head.[23] In addition to explicitly Buddhist soteriological rationales for deathbed practice, among the Heian nobility, the removal of dying persons to the *mujōin*—in aristocratic practice, often a private chapel or room at a temple or monastery where the dying individual might have patronage connections—also served the pragmatic purpose of isolating and confining the defilement of death, which had to be rigorously avoided by those involved in court ceremonials.[24]

The historicity of accounts of exemplary deaths is not always easy to evaluate. For example, the diary of the courtier Fujiwara no Sanesuke (957–1046), a contemporary of Michinaga, describes him as dying in acute discomfort, plagued by painful boils, occasional delirium, and loss of bowel control—thus suggesting that the account given in *Eiga monogatari* may be somewhat idealized.[25] What we can say, however, is that the prescriptions in the "deathbed practices" section of Genshin's *Ōjō yōshū* quickly became normative in elite circles for what an ideal death, one leading to liberation, was *supposed* to look like. At the same time, they formed the prototype for a number of subsequent *rinjū gyōgisho*, texts of deathbed ritual instruction or "deathbed manuals," as they might be termed. Such works were compiled in considerable numbers from the latter Heian period through early modern times; however, the eleventh through thirteenth centuries seem to have witnessed the greatest innovation in instructions for deathbed practice. Early modern *rinjū gyōgisho* in large

---

23   *Heike monogatari*, vol. 2, *Nihon koten bungaku taikei* (hereafter *NKBT*) 33, ed. Takagi Ichinosuke et al. (Tokyo: Iwanami Shoten, 1960), 440–442, 376–377; *Tale of the Heike*, trans. Helen Craig McCullough (Stanford: Stanford University Press, 1988), 436–338, 399–400. A list of individuals appearing in Heian- and Kamakura-period accounts who are said to have died holding the five-colored cords appears in Tsuji Zennosuke, *Nihon bukkyōshi* (Tokyo: Iwanami Shoten, 1944), 1:631–635. Tsuji regards this practice as reflecting an unfortunate trend toward increasing formalism in medieval Pure Land practice, an evaluation that reveals more about scholarly assumptions in Tsuji's time than about premodern understandings.

24   Nishiguchi Junko, "Where the Bones Go: Death and Burial of Women of the Heian High Aristocracy," in *Engendering Faith: Women and Buddhism in Premodern Japan*, ed. Barbara Ruch (Ann Arbor: Center for Japanese Studies, University of Michigan, 2002), 417–439 (422). For a detailed discussion of pollution in its relation to deathbed practices, see Jacqueline I. Stone, "Dying Breath: Deathbed Rites and Death Pollution in Early Medieval Japan," in *Heroes and Saints: The Moment of Death in Cross-cultural Perspectives*, ed. Phyllis Granoff and Koichi Shinohara (Newcastle: Cambridge Scholars Publishing, 2007), 173–246.

25   *Shōyūki* VIII, entries for Manju 4 (1027), 11/10–12/4, *Dai Nihon kokiroku*, ed. Tōkyō Daigaku Shiryō Hensanjo (Tokyo: Iwanami Shoten, 1976), 37–46. See also G. Cameron Hurst III, "Michinaga's Maladies: A Medical Report on Fujiwara no Michinaga," *Monumenta Nipponica* 34, no. 1 (Spring 1979): 101–112; and Hayami Tasuku, *Jigoku to Gokuraku: Ōjō yōshū to kizoku shakai* (Tokyo: Yoshikawa Kōbunkan, 1998), 141–145.

measure represent re-workings of this earlier material, and the present essay will focus on developments in the Heian and Kamakura periods. The majority of these texts adopt the basic features of Genshin's instructions: the removal of the dying to a separate place; the enshrinement of a buddha image with a cord fastened to its hand for the dying person to hold; the offerings of flowers and incense; the shielding of the dying person from talk of worldly affairs or the intrusion of those likely to arouse strong feelings, either of love or aversion; and the need above all to create a quiet and dignified atmosphere conducive to contemplation in one's last hours. Genshin's exhortation to the dying person is frequently quoted: "You should not visualize any form except the features of the Buddha. You should not hear any sounds except the Buddha's words of dharma. You should not speak of anything except the true teachings of the Buddha. You should not think of anything except birth in the Pure Land."[26] However, instructions for deathbed practice after *Ōjō yōshū* also reflect new developments, which will be summarized in the next three sections.

2 Appropriation across Traditions

Because of the popularity of *Ōjō yōshū* in later ages, Genshin has often been remembered primarily as a Pure Land teacher, and the sort of deathbed rituals he introduced have been assumed to be something peculiar to Pure Land Buddhism. However, scholarship has sometimes been too quick to read back into medieval times the clear-cut sectarian divisions of the early modern period and beyond. Aspiration for *ōjō* was a generic Buddhist goal, and the basic features of Genshin's instructions for deathbed practice were soon assimilated across institutional and sectarian divides, becoming adapted to the specific practices, iconography, and teachings of multiple Buddhist traditions. An early example is the *Rinjū gyōgi chūki* (Notes on deathbed practice) of Tanshū (1066–1120?), a monk learned in Hossō doctrine and with close ties to the Nara temples Kōfukuji and Saidaiji. Tanshū explicitly cites the instructions of the "bishop of Yokawa" (Yokawa Sōzu, that is, Genshin), assimilating them within a Nara Buddhist framework. Like a number of texts on deathbed ritual compiled subsequently to *Ōjō yōshū*, *Rinjū gyōgi chūki* takes the form of a series of articles of instruction (thirteen, in this case). Tanshū allows for aspiration to realms other than Amida's western Pure Land: if the dying person seeks birth in the Tuṣita heaven, he says, then an image of Maitreya should be substituted for that of Amida, and the dying person should visualize being born there.

---

26   *Ōjō yōshū, NST* 6:209; trans. from Dobbins, "Genshin's Deathbed Nembutsu Ritual," 170.

If death is not imminent, Tanshū suggests that a devotee of the *Lotus Sūtra* (*jikyōsha*) may expound its meaning for the dying person, or a companion in practice may read the *rishubun* section of the *Prajñāpāramitā-sūtra*. Reading the *rishubun* to the dying person would form a major component of deathbed ritual instructions with an esoteric orientation.[27] The dying person should also be encouraged to recite the bodhisattva precepts, or they may be recited for him, as an unrivalled source of merit. Tanshū further recommends performing the repentance rite of the bodhisattva Fugen (Skt. Samantabhadhra) to remove karmic hindrances that manifest at the time of death. His list of buddhas and bodhisattvas on whom the dying may rely for help in achieving right-mindfulness at the end include Śākyamuni, Maitreya, Yakushi, Fugen, Monju, Jizō, Kokūzō, Kannon, and Fudō.[28] Tanshū appears to have consulted Genshin's Chinese sources and added excerpts from them to his *Chūki* that are not found in *Ōjō yōshū*. For example, he quotes Daoxuan to the effect that all the good practices that the dying person has performed—such as doctrinal study, meditation, sūtra recitation, teaching others, or commissioning buddha images and stūpas—should be enumerated and praised by those attending at the deathbed, in order to inspire that person's joy and confidence. Later deathbed ritual instructions sometimes mandate that lists of the dying person's prior good deeds should be written out and read, and *ōjōden* accounts include examples of people who died holding in their hands such lists of their virtuous achievements.[29]

An important group of medieval deathbed ritual texts was produced within the Shingon *mikkyō* or esoteric tradition and represent that strand of thought retrospectively termed *himitsu nenbutsu*, or Pure Land esotericism. These texts

---

27   The *Rishubun* is one of several versions of the esoteric scripture *Liqu jing* (Jpn. *Rishukyō*, Sūtra of the guiding principle) and here appears to indicate fascicle 578 of the 600-fascicle *Dabore jing*, *T* no. 220. Reciting the *Rishukyō* was said to remove sins and karmic hindrances and to protect the practitioner from falling into the hells.

28   *Rinjū gyōgi chūki*, *DNBZ* 49:48–49. This work was discovered at the Chūshōin of Tōdaiji as part of a composite text, a transcription possibly dating to the Kamakura period, with the outer title *Yokawa Shuryōgon'in nijūgo zanmai Eshin Yasutane rinjū gyōgi*, consisting of Tanshū's instructions and the two sets of regulations for the Nijūgo zanmai-e given in note 16 above (Koyama, "Tōdaiji Chūshōin shozō 'Yokawa Shuryōgon'in nijūgo zanmai Eshin Yasutane rinjū gyōgi' no saikentō," 56–57). Its existence suggests a close connection between Tanshū's work and the deathbed protocols of the Nijūgo zanmai-e. Tanshū's authorship was determined by Ishii Kyōdō ("Shuryōgon'in nijūgo zanmai kisho ni tsuite," *Bussho kenkyū* 48 [1918]: 1–5).

29   For examples, see Ishida Mizumaro, *Ōjō no shisō* (Kyoto: Heirakuji Shoten, 1968), 249–252. Closely linked was the practice, chiefly attested in hagiographical literature, of holding in one's hand at the time of death a written vow to achieve the Pure Land (247–249).

assimilate Genshin's instructions to a *mikkyō* standpoint, typically identifying the deathbed *nenbutsu* with some form of ritual empowerment, and birth in a pure land, with realization of the nonduality of Amida and the *shingon* practitioner.[30] The earliest of these is the eight-article *Byōchū shugyōki* (Notes on practice during illness) by Jichihan (also Jitsuhan or Jippan, c. 1089–1144), who for a time was Tanshū's teacher.[31] Jichihan interprets Genshin's instructions for deathbed visualization from an esoteric perspective. As noted above, in his own articles of exhortation to the dying, Genshin had stressed contemplation of Amida Buddha's radiant light; this light, emitted from the curl of white hair between Amida's brows, Genshin asserted, will envelop the dying practitioner in the Buddha's compassion, eradicate his sins, focus his contemplation, and thus enable him to achieve birth in the Pure Land. Jichihan for his part recommends that the white curl be visualized as a transformation of the letter *hūṃ*, endowed with Amida's four inseparable mandalas. He also equates the name "Amida" with the three fundamental meanings of the letter "A": *A* indicating the originally unborn; mi, the non-self that is the great self; and *da*, moment-to-moment accordance with suchness. Jichihan may have been the first to present the deathbed *nenbutsu* as a form of empowerment or ritual union with the three secrets of the cosmic Buddha (*sanmitsu kaji*): the practitioner's reverent posture corresponds to the secret of the Buddha's body; the chanting of his name, to the secret of his speech; and the contemplation of the name's meaning, to the secret of his mind. Jichihan also recommended reliance on the esoteric deity Fudō Myōō to protect the practitioner and thwart the obstructions of both karmic hindrances and demonic influences at the moment of death. This role of Fudō as protector in the hour of death would become a standard feature of esoteric *rinjū gyōgi* texts. Like Genshin's *Ōjō yōshū* and Tanshū's *Rinjū gyōgi chūki*, Jichihan's text urges repentance to remove karmic hindrances; as specific forms of repentance, he suggests giving away one's clothing and other possessions or chanting mantras such as the Superlative Dhāraṇī of the Buddha's Crown (Skt. *uṣṇīṣavijayā dhāraṇī*, Jpn. Sonshō *darani*), the *kōmyō shingon*, or the name of Amida. The monk Kakuban (1095–1143),

---

30 For a more detailed discussion of esoteric versions of deathbed practice, see Jacqueline I. Stone, "The Secret Art of Dying: Esoteric Deathbed Practices in Heian Japan," in *The Buddhist Dead: Practices, Discourses, Representations*, ed. Bryan J. Cuevas and Jacqueline I. Stone (Honolulu: University of Hawai'i Press, 2007), 134–174.

31 *Byōchū shugyōki, Shingonshū anjin zensho* (hereafter *SAZ*), ed. Hase Hōshū (Kyoto: Rokudaishinbōsha, 1913–1914), 2:781–785. On Jichihan, see Marc Bunjisters, "Jichihan and the Restoration and Innovation of Buddhist Practice," *Japanese Journal of Religious Studies* 26, nos. 1–2 (1999): 39–82. I have followed Bunjisters in using the pronunciation "Jichihan."

later revered as the founder of "new doctrine" (*shingi*) Shingon, drew explicitly on Jichihan's *Byōchū shugyōki* in developing his own recommendations for deathbed practice. His nine-article *Ichigo taiyō himitsu shū* (Collection of secret essentials for life's end) also equates the *nenbutsu* with esoteric three secrets practice for union with the cosmic Buddha. He writes:

> Amida is Dainichi's function as wisdom. Dainichi is Amida's essence as principle.... When one contemplates in this way, then, without leaving the Sahā world, one is immediately born in [the pure land of] Utmost Bliss. One's own person enters Amida and, without transformation of Amida, becomes Dainichi. One's own person emerges from Dainichi; this is the subtle contemplation for realizing buddhahood with this very body.[32]

Both Jichihan and Kakuban stress union with the Buddha as the focus of the *shingon* practitioner's deathbed contemplation; in other words, the deathbed rite is recast in the model of an esoteric empowerment rite for realizing buddhahood through union with a deity. The deathbed scene in Kakuban's instructions is even arranged in a mandalic structure: four *zenchishiki* who assist the dying person's *nenbutsu* take up their positions around him so that together they reproduce the configuration of the five wisdom buddhas, the dying person occupying the central position of Dainichi.[33]

An esoteric approach to deathbed practice is also seen in the *Rinjū yōjin no koto* (Admonitions for the time of death) by the Shingon master Dōhan (1184–1252), dated 1234. Dōhan, too, emphasizes deathbed contemplation of the letter A: "The syllable A as existence arising through conditions corresponds to birth. The syllable A as the emptiness of nonarising corresponds to death. Thus dying in one place and being born in another is nothing other than the syllable A.... This is why Vairocana takes this single syllable as his mantra."[34] As deathbed invocations, Dōhan recommends reciting essential passages of the *Amida sūtra* or a range of esoteric mantras. One intriguing aspect of his ritual suggestions is that the practitioner face an image of the Shingon patriarch Kūkai (774–835) and invoke his compassionate aid in achieving birth in a pure land.[35]

---

32   *Ichigo taiyō himitsu shū, Kōgyō Daishi zenshū* (hereafter *KDZ*), ed. Tomita Kōjun (1935; rpt. Tokyō: Hōsenji, 1977), 2:1197–1220. The quoted passage appears at 2:1214.

33   *KDZ* 2:1215–1216.

34   *Rinjū yōjin no koto, SAZ* 2:792–795. The quotation is at 793.

35   Ibid., 792.

DEATHBED RITUAL PRACTICES

With the passage of time, instructions for deathbed practice also appear within the so-called "single practice" schools. Ryōchū (1199–1287), third patriarch of the Chinzei lineage of Hōnen's Jōdo sect, emphasizes in his *Kanbyō yōjinshō* (Admonitions in caring for the sick) the efficacy of simply chanting the *nenbutsu* at the last moment with faith in Amida's vow.[36] And in the early modern period, works appear in the Nichiren tradition stressing the unique deathbed efficacy of chanting the title or *daimoku* of the *Lotus Sūtra*.[37] The specific *honzon* to be enshrined at the deathbed scene, the texts to be read aloud to encourage the dying, and the incantations to be performed differ from one Buddhist tradition to another; so do understandings of the nature of the postmortem liberation being sought, which is variously represented as the realization of buddhahood or birth in a particular pure land or other superior realm. But the notion that a person's last hours should be ritually managed, as well as the basic techniques for so doing, cut across all divisions of "old" and "new," "exoteric" and "esoteric," in which we are accustomed to thinking of medieval Japanese Buddhism.

3   Elaboration, Interpretation, and the Production of Specialized Knowledge

Another characteristic of medieval deathbed manuals is an increasing elaboration, over time, of elements mentioned only briefly in Genshin's instructions. This reflects both an increased mining of Chinese Buddhist canonical sources for relevant passages and also, it would appear, an accumulation of both practical knowledge and specialized interpretation. For example, citing Chinese precedents, *Ōjō yōshū* says simply that the dying should be removed to a separate chapel (*mujōin*) or room to avoid the feelings of attachment aroused by the sight of familiar possessions and surroundings and be encouraged to hold five-colored cords affixed to the hand of a buddha image, which—depending on the source—may face either west or east. Later deathbed ritual instructions, however, discuss at length the arrangement of this separate room or chapel; how one should determine when the move is to be made and what

---

36   The *Kanbyō yōjinshō* (a.k.a. *Kanbyō goyōjin, Kanbyō yōjin*) is reproduced in Itō Shintetsu, *Nihon Jōdokyō bunkashi kenkyū* (Tokyo: Ryūbunkan, 1975), 447–461.

37   To my knowledge, the earliest Nichiren Buddhist *rinjū gyōgi* text is the *Chiyo migusa* traditionally attributed to Shinjōin Nichion (1572–1642) but possibly a slightly later composition. See also Jacqueline I. Stone, "The Moment of Death in Nichiren's Thought," in *Hokke bukkyō bunkashi ronso*, ed. Watanabe Hōyō Sensei Koki Kinen Ronbunshū Kankōkai (Kyoto: Heirakuji Shoten, 2003), 19–56.

advance preparations are necessary; the categories of attachment, whether two or three, from which the dying must strive to separate themselves by this relocation; how this transition to a liminal space should be understood; and how the dying should be cared for.

Tanshū already goes well beyond *Ōjō yōshū* in discussing advance preparations. From the time one becomes ill, he says, one should concentrate on accumulating merit. One should offer food, drink, and clothing to the three treasures and to the poor and ill; one should offer pure flax oil for lamps to the Buddha and to temples and stūpas. Sounding a note that would be echoed in several subsequent *rinjū gyōgi* texts, Tanshū warns against the use of *kitō* or prayer rituals to extend life as a form of delusive self-attachment. "The span of this lifetime is fixed for everyone. If such prayers were efficacious, then why would anyone die?"[38] Jichihan and Kakuban, on the other hand, both recommend that if it is possible to prolong one's life, one should seek medical help for illness—not out of self-love, but to extend one's opportunity for Buddhist practice. However, once it becomes clear that death is inevitable, one should immediately cease all such efforts and single-mindedly practice for one's last moments.[39] In contrast to the idealized accounts in *ōjōden* of devotees who foresee their death to the day and hour, some medieval *rinjū gyōgi* texts, beginning with Kakuban's *Ichigo taiyō himitsu shū*, frankly acknowledge that the approach of death may not be quite so obvious and recommend astrology or other forms of divination to determine whether one's illness will indeed prove fatal.[40]

As for the removal to the separate chapel, Kakuban says it expresses the intention to "abandon this impure, Sahā world and achieve the Pure Land of Utmost Bliss." It is also time to part from one's relations; one's last wishes should already have been communicated. One's only associates should now be three to five *zenchishiki*—presumably following Daochuo's instructions, cited by Genshin in his *Ōjō yōshū*, that anyone intent on achieving the Pure Land should "make a pact in advance with three to five people of like conviction." One should leave wealth, reputation, and family behind, just as Śākyamuni Buddha left his father's palace, or as Kūkai entered into perpetual meditation, becoming truly "homeless" (*shukke*) in both mind and body.[41] Kakuban identifies the dying person's move to the *mujōin* with both the literal departure from this world that is death and the spirit of world renunciation inherent in the act

---

38   *Rinjū gyōki chūki*, DNBZ 49:48b.

39   *Byōchū shugyōki*, SAZ 781; *Ichigo taiyō himitsu shū*, KDZ, 2:1198.

40   *Ichigo taiyō himitsu shū*, KDZ, 2:1199.

41   Ibid., 2:1199–2000.

of taking monastic vows. This homologizing of death to departure from the household life was also echoed in the practice, fairly widespread among Heian aristocrats, of deathbed tonsure (*rinjū jukai, rinjū shukke*), which was thought to aid one in the postmortem state.[42] A set of deathbed instructions contained in *Kōyōshū* (Collection of filial piety), attributed to Kakuban but probably a Kamakura-period text, recommends that the dying look upon the move to the *mujōin* as leaving the burning house of the threefold world. If death is not imminent, the transition should be made at an auspicious day and time, and on arriving, the sick should wash their hands, rinse their mouth, and invoke the aid of all buddhas and bodhisattvas in escaping birth and death.[43]

Virtually all of these texts follow *Ōjō yōshū* in recommending the burning of incense and scattering of flowers to create a dignified atmosphere, as well as the need to screen visitors, especially those who have recently consumed alcohol or any of the "five pungent roots," and to protect the dying person from the sight of objects or persons liable to arouse strong emotions. According to Genshin's text, the purpose of moving the dying to a separate place was to forestall the delusive feelings of attachment that may be provoked by the sight of familiar possessions and surroundings. This theme, too, undergoes considerable elaboration in later *rinjū gyōgisho*. Tanshū warns against the use of ornate clothes or bedding in the sickroom, lest they give rise to attachment. Two kinds of attachment, he says, bind people to the samsaric world: attachment to objects—such as possessions, wife, and children—and attachments to self; the dying should reflect on the impurity of the body and evanescence of worldly treasures.[44] The Pure Land teacher Ryōchū advises that, should no appropriate place be available, the dying person may remain in his own lodging cell, but it should be arranged in a manner different from usual, and he should be made to lie down before a buddha image.[45] *Kōyōshū* recommends for the death chamber a room that receives the light of the setting sun; if such is not available, a monastic cell or room in a lay household will suffice, but it should be purified and refurbished.[46] To the two categories of attachment warned against in Tanshū's deathbed instructions, the *Kōyōshū*'s compiler adds a third: that of attachment to rebirth in one or another of the various samsaric realms

---

42   On the practice of deathbed tonsure, see Takagi Yutaka, "Ōjōden ni okeru Hokke shinkō," in *Hokke shinkō no shokeitai*, ed. Nomura Yōshō (Kyoto: Heirakuji Shoten, 1976), 451–484 (478–483), and Mitsuhashi Tadashi, *Heian jidai no shinkō to shūkyō girei* (Tokyo: Zoku Gunsho Ruijū Kanseikai, 2000), 597–668.

43   *Kōyōshū, DNBZ* 43:26c.

44   *Rinjū gyōki chūki, DNBZ* 49:48c–49a.

45   *Kanbyō yōjinshō*, in Itō, *Nihon Jōdokyō bunkashi kenkyū*, 447.

46   *Kōyōshū, DNBZ* 43:26a.

that may appear in visions to the dying.[47] This text is particularly graphic in warning against the dangers of thoughts of attachment in one's last moments. "In the past, there have been cases of flies or ants appearing in a dead person's face. These insects were produced from the person's body because of lingering self-attachment. There have also been persons who turned into white worms that emerge from a woman's nose; these are men who died with lingering attachment to their wives." Even sacred objects can become the focus of delusive clinging; a case in point is "people who wander through saṃsāra because of their heedless love of ritual implements (*butsugu*) or objects of worship (*honzon*), thinking that by the power of these things they shall reach [the Pure Land of] Utmost Bliss. No matter what roots of great good you may have planted, never let your mind adhere [in your last hours to the objects of attachment]!"[48]

Once established in the chapel or room where he is to die, the sick person is to face west, either sitting up, if he prefers, or lying down with his head to the north, as the historical Buddha Śākyamuni is said to have done. As noted above, Genshin had cited variant opinions as to whether the buddha image should be installed facing west with the dying person placed behind it, as though following the Buddha to the Pure Land, or whether the image should face east, with the dying person directly facing it. Kakuban takes this to be a matter of personal choice; the buddha image facing west represents the dying person being embraced and drawn up (*injō*) into the Pure Land, while the image facing east symbolizes the coming of the Buddha to receive him (*raigō*).[49] Ryōchū stresses that the image should be of a height such that the dying person can readily gaze at it while lying down.[50] *Kōyōshū* recommends positioning the buddha image five to six *shaku* from the dying person as an appropriate distance.[51] Use of the five-colored cords also elicits considerable discussion in these texts. Kakuban says they should be prepared in advance and should measure one *jō* and two *shaku* in length each, totaling nine *shaku*. There is a method of preparing them, he notes, which should be conducted by someone who has received esoteric initiation (*kanjō*).[52] The unknown compiler of *Kōyōshū* specifies that

---

47   This specific formulation of the "three categories of attachment" (*san'ai*) that obstruct one at the time of death are first enumerated in Senkan's *Jūgan hosshinki* (Satō, *Eizan Jōdokyō no kenkyū*, 198–199). See also Kamii Monshō, "Rinjū ni okeru san'ai no mondai," *Indogaku bukkyōgaku kenkyū* 41, no. 2 (1993): 318–321.

48   *Kōyōshū*, DNBZ 43:25b–26a.

49   *Ichigo taiyō himitsu shū*, KDZ 2:1200. The distinction arises from variances in different Chinese accounts of deathbed practice at the Jetavana monastery. See ns. 3 and 4 above.

50   *Kanbyō yōjinshō*, in Itō, *Nihon Jōdokyō bunkashi kenkyū*, 447.

51   *Kōyōshū*, DNBZ 43:26b.

52   *Ichigo taiyō himitsu shū*, KDZ 2:1200.

DEATHBED RITUAL PRACTICES   199

their threads should be spun in a purified room by a woman approaching eighty (and thus, presumably, free from sexual impurity),[53] dyed the five colors by a holy man (*hijiri*), and woven under the supervision of someone who has received esoteric initiation; this method is not to be disseminated to people at large.[54] Such injunctions suggest that these five-colored cords were the same as those sometimes employed in esoteric rites (*mikkyō shuhō*) of the same period, to demarcate the altar space or for other ritual purposes.[55] According to esoteric ritual instructions, such cords were to be woven of the finest threads, purified in perfumed water, and woven by a prepubescent boy or girl, or alternatively, by an aged nun, while the ritualist was to empower the threads of each color with the corresponding mantras of the five buddhas.[56]

By reading medieval Japanese deathbed ritual texts chronologically, we can see in such elaborations the gradual production and accumulation of a body of specialized knowledge, both theoretical and practical, concerning deathbed practice. This development is closely related to another major characteristic of post-Genshin medieval *rinjū gyōgi* texts: the emergence of the individual

---

53   Presumably for the same reason, Hōnen admonishes that the cords should be woven by a child (*Ippyaku shijū gokajō mondō*, no. 71, *Shōwa shinshū Hōnen Shōnin zenshū* [hereafter *HSZ*], ed. Ishii Kyōdō [Kyoto: Heirakuji Shoten, 1955; rpt. 1974], 658). It appears that the cords were sometimes cut up afterwards and the pieces distributed to establish karmic connections (*kechien*) conducive to ōjō. Hōnen, however, explicitly rejects this practice (ibid., no. 103, 662).

54   *DNBZ* 43:26b.

55   One striking instance involves their use in a ritual directed toward the healing Buddha, Yakushi Nyorai (Bhaiṣajyaguru Tathāgata) and his six manifestations (*shichibutsu Yakushi*), to ensure safe childbirth or protect the dangerously ill. Revived by Genshin's teacher Ryōgen, this became one of the four major esoteric rites of Mt. Hiei (Paul Groner, *Ryōgen and Mt. Hiei: Japanese Tendai in the Tenth Century* [Honolulu: University of Hawai'i Press, 2002], 87–88). In this ritual, forty-nine mantra-empowered knots are tied in the cord, which is then fastened to the head, hands, feet, or body of the person for whom the ritual is being performed (see *Kakuzenshō*, *DNBZ* 53:60b–c). The symbolism in this case was presumably to draw the person, not up into the Pure Land, but back from proximity to death into the world of the living.

   One also finds scattered references to the use of cords in personal prayers not connected to the moment of death. The ninth-century *Nihon ryōiki* includes two such episodes: the ascetic Konsu prays for permission to receive Buddhist ordination while holding a rope fastened to the legs of a clay statue of the deity Shūkongōjin (Vajradhara), an esoteric form of Kannon (II:21), and an orphan girl prays for relief from poverty while holding a rope tied to an image of Kannon (II:34) (*Nihon ryōiki, Shin Nihon koten bungaku taikei* 30, ed. Izumoji Osamu [Tokyo: Iwanami Shoten, 1996], 94, 113; trans. Kyoko Motomochi Nakamura, *Miraculous Stories from the Japanese Buddhist Tradition: The* Nihon ryōiki *of the Monk Kyōkai* [Cambridge, MA: Harvard University Press, 1973], 189, 207).

56   See, for example, the *Suxidi jieluo jing*, *T* no. 893c, 18:689a; *Dapiluzhena chengfo jing su*, *T* no. 1796, 39:627a; and *Asabashō*, *T* (*zusō*) 9:563a.

200   STONE

known as the *kanbyō* ("one who attends the sick") or more commonly the *zenchishiki* as a deathbed ritual specialist.

4   The Role of the *zenchishiki*

In general Buddhist usage, a *zenchishiki* (Skt. *kalyāṇamitra*, "good friend") is simply a dharma teacher, one who leads another on the path of practice. But in medieval *rinjū gyōgi* texts, the *zenchishiki* (or simply *chishiki*) is specifically the one in charge of the deathbed scene, and the need for his presence and expertise is continually underscored by an emphasis on how difficult it is to maintain right thoughts at the crucial last moment, as well as the fearful consequences of not doing so. This emphasis can already be seen emerging in Tanshū's eleventh-century *Rinjū gyōgi chūki*:

> When one falls ill and approaches death, everything escapes one's control.... The winds of dissolution move through one like sharp swords, wracking one's body and mind.... The eyes no longer discern color and shape, the ears do not hear sound; one cannot move hands or feet or exercise the organs of sense. Even someone who is expecting this will find it hard to maintain right-mindfulness; all the more so, those of feeble attainments! ... Good or evil recompense [in the life to come] depends on one's single thought at the last moment.... Those who lose the advantage of this moment are very close to hell.[57]

Read chronologically, medieval *rinjū gyōgi* texts suggest that, at least by their compilers, the correct performance of the *zenchishiki* as a deathbed ritual specialist gradually came to be seen as equally and in fact even more important than that of the dying person in ensuring that individual's successful negotiation of the final moment and achievement of birth in the Pure Land. Following Daochuo's recommendation, cited in *Ōjō yōshū*, that the practitioner should

---

57   *DNBZ* 49:48a. The idea that inappropriate thoughts at the last moment can negatively affect one's rebirth can of course be found much earlier and is common to Indian religious traditions. See, for example, Franklin Edgerton, "The Hour of Death: Its Importance for Man's Fate in Hindu and Western Religions," *Annals of the Bhandarkar Institute* 8, part 3 (1926–1927): 219–249. Genshin paraphrases Tanluan (476–542) to the effect that one perverse thought at the last moment can lead to rebirth in the Avīci hell (*Ōjō yōshū*, *NST* 6:289). See also Tanluan's *Jingtu shiyi lun*, *T* no. 1961, 47:80a. In Japan, however, concerns about delusory thoughts obstructing one's attainment of the Pure Land do not seem to have become widespread until slightly after Genshin's time.

DEATHBED RITUAL PRACTICES

"make a pact in advance with three to five people of like conviction," several medieval *rinjū gyōgisho* recommend the presence of three to five *zenchishiki*; some, such as Kakuban's *Ichigo taiyō himitsu shū* or Ryōchū's *Kanbyō yōjinshō*, indicate a specific division of ritual and nursing tasks among several such individuals. In general, the *zenchishiki* was responsible for the physical requirements of nursing and for exhorting the dying in a proper attitude, such as "loathing this defiled world and aspiring to the Pure Land" (*onri edo gongu jōdo*) or maintaining their mental focus in the face of physical pain. He—the *zenchishiki* was usually a "he," a point addressed below—was responsible for reading religious texts to instruct the dying; for leading and maintaining the pitch and rhythm of the chanting that, regardless of its content, was central to virtually all deathbed practice; for interpreting the visions of the dying and warding off malevolent influences, including possessing spirits; for reading corporeal signs presaging the dying person's postmortem fate, and, if necessary, intervening ritually; and sometimes for conducting postmortem rites. Let us touch here on a few of these aspects.

Later Heian- and Kamakura-period deathbed ritual texts suggest a cumulative hands-on experience with nursing the sick and dying, not seen in *Ōjō yōshū*. Ryōchū's *Kanbyō yōjinshō* is especially detailed on the subject of nursing. Ryōchū recommends that a schedule of watches be set up and measured by burning incense, so that the *chishiki* may relieve one another. They should not relax vigilance because the illness seems to improve; death can occur at any time. Thus until the very end, a *chishiki* must not remove his eyes from the sick person even for a moment. Even when off duty, he should rest in a place where he can hear the patient's breathing. At night, lamps should be lit so that the dying person can see the Buddha image and so that the *chishiki* can clearly observe the dying person's countenance, for illness often worsens at night. The dying should not be forced to get up to urinate or defecate if unable to do so. In such cases, screens should be set up between the dying person and the Buddha image while the bedding is being changed. However, if death is imminent, such concerns should be set aside. In addition, the dying person's mouth should continually be moistened with paper soaked in water, to facilitate his continued *nenbutsu* chanting.[58] Ryōchū also advises on how to deal with

---

58 This suggests itself as an early precedent for what would later become the practice of offering *matsugo no mizu* or *shinimizu* ("last water" or "death water"), water used to moisten the mouth of a dying or deceased person as a parting service by friends and relatives; see Fujii Masao, *Bukkyō girei jiten* (Tokyo: Tōkyōdō Shuppan, 1977), 164–165. For some historically recent accounts of this custom, see Kimura Hiroshi, *Shi: Bukkyō to minzoku* (Tokyo: Meicho Shuppan, 1989), 2–29.

fractious and recalcitrant patients and with demands for inappropriate food, such as fish. One should never ask the dying, "Would you like anything?" as such questions can arouse desire and distract their thoughts from the Buddha. Conversation should be strictly curtailed and concern only liberation from the cycle of birth and death.[59]

But the *chishiki* was far more than a nurse. His chief responsibility lay in helping the dying person to focus his or her thoughts so as to be able achieve right-mindfulness at the end and thus birth in the Pure Land. Texts after Genshin increasingly stress the gravity of this responsibility. Tanshū says:

> As death approaches, one must depart from evil companions and seek out a good friend (*zenchishiki*). Master Daoxuan says, "The attendant (*kanbyōnin*) must never turn his back upon the sick person. Were he to do so, then deluded thoughts would arise furiously and in most cases destroy that person's right concentration." Moreover, the holy teachings expound, with regard to those persons [whose birth in the Pure Land is not yet settled] that by following a sage one enters into wisdom, and that by following a heretic, one enters into error. This is true throughout the course of life; how much more so at its end![60]

Kakuban specifies that at least one of the *chishiki* in attendance should "by all means be a person of wisdom, with aspiration for the way"; the sick person should think of the *chishiki* as the bodhisattva Kannon, who will lead him to the Pure Land, while the *chishiki* "should sit close by while observing his face and protect him by dwelling in the mind of compassion."[61] Ryōchū writes, "Were it not for the power of the *chishiki*'s compassionate encouragement, how could the sole great matter [of birth in the Pure Land] be fulfilled? Thus the sick person should think of the *chishiki* as the Buddha, while the *chishiki* should extend to the sick person the compassion one has for one's only child."[62]

Among the *chishiki*'s chief tasks was to lead the deathbed chanting, to encourage right thoughts on the part of the dying person. Tanshū is among the first to recommend repeatedly striking the "chimes of impermanence" (*mujō no kei*) to maintain rhythm. Kakuban recommends chanting in harmony with the dying person; Ryōchū urges that the *nenbutsu* be chanted at a pitch neither

---

59 *Kanbyō yōjinshō*, in Itō, *Jōdokyō bunkashi kenkyū*, 447–451.
60 *DNBZ* 49:48a. The citation from Daoxuan appears to be a paraphrase.
61 *Ichigo taiyō himitsu shū*, *KDZ* 2:1215.
62 *Kanbyō yōjinshō*, in Itō, *Jōdokyō bunkashi kenkyū*, 447.

DEATHBED RITUAL PRACTICES 203

too high nor too low but audible to the dying person and in rhythm with his breathing, an admonition often echoed in later deathbed ritual instructions.[63]

Yet however desirable it may have been thought to die with the *nenbutsu* or other holy mantras on one's lips, the harsh physiological reality is that many people lapse into unconsciousness before they die. What of dying persons who fall unconscious or become disoriented and are thus unable to chant? To my knowledge, the first deathbed ritual text explicitly to address this problem is Kakuban's *Ichigo taiyō himitsu shū*. In such instances, Kakuban says, the *chishiki* are to observe the dying person's breathing carefully and match their breathing to his, chanting the *nenbutsu* in unison on the outbreath, for a day, two days, a week, or as long as necessary until death transpires. "The rite for persons on their deathbed always ends with the outbreath," he warns. "You should be ready for the last breath and chant [the *nenbutsu*] together in unison." In this way the dying person can be freed of sins and achieve the Pure Land, because the power of Amida's original vow must inevitably respond to the invocation of his name. Moreover, the *chishiki* are to visualize their *nenbutsu*, chanted on the outbreath, as the six syllables *Na-mo-A-mi-ta-buḥ* in Sanskrit (Siddham) letters, entering the dying person's mouth with the inbreath, transforming into six sun disks, and dispelling with their brilliance the darkness of the obstructions of sins associated with the six sense faculties.[64]

Here we see for the first time an explicit statement that, when the dying person can no longer mentally focus or falls unconscious, responsibility for both chanting and visualization practice immediately shifts to the *chishiki*, whose own actions at the deathbed then become determinative of the dying person's *ōjō*. Kakuban reflects that the *Contemplation Sūtra*'s statement about sinful persons achieving the Pure Land by meeting a "good friend" at the time of death must refer to just such cases. "If one could maintain right thoughts [at the last moment]," he says, "what need would there be for a *chishiki*? But when wrong or [even merely] neutral thoughts appear, the *chishiki* can [help

---

63   *Rinjū gyōki chūki*, DNBZ 49:49b; *Ichigo taiyō himitsu shū*, KDZ 2:1215; *Kanbyō yōjinshō*, in Itō, *Jōdokyō bunkashi kenkyū*, 448.

64   *Ichigo taiyō himitsu shū*, KDZ 2:1216–1217. This represents Kakuban's esoteric reading of the *nissōkan* or contemplation of the [setting] sun, first of sixteen meditations leading to birth in Amida's Pure Land set forth in the *Guan Wuliangshou jing* (T 12:341c–342a). On esoteric understandings of the *nenbutsu* more generally, see James H. Sanford, "Breath of Life: The Esoteric Nenbutsu" (1994), rpt. in *Tantric Buddhism in East Asia*, ed. Richard K. Payne (Somerville, MA: Wisdom Publications, 2006), 161–189, and "Amida's Secret Life: Kakuban's *Amida hishaku*," in Payne and Tanaka, *Approaching the Land of Bliss*, 120–138, as well as Stone, "Secret Art of Dying."

204   STONE

the dying person and] save him from the suffering [that would otherwise confront him] at that time."[65]

Kakuban's emphasis on chanting on behalf of the dying until the last breath
would become a standard feature of subsequent instructions for deathbed
practice.[66] Similar admonitions occur in Ryōchū's *Kanbyō yōjinshō*. Ryōchū
places immense responsibility on the *chishiki* to encourage the dying person's
chanting of the *nenbutsu* as the "foremost essential"; should that person become disoriented or lose consciousness, the *chishiki* should make every effort
to rouse him by reciting gāthās in a loud voice and admonishing, "Don't you
realize that these are your last moments?" But if the dying person can no longer chant, the *chishiki* must chant for him; so long as the aural faculty is still
operative, simply hearing the *nenbutsu* alone will enable the dying to reach
the Pure Land. Ryōchū urges that the *kanbyō* continue chanting for two to four
hours after the breath has ceased, all the while transferring the merit of their
nenbutsu to the deceased person. "By its virtue," he says, "he will achieve *ōjō*,
even from the interim state (*antarābhava, chūu*)."[67] In such passages, the beneficial influence of the *chishiki*'s chanting is said to extend beyond the final moment into interim existence. At this point, deathbed practice begins to shade
off into the realm of postmortem rites.

Another important function of the *chishiki* was to ward off evil influences.
On this subject, *Ōjō yōshū* cites Shandao, who says only that if the dying see
images of painful punishment, those caring for them should aid them in performing repentance until their sin is eradicated and visions of Amida and his
retinue instead appear. Later Japanese deathbed ritual texts, however, greatly
expand the *chishiki*'s responsibilities in this area. For example, he may have to
interpret deathbed visions, which the dying themselves may not always recognize as inauspicious. This role of the *chishiki* is dramatized in an account
from the tale collection *Hosshinshū* (Tales of religious awakening), attributed to Kamo no Chōmei (1155–1216), in which a *hijiri* or holy man serving as

---

65   *Ichigo taiyō himitsu shū*, KDZ 2:1217.
66   See Ikemi Chōryū, "Rinjū nenbutsu kō: Kiku, kikaseru," *Nihongaku* 10 (1987): 199–208.
67   *Kanbyō yōjinshō*, in Itō, *Jōdokyō bunkashi kenkyū*, 454–456. The text has "one or two hours,"
     an "hour" corresponding to one of the twelve divisions of the day. A similar admonition
     occurs in the *Rinjū no yōi*, traditionally attributed to Jōkei (1155–1213), which also stresses
     that the *zenchishiki* should chant in rhythm with the dying person's breathing and even
     continue to chant into his ear for at least two hours after the breath has ceased. "Although
     he may to outward appearances be dead, consciousness may remain, or the spirit may not
     have departed but be lingering near the dead person. Even if he should be destined for the
     evil paths, because he hears the name, he may be born in the Pure Land from the interim
     state" (*Nihon daizōkyō* 64:26b). If authentic, this text would predate Ryōchū's by several
     decades. However, some scholars question Jōkei's authorship.

DEATHBED RITUAL PRACTICES 205

zenchishiki to a dying court lady guides her through a series of delusive death-bed visions. While he is encouraging her to chant the *nenbutsu*, she suddenly turns pale and appears terrified. "What are you seeing?" he asks. "Frightful persons are arriving with a fiery carriage," she replies. This of course is a clear omen of descent into the hells. The *hijiri* admonishes: "Firmly contemplate Amida Buddha's original vow and chant his name without slackening. By encountering a 'good friend' and saying the *nenbutsu* ten times [at the moment of death], even someone who has committed the five perverse offenses can reach the Pure Land. How much more is this true of someone [like yourself,] who has never committed such a serious sin!" Prompted by his instruction, the lady resumes her chanting. After a time, she regains her composure and appears delighted. Now she reports seeing a splendid carriage approaching, adorned with jewels and filled with heavenly maidens playing music. The scripturally informed reader knows this, too, for a disguise in which the guardians of hell approach dying evildoers, but the woman herself does not know it.[68] "You must not ride that carriage," warns the *hijiri*. "Just continue to contemplate Amida Buddha and believe that he will come welcome you." Later the woman reports a vision of a dignified, black-robed monk who approaches her and says, "Let's go now. You don't know the way, so I will guide you." "Don't even think of following him," says the *hijiri*. "On the way to [the land of] Utmost Bliss, one has no need of a guide. By entrusting yourself to the Buddha's compassionate vow, you will spontaneously arrive in that realm." Eventually, thanks to her *zenchishiki*'s guidance, the woman is able to die chanting the *nenbutsu*, her mind calmly fixed on the Buddha.[69]

Such delusive visions could be due not only to the dying person's own past evil deeds, but to external malevolent influences. Kakuban recommends that one *chishiki*, a person with long training and experience, should stand at the dying person's head and continuously recite the mantra of Fudō Myōō, to ward off demonic attacks.[70] From stories in *setsuwa* or medieval tales, we know that the dying were thought sometimes to fall victim to possessing spirits

68   See the *Guanfo sanmeihai jing* (*T* no. 643, 15:669a), which describes how the illusory gold carriage with its beautiful maidens (actually hell flames in disguise) lures evildoers to their retribution. Genshin quotes this passage in the last part of the *rinjū gyōgi* section of his *Ōjō yōshū* (*NST* 6:214–215), as does Ryōchū in his *Jōdo taii shō* (*Jōdoshū zensho* [hereafter *JZ*], 23 vols., ed. Jōdoshū Kaishū Happyakunen Kinen Keisan Junbikyoku [Tokyo: Sankibō Busshorin, 1970–1972], 10:722).

69   *Hosshinshū* IV:7, in *Hōjōki, Hosshinshū*, ed. Miki Sumito (Tokyo: Shinchōsha, 1976), 182–184. This story also appears in *Sangoku denki* IX:15 (*DNBZ* 92:317a–b). In that version, auspicious signs accompanying the woman's death—purple clouds, fragrance, radiant light, and music—are described, indicating that she has undoubtedly achieved *ōjō*.

70   *Ichigo taiyō himitsu shū*, *KDZ* 2:1215.

(*mononoke*), and the *chishiki* then had to double as exorcist.[71] The *Kōyōshū* advises that while such spirits may deceive human eyes, they can readily be exposed by the simple expedient of hanging up a mirror, because *mononoke* are unaware of their own shadow.[72] By the late Kamakura period, we find clear evidence of a belief that malevolent influences can even mimic the appearance of Amida Buddha himself, and detailed instructions are provided for distinguishing genuine manifestations of the *raigō* from deceptive ones. For example, unlike the Buddha in a true *raigō* vision, a demonic apparition will not arrive riding on purple clouds. The golden hue of its body will resemble the gilt of a painted image, rather than the pellucid, all-pervading light emanating from Amida himself. And a vision of the "real" Amida will be visible with the eyes open or shut, while a demonic apparition will not, and so on.[73] One can imagine that the content of a person's deathbed visions, if known, might easily prompt others to draw conclusions about that individual's postmortem fate. Perhaps for this reason, in a version of what today we might call patient confidentiality, Ryōchū warns: "Whether they are good or evil, a *chishiki* should never reveal these [deathbed visions] to others."[74]

Karmic hindrances indicative of an unfortunate rebirth could manifest at the time of death, not only as ominous visions but also as corporeal signs. Kakuban's instructions specify which esoteric rites the *chishiki* should perform and what mantras he should chant immediately after the person's death, should that person have manifested some physical sign presaging a descent into the lower realms. For example, should the newly deceased have evinced any signs of falling into the hells, Kakuban recommends that the *zenchishiki* act at once to save that person by performing the Buddha Eye, Golden Wheel, Shō Kannon, or Jizō rites; or by reciting the *Rishukyō*, the names of the fifty-three buddhas, or the Jeweled Casket or Superlative dhāraṇī, or the Mantra of Light; or by performing the Jeweled Pavilion (*hōrō*) rite or reciting the "Bodhisattva Preaching Verses" chapter of the *Flower Ornament Sūtra* or the *Lotus Sūtra*, and so forth. Here Kakuban cites from the esoteric Chinese scripture *Shouhu guojiezhu tuoluoni jing* (Sūtra of dhāraṇīs for protecting the nation and the ruler), which gives fifteen signs that the dying will fall into the hells (such as crying

---

71   See, for example, *Goshūi ōjōden* 1:8, *ZNBS* 1:647, and the death of Yoshida no Saikū in *Hosshinshū* VII:5, Miki, *Hōjōki, Hosshinshū*, 314–315.

72   *Kōyōshū*, *DNBZ* 43:19b–c.

73   These and other distinctions are appended to a transcription of Ryōchū's text made by the Jōdo monk Ryūgyō (1369–1449), who gives them as citations from a work called *Nōsenshō* by one Rengedani Sōzu of Mt. Kōya and from another, unidentified account (*ichigi*). See Itō, *Jōdokyō bunkashi kenkyū*, 445–446.

74   *Kanbyō yōjinshō*, in Itō, *Jōdokyō bunkashi kenkyū*, 452.

aloud with grief or choking with tears, urinating or defecating without awareness, refusing to open the eyes, foul breath, lying face down, or refusing to follow the *zenchishiki*'s instructions [!]); eight signs of falling into the realm of
hungry ghosts (such as burning with fever or suffering from continuous hunger
or thirst); and five signs presaging a descent into the bestial realm (such as
contorting of the hands and feet, foaming at the mouth, or sweating from the
entire body)—all requiring the *chishiki*'s immediate ritual intervention.[75]

As noted above, the protocols of the Nijūgo zanmai-e, which was formed as
an association of monks dedicated to helping one another carry out disciplines
leading to birth in the Pure Land, emphasize both encouraging the deathbed
practice of fellow members and, after their death, performing on their behalf
the ritual of the *kōmyō shingon*, sprinkling the corpse with mantrically empowered sand.[76] Kakuban's recommendations for ritual intervention to rescue the
dying from the lower realms—like Ryōchū's directive that attendants should
continue chanting after the individual's death to redirect that person's wandering spirit from the interim state to the Pure Land—similarly extended the
chishiki's role past the moment of death into the postmortem realm.

The thrust of medieval deathbed ritual instructions was increasingly to
construct the *zenchishiki* as a sort of deathbed specialist. With him rested the
ritual control of the final moment, with its brief window onto the possibility
of escape from samsaric suffering. Soteriological control of one's last moments
could thus be safely entrusted to an expert who knew what he was doing. Over
time, it is he, even more than the dying person, who comes to be represented
as ultimately responsible for that person's success or failure in reaching the
Pure Land. Thus by the later Kamakura period, the compiler of *Kōyōshū* writes:

---

75   *T* no. 997, 19:574a, cited in *Ichigo taiyō himitsu shū*, KDZ 1:1217–1219. The sūtra itself merely
lists these signs, while Kakuban prescribes specific ritual interventions. This sūtra passage seems to have been a popular medieval text for knowing about deathbed signs. A
copy of it accompanies one extant transcription of Jichihan's *Byōchū shugyōki* (see Ōtani,
"Jichihan *Byōchu shugyōki* ni tsuite," 44). It is also cited by Nichiren (1222–1282) in a passage dealing with the interpretation of corporeal signs at the time of death ("Myōhō-ama
gozen gohenji," *Shōwa teihon Nichiren Shōnin ibun*, ed. Risshō Daigaku Nichiren Kyōgaku
Kenkyūjo [Minobu, Yamanashi prefecture: Minobusan Kuonji, 1952–1959; rev. 1988],
2:1535), and by Ryōchū, in his *Jōdo taii shō*, *JZ* 10:720–721.

76   This is specified in both sets of extant regulations for the Society, the 986 *Kishō hachikajō*
(article 2), and the 988 *Yokawa Shuryōgon'in nijūgo zanmai kishō* (article 4). See Koyama,
"Tōdaiji Chūshōin shozō 'Yokawa Shuryōgon'in nijūgo zanmai Eshin Yasutane rinjū gyōgi'
no saikentō," 86–87 and 76. The use in Japan of mantrically empowered sand in funerary
practices dates back at least to the ninth century and, as described in Mariko Walter's
Chapter 7 in this volume, still figures in Tendai and Shingon funerals today.

"In most cases, the fact that people achieve their aspiration for the Pure Land is due solely to the ability of the *zenchishiki*."[77]

5 Criticism of Deathbed Rites

Despite a growing interest during the medieval period in deathbed ritual, not all Buddhists endorsed such practices. Occasionally, criticism was raised, usually on doctrinal grounds. For example, the Shingon monk Kakukai (1142–1223) suggests that, for Buddhists, who should understand the emptiness and nonduality of all things, there is something improperly self-obsessed about fixing one's aspirations on a particular postmortem destination:

> When we calmly contemplate the arising and perishing of the dharmas, we cannot be attached to [Maitreya's] Heaven of Satisfaction, nor to [Amida's Pure Land of] Utmost Bliss…. If we simply purify the mind, we shall feel no distress, even if we should assume the forms of such [lowly] creatures as dragons and *yakṣas*…. Our partiality for the human form and our bias against the strange forms of other creatures are due to our lack of understanding. Regardless of transmigration, we shall suffer no discomfort….[78]

This position leads Kakukai to criticize the practice of relying on a *zenchishiki* in one's last moments:

> The circumstances of our final moments are by no means known to others, and even good friends (*zenchishiki*) will be of no assistance. Since one's own and others minds are separate, even if they perform the same contemplation, another's thinking is likely to differ from one's own. And as for those whose thought differs from one's own, it would be better not to have them around [in one's last moments]…. I think it is quite splendid to die as did the likes of [the recluse] Gochibō, abiding in a correct state of mind with his final moments unknown to any others.[79]

---

77 *DNBZ* 43:28a.

78 *Kakukai Hōkyō hōgo, Kana hōgoshū*, NKBT 83, ed. Miyasaka Yūshō (Tokyo: Iwanami Shoten, 1964), 57; trans. from Robert E. Morrell, *Early Kamakura Buddhism: A Minority Report* (Berkeley: Asian Humanities Press, 1987), 99–100, slightly modified.

79 *Kakukai Hōkyō hōgo*, NKBT 83:57; trans. from Morrell, *Early Kamakura Buddhism*, 100, slightly modified. The ascetic Gochi-bō Yūgen was a relative and disciple of Kakuban. He practiced in reclusion on Mt. Kōya, and there is indeed no record of his final moments.

DEATHBED RITUAL PRACTICES 209

In his later years, Hōnen (1133–1212), founder of the exclusive *nenbutsu* movement, also minimized the need for the presence of a *zenchishiki*. Where Kakukai had objected to the false discrimination and lingering self-attachment implicit in attempts to control one's last moments to soteric advantage, Hōnen saw reliance on the *zenchishiki*'s assistance as potentially undermining the devotee's trust in the vow of Amida and in the power of the *nenbutsu* that he or she had been chanting even in ordinary times. In a letter to a daughter of the retired emperor Go-Shirakawa, declining to act as *zenchishiki* at her deathbed, Hōnen admonished, "You should abandon the thought of an ordinary person (*bonbu*) as your good friend, and instead rely on the Buddha as your *zenchishiki*.... Who would [be so foolish as to] relax one's reliance on the Buddha and turn [instead] to a worthless, ordinary *zenchishiki*, thinking slightingly of the *nenbutsu* one has chanted all along and praying only for right thoughts at the last moment? It would be a grave error!"[80] Hōnen did not reject the *zenchishiki*'s presence at the deathbed, and at times even encouraged it, but did not see it as indispensable. "Because of the *nenbutsu* that you have chanted all along, even without a *zenchishiki* in your last hours, the Buddha will come to welcome you."[81] Such statements are consistent with Hōnen's position that birth in the Pure Land comes about through wholehearted reliance on the "other power" (*tariki*) of the Buddha Amida, rather than the virtue of one's own efforts (*jiriki*), and that only the *nenbutsu* is the practice according with Amida's original vow. Thus for Hōnen, while the chanting of *nenbutsu* in one's last moments remained vital, it was understood as an extension of one's ordinary practice and did not necessarily require a *zenchishiki*'s ritual assistance. A more radical view was taken by Hōnen's disciple Shinran (1173–1262), who is often said to have carried Hōnen's emphasis on salvation solely through reliance on Amida to its ultimate conclusion. Shinran understood the certainty of salvation as occurring, not at the moment of death, when one would achieve birth in the Pure Land, but at the moment when, casting off all egoistic reliance on one's own virtues and entrusting oneself wholly to Amida, one is seized by the Buddha's compassion, never to be let go, and faith arises in one's heart. This led him to reject the need for deathbed practices altogether. "When faith is established, one's attainment of the Pure Land is also established; there is no need for deathbed rituals to prepare one for Amida's coming," Shinran

---

80 "Shōnyo-bō e tsukawasu onfumi," *HSZ* 545–546.

81 *Ōjō jōdo yōjin*, *HSZ* 562. See also the discussion of Hōnen's views of the last moment in his biography *Enkō Daishi gyōjō ezu yokusan*, *JZ* 16:372–376; in English, see Harper Havelock Coates and Ryugaku Ishizuka, *Honen the Buddhist Saint: His Life and Teaching* (Kyoto: Chionin, 1925), 438–441.

wrote. He also said, "Those whose faith is not yet established are the ones who await Amida's coming at the time of death."[82]

Criticism of deathbed ritual, like deathbed ritual itself, crossed sectarian lines; critics were to be found both among established traditions and new movements. These remained largely isolated objections and did not harden into sectarian positions. For example, despite Hōnen's own admonitions against relying on a *zenchishiki* rather than Amida, some of Hōnen's immediate and second-generation disciples understood the presence of a *zenchishiki* at the deathbed as absolutely essential. Benchō (a.k.a. Ben'a or Shōkō, 1162–1238), the second patriarch of the Pure Land sect, even wrote, "At the time of death, practitioners of the exclusive *nenbutsu* (*ikkō*) should make use of a *zenchishiki*. This is what Hōnen Shōnin instructed."[83] And Benchō's disciple Ryōchū, as we have seen, was the author of the detailed deathbed instruction manual *Kanbyō yōjinshō*, emphasizing the importance of the *zenchishiki* in one's last hours. Despite occasional criticism from individuals in the Kamakura period and later, formal deathbed practices, including the employment of *zenchishiki* as ritual specialists, spread beyond monastic and aristocratic circles to reach a wider social range.

6   Who Were the *zenchishiki*? Some Preliminary Findings

Genshin's instructions for deathbed contemplation in *Ōjō yōshū* assume a monastic context; as we have seen, the sort of practices he recommends were first formally instituted within the Nijūgo zanmai-e, a society of renunciates. By the eleventh century, however, such practices were being adopted in aristocratic circles, and court diaries sometimes record the name of the cleric or adept summoned to act as *zenchishiki* for a particular noble. Who were these monks who served as deathbed attendants? Can we generalize in any way about their position in the monastic world, or about the social location of those who sought their services? While further research is needed, some tentative conclusions may nonetheless be proposed.

Court diaries suggest that, while monks who held temple administrative positions or high rank in the Bureau of Monastic Affairs (Sōgō) might occasionally perform deathbed rites for family members or aristocratic patrons, those monks summoned repeatedly to perform this service for court nobles tended

---

82   *Mattōshō* 1 and 18, *Shinran chosaku zenshū*, ed. Kaneko Daiei (Tokyo: Daizō Shuppan, 1964), 580, 608.

83   *Shōkō-bō ni shimesarekeru onkotoba* 17, HSZ 747.

DEATHBED RITUAL PRACTICES   211

not to be part of the ecclesiastical hierarchy but were rather ascetics or semi-reclusive monks, sometimes based at *bessho*, literally "places apart," retreats often affiliated with leading monasteries but on their outskirts or in other locations altogether. Referred to variously by such titles as *hijiri* ("holy man"), *shōnin* ("holy man"), or *ajari* (esoteric master), these monks were often *nenbutsu* practitioners and also skilled in esoteric rites; frequently they seem to have enjoyed a reputation for exceptional ascetic practice, spiritual attainments, or thaumaturgical powers.[84] Several such adepts find mention, for example, in *Gyokuyō*, the diary of the regent Kujō Kanezane (1149–1207). These include Honjō-bō Tankyō (or Honshō-bō Tangō, n.d.), of the Ōhara *bessho*, who served as *zenchishiki* at the deathbed of Kanezane's elder sister, the former imperial consort Kōkamon'in.[85] In 1185, when the Taira were defeated by the Minamoto, Tankyō acted as *zenchishiki* to both Taira no Munemori and his son Kiyomune, preaching to them before they were beheaded, an episode poignantly related in *Tale of the Heike*.[86] According to the historical record *Azuma kagami* (Mirror of the East), it was reported that "both took refuge in [Tankyō] Shōnin's preaching and gave up all thought of resentment, dwelling in aspiration for the Pure Land."[87] In this case, Tankyō as *zenchishiki* would have been responsible for ensuring that these defeated Taira leaders did not depart this life bearing grudges that could transform them into dangerous vengeful ghosts. Tankyō also provided his ritual services at the death of retired emperor Go-Shirakawa in 1192.[88] Another example is the adept Chizen, a *Lotus Sūtra* devotee (*jikyōsha*) also versed in the esoteric rites of Fudō Myōō, who served as a ritualist to Kanezane and his family.[89] In 1186, for example, he prayed for Kanezane's consort to recover from illness, using the *senju darani* (dhāraṇī of the thousand-armed

---

84   On the importance to the nobility of practitioners of this kind, see, for example, Hayami Tasuku, *Heian kizoku shakai to bukkyō* (Tokyo: Yoshikawa Kōbunkan, 1975), 147–154.

85   *Gyokuyō*, Yōwa 1 (1181), 12/1–4. Kanezane records that he and Tankyō chanted the *nenbutsu* with her, while an unidentified "repentance rite monk" (*senbōsō*) was summoned to chant from the other side of a screen. Sonchū Sōzu, Kōkamon'in's half-brother, was also present at her side, reciting the Fudō mantra (12/4). The following year, Tankyō led a memorial service for Kōkamon'in; on that occasion, Kanezane referred to him as having acted as her *zenchishiki* (*Gyokuyō*, Juei 1 [1182], 11/18). See Gyokuyō, ed., Imaizumi Teisuke, 3 vols. [Tokyo: Kokusho Kankōkai, 1906–1907], 2:539–540, 581).

86   *Heike monogatari*, vol. 2, *NKBT* 33:368–371; McCullough, *Tale of the Heike*, 395–397.

87   Genryaku 2 (1185), 6/21, *KT* 32:161.1.

88   Gyokuyō, Kenkyū 3 (1192), 3/13, 3:798. Kanezane records that Tankyō acted as *zenchishiki*, together with Ninnaji-no-miya Shōken Sōjō (Shukaku, 1150–1202), who was Go-Shirakawa's second son. *Azuma kagami* mentions only Tankyō, who is referred to as Ōhara Honjō-bō Shōnin (Kenkyū 3, 3/16, *KT* 32:461–462).

89   See Kikuchi Hiroki, "Go-Shirakawa inseiki no ōken to jikyōsha," *Meigetsuki kenkyū* 4 (1999): 165–184 (172–177).

Kannon).[90] An accomplished mountain ascetic, he also made the Kumano pilgrimage on Kanezane's behalf on multiple occasions.[91] Chizen served in 1176 as *zenchishiki* at the death of Kanezane's father and was also summoned at the death of his son.[92] Still other examples include Ashō-bō Inzei (or Insai, n.d.), known as the "*hijiri* of Chōrakuji," a temple in the Higashiyama area, who attended the deathbed of the retired emperor Takakura (d. 1181),[93] and the esoteric adept and *nenbutsu* monk Butsugon, who, like Chizen, served as preceptor, ritualist, and healer to Kanezane's family. Butsugon acted as *zenchishiki* at the deathbed of Kanezane's former wet-nurse, Mikushige-dono (d. 1171), and was among the monks summoned when Kanezane's son died suddenly, administering the precepts to him posthumously.[94]

As these examples suggest, monks who served the nobility as deathbed *zenchishiki* tended to be the same individuals who also provided them with prayers for safe childbirth and recovery from illness, who conducted exorcisms, conferred the precepts, and carried out memorial rites. In short, in court circles, by the end of the twelfth century, attendance as *zenchishiki* at the deathbed had joined the many ritual services that such monks typically performed for their highborn clients.

In another pattern, also datable to around the twelfth century, we find monks living in *bessho* or other mountain temples outside the capital who received dying patrons into their chapels, assisting their deathbed rites and sometimes also performing their funeral and seeing to the disposal of the body.[95] In one *ōjōden* account, shortly before his death, the former governor of Shinano, Fujiwara no Nagakiyo (1031–1096), speaks to his brother, the scholar-monk Gyōken, and announces his intention to die in the lodging temple of a "meditation monk" (*zensō*) of Sōrinji, with whom he had made a prior arrangement to this effect. This monk, he says, has also agreed to handle his burial."[96] Significantly, Nagakiyo turns for this purpose, not to his brother, a scholar-monk following the clerical career track culminating in appointment to the

---

90 *Gyokuyō*, Bunji 2, 4/19, 3:188.

91 Kikuchi, "Go-Shirakawa inseiki no ōken to jikyōsha," 174–176.

92 *Gyokuyō*, Angen 2 (1176), 3/23, 1:564, and Bunji 4 (1188), 2/19–20, 3:499.

93 *Gyokuyō*, Jishō 5, 1/12, 2:464. On Inzei, see Ōtsuka Ayako, "Kenreimon'in Tokushi no kaishi Inzei ni tsuite," *Bukkyō bungaku* 15 (1991): 65–78, and Muramatsu Kiyomichi, "Ashō-bō Inzei ni tsuite," *Taishō Daigaku Sōgō Bukkyō Kenkyūjo nenpō* (1993): 61–79.

94 *Gyokuyō*, Shōan 1, 7/20, 1:157, and Bunji 4, 2/19–20, 3:499–500. On Butsugon, see also Sakagami Masao, "Butsugon-bō Shōshin ni tsuite," *Bukkyō ronso* 26 (1982): 145–149.

95 On monks ritually "opening" cemeteries and making them accessible to aristocratic patrons, see Katsuda Itaru, *Shishatachi no chūsei* (Tokyo: Yoshikawa Kōbunkan, 2003), 166–168.

96 *Shūi ōjōden* 11:17, *ZNBS* 1:337.

DEATHBED RITUAL PRACTICES 213

Bureau of Monastic Affairs, but to a *zensō* or "meditation monk." Funaoka Makoto has identified such *zensō* as monks committed primarily to practice or ascetic disciplines (including but not necessarily confined to "meditation"), as opposed to the elite *gakuryo*, or scholar-monks. They were outside the status system of official monastic posts and appear to have overlapped the category of *bessho hijiri*, or monks practicing at retreats affiliated with but outside the major temples. Sōrinji, where Nagakiyo went to die, is said to have been a *bessho* belonging to the Tendai school and was located in Higashiyama, near the charnel grounds on the eastern edge of the capital. Both *zensō* and *bessho hijiri* also appear to have performed deathbed and funerary rites for a range of clients. It was because of pollution issues, Funaoka argues, that monks such as these, rather than career-track scholar-monks holding official clerical appointments, came to specialize in death-related ritual services, including deathbed practices and funerals.[97] Among those monks with aristocratic ties, the categories of *hijiri* and scholar-monk occasionally overlapped; for example, the adept Butsugon, mentioned above, was at one point the head of instruction (*gakutō*) for the Daidenbōin cloister at the Shingon monastery at Mt. Kōya.[98] Nonetheless, Funaoka's distinction is a helpful one. Monks engaged in rites for nation protection had to observe the same strictures of pollution avoidance observed in worship of the *kami* or local deities, including an exorcistic period of purification (*imi*), usually thirty days, following the performance of funerals or other contact with death. Thus it was often monks outside the system of official temple posts or the scholastic career track culminating in Sōgō appointments who assumed the major responsibility for deathbed and funerary ritual.[99]

Outside monastic settings, deathbed practices spread first among the nobility. In particular, the more elaborate forms of deathbed rites, involving multiple ritual specialists, were probably confined to elite circles. To have had three or four *zenchishiki* in attendance—as Kakuban recommends—for "a day, two days, a week, or as long as necessary until death transpires" would

---

97   *Nihon Zenshū no seiritsu* (Tokyo: Yoshikawa Kōbunkan, 1987), esp. 90–94.

98   *Kōyasan ōjōden* 13, *ZNBS* 1:700. See also "Kaisetsu," 758.

99   On pollution taboos at major Buddhist temples and ceremonies, see, for example, Taira Masayuki, "Sesshō kindan no rekishiteki tenkai," in *Nihon shakai no shiteki kōzō: Kodai, chūsei*, ed. Ōyama Kyōhei Kyōju Taikan Kinenkai (Kyoto: Shibunkaku, 1997), 149–171 (151–153). On monks without formal clerical appointments as the primary purveyors of death-related practices in the Heian period, see Stone, "The Dying Breath," esp. 203–206; and Uejima Susumu, "'Ō' no shi to sōsō: Kegare to gakuryo, hijiri, zenshū," *Kōkogaku to chūseishi kenkyū* 4: *Chūsei jiin: Bōryoku to keikan*, ed. Ono Masatoshi, Gomi Fumihiko, and Hagiwara Mitsuo (Tokyo: Kōshi Shoin, 2007), 127–163.

have required considerable financial outlay. *Kōyōshū* addresses the economics of such arrangements, where it says, "The presence of appropriate persons should be arranged in advance, and they should always be given donations and treated courteously, in recompense for their assistance at the time of death."[100] Clearly, this would have been beyond the means of many people. Nonetheless, if we go by the evidence of *ōjōden* and *setsuwa*, even persons of very low status occasionally appear to have engaged in simple forms of ritualized deathbed practice, assisted by a *zenchishiki*. The early Kamakura-period tale collection *Senjūshō*, for example, tells of a lowly monk of Sagami who tends to a destitute widow when she falls ill. He begs for money and food for her care and teaches her to chant the *nenbutsu*, thus presumably enabling her to achieve *ōjō*.[101]

As Imai Masaharu has noted, by the mid-Kakamura period, high-ranking warriors had begun to adopt formal deathbed ritual as part of a broader appropriation of aristocratic culture.[102] Yoshitoki (d. 1224), the second Hōjō regent, had at his deathbed the assistance of a *zenchishiki* identified as Tango Risshi, who encouraged him in chanting the *nenbutsu*.[103] However, warrior appropriation of deathbed practices and the rhetoric surrounding them also exacerbated fears about the karmic hindrances of warriors as "evil men" (*akunin*). Jonathan Todd Brown has shed light on how Ta'amidabutsu Shinkyō (1237–1319), successor to Ippen as leader of the Jishū, skillfully secured this fledgling movement an institutional base among the *bushi* of the eastern provinces by emphasizing how hard it is for those professionally engaged in the sin of killing to reach the Pure Land, and thus the immense benefits to be gained by any warrior who supported a local Jishū practice hall, thus ensuring himself the presence of a *chishiki* in his last hours.[104] In time of armed conflict, warriors also had to be concerned about the dangers of being struck down on the battlefield

---

100   *DNBZ* 43:27b. This represents a rare reference in *rinjū gyōgi* texts to the financing of deathbed rites.

101   *Senjūshō* VII:3, *Senjūshō zenchūshaku*, ed. Senjūshō Kankōkai, 2 vols. (Tokyo: Kasama Shoin, 2003), 204–210.

102   *Chūsei shakai to Jishū no kenkyū* (Tokyo: Yoshikawa Kōbunkan, 1985), 357–358. Imai suggests in this regard that in *Tale of the Heike* one sign of aristocratic influence on the Taira clan is their desire to employ *zenchishiki* at the end. The most famous instance is of course that of Taira no Koremori, who in his determination to escape the realm of rebirth, drowns himself in the sea off Kumano. He has the novice Takiguchi Nyūdō accompany him in the boat and preach to him on the futility of worldly attachments and the certainty of Amida's salvation (*Heike monogatari*, vol. 2, *NKBT* 33:280–284; McCullough, *Tale of the Heike*, 348–350).

103   *Azuma kagami*, Gennin 1, 6/13, *KT* 33:18.

104   Jonathan Todd Brown, "Warrior Patronage, Institutional Change, and Doctrinal Innovation in the Early Jishū" (Ph.D. diss., Princeton University, 1999), esp. 198–210, 401–407.

DEATHBED RITUAL PRACTICES 215

by swords or arrows with no chance to think of the Buddha or to invoke his name. This led, in later medieval times, to the institution of "camp priests" (*jinsō*), who accompanied their warrior patrons to the battlefield and, in advance of the fighting, literally "conferred [on them] the ten *nenbutsu*." This meant chanting "*Namu Amida butsu*" ten times on a single outbreath—that is, a performance of an ideal death that was ritually conferred by the monk on his patron in a truncated but nonetheless obvious extension of the *zenchishiki*'s deathbed role.[105]

Was the *zenchishiki* necessarily a monk? Most commonly, yes, and especially where specialized prayer rites were sought, such as those stipulated by Kakuban to save a dying or newly deceased person from the evil realms, the services of a learned cleric or adept would have been required. But lay people may in some cases have played a role. *Kōyōshū* observes that "it is undesirable to have a lot of people around [at the deathbed] who are without understanding. Even if those present are monks, if they lack understanding and mill about, it will not be good. But even lay people should not be excluded if they understand what to do."[106] Outside monastic communities, where the dying person was a well-to-do lay patron, it seems probable that other lay persons may have assisted the *zenchishiki* in a nursing capacity, even if they did not have major ritual responsibilities. It is also possible that, within medieval *nenbutsu* associations (*kessha*) that included lay followers, lay people may have encouraged one another's *nenbutsu* chanting in their last hours, although determining this would require further research. To what extent women may have served as *zenchishiki* at the deathbed also requires further investigation. Medieval *rinjū gyōgi* texts do not address this issue explicitly but often presume a male viewpoint, such as Ryōchū's *Kanbyō yōjinshō*, which admonishes, "Apart from two or three *chishiki* and nurses (*kanbyō*), others should not be permitted access [to the dying person], whether they are intimates or strangers. Above all, his wife and children should not be allowed to approach."[107] Here the issue is not the fitness of women to serve as *zenchishiki* but the need to avoid arousing thoughts of attachment in the dying person. In literary sources it is almost always women who are represented as hindering the deathbed contemplations

---

105 On the battlefield practice of Jishū clerics, see Imai Masaharu, *Chūsei shakai to Jishū no kenkyū*, 365–378; Ōhashi Shunnō, *Ippen to Jishū kyōdan* (Tokyo: Kyōikusha, 1978), 143–151; Sybil Anne Thorton, "Propaganda Traditions of the Yugyō Ha: The Campaign to Establish the Jishū as an Independent School of Japanese Buddhism (1300–1700)" (Ph.D. diss., University of Cambridge, 1988), 76–111; and Brown, "Warrior Patronage, Institutional Change, and Doctrinal Innovation in the Early Jishū," 444–450.

106 *DNBZ* 43:27b–c.

107 In Itō, *Jōdokyō bunkashi kenkyū*, 448.

of men, and not the other way around.[108] Nonetheless, a few scattered references in premodern sources show that women occasionally assisted ritually at the deathbed. Following the death of his consort in 1002, the courtier Fujiwara no Yukinari recorded in his diary that she had been attended in her last hours by himself and by the nun Shakuju, with whom she had a prior agreement.[109] Nishiguchi Junko has noted an instance in which two Jishū nuns in Kyoto, Kyōbutsu-bō and Gyōichi-bō, served in 1345 as *zenchishiki* at the deathbed of Zenni Kenshin, the widow of Nakabara Morosuke; these nuns may originally have been members of the Nakabara house, which would suggest that nuns may have assisted female family members in this capacity.[110] By the early modern period, however, we find explicit prescriptions against women serving in the *zenchishiki* role. A manual for deathbed practice by the eighteenth-century monk Jikū (a.k.a. Shōken, 1646–1719), reads, "If he has the *bodhi* mind, anyone who can be of aid to the sick person should be permitted and employed [to serve as *zenchishiki*], even a man's own son. But a woman, even if she has faith, should never be so employed. This is because she is the source of the impurity of birth."[111] Such admonitions are not uncommon in *rinjū gyōgi* texts of Jikū's time and would seem to reflect increased fears about the polluting nature of female biological processes that emerged in the late medieval and early modern periods, as discussed in Hank Glassman's essay, Chapter 5 in this volume.[112]

Ōjō yōshū and other Heian-period instructions for deathbed practice are written in Sino-Japanese (*kanbun*). But beginning with Ryōchū's *Kanbyō yōjinshō* in the latter Kamakura period, such deathbed manuals tend increasingly to be written in the more accessible Japanese *kana majiri bun*. *Kōyōshū*

---

108 See, for example, *Hosshinshū* IV:5, Miki, *Hōjōki, Hosshinshū, 176–179*, and Shasekishū, IV: 5 and IV:6, *NKBT* 85, ed. Watanabe Tsunaya (Tokyo: Iwanami Shoten, 1966), 188–190; trans. Robert E. Morrell, *Sand and Pebbles (Shasekishū): The Tales of Mujū Ichien, A Voice for Pluralism in Kamakura Buddhism* (Albany: State University of New York Press, 1985), 146–147.

109 *Gonki* 1, *Chōhō* 4, 10/16, *ST* 4:274.

110 *Shishuki*, cited in Nichiguchi Junko, "Josei to mōja kinichi kuyō," in *Hotoke to onna*, ed. Nichiguchi Junko (Tokyo: Yoshikawa Kōbunkan, 1997), 219–246 (234–236).

111 *Rinjū setsuyō*, in *Rinjū gyōgi: Nihonteki tāminaru kea no genten*, ed. Kamii Monshō et al. (Tokyo: Hokushindō, 1993; rpt. 1995), 168–169.

112 However, some instances from early modern *ōjōden* suggest that such injunctions were not always observed. For example, the pious Kintarō (d. 1860), third son of Fujiya Jūemon of Okazaki in Nukada village, Mikawa province, who died at age seventeen, requested that his grandmother, the nun Jōryō, act as his *zenchishiki* (*Mikawa ōjō kenki* 1, in *Kinsei ōjōden shūsei*, ed. Kasahara Kazuo, 3 vols. [Tokyo: Yamakawa Shuppan, 1978–1980], 1:359–360). It is not clear whether elderly women, especially nuns, would have been considered free from female pollution or whether such cases simply illustrate a gap between prescriptive standards and on-the-ground practice.

DEATHBED RITUAL PRACTICES 217

cites passages from Chinese scripture and then immediately explains their meaning in Japanese, suggesting that its instructions were addressed to less highly educated ritualists than were earlier manuals of this kind. In the Tokugawa or early modern period (1603–1868), as described in Chapter 6, by Duncan Williams, Buddhist temples were incorporated into the shogunal apparatus of social control, and families were required to affiliate with a local Buddhist temple that performed their funerals and memorial rites and also often housed their family graves. At this time, deathbed practices seem to have joined the standard repertoire of death-related practices that came to constitute the major social role, and economic base, of Buddhist temples. For example, a diary kept by the priest Ankokuin Nichikō (1626–1698) of the Nichiren sect contains such entries as: "Having heard that [our parishioner] Kinmaro's present illness had suddenly worsened, I sent my disciple Heiroku Mon'ya to encourage him in the essentials for practice at the time of death, and at the earnest request [of his family], I inscribed a *honzon* [object of worship; in this case, the calligraphic mandala of the Nichiren sect] to be placed in the coffin."[113] Early modern *ōjōden*, revived as a genre following the publication in printed editions of their Heian precursors, also suggest that deathbed ritual, along with funerals and mortuary rites, may have become one of the standard ritual services provided by local temples. The devout men and women of these early modern hagiographies are frequently depicted as having the assistance of a priest or spiritual adviser in their last hours.[114] By this point, however, the *zenchishiki*'s role was no longer performed chiefly by *hijiri* or other semi-reclusive adepts but had become a routine religious activity of village priests.

7   In Conclusion: a Note on Early Modern Instructions for Deathbed Practice

As deathbed practices joined the standard repertoire of ritual services offered by local priests to their parishioners in the Tokugawa period, one notes also a corresponding routinization in the performance of these practices. Early modern *rinjū gyōgi* texts cite extensively from their medieval precursors but contain few innovations in the treatment of the dying per se; on the whole, they

---

113   *Setsumoku nikka*, Jōkyō 3 (1686), 4/8, *Nichirenshū shūgaku zensho*, ed. Risshō Daigaku Nichiren Kyōgaku Kenkyūjo, 23 vols. (Tokyo: Sankibō Busshorin, 1968–1978), 12:389.

114   For deathbed practice as reflected in early modern *ōjōden* and other sources, see, for example, *Nihon bukkyō* 39 (1976): *Tokushū: Kinsei ōjōden*; Hasegawa Masatoshi, *Kinsei nenbutsusha shūdan no kōdō to shisō: Jōdoshū no baai* (Tokyo: Hyōronsha, 1981), 186–198; and Kamii et al., *Rinjū gyōgi*, 435–463.

218   STONE

seem much less concerned than earlier works of this kind with the details of
how to fend off demonic influences, interpret deathbed visions, or accurately
gauge the moment of the last breath. This may hint indirectly at shifts in the
funerary practice of this era, whose development in Sōtō Zen is discussed by
Williams in Chapter 6 in this volume. The early modern Buddhist funeral was
understood not merely as transferring merit to the deceased to aid that person
in the next life, but as actually effecting his or her enlightenment or birth in the
Pure Land. Since the funeral proper had assumed such overriding soteriological importance and would in most cases be performed by the same priest who
acted as *zenchishiki* at the time of death, there may no longer have been the
same perceived need to assess continually the portents manifested during the
deathbed rite.

What does stand out as new in these early modern *rinjū gyōgisho* is a heightened attention to the treatment of the body after death and its preparation
for burial, something rarely addressed in medieval deathbed ritual texts. This
too may reflect shifts in Tokugawa Buddhist funerary practice. Premodern funerary rites—except for rituals accompanying cremation or the installation
of remains—were usually conducted without the body of the deceased being
present, but in the early modern funeral, the corpse held a position of central ritual focus.[115] Tokugawa-period *rinjū gyōgi* texts often warn, for example,
against touching the body while it is still warm (considered a sign that consciousness is still present), which is said to cause intolerable pain. To place a
corpse while still warm in the coffin is equivalent to murder. *Chiyo migusa*, a
seventeenth-century text of deathbed instructions in the Nichiren sect, strictly admonishes against touching the body for ten to twelve hours after death.
"After twelve hours, you may wash [the body] and place it in the coffin."[116] The
Shingon monk Jōkū (1693–1775) recommends forty-eight hours as the proper
period to wait before encoffining. Like the authors of other Tokugawa-period
deathbed instructions, Jōkū strictly enjoins against bending the limbs of a
newly dead person to facilitate burial; instead, pouring a small amount of
mantrically empowered sand into the mouth or on the chest of the corpse will
prevent rigor mortis.[117] These admonitions are echoed by the Pure Land monk
Jikū, mentioned above, who also comments on the sin of preparing a body for

---

115   William M. Bodiford, *Sōtō Zen in Medieval Japan* (Honolulu: University of Hawai'i Press,
       1993), 185–186.
116   *Kinsei bukkyō no shisō*, NST 57, ed. Kashiwabara Yūsen and Fujii Manabu (Tokyo: Iwanami
       Shoten, 1973), 449. The text has "five or six hours," one "hour" corresponding to one of the
       twelve divisions of the day. The *Rinjū no yōi*, attributed to Jōkei, also gives this same warn-
       ing as "an admonition of people of old" (*Nihon daizōkyō* 64:26b). See n. 67 above.
117   *Jōbutsu jishin*, SAZ 2:828–829.

DEATHBED RITUAL PRACTICES   219

burial while it is still warm. "If the body's warmth has not yet dissipated, that means the *ālaya* consciousness has not departed. When you hurt the body [before consciousness has departed,] that becomes the karma of taking life. And if it is your parent, you commit the sin of killing a parent. This is absolutely to be avoided."[118] Jikū additionally voices opposition to a number of mortuary practices current in his day, such as use of the *kyō katabira*, a robe for wrapping the body on which sūtras, mantras, or other holy texts have been inscribed, or placing the body before the Buddhist altar prior to burial as though it were an offering. The corpse should be screened from the altar because of its impurity.[119] Kaen (1693–1780), also of the Pure Land sect, additionally criticizes the contemporary practice of arranging the corpse in a formal pose to suggest an ideal death: "What value is there in placing the body [in the nirvāṇa position] with the head to the north and facing west? Some people have the hands of the deceased hold a cord or banner [tied to the hand of the buddha image], even after the spirit has departed. This is like closing the gates after the robbers have left. And as for making the deceased hold a rosary: a rosary is a Buddhist implement for counting the *nenbutsu* [recited by living practitioners]. What merit is there in having a corpse hold one?"[120] Kaen's criticisms not only reflect the attention paid to the body in Tokugawa-period *rinjū gyōgi* texts but also suggest that specific bodily postures originally recommended as proper conduct for the dying (such as facing west or holding a rosary) were being transposed to the postmortem arrangement of the corpse.

As described in *Ōjō yōshū*, deathbed practice is a contemplation performed by dying persons to focus their last thoughts and thus achieve birth in the Pure Land, forever escaping the cycle of samsaric rebirth. For Genshin, the dying are the primary agents of their own liberation: the attendants' responsibility is merely one of encouragement. Sustaining "right thoughts at the last moment," however, is an extremely demanding goal, even for those trained in meditation; proper mental focus at the time of death could all too easily be subverted by physical pain; by fears, regrets, and emotional attachments; or by loss of consciousness. Especially as deathbed rites spread outside monastic circles and began to be performed as a religious service for lay persons, the role of the *zenchishiki* began to shift from an ancillary one to that of primary ritualist, a shift that, over time, increasingly strengthened the continuity between deathbed practice and funerary rites. In the development of instructions for deathbed practice from *Ōjō yōshū* in the late tenth century up through early modern

---

118   *Rinjū setsuyō*, in Kamii et al., *Rinjū gyōgi*, 170.
119   Ibid., 166, 170.
120   *Rinjū yōjin*, in Kamii et al., *Rinjū gyōgi*, 211–212.

times, one can trace a gradual process in which attempts to positively affect one's postmortem state by ritual means shifted first from the dying individual's own practice to the actions of the *zenchishiki,* and then from the salvific power of deathbed practice to increasing emphasis on that of funerary and mortuary rites. Although not all monks of the Heian and Kamakura periods routinely engaged in such activities, the emergence of the *zenchishiki* as a deathbed specialist represents a significant step in the larger process by which Buddhist monks came to dominate the performance of death-related practices.

PART 3

Turn to the Nembutsu as the Sole Solution

Hōnen on Attaining Pure Land Rebirth: the Selected Nenbutsu of the Original Vow

Allan A. Andrews

1 Hōnen in the History of East Asian Pure Land Buddhism

Perceived from the perspective of the development of the Pure Land tradition in East Asia, Hōnen (1133–1212) is situated at an important juncture. Not only did he introduce Shandao's populist Pure Land thought to Japan, he also contributed to the transformation of continental forms of Pure Land Buddhism into distinctly Japanese forms.[1] Institutional Pure Land Buddhism in Japan prior to Hōnen was based upon continental models—largely monastic and emphasizing contemplative practice; after Hōnen it became entirely a layperson's Buddhism, emphasizing devotion. Thus, a study of Hōnen's Pure Land thought can give us insights into the varieties of Pure Land, both geographically and typologically. We will first characterize Hōnen's position on how to attain Pure Land rebirth and then return to these geographical and typological considerations.

For exploring Hōnen's views we will utilize only fully authenticated works, those either entirely or partially autographed by him.[2] We will rely primarily on his *Passages on the Selected Nenbutsu of the Original Vow* (*Senchaku hongan nenbutsu shū*), but will also utilize the *Seven Article Admonition* (*Shichikajō*

Source: Andrews, Allan A., "Hōnen on Attaining Pure Land Rebirth: The Selected Nenbutsu of the Original Vow," *Pacific World* 6 (2004): 89–107.

---

1 Elements of Shandao's thought had been introduced to Japan prior to Hōnen by Genshin (942–1017) and Yōkan (1033–1111). By "populist" I refer to that Chinese Pure Land tradition that reached its fullest expression in Shandao (613–681) and shaped its teachings to address and guide to liberation the largest number of persons possible, both clergy and laity and of whatever social stratum or spiritual capacity.

2 Only seven or eight texts exist in manuscripts bearing Hōnen's handwriting: the *Senchaku hongan nenbutsu shū*; the *Shichikajō seikai*; the letter to Kumagae Naozane dated second day, fifth month; three partial letters to Shōgyōbō, undated; a single line of text and Hōnen's signature on the so-called *Ichigyō ippitsu Amida kyō* (*One-line-one-brush Amitābha Sutra*); and possibly the *Ichimai kishōmon*; see Tōdō Kyōshun and Itō Yuishin, "Hōnen Shōnin shinpitsu ruishū kaisetsu," in *Jōdoshū kaishū happyakunen kinen Hōnen Shōnin Kenkyū*, ed. Bukkyō Daigaku Hōnen Shōnin kenkyūkai (Tokyo: Ryūbunkan, 1975).

seikai) and his letter to Kumagae Naozane dated second day, fifth month.[3] Other texts traditionally attributed to Hōnen may be authentic, but the *Passages* is Hōnen's only comprehensive doctrinal work, and the two other fully authenticated texts we will use contain important statements on practice for rebirth.

2   Hōnen on Attaining Pure Land Rebirth: the Nenbutsu of Calling on the Name

It is widely believed that Hōnen espoused as practice for rebirth "sole nenbutsu" (*senju nenbutsu*, "sole practice nenbutsu"), that is, the exclusive cultivation of vocal nenbutsu. While this assumption is problematic and will be reexamined below, it is true that Hōnen propounded vocal nenbutsu, calling on the name of Amida Buddha, as the best practice for Pure Land rebirth. Hōnen employed two quite different rationales for asserting the superiority of vocal nenbutsu. The first of these he presents in the second chapter of his *Passages on the Selected Nenbutsu of the Original Vow* where he differentiates the "right practices" (*shōgō*) for Pure Land rebirth from ineffective "mixed practices" (*zōgō*), and further differentiates the right practices into the "assured right practice" (*shōjō no gō*) and "assisting right practices" (*jogō*).[4] The right practices are first, reading and reciting the *Amitābha Contemplation Sutra* (*Kan Muryōjuhutsu kyō*),[5] *Amitābha Sutra* (*Amida kyō*), and *Sutra of Limitless Life* (*Muryōju kyō*); second, contemplating (*kanzatsu*) and meditating (*okunen*) on the Pure Land and Amida Buddha; third, venerating Amida; fourth, calling vocally (*kushō*) the name of Amida; and fifth, singing praises and making offerings to that Buddha. Of these, he designates number four, vocal nenbutsu, as the assured right practice, that is, the practice certain to result in Pure Land rebirth because it is in conformity with the practice designated by the eighteenth vow of Amida Buddha.[6] This conformity of vocal nenbutsu to the eighteenth vow involves Hōnen's second rationale, which we will examine shortly.

---

3   Probably written in 1204; see Akamatsu Toshihide, *Zoku Kamakura Bukkyō no kenkyū* (*Further Studies on Kamakura Period Buddhism*; Kyoto: Heirakuji Shoten, 1966), p. 297.

4   Hōnenbō Genkū, *Passages on the Selected Nenbutsu of the Original Vow* (*Senchaku hongan nenbutsu shū/Senchakushū/Senjakushū*, T. 2608), T83.2c.

5   I will not use diacritical marks in words derived from Sanskrit when they occur in titles I have translated into English.

6   This formulation Hōnen obtained from Shandao (*Commentary on the Contemplation Sutra* [*Kuan Wu-liang-shou-fo-ching shu/Kan Muryōjubutsukyō sho*, T. 1753, T37.272a–b]), who derived it from the *Discourse on the Sutra of Limitless Life and Verse in Aspiration for Rebirth* (*Wu-liang-shou-ching yu-p'o-t'i-she yuan-sheng chieh, Muryōjukyō ubadaisha ganshō ge* [also known in Japanese under the abbreviated names: *Ōjō ron* and *Jōdo ron*], * *Sukhāvatīvyūha*

The remaining right practices, that is, those other than calling on the name, are designated by Hōnen as "assisting practices." Although here he does not explain how they assist vocal nenbutsu, in Chapter 4 he calls them "supporting practices" (*jojō*) in that they generate karma that produces the same result as vocal nenbutsu.[7]

As we can see, the right practices are all exclusively Pure Land practices, focusing on Amida or the Pure Land. Any practice directed toward some other buddha, as well as more general practices such as charity (*danna*; Skt. *dāna*) and observance of the Buddhist precepts, are rejected as largely ineffective.

In Chapter 3 of the *Passages* Hōnen presents the second of his two basic rationales for the superiority of nenbutsu. There he claims that calling on the Buddha is the best practice for Pure Land rebirth because it is the practice selected by Amida for his eighteenth bodhisattva vow. The eighteenth is the well known vow of the *Sutra of Limitless Life*, which Hōnen read as promising Pure Land rebirth for all who call on Amida with deep faith ten times or more.[8] Hōnen maintains, moreover, that Amida chose calling on his name as the practice of this vow because the name possesses all of his "ten thousand" karmic merits, or kinds of wholesome karma, which will be acquired by sentient beings who call the name, and because it is an easy practice whereas other practices are difficult. This principle of the ease of the selected practice, nenbutsu, revealed to Hōnen not only the inferior capacity of sentient beings in an age of final dharma (*mappō*), but also the Buddha's soteric intentions. Because of his great compassion Amida sought to bring about the universal, egalitarian salvation of all sentient beings of whatever ability, merit, station, or gender. "And thus was it not," Hōnen asks, "for the purpose of equally and universally (*byōdō*) bringing about the rebirth of all sentient beings that the difficult [practices] were rejected and the easy adopted as the [practice] of the original vow?"[9] Thus, vocal nenbutsu is the easy practice endowed with Amida's ten thousand merits guaranteed to make rebirth available to every sentient being.

We should also note that Hōnen explicitly interprets the nenbutsu of this vow as vocal nenbutsu. He does this by identifying the "ten nen" (*jū nen*) of the vow with the "ten nen" in the passage in the *Amitābha Contemplation Sutra* on the rebirth of the very worst of human beings. That well known passage reads,

---

    upadeśa, T. 1542), attributed to Vasubandhu, where these five practices are called the "five gates of buddha-reflection" (*wu nien-men/go nenmon*).

7 Hōnen, *Passages*, T83.7b.

8 Hōnen, *Passages*, T83.4b–6c. The vow is found at T12.268a.

9 Hōnen, *Passages*, T83.5c.

... [he] makes them call (*shō*) without interruption [until they] complete ten nenbutsu (*jū nen*), calling "Namu Amida Butsu."[10]

For Hōnen the "ten nen" of the vow, that is, the selected practice of the vow, was definitely vocal rather than contemplative nenbutsu.

3   Hōnen and "Sole Practice Nenbutsu"

While it is generally thought that Hōnen taught "sole practice nenbutsu" (*senju nenbutsu*), that is, the cultivation of vocal nenbutsu exclusively, this is not supported by his arguments in the *Passages*, nor by any of his fully authenticated writings.[11] First of all, according to his exclusive versus mixed rationale for the superiority of nenbutsu, Pure Land practices other than vocal nenbutsu— such as chanting Pure Land sutras, making offerings to Amida, and meditatively contemplating the physical features of Amida—are called assisting practices, those practices which contribute to bringing about rebirth. Further, Hōnen does not claim that practices other than the "right" practices are entirely ineffective for rebirth. While he maintains that of those who cultivate the mixed practices only one or two out of a hundred will attain Pure Land rebirth,[12] nonetheless, even this ratio would indicate that the mixed practices are effective to some degree. Moreover, in regard to Hōnen's second rationale for the superiority of vocal nenbutsu, in spite of the privileged status that he claims was bestowed upon vocal nenbutsu by the eighteenth vow, he does not therefore entirely reject other practices. Regarding the status of practices not selected by the vow he cites this passage from the Tendai Pure Land classic, *Essentials of Pure Land Rebirth* (*Ōjō yōshū*),

> Question: All good works, each and every one, have their benefits. Each and every one can earn rebirth. Why do you urge only the single dharma-gate of nenbutsu?
>
> Answer: That we now urge nenbutsu does not hinder cultivation of the various other excellent practices. It is just that anyone—man or woman, noble or commoner, whether walking, standing, sitting, or lying, and regardless of time, place, or any other conditions—can cultivate it without

---

10   *Amitābha Contemplation Sutra* (*Fo-shou kuan Wu-liang-shou-fo ching/Bussetsu kan Muryōjubutsu kyō*, T. 365), T12.346a.

11   With the possible exception of the *Ichimai kishōmon*.

12   T47.439b–c.

difficulty. Moreover, there is nothing to equal the convenience of nenbutsu for those seeking rebirth at the time of death.[13]

Thus, even while claiming that vocal nenbutsu is the vow-selected practice, Hōnen agrees with the view of the *Essentials* and does not insist that other practices are useless for achieving rebirth.

Finally, in Chapter 12 of the *Passages* where Hōnen subordinates the practices taught in the *Amitābha Contemplation Sutra* to the nenbutsu of the eighteenth vow, he nonetheless acknowledges that any of the thirteen contemplations of the *Contemplation Sutra* and all of the practices called "three kinds of meritorious conduct" (*sampuku*) set out in that scripture—such as filial piety, observing the precepts, arousing aspiration for enlightenment, and reading and reciting the Mahayana scriptures—can become good karma for rebirth in the Pure Land.[14]

Thus we see that in his major work, the *Passages*, Hōnen does not espouse "sole nenbutsu." As a matter of fact, only once in the *Passages* does he use the term, "sole nenbutsu practice" (*senju nenbutsu*). This is at the end of that work where he praises Shandao, calling him "the guide to sole nenbutsu practice" (*senju nenbutsu no dōshi*).[15]

Yet, in his own times Hōnen certainly had a reputation as a radical teacher of sole practice nenbutsu. For example, the *Kōfukuji Temple Petition* (*Kōfukuji sōjō*) identifies him as the leader of a nenbutsu sect (*nenbutsu no shū*) who promotes the sole practice of the nenbutsu,[16] and the *Miscellany of Foolish Views* (*Gukanshō*) of Jien (1155–1225) claims that Hōnen promoted sole practice nenbutsu.[17] Indeed, Hōnen's statements on this issue were somewhat ambiguous. While he acknowledged the efficacy of practices other than nenbutsu, in his writings he constantly urges the sole or exclusive practice of nenbutsu.

---

13   Hōnen, *Passages*, T83.5c; Genshin, *Ōjōyōshū* (*Essentials for Pure Land Rebirth*, T. 2682), T84.76c.

14   Hōnen, *Passages*, T83.14c–15c.

15   Hōnen, *Passages*, T83.20a.

16   Robert E. Morrell, *Early Kamakura Buddhism: A Minority Report* (Berkeley: Asian Humanities Press, 1987), p. 75; Kamata Shigeo and Tanaka Hisao, eds., *Kamakura kyū-Bukkyō* (*Traditional Kamakura Period Buddhism*; Tokyo: Iwanami Shoten, 1971), p. 32.

17   Delmer M. Brown and Ichirō Ishida, *The Future and the Past: A Translation and Study of the Gukanshō* (Berkeley: University of California Press, 1979), p. 171; Ikawa Jōkei, ed., *Hōnen Shōnin den zenshū* (*The Complete Biographies of Hōnen Shōnin*, rev. ed.; Takaishi, Osaka Pref.: Hōnen Shōnin den zenshū kankōkai, 1967), p. 975.

228   ANDREWS

4   The Quantity of Nenbutsu Required for Rebirth

Another issue concerning Hōnen's teachings on nenbutsu is the quantity of
nenbutsu necessary for Pure Land rebirth. This is a significant issue because
different quantities of nenbutsu imply differences in the way nenbutsu functions to effect rebirth and rebirth for different types of persons. First of all,
Hōnen interprets the number of nenbutsu specified in the eighteenth vow
quite inclusively as any quantity from ten repetitions up to that accumulated
over a lifetime of cultivation, or from ten down to even one calling,[18] while noting that some other interpreters understood it in a much more narrow sense
as exactly ten or as ten or less invocations. In general, however, Hōnen urged
aspirants to produce as many nenbutsu as possible, both on a day-to-day basis
and throughout their lives.

   In Chapter 9 of the *Passages* he specifies that one's Pure Land practices—
presumably the exclusively Pure Land practices set out in Chapter 2—should
be cultivated in a fourfold manner (*shi shuhō*): first, lifelong, second, reveren-
tially, third, exclusively, and fourth, ceaselessly. He singles out the first of these,
lifelong cultivation, as the most important because without it the remaining
three modes would not be consummated.[19] Moreover, this position was not
merely theoretical for Hōnen. Several early biographical texts indicate that
Hōnen himself cultivated an enormous quantity of nenbutsu daily, sixty thousand repetitions or more.[20] And in his letter to Kumagae Naozane, as we will
see below, Hōnen urges Naozane to pursue up to sixty thousand nenbutsu per
day.[21] When we calculate that at the rate of one nenbutsu per second, it would
take sixteen and two-thirds hours to accomplish sixty thousand repetitions,
and we get a sense of the total commitment and enormous amount of exertion
that Hōnen thought necessary to assure entry into the Pure Land.

   Hōnen's view that assurance of rebirth required the generation of as many
nenbutsu as possible over a lifetime was the conventional view of his times, the

---

18   Hōnen, *Passages*, T83.6b21–25.

19   Hōnen, *Passages*, T83.13a–b. The fourfold manner of practice, like many of Hōnen's key
      doctrinal positions, was derived by Hōnen from Shandao (T47.439a7–18), but is not ex-
      clusive to Pure Land piety. It is a general Mahayana prescription for bodhisattva practice
      found, for example, in the *Abhidharmakośa Śastra* (T.1558.29.141), and in Vasubandhu's
      Commentary on the Compendium of the Mahayana (T.1595.31.209), which were modified
      by Shandao to conform to his exclusivistic Pure Land devotionalism.

20   *Chion kōshiki*, Ikawa, *Hōnen Shōnin den zenshū*, p. 1036; and *Sammai hottokuki*, in Ishii
      Kyōdō, ed., *Shōwa shinshū Hōnen Shōnin zenshū* (hereafter Shsz) (Kyoto: Heirakuji Shoten,
      1955), p. 864.

21   Ōhashi Toshio (Shunnō), ed., *Hōnen-Ippen* (*Hōnen and Ippen*; Tokyo: Iwanami Shoten,
      1971), pp. 166–167.

twelfth century, but there were alternative views with important implications. Some of Hōnen's disciples interpreted the *Sutra of Limitless Life* as requiring only one nenbutsu. This can be justified not only by an interpretation of the eighteenth vow's "ten-nenbutsu" passage, but also by the so-called "vow fulfillment passage" of that sutra which promises rebirth to all who produce even one nenbutsu (*ichinen*).[22] The implication of this view is that rebirth is accomplished primarily by faith in Amida and his vow rather than by the good karma generated by many nenbutsu, and further that evil-doers can be reborn by this faith and the power of Amida's vow despite their bad karma. In this interpretation, many repetitions of the nenbutsu can be seen as an attempt to expunge bad karma and thereby through self-effort become worthy of Pure Land rebirth, rather than to utter the nenbutsu but once in reliance upon the Other Power of Amida's compassionate promise in the vow. Varieties of this position were espoused by several of Hōnen's disciples—by Shinran, whose views are well known, and also apparently by others such as Kōsai and Hōhombō Gyōkū.

Either justifiably or unfairly, the teaching on rebirth by just one nenbutsu was associated early on with the radical view called "encouragement of evil conduct" or "unhindered evil" (*zōaku muge*), the notion that one can with impunity violate the Buddhist precepts—for example, against meat-eating and sexual misconduct—because Amida saves in spite of their bad karma those who call on him.[23] In his *Seven Article Admonition* (*Shichikajō seikai*) Hōnen emphatically condemned this distortion of his teachings, without explicitly rejecting, however, the view of rebirth by just one nenbutsu.[24] And in 1206 he expelled from his community of disciples the monk Hōhombō Gyōkū, allegedly for teaching encouragement of evil conduct.[25]

On the other hand, in Hōnen's age, rebirth by ten nenbutsu implied rebirth achieved only or especially at the time of death because of the close association of this specific quantity of nenbutsu with the passage from the *Amitābha Contemplation Sutra* just cited on the rebirth of the worst of beings by ten nenbutsu uttered at the moment of death. Among aristocrats and clergy the cultivation of nenbutsu at times of critical illness or at the approach of death was a common practice. The general view was that nenbutsu cultivated at this juncture had the power to expunge extraordinary amounts of evil karma, as depicted in the *Contemplation Sutra*, and thus to bring about the rebirth of

---

22   T12.272b.
23   See *Kōfukuji sōjō* in Kamata and Tanaka 1971, p. 40 and Morrell 1987, p. 86.
24   Shsz 1955, p. 788.
25   Itō Yuishin, *Jōdoshū no seiritsu to tenkai* (*The Establishment and Development of the Pure Land Denomination*; Tokyo: Yoshikawa Kōbunkan, 1981), pp. 127–130.

even grievous transgressors. A related view was that this deathbed nenbutsu was effective because it established the "right reflection" or "right thought" (*shōnen*) at the very moment of death, and thus it was thought important to constantly cultivate nenbutsu throughout one's life so as to be well practiced and prepared to generate the "right reflection" at death, or in the event that death was untimely so as to be in possession of the "right reflection" at the last moment. These views emphasizing deathbed nenbutsu tended to see nenbutsu as expiatory, and also saw it as a consciousness purifying form of meditative practice, deemphasizing its relationship to the eighteenth vow.[26]

In his authenticated works Hōnen did not emphasize deathbed nenbutsu. And as a matter of fact, in Chapter 12 of the *Passages* he declines to identify the deathbed ten nenbutsu of the worst of beings with the nenbutsu of the eighteenth vow, equating it rather with one of the so-called "non-meditative wholesome practices" (*sanzen*) of the *Contemplation Sutra*, reading and reciting Mahayana scriptures.[27]

5   Honen and Self Power versus Other Power Nenbutsu

Thus, we see that Hōnen urged those seeking Pure Land rebirth to cultivate enormous quantities of nenbutsu, both on a day-to-day basis and over a lifetime. This could be considered Self Power practice, that is, the attempt to save oneself through the accumulation of many meritorious acts rather than to rely on the saving power of the Buddha. We must remember, however, that for Hōnen the merit or good karma of nenbutsu cultivation ultimately derived from Amida, who had invested the nenbutsu with ten thousand merits by means of his many eons of purified bodhisattva cultivation (*shōjō no gyō*).[28] For Hōnen, utterance of the nenbutsu was always "the practice of the original vow" (*hongan nenbutsu gyō*).[29] Indeed, the significance of Hōnen's concept "selected nenbutsu of the original vow" (*senchaku hongan nenbutsu*), the main theme of the *Passages* and the idea around which his thought is structured, is that nenbutsu is the practice intentionally chosen and endowed by Amida's vow with that buddha's extraordinary karmic power. Thus, for Hōnen the nenbutsu is the means of acquiring the karmic merit earned by Amida during

---

26   For the *locus classicus* on deathbed rebirth, see Genshin, *Ōjōyōshū*, T.84.69a–71b and Allan Andrews, *The Teachings Essential for Rebirth: A Study of Genshin's Ōjōyōshū* (Tokyo: Sophia University Press, 1973), pp. 82–86.

27   T.83.16a.

28   *Muryōjukyō*, T.12.267c8; *Senchakushū*, T.83.4c28.

29   T.83.16b13–20.

HŌNEN ON ATTAINING PURE LAND REBIRTH   231

his bodhisattva career. We might ask, If the nenbutsu has such extraordinary karmic merit, then why are such large quantities required? Shouldn't just a few, ten, or even one utterance be adequate? Hōnen, in his authenticated works, never asked himself that question. We can find the suggestion of an answer in his letter to Kumagae Naozane, where he tells Naozane that if he cultivates up to sixty thousand nenbutsu per day then even minor violations of the Buddhist precepts will not impede his rebirth. This means that Hōnen thought nenbutsu expunged bad karma, and we might speculate that he urged constant nenbutsu cultivation so as to remove bad karma whenever it occurred.[30] In the *Passages* we find that Hōnen indeed acknowledges the power of nenbutsu to extinguish even the weightiest bad karma, as for example in the situation described in the *Contemplation Sutra* for the rebirth of the worst type of person (*gehon geshō*) by ten nenbutsu cited above. This sutra goes on to claim,

> Because of calling on the Buddha's name, with each reflection (*nennen no naka ni*) they remove [the evil karma generated by] eighty billion eons of samsaric offenses.[31]

However, in the *Passages* Hōnen rarely refers to the removal of bad karma by nenbutsu except in relation to this section of the *Contemplation Sutra* and the parallel section on the rebirth of the "best of the worst" (*gehon jōshō*) by just one nenbutsu.[32] Moreover, these grievous transgressors, persons so depraved as to have committed the "ten evil acts" or the "five irredeemable offenses" were not the primary target of Hōnen's teachings.[33] He considered virtually all sentient beings living in an age of final dharma, the relatively virtuous as well

---

30   This was a traditional function of nenbutsu; see *Ōjōyōshū*, T84.66c–67a and Andrews, *Teachings*, pp. 72–73. Matsunaga and Matsunaga claim that Hōnen emphasized the cultivation of large quantities of nenbutsu as a means to exorcise or remove "sin," i.e., bad karma. However, to support this view they cite Hōnen's unauthenticated writings, works so numerous and varied that one or another can be used to support almost any opinion about Hōnen. See Daigen Matsunaga and Alicia Matsunaga, *Foundations of Japanese Buddhism*, vol. II (Los Angeles: Buddhist Books International, 1976), pp. 61–62.

31   *Amitābha Contemplation Sutra*, T12.346a18–20.

32   For Hōnen's references to rebirth by ten or one nenbutsu see *Passages*, Chapter 10, T83.13b6–29 and Chapter 12, T83.16a8–15. In these references Hōnen does identify the deathbed nenbutsu of these evil persons with the nenbutsu of the eighteenth vow, emphasizing that only because this nenbutsu has been empowered by the vow of Amida is it able to remove such extraordinarily bad karma. Yet, as we have pointed out, in his classification of the practices of the *Contemplation Sutra* he declines to identify the nenbutsu of these miscreants with the nenbutsu of the vow.

33   The ten evil acts (*jūaku*) include the taking of life, theft, falsehood, adultery, greed, and wrath, and the five irredeemables (*gogyaku*) include patricide and matricide.

as unrepentant perpetrators, as equally the ordinary deluded persons (*bonbu*) for whom Amida had pledged his vows.[34]

If not primarily as exorcism of bad karma, then how did Hōnen understand that nenbutsu functioned to bring about Pure Land rebirth? First of all, though an innovative thinker, Hōnen was nonetheless a Buddhist thinker and believed deeply in the fundamental role of karma—as he put it, "cause and effect"[35] (*inga*)—in producing both bondage and liberation. He did not often exposit on the role of karmic causation in bringing about Pure Land rebirth, perhaps because the role of karma was such a given within his Buddhist worldview, but in Chapter 9 of the *Passages* he quotes a Chinese text, the *Standard Interpretations on the Western Land (Hsi-fang yaochueh shih-i t'ung-kuei/Saihō yōketsu shakugi tsūki)* as saying that

> ... lifelong practice [of nenbutsu] means constantly generating pure causation (*jōin o nasu*) from first arousing the aspiration for enlightenment to [the realization of] enlightenment without ever backsliding.[36]

Of course, as we have noted, for Hōnen this pure causation ultimately derived from the bodhisattva practices performed by Amida.

In addition to this power of the nenbutsu to expunge bad karma and generate good karma for rebirth, there was another way Hōnen saw nenbutsu functioning to bring about Pure Land rebirth. This was by establishing a devotional bond of mutual care and concern between the practitioner and Amida. This devotional character of nenbutsu is clarified by Hōnen in Chapter 2 of the *Passages* where he discusses the advantages of exclusive versus mixed practice. He says,

> Those who cultivate the right and assisting practices become extremely intimate and familiar with Amida Buddha. Thus it says in a prior passage of the *Commentary [on the Contemplation Sutra* by Shandao],[37] "When sentient beings engage in cultivation and with their mouths always call on the Buddha, the Buddha hears them; when with their bodies they always venerate and worship the Buddha, the Buddha sees them; when in their minds they always reflect on the Buddha, the Buddha knows them; when

---

34   In traditional language we would say that evil as well as good persons were equally the primary objects of Hōnen's teachings (*zennin akunin byōdō shōki*); see Kasahara Kazuo, ed., *Nyonin Ōjō* (Tokyo: Kyōikusha, 1983), pp. 37–38.

35   Hōnen, *Passages*, T83.15b.

36   Hōnen, *Passages*, T83.12c; 134.6–7. See also Chapter 12, T83.15b.

37   T37.268a6–9.

sentient beings meditate (*okunen*) on the Buddha, the Buddha meditates on them. Because none of the three modes of either that [Buddha's] or these [sentient beings'] karmic action is ever relinquished, we call this the intimate karmic condition."[38]

As we see, cultivation of nenbutsu was for Hōnen an act of devotion expressing adoration for and reliance upon Amida as a personal savior. It was an intense, exclusive, and constant worship of the Buddha which elicited a like response, enormously magnified in degree. Thus, for him the "right practices" were best not only because they generate good and annul bad karma, but also because they generate a karmic bond of mutual intimacy and care between devotee and soter that will protect the devotee during life and assure his or her birth in the Pure Land at death.[39]

Within classical Pure Land Buddhist thought, devotion to Amida is of course expressed as the three attitudes necessary for Pure Land rebirth (*sanjin*) set out in the *Contemplation Sutra*: first, sincerity (*shijō shin*), second, deep belief in Amida and corresponding acknowledgment of one's own fallen condition and helplessness (*jinshin*), and third, aspiration for rebirth (*ekō hotsugan shin*). Consonant with his understanding of the devotional character of nenbutsu, Hōnen also firmly believed that these three attitudes were essential to effective nenbutsu cultivation.[40]

---

38   Hōnen, *Passages*, T83.3b27–3c2. "A prior passage" means prior to the primary passage of this chapter. This is from Shandao's interpretation of Śākyamuni's pronouncement in the ninth contemplation of the *Contemplation Sutra* that those who cultivate buddha-reflection are embraced and never abandoned by the light emanating from Amitābha's body. The three modes of karma, i.e., of action and its results, are vocal, physical, and mental karma, or speech, act, and thought.

39   During one's life the nenbutsu provides protection from evil spirits, sudden illness, untimely death, and all misfortunes and calamities; see Hōnen, *Passages*, Chapter 15, T83.18a.

40   Hōnen, *Passages*, Chapter 8, T83.12a28–b3. Unlike Shinran, who was strongly influenced by Tanluan and for whom faith in the power of the vow and the nenbutsu vitiated the need for incessant nenbutsu cultivation, Hōnen's view of the function of faith derived from Shandao, for whom faith enabled practice. For Hōnen, faith in Amida, the vows, and the nenbutsu provided the motivation and inspiration for assiduous practice. For example, in Chapter 8 of the *Passages* (T83.10a16–11a11) we find Hōnen citing Shandao that,

"... deeply believing (*jinshin*)—and I implore all practitioners [to do this]—is to believe whole-heartedly in the Buddha's words, and with no regrets about the past to firmly decide to practice according to these. What the Buddha charges you to reject, reject. What he charges you to cultivate, cultivate. What he charges you to avoid, avoid. This is called conforming to the Buddha's teachings, conforming to the Buddha's intentions, conforming to the Buddha's vows. This is to be a true disciple of the Buddha.... Next there is establishing [deep] faith in relation to cultivation, and there are two kinds of cultivation [we should have deep faith in]: (1) right cultivation and (2) mixed cultivation."

234   ANDREWS

In summary we can say that while Hōnen did acknowledge that nenbutsu can expunge even the most evil karma and make rebirth possible for the most heinous offenders converted to Pure Land faith only upon their deathbeds, he urged his contemporaries to cultivate every day throughout their lives as much nenbutsu as possible, the richly meritorious nenbutsu of the vow, so as to accumulate as much good karma for rebirth as possible, but also to create a caring, loving, and saving bond with Amida.

6   Hōnen on the Buddhist Precepts

While Hōnen's position in the *Passages* on the practices for rebirth is systematic and fairly clear, we find in his *Seven Article Admonition* what seems like a glaring contradiction to that position. This involves the role of the Buddhist precepts, the fundamental guides to moral conduct for Buddhists. In the *Passages* Hōnen explicitly relegates the observance of the precepts to the status of "mixed cultivation"[41] and declares it to be a practice not selected by the original vow and therefore unnecessary for Pure Land rebirth.[42] However, in the *Seven Article Admonition* he orders his disciples,

> Cease and desist the following: claiming that the nenbutsu dharmagate does not include the observance of precepts, urging sexual misconduct, liquor-drinking and meat-eating, calling those who observe the precepts "cultivators of mixed practices," and teaching that those who rely on Amida's original vow need have no fear of committing evil deeds.[43]

And he adds,

> With regard to the above, the precepts are the foundation of the buddhadharma. While various forms of cultivation are pursued [by different persons], these same [precepts] should be observed by all. Thus, preceptor Shandao would not raise his eyes to view a women. The import of this form of behavior goes beyond the basic monastic rules (*hon ritsu*) [and involves basic morality]. For Pure [Land] practitioners (*jōgō no tagui*) not

---

In other words, for Shandao and for Hōnen, deep faith meant to believe deeply that the nenbutsu of the vow is the practice that will certainly result in Pure Land rebirth, and consequently, one should cultivate it assiduously.

41   T83.3b.

42   T83.5c–6a.

43   Shsz, p. 788.

HŌNEN ON ATTAINING PURE LAND REBIRTH

to conform [to the precepts] is to lose all the teachings inherited from the *tathāgata*-s and to ignore the example of our patriarchs.[44]

Here Hōnen contradicts the position he took in the *Passages* and emphatically demands of his disciples that they observe the precepts.

There are several ways we can attempt to understand this contradiction. While the *Passages* was a theoretic statement of doctrines, the *Seven Article Admonition* was a response to charges by Hōnen's critics of serious abuses by him and his disciples. It was a pragmatic and passionate attempt to correct those abuses and fend off persecution of his movement. As we can see, this particular admonition (number four) focuses on the gross distortion of his teachings called unhindered evil. Perhaps in these circumstances Hōnen felt constrained to enjoin the observance of precepts in spite of the position he took earlier in the *Passages*. Indeed, he may have changed his views on this matter between the composition of the *Passages* in 1198 and the issuing of the *Seven Article Admonition* in 1204. Yet, Hōnen's position on the precepts in the *Seven Article Admonition* seems like a pragmatic compromise with principle in the face of external pressure.

Fortunately, another of Hōnen's authentic writings touches on the subject of the precepts and gives us an opportunity to more fully understand his position. This is his letter to Kumagae Naozane, probably composed also in 1204 but prior to the *Seven Article Admonition*.[45] Kumagae Naozane, a.k.a. Rensei (1141–1208), was a warrior from the eastern provinces who had distinguished himself in the Gempei War of 1180–1185 and became a close vassal of the warrior chieftain or Shōgun, Minamoto Yoritomo.[46] But then in 1187 he had a falling out with Yoritomo, and in 1191 or 1192 entered the Buddhist clergy. Later he journeyed to Kyoto and became Hōnen's disciple, probably in 1194.[47] Subsequently he left Hōnen's center and traveled about, but apparently stayed in touch with Hōnen by correspondence. Hōnen's letter to Naozane is dated the second day of the fifth month and is in response to a no longer extant letter from Naozane in which Naozane apparently asked Hōnen about the advisability of pursuing certain practices. Hōnen responded:

---

44   Ibid.

45   Akamatsu, *Zoku Kamakura Bukkyō no kenkyū*, p. 297; traditionally dated 1193–1194.

46   Naozane also became the protagonist of a *no* play and several *kabuki* dramas.

47   Akamatsu, *Zoku Kamakura Bukkyō no kenkyū*, pp. 290–295; Fumiko Miyazaki, "Religious Life of the Kamakura Bushi: Kumagai Naozane and His Descendants," *Monumenta Nipponica* 47, no. 4 (1992): pp. 437–439.

I was so pleased to receive your letter. Indeed, since last [I received a letter from you or saw you] I was very worried, and I am very pleased at what you have written. Please read what I am going to write about "just nenbutsu" (*tan nenbutsu*).

Nenbutsu is the practice of the Buddha's original vow. Because observance of precepts, recitation of sutras, incantations, contemplation of buddha-nature (*rikan*), and so on are not the practices of that Buddha's original vow, those who seek [the land of] Boundless Bliss should without fail first cultivate the practice of the original vow, and then in addition to that, if they want to add other practices, they may do so. Also, [to cultivate] just the nenbutsu of the original vow is alright. Those who seek [the land of] Boundless Bliss without cultivating nenbutsu, cultivating only practices other than nenbutsu, will not be able to attain rebirth in Boundless Bliss....

Also, sexual relations with women (*nyobon*) is definitely [a violation of] the precept forbidding sexual relations (*fuinkai*). And disinheritance of one's children is definitely [a violation of] the precept forbidding anger (*fushinkai*). Because the observance of the precepts are not in the original vow, you should observe them only as much as you can manage (*taetaran ni shitagaite tamotase tamau beku sōrō*).... To utter just nenbutsu (*tada nenbutsu*) thirty, fifty, or sixty thousand times a day with all your heart is the practice certain to achieve rebirth. Other good works are for when you have time to spare from nenbutsu. But if you utter sixty thousand nenbutsu a day, what other practices need you do? If you diligently, with all your heart, cultivate thirty or fifty thousand nenbutsu per day, then even if you violate the precepts a little that ought not prevent your rebirth....

However, even though the practice of filial conduct (*kōyō no gyō*) is not in the Buddha's original vow, [your mother] is eighty-nine years old. What you are fully prepared and waiting for [the death of your mother] will probably happen this year or soon. It is very sad. But whatever happens should not pose a problem [for you]. You are the only one who is waiting with her, and you must without fail [continue to] wait with her....[48]

Apart from a theoretic, doctrinal context, and absent external pressures, this was Hōnen's heartfelt advice to a disciple. First of all we should note that he instructs Naozane that nenbutsu, especially when cultivated to the utmost of one's ability throughout each day, is solely sufficient for Pure Land rebirth

---

48   Ōhashi, *Hōnen-Ippen*, pp. 166–167.

because it is the practice designated by the Buddha's original vow. Other practices not selected by the vow can be helpful, but should be cultivated only after nenbutsu and to the extent that they do not interfere with nenbutsu cultivation. This clarifies what Hōnen meant by "sole practice nenbutsu" (*senju nenbutsu*). He clearly meant that for Pure Land rebirth one need cultivate "just nenbutsu" (*tada nenbutsu*).

Hōnen goes on to advise Naozane that this is true also in relation to precept observance. Like all "mixed practices," precepts observance is not necessary, though it may be marginally helpful *in addition* to nenbutsu. Hōnen's comment that violating the precepts a little ought not to hinder Naozane's rebirth if he has cultivated thirty or fifty thousand nenbutsu per day indicates, as we remarked above, that Hōnen acknowledged that nenbutsu expunges bad karma, but it also shows that Hōnen saw precept observance as primarily useful for preventing the accumulation of evil karma. And, by advising Naozane to observe the precepts only as much as he could manage, Hōnen probably meant that while nenbutsu is easy and convenient for anyone in any circumstances (as stated in the passage from the *Essentials of Pure Land Rebirth* quoted by Hōnen and cited above), strict observance of the precepts is difficult and requires special circumstances, specifically those of a monastic setting. Naozane was a so-called "lay priest" (*nyūdō*). A lay priest was a person who had entered the clergy after pursuing a secular career, and in many cases while still remaining to some degree a householder. Because Naozane still had a wife, mother, and children, he had many secular bonds and obligations. Therefore, it would have been difficult and perhaps inconsiderate and unjust of him in his circumstances to have rigorously observed the monastic precepts. However, as we have seen, Hōnen definitely viewed bad karma as a hindrance to Pure Land rebirth, and for Hōnen as for any Buddhist, the surest way to avoid bad karma was to observe the precepts. Thus, he advises Naozane to observe them as much as he can manage, that is, to the extent that he is able within his circumstances. In response to Naozane's questions Hōnen advises him that within his circumstances he should avoid having sexual relations with his wife and not disinherit his son, but fulfill his filial obligations by remaining at home with his mother until she dies.[49]

Hōnen's advice in this letter helps us to resolve the apparent contradiction we noted between his views on observance of the precepts in the *Passages* on the one hand and in the *Seven Article Admonition* on the other hand. Although

---

49 Although filial behavior is not a requirement of the Buddhist precepts, it is enjoined in the *Contemplation Sutra* (T12.341c9–12), and Hōnen remarks in the *Passages* that it does generate karma for rebirth (T83.15a8–12).

not necessary for Pure Land rebirth, he apparently thought that everyone should attempt to observe the precepts as much as their circumstances would allow so as to avoid the accumulation of bad karma. For those who were regularly ordained monks he would have probably urged a rigorous observance, for lay priests a less strict conformance as dictated by their particular circumstances, and for laypersons a sincere attempt to observe at least the primary rules, such as those forbidding the taking of life, stealing, and lying.[50] On the other hand, given the special circumstances of an age of final dharma when virtually all human kind have become just "ordinary deluded beings" (*bonbu*), he was convinced that strict observance of precepts was almost impossible. While in the *Passages* Hōnen attempts to explain why Amida had selected nenbutsu rather than other practices for his vow, he remarks,

> If observance of the [lay] precepts and monastic rules had been made [the practice of] the original vow, then those who violate or who have not taken the precepts would have no hope of rebirth at all. Yet those who observe the precepts are few, while those who violate the precepts are extremely numerous.[51]

Thus, while one should avoid evil conduct by attempting to observe the precepts, one's major efforts should be dedicated to the cultivation of nenbutsu. If one's nenbutsu cultivation is of sufficient quality and quantity, one will be reborn in spite of one's bad karma.[52]

7   The Varieties of Pure Land Buddhism

Finally, let us return as promised to a consideration of the varieties of Pure Land Buddhism. At the beginning of this study I ventured the view that Hōnen contributed to the transformation of continental forms of Pure Land Buddhism into distinctly Japanese forms. By this I mean that institutional Pure

---

50   Hōnen himself strictly observed the precepts throughout his life.

51   T83.5c25–6a5.

52   In traditional studies of Hōnen's position on the precepts a passage from the *Gekishu seppō* (Shsz 1955, p. 243), the *Mappō tōmyōki*, is frequently cited to show that Hōnen viewed the observance of precepts in an age of final dharma as totally irrelevant to rebirth (see, for example, pages 91–92 in Robert F. Rhodes, trans., "Saichō's *Mappō Tomyoki: The Candle of the Latter Dharma*," *The Eastern Buddhist* 1, no. 311 [1980]: pp. 79–103). However, the authenticity of the *Gekishu seppō* is not confirmed by an autographed manuscript, thus it might be an apocryphal work.

Land Buddhism in Japan prior to Hōnen was based upon continental models—largely monastic and emphasizing contemplative practice—but after Hōnen it became entirely a layperson's Buddhism, emphasizing devotion. An adequate defense of this thesis is far beyond our limitations of time and space here, but let me briefly consider the ways in which Hōnen's teachings on practice facilitated participation by laypersons in Pure Land Buddhism. In addition to his rejection of earlier Buddhist mystical, monistic systems of thought and of the complex rituals associated with them,[53] Hōnen, as we have documented, rejected the core practices of Buddhist monasticism—meditation and observance of the precepts. His rejection of meditation, that is, contemplations of the Pure Land and its beings (*kanzatsu, kambutsu*), was total and definitive for the Pure Land tradition that followed him.[54] As we have seen, the complex visionary meditations that dominated the Pure Land tradition prior to Hōnen, and that even for Shandao continued be an important form of practice, were replaced by the simple devotional act of calling on the name of the Buddha.

With regard to the value of precept observance, we first acknowledged contradictions between the positions taken by Hōnen in the *Passages* on the one hand and in the *Seven Article Admonition* on the other, and then explored how Hōnen clarified the relation of the precepts to the nenbutsu in his letter to Kumagae Naozane.[55] There he unequivocally declares that the cultivation of nenbutsu is absolutely essential for the attainment of rebirth, while

---

53   While Matsunaga and Matsunaga (*Foundations*, p. 61) claim that Hōnen participated in ordination rites using esoteric tantric ritual, this claim is dubious. (It is probably based upon the assertion of Ishida Mizumaro on page 266 of "Hōnen ni okeru futatsu no seikaku," in *Jōdokyō no tenkai* [Tokyo: Shunjūsha, 1967], pp. 264–268, but Ishida moderated his view considerably in his revision, "Hōnen no kairitsu kan," in *Nihon Bukkyō ni okero kairitsu no kenkyu* [Tokyo: Nakayama Shobō, 1986], pp. 313–322.) That Hōnen ordained Kujō Kanezane and two other aristocrats and that he conferred the Buddhist precepts on Kanezane, his wife, and his daughter when they were ill is certain (*Gyokuyō* and *Meigetsuki*; Ikawa, *Hōnen Shōnin den zenshū*, pp. 966–968). That he did so by means of esoteric rites is speculation. An early biography, the *Genkū Shōnin shinikki*, does claim that Hōnen participated in esoteric rituals (Alan A. Andrews, "A Personal Account of the Life of the Venerable Genkū," in *Religions of Japan in Practice*, ed. George J. Tanabe, Jr. [Princeton: Princeton University Press, 1999], p. 376.), apparently while still residing at Kurodani prior to 1174, but this claim is also dubious; see discussion of the process of compilation of the *Genkū Shōnin shinikki* in Tamura Enchō, *Hōnen Shōnin den no kenkyū* (Kyoto: Hōzōkan, 1972), pp. 16–21 and 292.

54   The issue of Hōnen's alleged personal participation in contemplative exercises must be treated separately from his teachings on this issue.

55   The original manuscript of Hōnen's letter to Naozane, written in Hōnen's own hand, has been preserved and is therefore unquestionably authentic; see Tōdō and Itō, "Hōnen Shōnin shinpitsu ruishū kaisetsu."

the observance of the precepts is of only marginal value. Based on the advice he gives to Naozane we can conclude that for Hōnen one could be a layperson, pursuing a lifestyle completely unobservant of the Buddhist behavioral precepts as such, and yet cultivate the requisite quantity and quality of nenbutsu for Pure Land rebirth. Finally, in exploring the character of Hōnen's nenbutsu we discovered that while he urged sustained cultivation of enormous quantities of nenbutsu and saw this nenbutsu as accruing good karma for rebirth (albeit the karmic merit derived from that which Amida had invested in the nenbutsu), he also taught that sincere and deeply believing nenbutsu cultivation establishes an intimate and caring bond between the cultivator and the Buddha, and at death the Buddha would therefore welcome the devotee into the Pure Land. As James Foard has pointed out,[56] Hōnen was one of those early Kamakura Buddhist leaders who participated in a devotional movement that eliminated the necessity of institutional or sacerdotal mediation and made salvation immediately available to laypersons. Thus, with few exceptions, after Hōnen Japanese Pure Land Buddhism became a layperson's Buddhism.[57]

---

56   James Foard, "In Search of a Lost Reformation," *Japanese Journal of Religious Studies* 7, no. 4 (1980): pp. 261–291.

57   The primary exceptions are the Jishū and Ōbaku Zen.

Hōnen and Popular Pure Land Piety: Assimilation and Transformation

Allan A. Andrews

This study will explore one of the many complex issues in the development of Japanese Pure Land Buddhism.* From a broad perspective Japanese Pure Land can be seen as a component of the East Asian Pure Land tradition. It was based on Chinese texts, ideas, and practices, some of which had been derived from India and central Asia. Yet the Japanese did not simply preserve what they had received from China; they made distinct contributions to East Asian Pure Land Buddhism. Japanese modifications of the received tradition began in the Nara period (646–794) soon after the introduction of Pure Land Buddhism to Japan (Shigematsu 1964, 13–60), continued during the early Heian period (794–ca. 1000; Inoue 1975, 83–156), and in the late Heian (ca. 900–1185) and early Kamakura periods (1185–ca. 1250) produced major transformations. The thought of Hōnen-bō Genkū (1133–1212) is especially remarkable for its departures from earlier Pure Land. His innovations and those of his disciples not only greatly altered the Pure Land tradition, they initiated a new phase of Japanese religious history called Kamakura New Buddhism. Whence did Hōnen derive his new ideas? Did he get them directly from Chinese texts as he claimed, or was he influenced by indigenous Japanese thought?

It was posited several decades ago by both Hori Ichirō and Ienaga Saburo that Hōnen was the inheritor of a rich fund of popular Japanese ideas and practices which he systematized into the thought of his Pure Land School (Jōdo shū) on the basis of continental, i.e., Chinese, Buddhist doctrines and texts.[1]

Source: Andrews, Allan A., "Hōnen and Popular Pure Land Piety: Assimilation and Transformation," *Journal of the International Association of Buddhist Studies* 17(1) (Summer 1994): 96–110. © International Association of Buddhist Studies.

---

* An earlier version of this study was delivered to an Association for Asian Studies panel on Japanese Pure Land Buddhism in March 1993. I wish to thank respondent Jacqueline Stone, fellow panelists and my colleague Kevin Trainor for helpful suggestions.

1 Hori 1953, 324–25; Ienaga 1963, 26–28. Hori actually locates the sources of Hōnen's systemization in the *Ōjōyōshū* and criticizes Hōnen for an incomplete systemization. Ienaga was primarily concerned with the derivations of Shinran's ideas, but the systemization which he credits to Shinran began, of course, with Hōnen. I might add that while Hōnen discovered continental Pure Land thought in the *Ōjōyōshū*, he then bypassed that text and drew directly upon continental thinkers like Shan-tao.

242 ANDREWS

Like these two scholars, Japanese historians in general have tended to emphasize the importance of Hōnen's indigenous, popular legacy (Ienega, Akamatsu
and Tamamuro 1967–68, 1.327–41, 2.31–32; Inoue 1975, 315–18), while Pure Land
denominational scholars have tended to deemphasize the Japanese compo-
nents of Hōnen's thought and accentuate his debt to continental ideas (Ishida
1952, 96–103; Fujiwara 1957, 215–21; Ishii 1969, 158–60). I would like to begin
sorting out what Hōnen derived from late Heian popular Pure Land piety, what
he acquired from continental thought, and how he related these diverse influences. Here I will explore the origins of just one of Hōnen's ideas, his view on
effective practice for Pure Land rebirth.

Hōnen taught that the only practice necessary for rebirth into Amida
Buddha's Pure Land was vocal *nembutsu*, that is, calling upon Amida (Sanskrit,
Amitābha/Amitāyus) with the invocation, "*namu* Amida Butsu," "Homage to
Amida Buddha," or, "I take refuge in the Buddha of Limitless Light and Life."
My thesis is that Hōnen derived from popular[2] Pure Land piety this position
on sole nembutsu cultivation, augmented and systemized it by means of con-
tinental thought, and related this systemized thought to a Pure Land scriptural
canon, enhancing its credibility and emphasizing its autonomy.

For information on the popular piety which may have influenced Hōnen
I will refer to Japanese scholarship on Heian period "accounts of rebirth"
(*ōjōden*); I will consider Shan-tao (613–81) the major continental influence
upon Hōnen; and I will utilize Hōnen's *Passages on the Selected Nembutsu of
the Original Vow* (*Senchaku hongan nembutsu shū*)[3] as the most important and
only fully authenticated formulation of his thought.

1 Hōnen and Popular Pure Land Piety of the Late Heian Period

It is well known that Hōnen claimed sole cultivation of vocal nembutsu as the
best practice for Pure Land rebirth. In Chapter 2 of his *Passages* he maintains
that exclusive Pure Land cultivation is much more effective than "adulterat-
ed practices" (*zōgyō*), and that among Pure Land practices, calling on Amida
Buddha's name is the "assured act" (*shōjō no gō*) certain to bring about rebirth
(*T.* 83.2c14–4b20);[4] in Chapter 3 he claims that vocal nembutsu is the sole

---

2 By "popular" I mean the religion of both clergy and lay persons of all classes and occupations
  except that of the nobility and upper echelon warriors; see Inoue 1975, 158, n. 1.
3 See References for fuller bibliographic information.
4 This reference is to volume number 83, page 2, tier "c," line 14, to page 4, tier "b," etc., of "*T.*,"
  the *Taishō shinshū daizōkyō*.

practice selected by Amida and guaranteed by his eighteenth original vow for the rebirth of all sentient beings (*T.* 83.4b–6c); in Chapter 6 this nembutsu is presented as the best practice for an age of final Dharma (*mappō*; *T.* 83.8b–9a); and in Chapter 12 Hōnen explicitly rejects meditation, observance of precepts, recitation of scripture, filial behavior, the performance of good deeds and other "meditative and non-meditative meritorious acts" (*jōsan nizen*) because he claims they were not selected by the eighteenth vow (*T.* 83.14c–17a). In short, Hōnen maintained that calling the Buddha's name was the best and only practice necessary for rebirth.

As we have indicated, our concern is to determine whence Hōnen derived these views. He claimed that he obtained them from the Mahāyāna scriptures as interpreted by the continental master Shan-tao (*T.* 83.19a5–12). In a moment we will examine to what extent this claim was justified, but first let us summarize the popular Pure Land piety of Hōnen's time and especially its beliefs on how to be reborn in the Pure Land.

Some of the most revealing glimpses into popular Buddhism of the late Heian period, the eleventh and twelfth centuries, are provided by six collections called "accounts of Pure Land rebirth" (*ōjōden*). The earliest, *Nihon Gokuraku ōjōki*, was compiled in 985 by Yoshishige no Yasutane, and was followed over a century later by the *Zoku honchō ōjōden* of Oe no Masafusa in 1101–04, by the *Shūi ōjōden* and *Goshūi ōjōden* of Miyoshi no Tamayasu compiled between 1111 and 1139, the *Sange ōjōki* by Shami Renzen soon after 1139, and the *Honchō shinshū ōjōden* by Fuji no Munetomo between 1134 and 1139 (Inoue and Ōsone 1974, 711–760). All together they contain some 340 vignette describing the faith, practices and rebirth of mostly contemporaneous persons into Amida's Pure Land. And while these stories cannot be taken as historical fact, they nonetheless give us considerable insight into the views of the compilers and of their contemporaries on the availability and means to Pure Land rebirth. Hori, Ienaga, Shigematsu and Inoue have conducted extensive studies of these compilations (Hori 1953, 304–17; Ienaga 1963, 1–44 and 201–218; Shigematsu 1964, 122–309; Inoue and Ōsone 1974, 711–760; Inoue 1975, 158–265).[5] They find that the subjects of the rebirth tales are persons of all classes and circumstances—nobility and commoners, warriors and free cultivators, lay persons and clergy, women as well as men—but that those from the lower ranks of society are more numerous, that women, both lay and clerical are well represented, and that *hijiri* and *shami*, the evangelists and leaders of popular Buddhism, are prominent. The *hijiri* were clergy who left the

---

5   Moreover, Kotas 1987 summarizes much of the Japanese scholarship on the *ōjōden* and translates a number of tales.

degenerating centers of monastic Buddhism to pursue an ascetic, fervid religious life either as recluses dwelling at monastic retreats (*bessho*), or as itinerants circulating among the populace in towns and villages. The *shami* were unordained "householder novices" (*zoku shami*) or "wayfarers" (*nyūdō*) who, while remaining married and in lay occupations, assumed an austere lifestyle, engaged in assiduous devotions and performed various religious functions for their fellow townspeople and villagers (Hori 1958; Itō 1969; Inoue 1975, 215–56).

As depicted in the accounts of rebirth, the Pure Land piety of this mixed populace had the following features: belief in the advent of the final age of the Dharma (*mappō*), conviction of heavy karmic burden, anxiety about reincarnation in hell, simultaneous participation in an eclectic *Lotus Sūtra*, Kannon, Miroku, Amida and Jizō devotionalism, as well as practice of various austerities and esoteric rituals, all in pursuit of this-worldly benefits as well as Pure Land rebirth. The practices depicted most frequently as eventuating in Pure Land rebirth are *Lotus Sūtra* veneration, especially chanting and copying the sūtra, and Pure Land nembutsu, especially ontemplation of Amida.[6] Frequently both kinds of devotion are pursued by the same person (Shigematsu 1964, 171–232).

These collections also reveal shifts in beliefs and practices from the earlier compilation of 985 to those compiled in the twelfth century. They show a heightened sense of personal evil and an increased anxiety, amounting to almost a certainty, of falling after death into a Buddhist hell. Amida and Jizō come to be emphasized as soters who have vowed to save their devotees from this fate.[7] Exclusive devotion, especially to Amida or the *Lotus Sutra*, becomes more frequent. Vocal nembutsu becomes more common, and these later collections also show a tendency toward cultivation of huge quantities of vocal nembutsu—10,000 or 100,000 nembutsu per day or 1,000,000 during a fixed period. Sole cultivation of vocal nembutsu makes its appearance in a few tales as well.[8] There is a noticeable increase in the incidence of rebirth of "evil persons" (*akunin*)—butchers, warriors, skeptics, and flagrant offenders—and especially of their conversion upon their deathbeds and rebirth by just a few

---

6 The locus classicus of this exercise is the *Kuan Wu-liang-shou-fo ching* / *Kan Muryōjubutsu kyō*; see Ryukoku University 1984 or Muller, *Sacred Books of the East*, vol. 49. For discussions of this exercise in Japan and China, see Andrews 1973 and 1993.

7 Found by Inoue (1975, 230–254) also in the contemporaneous tale collection, *Konjaku monogatari shū*.

8 Inoue (1975, 250–51) identifies only four instances in the *ōjōden* and two in the *Konjaku monogatari shū*, but because all these cases describe the practices of commoners, including those leaders and evangelizers, the *hijiri* and *shami*, he maintains that such exclusive devotion to Amida and sole nembutsu cultivation must have been fairly common in this period.

utterances of the Buddha's name.[9] And finally, fanatical rebirth-suicide—devotees immolating or drowning themselves in expectation of immediate Pure Land rebirth—are more frequently depicted as well.

These eleventh century accounts also reveal a shift in the types and activities of the *hijiri* and *shami*. The *hijiri* more frequently emerge from their retreats and interact with laymen as itinerants who travel about from village to village (Itō 1984). Both *hijiri* and *shami* become more involved with Pure Land piety and in general they assume the roles of evangelizers and leaders of popular Buddhism, instructing and organizing the populace as preachers, healers and magicians in the style of the famous "*hijiri* of the market place," Kūya (893–972). For example, they serve as priests of local temples and shrines, organize Pure Land and other devotional groups (*nembutsu shu*, etc.), lead pious ceremonies (*nembutsu kō*, *mukae kō*, etc.), collect meritorious donations for temple and village projects, conduct funerals, exorcise malevolent spirits, heal the sick, organize social service projects, and in general serve the many needs of the populace while recruiting them to Buddhist faith and especially to Pure Land piety (Inoue 1975, 226–56). However, despite these tendencies the rebirth accounts nonetheless reflect a Pure Land piety at the close of the Heian period that continued overwhelmingly to be incorporated into an eclectic popular devotionalism of many faiths and practices.[10]

When we compare this popular Pure Land piety with Hōnen's teachings on sole cultivation of vocal nembutsu it is clear that several of its tendencies coincide with Hōnen's positions: emphasis on the vows of Amida, on exclusive Pure Land devotion, on vocal nembutsu, on affirmation of the rebirth of commoners, women and even evil persons by vocal nembutsu, and their emphasis on sole nembutsu cultivation. It would seem reasonable to conclude, as some Japanese historians have, that Hōnen was strongly influenced by his contemporary, popular milieu.

We should also note that during his lifetime Hōnen had ample opportunity to absorb popular influences. Much of his clerical career was spent among the rural populace and close to those popular evangelists, the *hijiri* and *shami*. From the age of nine until his mid-teens he served in a provincial temple and was no doubt exposed to all sorts of popular piety. At age fifteen he received priestly ordination upon Mt. Hiei, but within a few years retired from Tendai's

---

9   Ienaga (1963, 14–18) identifies 19 such cases in the twelfth century *ōjōden*.

10   We must keep in mind that the rebirth accounts by their very nature emphasize Pure Land piety and tell us less about important trends in other varieties of popular religion. Thus our claim is not that they reveal an overall shift toward Pure Land piety, but just that they show some trends within popular piety as a whole and within Pure Land devotionalism in particular.

ecclesiastical center to a rural monastic retreat (*bessho*) on the western slopes of Mt. Hiei, called Kurodani, where he dwelt for twenty-five years (Tamura 1972, 61–103). Kurodani, like all such monastic retreats, served as a center where *hijiri* congregated and from whence they departed to preach and evangelize in the towns and villages (Takagi 1973, 357–375; Kikuchi 1982). While Hōnen himself does not appear during those twenty-five years to have left Kurodani to proselytize, he was nonetheless in close contact with these leaders of popular piety (Itō 1981, 42–72). Moreover, after his departure from Kurodani in 1175 Hōnen established a teaching center at Yoshimizu in the suburbs of the capital where he taught scores of disciples and followers.[11] Many of these adherents then went out into the city and countryside in *hijiri* fashion, spreading the sole-nembutsu faith among the populace (Ōhashi 1972, 143–47; Tamura 1959, 148–56; Itō 1969 and 1981, 73–136). Throughout his career, Hōnen was well positioned both to be influenced by, and exert influences upon, popular piety.

2   Hōnen and Shan-tao on Practice

Yet, whatever popular influences we may detect in Hōnen's thought, as we have noted, Hōnen himself claimed that his teachings were based on the interpretations of Shan-tao. Thus we must examine Shan-tao's position on effective practice.

Shan-tao twice concisely formulated correct and effective Pure Land practice, once in his *Wang-sheng li-tsan chieh* (Hymns in Praise of Pure Land Rebirth) and again in his *Kuan Wu-liang-shou-fo-ching shu* (Commentary on the Amitabha Contemplation Sūtra). The former (*T.* 47.438c–439a) urges (1) veneration of Amitābha with offerings of incense and flowers, (2) singing the praises of Amitābha, his entourage and his Pure Land, (3) contemplating Amitābha, his entourage and his land, (4) vowing and praying to be reborn in the Pure Land, and (5) dedicating all one's own karma and the good karma of others to mutual rebirth in the Pure Land. This formulation completely omits the practice of calling on the name, except perhaps as an implicit accompaniment to veneration or contemplation. The *Commentary on the Contemplation Sūtra* formula (*T.* 37.272a–b)[12] gives priority to invoking the Buddha's name, but also recommends accompanying this with the practices of reciting the

---

11   In 1204 some 170 disciples and followers indicated their assent to Hōnen's teachings by signing his *Shichikajō seikai* (Seven Article Pledge); see Tamura 1959, 146–48 and Nakano 1985.

12   Cited by Hōnen in Chapter 2 of his *Passages, T.* 83.2c16–22.

HŌNEN AND POPULAR PURE LAND PIETY

Pure Land sūtras and contemplating, venerating, and praising Amitābha. In another of Shan-tao works, his *Kuan-nien A-mi-t'o-fo hsiang-hai san-mei kung-te fa-men* (Methods and Merits of Samādhi of Contemplation and Reflection upon Amitābha), he prescribes contemplating the auspicious signs of the Buddha's physical body, but also urges as many as ten thousand to one hundred thousand daily invocations of the Buddha's name, interspersed with other devotional acts such as reciting scripture, making offerings and singing praises (*T.* 47. 23b8–14). In general, Shan-tao was an austere monastic and a fervent devotee who insisted on total dedication to Amitābha through constant, ardent engagement in an array of devotional activities.

Yet, fundamental to Shan-tao's thought were two tenets: First, that he and virtually all of his contemporaries were helpless, morally degenerate "ordinary persons" (*fanfu*) living in an age of final Dharma, and second, that for such persons the practice most certain to result in Pure Land rebirth was the act empowered by the eighteenth vow, calling on the Buddha's name.[13] Shan-tao's position on practice was, therefore, ambivalent. While on the one hand he frequently urged constant performance of the most arduous contemplations and devotions, on the other hand he thought that most persons were capable of little more than calling on the Buddha's name.

Hōnen himself (*T.* 83.14c17–20) and modern Pure Land denominational scholars (Ishida 1952, 96; Fujiwara 1957, 215 and 218; Ishii 1969, 526–27) have heavily based their claim of Shan-tao's advocacy of sole invocational nembutsu on a passage in Shan-tao's *Commentary on the Contemplation Sūtra* interpreting Śākyamuni's final transmission of his *Contemplation Sūtra* discourse to Ānanda. This passage reads,

> [The section of the *Contemplation Sūtra*] from, "The Buddha said to Ananda, 'Keep these words well! [To keep these words is to keep the name of the Buddha of Limitless Life.']," rightly reveals the bestowal of Amitābha's name for transmission to future generations. Even though [Śākyamuni] had hitherto taught the benefits of the meditative and non-meditative Dharma-gates, [he] saw that the meaning of [Amitābha] Buddha's original vow consisted in sentient beings calling solely and exclusively on the name of Amitābha Buddha.[14]

---

13   In the first section of his *Commentary on the Contemplation Sūtra*, *T.* 37.245–251, Shan-tao argues at length for the degeneracy of his age and the decadent condition of his contemporaries. He interprets the eighteenth vow as urging invocation at *T.* 47.27a16–19 and *T.* 47.447c23–26.

14   *T.* 37.278a23–26 by Shan-tao, interpreting *T.* 12.346b15–16 of the *Contemplation Sūtra*, cited by Hōnen in his *Passages* at *T.* 83.14c17–20.

Here Shan-tao seems to be saying that Śakyamuni Buddha wanted Ānanda to convey to sentient beings in the future not the contemplations and ethical practices which he had just taught in the *Contemplation Sūtra*, but rather the sole practice of invocational nembutsu urged by Amitābha himself in his eighteenth vow. However, this is but one terse and ambiguous passage in all of Shan-tao's voluminous writings, and to use it to relegate categorically buddha-contemplation to the status of an inferior practice would be to oversimplify Shan-tao's rich thought.[15]

Although there are scattered about in Shan-tao's writings passages which urge invocation to the exclusion of contemplation (e. g., *T.* 47. 439a24–26), we should keep in mind as well first that Shan-tao frequently urged observance of the Buddhist precepts and performance of rites of repentance, and secondly that three of this five works are liturgical designed for use in ritualistic worship services.

Was Hōnen therefore justified in ascribing his position on sole nembutsu to Shan-tao's interpretations? On the one hand, Shan-tao did interpret the practice of the eighteenth vow as calling on the Buddha's name and urge this practice as best for his contemporaries. On the other hand, his writings enthusiastically encourage the cultivation of buddha-contemplation and other Pure Land devotional practices. Thus, while Hōnen did not find "sole nembutsu" *per se* in the writings of Shan-tao, he was clearly influenced by Shan-tao's powerful arguments for the special status and efficacy of invocation.

However, aside from Shan-tao's position on buddha-recollection itself, there was another feature of his thought, a more basic feature, which was a prerequisite for Hōnen's formulation of a sole nembutsu doctrine. Before Hōnen could conceive of nembutsu as among all practices a superior practice which should be cultivated solely, it was necessary for him to perceive Amida as a special object of devotion to be worshiped to the exclusion of all other soters and sacralities. In Japan, the tendency had been to subsume Pure Land piety within either non-Pure Land doctrinal systems or, as we have seen, within an eclectic popular matrix. Moreover, even by the twelfth century exclusive devotion to Amida, according to the accounts of rebirth, had barely begun to emerge. In China,

---

15   Some Pure Land denominational scholars also claim that the *Commentary on the Contemplation Sūtra* was Shan-tao's final and most mature work (for example, Fujiwara 1957, 204–09), and therefore that its position on the priority of the eighteenth vow's vocal nembutsu should take precedence over passages in Shan-tao's other works urging contemplative and other practices. While the *Commentary on the Contemplation Sūtra* is probably Shan-tao's most mature work, there is no historical evidence that it is his last composition.

on the contrary, the line of Pure Land teachers from T'an-luan (ca. 488–554) to Shan-tao had for centuries been exclusively focused on Amitābha Buddha. Shan-tao rejected totally any spirituality except that committed to Amitābha and Pure Land rebirth. Thus the practices he recommends, as we have seen above, were all practices expressing devotion to Amitābha. Hōnen encountered in Shan-tao this exclusive commitment to Pure Land rebirth and exclusive reliance on practices in devotion to Amitābha. And this exclusive focus on Amitābha made it possible for Hōnen to formulate the even more thoroughgoing exclusiveness of his sole nembutsu position.[16]

3 Hōnen's Transformation of Popular Pure Land Piety

As I proposed above, it is my view that Hōnen drew from both his contemporary religious milieu and from continental thought and that he synthesized these influences so as to systemize a unique doctrinal position. Let me make three points: First, that Hōnen used continental thought to extract the sole nembutsu idea from its Japanese multi-faith, multi-praxis popular matrix; secondly, that he borrowed from Shan-tao certain of Shan-tao's notions on Pure Land praxis and used these to formulate a system of doctrines around the idea of sole nembutsu; and thirdly, that Hōnen related his teachings on sole nembutsu practice to a Pure Land scriptural canon, thus supplying them with some legitimacy and considerable autonomy.

Regarding the first point, based upon Shan-tao's exclusive commitment to Amitābha and his insistence upon the cultivation of Pure Land practices only, Hōnen was able first to extricate in theory Pure Land piety from its eclectic popular mix. Then based upon this exclusive Pure Land devotionalism and Shan-tao's high regard for buddha-invocation he was able to develop his subsequent position of just one Pure Land practice, thereby extracting vocal nembutsu also from its eclectic amalgam. In some ways the highly focused Pure Land exclusivity Hōnen derived from Shan-tao was more important for Hōnen's historical role than his better known position on sole nembutsu, because it made possible, after centuries of co-option and subordination, the formulation by Hōnen of autonomous forms of doctrine and praxis essential for the development of the various Kamakura period Pure Land sectarian groups.

---

16   Hōnen develops his exclusive Pure Land stance initially in Chapter 1 of his *Passages*, basing his position on citations from Tao-ch'o (562–645) and other continental masters, and subsequently amplifies this doctrine drawing heavily on Shan-tao.

My second point is that Hōnen borrowed from Shan-tao certain of Shan-tao's notions on Pure Land praxis and used these to formulate a system of doctrines around the idea of sole nembutsu. As noted above, by the seventh century in T'ang China Shan-tao had already devised a rich system of Pure Land praxis. He saw the *nien-fo*, i.e., nembutsu, empowered by the eighteenth vow as the major act establishing a nexus of mutual devotedness between sentient being and buddha (*T.* 37.268a4–13), an act to be cultivated with sincere, deep and focused faith (*T.* 37.270c–273b), reverently, exclusively, constantly and to the end of one's life (*T.* 47.439a7–18). All this, as well as the identification of the *nien-fo* of the eighteenth vow with the utterance of the Buddha's name ten times as described in the *Contemplation Sūtra*, had already been worked out by Shan-tao. These systemic ideas and others were borrowed by Hōnen, enriching his notion of sole nembutsu and providing a rationale for its effectiveness.[17]

My third point is that Hōnen associated his teachings on sole nembutsu with a Pure Land canonical corpus, thereby enhancing their legitimacy and establishing their autonomy in relation to other doctrinal systems. There can be no question that a major concern of Hōnen in his *Passages* was to authenticate his teachings by showing how they were based upon Pure Land and other Mahāyāna scriptures. In the opening chapter he claims for his Pure Land School a canon called "the three part Pure Land scripture" (*jōdo sambukyō*), consisting of the *Wu-liang-shou ching* / *Muryōju kyō* (Sūtra of Limitless Life), *Kuan Wu-liang-shou-fo ching* / *Kan Muryōjubutsu kyō* (Sutra of Contemplation on the Buddha of Limitless Life, or Amitabha Contemplation Sutra), and the *O-mi-t'o ching* / *Amida kyō* (Amitābha Sūtra).[18] Subsequent chapters of the *Passages*, with the exception of chapters 2, 9, 14, and 15, begin with a citation from one of these scripture intended to justify a particular claim regarding sole nembutsu or some related doctrine. (Chapters 2, 9, 14, and 15 begin with citations from the works of Shan-tao, which for Hōnen also had canonical authority.) This direct link to a defined set of scriptures associated with the Buddha Amitābha was also intended to liberate Pure Land doctrines from dependence on the canons of other schools, thereby giving these doctrines autonomy as well as legitimacy.

---

17 See Hōnen's *Passages on the Selected Nembutsu*, *T.* 83.9a23–b7; 9c3–12b25; 12b27–c10; 4b26–c6.

18 The influence of Shan-tao is apparent here also. These three sūtras were the ones he recommended reading and reciting in one of his formulations of Pure Land practice (see section 3 above and *T.* 37.272b2). On Hōnen's formulation of this canon and other features of his Pure Land School, see Andrews 1987.

4   Conclusion

Let me conclude by reiterating that Hōnen did not simply adopt the raw features of popular faith into his teachings. He returned to the Chinese sources of much of Japanese popular Pure Land piety[19] and used those texts and teachings to modify, systematize and defend popular Japanese beliefs and practices. Moreover, this hybrid character of Hōnen's thought was important for the further development of Japanese Buddhism: Because it was based upon popular ideas and practices, Hōnen's thought had great popular appeal, and because it now constituted a system of doctrines invested with credibility and autonomy, it was able to serve, with later modifications of course, as the basis for several institutionalized Buddhist sects—the Jōdo Shū, the Jishū and the Jōdo Shinshū.

References

Andrews, Allan A. 1973. *The Teachings Essential for Rebirth: A Study of Genshin's Ōjōyōshū*. Monumenta Nipponica Monograph. Tokyo: Sophia University Press.

Andrews, Allan. 1987. "The Senchakushū in Japanese Religious History: The Founding of a Pure Land School." *Journal of the American Academy of Religion* 55.3.

Andrews, Allan. 1989. "Genshin's Essentials of Pure Land Rebirth and the Transmission of Pure Land Buddhism to Japan, Part One: The First and Second Phases of Transmission of Pure Land Buddhism to Japan—The Nara Period and the Early Heian Period." *Pacific World: Journal of the Institute of Buddhist Studies*. (N. S.) 5.

Andrews, Allan. 1990. "Genshin's *Essentials of Pure Land Rebirth* and the Transmission of Pure Land Buddhism to Japan, Part Two: The Third Phase of Transmission of Pure Land Buddhism to Japan—A Quantitative Survey of the Resources Utilized by Genshin's *Essentials of Pure Land Rebirth* for the Cultivation and Efficacy of Nembutsu" *Pacific World: Journal of the Institute of Buddhist Studies*. (N.S.) 6.

Andrews, Allan. 1991. "Genshin's *Essentials of Pure Land Rebirth* and the Transmission of Pure Land Buddhism to Japan, Part Three: The Third Phase of Transmission of Pure Land Buddhism to Japan—An Examination of the Continental Ideas and Modes of

---

19   Inoue and others (Shigematsu 1964; Satō 1956; Andrews 1989, 1990, 1991) have documented the impact of Chinese Pure Land upon early and mid-Heian Japanese Pure Land devotionalism, especially upon the *Ōjōyōshū*, and the impact of this text in turn upon popular piety.

Nembutsu Introduced by Genshin's *Essentials of Pure Land Rebirth.*" *Pacific World: Journal of the Institute of Buddhist Studies.* (N.S.) 7.

Andrews, Allan. 1993. "Lay and Monastic Forms of Pure Land Devotionalism: Typology and History." *Numen* 40.

Fujiwara Ryōsetsu. 1957. *Nembutsu shisō no kenkyū* [Studies on nembutsu thought]. Kyoto: Nagata Bunshodō.

Hōnen. *Passages on the Selected Nembutsu of the Original Vow* (Senchaku hongan nembutsu shū). *T.* 2608.

Hori Ichirō. 1953. *Shūkyōshi hen* [Religious history]. Waga kuni minkan shinkoshi no kenkyū 2 [Researches on the folk beliefs of our land 2], Tokyo: Shogen Shinsha.

Hori Ichirō. 1958. "On the Concept of *Hijiri* (Holy-man)." *Numen* 5.2: 129–160, and 5.3: 199–232.

Ienaga Saburō. 1963. *Chūse Bukkyō shisōshi kenkyū* [Studies in the history of medieval Buddhist thought]. Rev. ed. Kyoto: Hōzōkan.

Ienega Saburō, Akamatsu Toshihide, and Tamamuro Taijō, eds. 1967–68. *Nihon Bukkyō shi* [A history of Japanese Buddhism]. 3 vols. Kyoto: Hōzōkan.

Inoue Mitsusada, and Ōsone Shōsuke. 1974. *Ōjōden-Hokegenki* [Accounts of Rebirth and Miraculous Tales of the Lotus Sūtra]. Nihon shisō taikei 7. [Compilation of Japanese thought 7]. Tokyo: Iwanami Shoten.

Inoue Mitsusada. 1975. *Nihon Jōdokyō seiritsushi no kenkyū* [Studies in the history of the establishment of Japanese Pure Land Buddhism]. Rev. ed. Tokyo: Yamakawa Shuppansha.

Ishida Mitsuyuki. 1952. *Nihon Jōdokyō no kenkyū* [Studies on Japanese Pure Land Buddhism]. Kyoto: Hyakkaen.

Ishii Kyōdō. 1969. *Senchaku shū zenkō* [Commentary on the *Senchaku shū*]. Kyoto: Heirakuji Shoten.

Itō Yuishin. 1969. "Amida no *hijiri* ni tsuite: Minkan Jōdokyō e no ichi shiten" [Amida *hijiri*: A perspective on popular Pure Land Buddhism]. *Nihon Jōdokyōshi no kenkyū.* Eds. Fujishima and Miyazaki. Tokyo: Heiryakuji Shoten.

Itō Yuishin. 1981. *Jōdoshū no seiritsu to tenkai* [The establishment and development of the Pure Land Denomination]. Tokyo: Yoshikawa Kōbunkan.

Itō Yuishin. 1984. "Jōdo shinkō to *hijiri* no katsudo" [Pure Land faith and *hijiri* activities]. *Amida Shinkō* [Amida faith]. Ed. Itō Yuishin. Minshū shūkyōshi sōsho [History of folk religion series]. Tokyo: Osankaku Shuppan K. K.

Kikuchi Yujirō. 1982. "Kurodani Bessho to Hōnen" [Kurodani monastic retreat and Hōnen]. *Hōnen.* Eds. Itō Yuishin and Tamayama Jōgen. Nihon meisō ronshū 6 [Studies of eminent clergy 6]. Tokyo: Yoshikawa Kōbunkan.

Kotas, Fredrick J. 1987. "Ōjōden: Accounts of Rebirth." Diss. University of Washington.

Kuan Wu-liang-shou-fo ching / Bussetsu kan Muryōjubutsu kyō. (Amitābha Contemplation Sūtra.) *T.* 365.

Muller, F. Max, ed. 1969. *Buddhist Mahdāyāna Texts.* Sacred Books of the East 49. 1894. New York: Dover Publications.

Nakano Masaaki. 1985. "Nisonin shozō *Shichikajō seikai* ni tsuite" [On the *Seven Article Pledge* text of Nisonin Temple]. *Hōnen Shōnin to Jōdo Shū* [Hōnen Shōnin and the Jōdo Denomination]. Eds. Itō Yuishin and Tamayama Jōgen. Nihon Bukkyō shūshi ronshū 5 [Studies on the denominational history of Japanese Buddhism 5]. Tokyo: Yoshikawa Kōbunkan.

Ōhashi Toshio. 1972. Hōnen: *Sono kōdō to shisō* [Hōnen: His life and thought]. Tokyo: Hyōronsha.

O-mi't'o ching / Bussetsu Amida kyō. (Amitabha Sūtra.) *T.* 366.

Ryukoku University Translation Center, trans. 1984. *The Sūtra of Contemplation on the Buddha of Immeasurable Life as Expounded by Śākyamuni Buddha.* Ed. Meiji Yamada. Kyoto: Ryukoku University.

Satō, Tetsuei. 1956 "Eizan ni okeru Jōdokyō no keitai" [The development of Pure Land Buddhism on Mt. Hiei in the Tendai School]. *Bukkyō no kompon shinri* [The fundamental truths of Buddhism]. Ed. Miyamoto shōson. Tokyo: Sanseidō.

Shan-tao. *Kuan Wu-liang-shou-fo-ching shu / Kan Muryōjubutsukyō sho* [Commentary on the Amitabha Contemplation Sūtra]. *T.* 1753.

Shan-tao. *Wang-sheng li-tsan chieh / Ōjō raisan ge* [Hymns in Praise of Pure Land Rebirth]. *T.* 1980.

Shan-tao. *Kuan-nien A-mi-t'o-fo hsiang-hai san-mei kung-te fa-men / Kannen Amida Butsu sōkai sammai kudoku hōmon* [Methods and Merits of Samadhi of Contemplation and Reflection upon the Ocean-like Aspects of Amitabha Buddha]. *T.* 1959.

Shigematsu Akihisa. 1964. Nihon Jōdokyō seiritsu katei no kenkyū [Studies on the process of establishment of Japanese Pure Land Buddhism]. Kyoto: Heirakuji Shoten.

Taishō shinshū daizōkyō [Taishō Period revised edition of the Buddhist Canon]. 1924–32. Eds. Takakusu Junjirō and Watanabe K. 100 vols. Tokyo: Taishō Shinshū Daizokyō Kankōkai.

Takagi Yutaka. 1973. *Heian jidai Hokke Bukkyōshi kenkyū* [A study of the history of Heian period Lotus Buddhism]. Kyoto: Heirakuji shoten.

Tamura Enchō. 1959. *Hōnen.* Jimbutsu sōsho 36 [Biographical series 36]. Tokyo: Yoshikawa Kobunkan.

Tamura Enchō. 1972. *Hōnen Shōnin den no kenkyū* [Studies on the biographies of Hōnen Shōnin]. Rev. ed. Kyoto: Hōzōkan.

Wu-liang-shou ching / Bussetsu Muryōju kyō [Sūtra of Limitless Life]. *T.* 360.

Character List

akunin	悪人
bessho	別所
fanfu	凡夫
hijiri	聖
Hōnen-bō Genkū	法然房源空
Jōdo shū	浄土宗
jōsan nizen	定散二善
Kūya	空也
mappō	末法
mukae kō	迎講
nembutsu	念佛
nembutsu kō	念佛講
nembutsu shu	念佛衆
nien-fo	念佛
nyūdō	入道
ōjōden	往淨傳
shami	沙彌
Shan-tao	善導
shōjō no gō	正定業
T'an-luan	曇鸞
Tao-ch'o	道綽
zōgyō	雑行
zoku shami	俗沙彌

Socio-Economic Impacts of Hōnen's Pure Land Doctrines: an Inquiry into the Interplay between Buddhist Teachings and Institutions

Martin Repp

One of the leading figures of the new Buddhist schools of the Kamakura period, Nichiren 日蓮 (1222–1282), harshly criticized Hōnen 法然 (1133–1212), the acclaimed founder of the Pure Land school, for focusing only on Amida Buddha and the Pure Land sutras and thereby neglecting the other buddhas and sacred scriptures.[1] In his main work *Risshō ankoku-ron* 立正安國論 (Treatise on Establishing the Right [Teaching] for the Safety of the Country) he states in particular the devastating socio-economic consequences of such doctrines:

> The rulers of the nation contributed counties or villages so that the [Dharma] lamps might continue to burn bright before the images, while the stewards of the great estates offered [*kuyō* 供養] their fields and gardens (to provide for the upkeep of the temples).
>
> But because of this book by Hōnen, this *Senchaku Shū*, the Lord Buddha Shakyamuni is forgotten and all honor is paid to Amida, the Buddha of the Western Land.... If temples are not dedicated to Amida, then people no longer have any desire to support them or pay honor [*ku* 供] to the Buddhas enshrined there; if monks do not chant the Nembutsu, then people quickly forget all about giving these monks alms [*se* 施]. As a result, the halls of the Buddha fall into ruin, scarcely a wisp of smoke rises above their mossy tiles; and the monks' quarters stand empty and dilapidated, the dew deep on the grasses in their courtyards. And in spite of such conditions, no one gives a thought to protecting the Law or to restoring the temples. Hence, the sage monks who once presided over the temples leave and do not return, and the benevolent deities who guarded the Buddhist teachings depart and no longer appear. This has all come about because of this *Senchaku Shū* of Hōnen. How pitiful to think that in

Source: Repp, Martin, "Socio-economic Impact of Hōnen's Pure Land Doctrines: An Inquiry into the Interplay between Buddhist Teachings and Institutions," in Ugo Dessì (ed.), *The Social Dimension of Shin Buddhism*, Leiden, Boston: Brill, 2010. pp. 11–58.

[1] I would like to thank Galen Amstutz for correcting the English of this article and for helpful suggestions.

the space of a few decades [*sūjūnen* 数十年], hundreds, thousands, tens of thousands of people have been deluded by these devilish teachings and in so many cases confused as to the true teachings of Buddhism [*Bukkyō* 佛教]. If people favor perverse doctrines and forget what is correct, can the benevolent deities be anything but angry? If people cast aside doctrines that are all-encompassing and take up those that are incomplete, can the world escape the plots of demons? Rather than offering up to ten thousand prayers for remedy, it would be better simply to outlaw this one evil doctrine that is the source of all the trouble!

YAMPOLSKY 1990: 25; NSI 2: 1464–1465

In this passage Nichiren blames Hōnen's main systematic work, the *Senchaku-shū* 選擇集, for the disastrous situation of his time that temple buildings had fallen into decay due to lack of financial support and monks had deserted their monasteries. In other words, he draws a causal connection between Hōnen's new Pure Land doctrines and their socio-economic impact on Buddhist institutions. Nichiren goes even further in his criticism when blaming Hōnen for threatening the peace and stability of the Japanese nation as a whole. Considering that the *Risshō ankoku-ron* was written in 1260 (Yampolsky 1990: 12) and that the *Senchaku-shū* was composed in 1198, the disastrous effects of Hōnen's teachings must have occurred during the six decades in between. Hōnen taught that human beings can attain ultimate liberation (*gedatsu* 解脱) from suffering only through the exclusive practice of the *nenbutsu* (*senju nenbutsu* 專修念佛). In an elaborate discourse on the basis of the three Pure Land sutras and the teachings of Chinese Pure Land teachers he argued that during his time of the "Final Dharma" (*mappō* 末法) there was no other possibility to attain certain liberation. In consequence, all other practices, such as giving donations or leaving the family to become monk or nun, are viewed as being only of relative value.

The present study attempts to elaborate the social and economic impacts of Hōnen's doctrine. In the background stands the methodological consideration that Buddhist studies and studies on religions in Japan tend to focus on doctrinal discourses or religious 'ideas' and thereby to neglect social, economic and political contexts.[2] As it is well known, a major step to elaborate the relationship between religious doctrines and economic life was undertaken by Max Weber in his groundbreaking work *The Protestant Ethic and the Spirit of*

---

2 In two reviews I have demonstrated how the negligence of historical contexts results in insufficient analyses or even wrong depictions of the subject matter under scrutiny. Cf. Repp (2002a; 2002b).

Capitalism. Apart from sociology of religion, approaches by historians investigating religion in socio-economic contexts also have to be mentioned, such as Kuroda Toshio (1996a; 1996b; 1996c) and Mikael Adolphson (2000) for medieval Japanese history.[3] Following basically this direction, the present study now tries—from the side of religious studies—to bridge the gap between doctrinal studies on the one hand, and historically oriented socio-economic research on the other hand.[4] Therefore the theme of this paper is mainly concerned with social and economic impacts that Hōnen's teachings exerted.[5]

Leaving here aside the question whether Nichiren's criticism quoted above is a polemic exaggeration or not, it serves here as starting point for examining other related religious texts under the guiding question of their social and economic implications. Re-reading these texts under such perspective brings to light not only the immediate socio-economic context of religious doctrine, but sheds also new light on these teachings themselves and thereby provides a more comprehensive understanding of these doctrines. For heuristic reasons, this study will not follow the historical development, but will give an account more or less in reverse historical order, i.e. moving from the results to the cause. Thus, I will proceed from Nichiren's later critique to earlier criticism of Hōnen's teaching by contemporary religious authorities, especially the Tendai and Hossō schools (cf. Sections 1 and 2). After briefly sketching the persecution of Hōnen and his movement (Section 3), finally I will investigate Hōnen's own writings under the guiding question of their socio-economic implications (Section 4). In this section I will occasionally contrast his way of thinking with Heian Buddhism, especially the Tendai tradition in which he was raised. Thereby the specific character of his doctrine will become clearer.

---

3 For reasons of space, I refrain in this study from elaborating the problem of Buddhism and politics in the case of Hōnen. I also do not treat here the problem of 'Buddhist ethics' which recently became quite a popular subject, since I am concerned here with the problem of socio-economic facts, and not with ethical norms.

4 For Chinese Buddhism, Jaques Gernet (1995) has done this in his groundbreaking work *Buddhism in Chinese Society: An Economic History from the Fifth to the Tenth Centuries* which was published first in 1956.

5 Thereby this study leaves the complementary question of the economic and social factors leading to his doctrines as a task for future investigation. Further, since this paper limits itself to examine mainly (but not only) religious sources, it is hoped that historians will be stimulated to research also contemporary secular texts and thereby help to bridge the gap between different academic disciplines from their side. The basic methodological problem of many specialized studies today is that they artificially separate certain phenomena from their context and thereby provide inadequate pictures of reality. However, since the reality with which any kind of academic discipline is concerned is an extremely complex and interwoven entity, the development of interdisciplinary research is required in order to grasp it adequately.

In the concluding part, the findings of this study will be viewed in the perspective of subsequent Japanese history. It seems that the *Wirkungsgeschichte* of Hōnen's religious concept of equality can be found more in Jōdo Shinshū than in Jōdoshū. Here, its application can be found in socio-religious terms.

1 Criticism of Hōnen's Teaching by the Tendai School

The first official criticisms launched against Hōnen concerned more his followers and their behavior than his own person or teachings. In 1204, the Tendai abbot Shinshō 真性 sent Hōnen a letter complaining about certain abuses among his "stupid" (*guchi* 愚痴) and "fanatic" (obstinate or one-sidedly clinging, *henshū* 偏執) followers.[6] They "destroy *shingon* 信言 and *shikan* 止観" (the esoteric and contemplative Buddhist practices of Tendai), "slander the other buddhas and bodhisattvas" (except of Amida Buddha), urge believers of other teachings and practices to abolish them and follow only the "gate of the *nenbutsu*" (*nenbutsu-mon* 念仏門), break the Buddhist rules of conduct (or discipline, *kai* 戒), and, all in all, they pursue "heretic teachings" (*jahō* 邪法). Hōnen responded by a formal *Written Pledge in Seven Articles* (*Shichi kajō kishō-mon* 七箇條起請文; HSZ: 787–793), in which he strongly admonished his disciples to refrain from such abuses; at the end of the text he had the document signed by 180 of his disciples.

Since Hōnen was a Tendai monk, this was an intra-monastic criticism of certain abuses among his immediate disciples. The fact that the names of his disciples appear in this official document indicates that they have to be distinguished from the wider circle of Hōnen's followers, namely the larger *nenbutsu* movement centering around Hōnen and his disciples. This document mentions also their attempt to convert other Buddhist believers to the *nenbutsu-mon*, which implies reduction in membership and support of the Tendai institution. Apart from this criticism, no other specific elements of social or economic impacts by Hōnen's teaching are mentioned here. The next document is more detailed in this respect.

2 Criticism of Hōnen's Teaching by the Hossō School

Whereas the Tendai criticism still was an intra-monastic affair, subsequent developments led to public conflicts. This occurred in the following year (1205)

---

6   The Tendai accusations are contained in Hōnen's response mentioned next; cf. HSZ: 787–789.

SOCIO-ECONOMIC IMPACTS OF HŌNEN'S PURE LAND DOCTRINES   259

when monks from Kōfukuji in Nara submitted an official petition to the imperial court in Kyōto in order to have the excesses of the sole *nenbutsu* (*senju nenbutsu*) teaching stopped as well as the "heretical" transgressions of Hōnen and his disciples. Like the previous Tendai admonition, this document indicates that Hōnen's teaching had begun to polarize the Buddhist community and thus added a new confrontation to the already existing conflicts among the traditional eight schools of the Heian period. The *Kōfukuji Petition* (*Kōfukuji sōjō* 興福寺奏状), was drafted by the famous scholar monk Jōkei Gedatsu-bō 貞慶解脱房 (1155–1213) (NST 15: 32–42; Morrell 1987: 75–88). What is important here is that the conflict surrounding Hōnen's movement for the first time was dragged from an intra-monastic conflict to a political level.[7] The *Kōfukuji Petition* is accompanied by a letter which mentions that previous attempts to "quell the annoyance" were not effective, on the contrary, the "agitation by Genkū's [Hōnen] followers" increased.[8] Since the main monasteries apparently were not able to handle this new movement anymore, they turned to political authorities. Hence, the letter states the purpose of the petition, that Kōfukuji launched this attempt to get it under control. When mentioning that lay followers posed problems, this letter (like the previous Tendai admonition) distinguishes between the inner circle of Hōnen's clerical disciples and the wider group of lay followers. This indicates that by then Hōnen's teaching had resulted in a broader movement which began to pose a socio-religious problem not only for the monasteries, but also for the public. Moreover, according to the petition, by then (1205) the social increase of Hōnen's movement was accompanied by a geographical spread throughout several provinces towards the north (Hokuriku) and east (Tōkai) of the old and the new capital, Nara and Kyōto (Morrell 1987: 86). Hence, the letter requests that an Imperial Proclamation should be sent throughout the whole country in order to restrain this movement (Morrell 1987: 88).

The *Kōfukuji Petition* addresses Hōnen's "defects" (or "errors," *ketsu* 欠) in nine articles, which mostly concern religious criticism of Hōnen's Pure Land teaching and practice. They criticize the errors of "establishing a new teaching" based on the principle of the exclusive *nenbutsu* practice (Article 1), designing new images for worship (Art. 2), slighting Śākyamuni (Art. 3), neglecting

---

7 It may contain also an indirect criticism against the Tendai school, since the rivalries between Tendai and Kōfukuji's Hossō school had a long history and were still continuing. In such case, the *Kōfukuji Petition* raised the initial intra-monastic affair to an inter-monastic as well as public level.

8 Morrell (1987: 88). This letter refers also to the previous Tendai criticism and Hōnen's response, as well as to an "order of prohibition" issued by the Retired Emperor Go-Toba which to my knowledge is not extant anymore.

the *kami* (Art. 5), ignoring the true character of the Pure Land (Art. 6), and misunderstanding the *nenbutsu* practice (Art. 7). Two articles address social and political issues such as vilifying monks and bringing disorder to the nation (Arts. 8 and 9). For our question first of all Article 4 is of immediate interest, the "Error of neglecting the multitude of good (practices)" (*manzen* 万善) which states:

> Numerous sectarian positions arise as occasion demands, and we partake of the good ambrosial medicine (of the Buddha's varying teachings) each according to our karmic predispositions. They all are aspects of the True Law which our great teacher Śākyamuni gained for us by difficult and painful labor over innumerable aeons. Now to be attached to the name of a single Buddha is completely to obstruct the paths essential for deliverance.
>
> MORRELL 1987: 78

This article further states that there are rumors spread by people saying that when reciting the *Lotus Sutra* one would fall into hell. "Hearing such opinions, people who earlier recited the eight or ten scrolls (of the *Lotus*) now reject it forever" (Morrell 1987: 78). Moreover, many people switch their religious affiliation as follows:

> Apart from these (who reject the *Lotus*) are others who once took refuge in the *Garland* and *Wisdom* sutras, or who developed spiritual affinities with esoteric (Shingon) or (Tendai) meditation (*shikan*) practices. Now, eight or nine out of ten give them up. As numerous as clods of dirt or sand are those who belittle or ridicule the building of temples and pagodas and the fashioning of sacred images. Lacking in both virtues and wisdom, they have little to hope for in the present or in the future.
>
> The Shōnin [Hōnen] is an intelligent man and certainly has no intention willfully to slander the Law! It is simply that among his disciples not a few are fools who are unable to comprehend the situation and so commit these evils.
>
> MORRELL 1987: 78

This article first emphasizes that the diversity of Buddhist teaching and practices necessarily corresponds with the various karmic dispositions of individual believers in order to attain ultimate liberation. At the same time, such a comprehensive approach allowed the diverse schools also to relate to and acknowledge each other by complementing each other. Already the previous articles attack the reductionism of the *senju nenbutsu* (or *ikkōshū* 一向宗) followers by maintaining that the "sacred teaching" of the Buddha cannot be reduced to calling the name (*shōmyō* 称名) of a single Buddha, Amida (Article 1), that the "other practices" (*yogyō* 余行) cannot be excluded (Art. 2), and that the "other Buddhas" (*yobutsu* 余仏) must be revered as well (Art. 3). Hōnen's exclusivist teaching results in reductionism which is unheard of in Buddhist tradition. Article 6 maintains that even in the Pure Land tradition a "variety of religious practices" was always acknowledged and guaranteed religious liberation (Morrell 1987: 81). It states: "If the *nembutsu* is not accompanied by other practices, then we will be lacking in good karma. The two approaches are complementary. How then can those who practice other methods be excluded from reception (*injō* [引摂]) into the Pure Land?" (Morrell 1987: 82).

The fourth article also mentions the social consequences of Hōnen's teaching and practice when stating that 90% of Buddhist believers are abandoning the traditional schools and converting to his new Pure Land movement. It is probably impossible today to verify such a figure. However, even if this statement is exaggerated for polemic reasons, it still indicates that a significant number of adherents of the established schools changed their 'karmic relation,' that is their religious affiliation, by joining the movement around Hōnen. Nichiren's statement quoted in the beginning confirms that this movement must have grown considerably. Hence, the loss of membership must have had grave impact on the Buddhist temple establishment of the time. In the next sentence, the petition deplores the economic consequences of such an enormous shift in religious allegiance. The numerous *nenbutsu* followers belittle the construction of temples and pagodas, as well as the carving of Buddhist statues. Thus, already in 1205—that is 55 years before Nichiren deplored the bad consequences of Hōnen's doctrine—its social and economic impact is felt considerably.

The fifth article criticizes that Hōnen's followers disrespect the spirits and deities (*reijin* 霊神). Thereby they do not revere the union into which buddhas and the *kami* 神 entered in Japan. The petition reminds that the buddhas have a close connection with the local *kami* since they accommodated themselves to the religious situation of this country and had left their traces (*suijaku* 垂跡) in form of the *kami* long ago; hence, the *kami* were turned into avatars (*gongen* 権現) of the buddhas. In other words, the *nenbutsu* followers reject the important Buddhist *honji suijaku* 本地垂跡 (original ground and traces) teaching from the Heian period, which enabled Buddhism to accommodate indigenous beliefs and thereby to establish itself in Japan. The petition provides examples of famous priests who revered the indigenous deities, such as the Tendai founder Saichō 最澄 (767–822), who prayed at the Usa Hachiman Shrine in

Kyūshū as well as at the Kasuga Shrine in Nara. This leads to the social, economic and political context of the *honji suijaku* doctrine. First of all, Buddhism as a foreign religion somehow had to find ways to reconcile with indigenous *kami* beliefs, especially because the *kami* were closely connected with the land. For example, when Buddhist temples were built, the local *kami* had to be appeased by elevating them to protective deities of the new establishment. Or when noble families added to their traditional *kami* worship also the veneration of foreign buddhas and built clan temples, the new "deities" had to be reconciled with the clan shrines. This resulted in a dual system combining shrine and temple (*jisha* 寺社). A famous example of such a pair was Kasuga Shrine and Kōfukuji (as mentioned in the petition), both at the same time serving for, and being sponsored by, the Fujiwara clan. Further, on the state level, when Nara was established as constant capital for a newly centralized state, the government officially asked the Hachiman deity in Usa to grant permission for constructing the central state temple Tōdaiji with the grand Buddha statue, intended to serve as religious symbol for a unified state.[9]

When Hōnen's followers now began to disrespect the indigenous *kami*, they damaged a closely interwoven system of interplay between native and foreign religion, between Buddhist temples and noble patrons, and between the court and the Buddhist temple establishment. Such a socio-religious system had been established during a long time beginning with the Nara period. When neglecting one important element such as the *kami*, the social, economic and political system as a whole was threatened. This is also the background for Nichiren's complaint quoted above that the "benevolent deities who guarded the Buddhist teachings [have] departed" because they were neglected by Hōnen's followers.

As mentioned above, the *Kōfukuji Petition* argues in Article 6 that the *nenbutsu* and the other practices supplement each other. However, the problem is not only one on the horizontal level of 'diversity' versus 'one practice.' This conflict extends to the vertical dimension as well, as the following passage of this article states, which is crucial for our study:

> However, people today neglect the root and go for the branches, rely on the inferior [*retsu* 劣] and scorn the superior [*shō* 勝]. How could they be

---

9 The deity, known for protecting the country from foreign dangers, consented through oracle. However, he demanded also that a shrine for him would be erected next to the state temple on Tamuke-yama. In gratitude for this cooperation, Hachiman received the Buddhist title of a bodhisattva. This is one of the first cases that a Japanese deity was granted a Buddhist title and in this combination emerged as a Buddhist incarnation. Cf. Repp (2002c: 176–177).

in conformity with the purpose of the Buddha? On the day when an august emperor designates, at the court where he conducts affairs of state, the officials to act on his behalf, he requests service from the wise and the foolish [*kengu-shina* 賢愚品], each according to their abilities, and from families both of high and low status [*kisen-ke* 貴賤家]. But to the foolish he does not entrust a position which would not be within their capacity even if they were to apply themselves from morning till night; and a person of low social status cannot advance to the rank of the nobility even if he is diligent in public affairs. In his own country the Great King of Enlightenment dispenses his ranks of Nine Stages [*kubon no kaikyū* 九品の階級] (described in the *Sutra of Meditation on Amida Buddha*) at the gate where the wise and the foolish come to his court. His principle of selection is surely that one receives in accord with his performance in observing virtuous behavior in former lives. It would be an excess of stupidity for one to rely entirely on the Buddha's power without taking into account his own condition in life.

> MORRELL 1987: 82; NST 15: 37–38

With these words, the *Kōfukuji Petition* characterizes the medieval socio-religious worldview quite clearly. The diversity of practices is necessary in order to accumulate many merits which affect the process of liberation. Here, diversity on a horizontal level transforms into a vertically structured hierarchy. In such a pyramid of diverse practices and teachings, each person has to strive to climb up the stages by accumulating merits as much as possible (cf. Section 4.2.4). When reducing practices to one only and relying on Amida's power alone, the pyramid must collapse. Here lies the subversive potential of Hōnen's teaching which negates the 'self-power' and emphasizes reliance on the 'other-power.' Moreover, by alluding to the distinction of high and low at the imperial court, the petition indicates that the social and the religious orders conform, or have to conform, to each other. In fact, the religious model of the nine stages (*kubon* 九品) of birth into the Pure Land originally derives from the system of court ranks in China. The compiler(s) of the *Contemplation Sutra* projected first this social rank system into the metaphysical realm, and later sources, such as the *Kōfukuji Petition* here, projected this pyramid again back into this world in order to confirm and stabilize the existing social order. Here, the hierarchies of this world and those in the world beyond affect each other reciprocally. The petition claims that the religious hierarchical order has to be maintained and thereby it must conform to the social order. There is no place for a socio-religious revolt whatsoever. After all, as the petition states: "Although we all sink (in this world of birth-and-death), the foolish sink straight down, and although we rise together, the wise quickly float like a bowl (on water)" (Morrell 1987: 83). Yet, "these [*nembutsu*] people dismiss such considerations" concerning the necessity to cultivate wisdom and morality (Morrell 1987: 83). Article 7 gives the principal admonition for the preservation of the existing socio-religious order: "Seek for mutual harmonization and do not delight in wanton opposition" (Morrell 1987: 85).

Whereas Articles 6 and 7 concern the impact of Hōnen's teaching on society, Article 9 on the "error of bringing disorder to the nation [country]" addresses its political consequences. Since the *Kōfukuji Petition* is submitted to the imperial court, this article certainly bears the gravest weight. It begins by stating:

> The Buddha's Law and the Imperial Law [*buppō-ōbō* 仏法・王法] are as body and mind: each should see to the well-being of the other, and then the welfare of the state will be assured. In these times, the Pure Land movement [lit. "gate," *jōdo no hōmon* 浄土の法門] has begun to arise and the activities of the Sole-practice to flourish. But can we also say that these are times when the imperial power has been restored? Moreover, the Three Learnings [*sangaku* 三学] (morality, wisdom, meditation) are about to be abandoned and the Eight Sects are declining. Time and again how the government of society is in disarray!
>
> What we wish is that the Nembutsu and the other sects would be as compatible as water and milk, and that the Buddha's Law would forever harmonize heaven and earth. But although the various (traditional) sects all believe in meditation on the Buddha (*nembutsu*) and harbor no ill designs against that movement, the Sole-practice followers deeply despise the other sects and will not share the same seat with them. They carry their conduct to this extreme, being as difficult to accommodate as fire and water.... In these Latter Days, if the Sole-practice people succeed in their campaign, the attitude of the government will be to see the other sects as so much rubbish. And even if it did not come to the point of their actually being banned, the Eight Sects would truly be as if they did not exist!
>
> MORRELL 1987: 86–87; NST 15: 41

This article begins with the traditional doctrine that imperial law (*ōbō*) and Buddhist law (*buppō*) conform to each other for the sake of mutual benefit (cf. Kuroda 1996b). By complementing each other they constitute a dual system. However, Hōnen's exclusive *nenbutsu* practice destroys not only the comprehensive and hierarchical system of salvation practiced in traditional schools, but endangers thereby also the sensitive power balance between religion and

SOCIO-ECONOMIC IMPACTS OF HŌNEN'S PURE LAND DOCTRINES 265

state. In other words, when Hōnen's movement reduces this comprehensive religious pyramid to a single practice, it destroys the socio-political pyramid of the time; in other words, it is subversive. The article observes that the "Pure Land Gate" is flourishing, whereas the traditional eight schools are declining. Then it even expresses the fear that the government may tolerate this movement up to the point that if Hōnen's movement would further succeed, it would endanger the very existence of the traditional schools being closely interlinked with aristocratic society and imperial court. Thus, this article expresses a sense of deep crisis among traditional schools. Fighting thus on two fronts, the threat of a new Buddhist movement and the danger of losing state support, the petition appears here to be nothing less than a desperate struggle for survival. This is also expressed in a subsequent passage of the petition which reminds the Japanese court of previous state suppressions of Buddhism in India and China in order to illustrate the gravity of the present situation in Japan. It is with such a sense of urgency that the petition further poses the question: "If an admonition is not forthcoming at this time, then how will future perplexities be resolved?" (Morrell 1987: 87). And while admitting that Buddhism "has had its problems since antiquity," it points out that (because of the serious present situation) "this common appeal by all the Eight Sects is unprecedented" (Morrell 1987: 87). Hence, the petition appeals to the court to issue an Imperial Decree "calling for the correction of the doctrine of the Sole-practice … as advocated by Genkū" (Morrell 1987: 87).

Today, it is difficult to estimate the extent of the danger that Hōnen's movement posed for the established schools. However, the "unprecedented" submission of such petition by "all the Eight Sects" (as it claims), as well as its contents, suggest that they felt a real threat and were prepared to fight for their own survival.

3 Prohibition and Persecution of Hōnen's Movement according to Jien's *Gukan-shō*

It seems that the court did not take immediate action after the submission of the *Kōfukuji Petition*. In all likelihood, one of the reasons was that Hōnen and his disciples already had supporters within the court who were able to shield them against attacks by the established schools.[10] The situation, however, was going to change suddenly and result in official prohibition of the exclusive *ne-*

---

10   Among them was the (former) regent Kujō Kanezane, who had requested from Hōnen a systematic outline of his doctrine which resulted (1198) in the composition of his major

nbutsu teaching and the persecution of Hōnen and his movement. The occasion for such abrupt change in government policy is recorded by Kanezane's brother Jien 慈円 (1155–1225), a four-time Tendai abbot and a critic of Hōnen (cf. Brown and Ishida 1979: 237). In his work *Gukan-shō* 愚管抄 (Notes of My Foolish Views, 1219) he presents the fateful event as follows:

> Also during the Ken'ei years (1206–1207) there was a religious man named Hōnen. Close to this time, while living in Kyōto, he established the *nembutsu* school [*nenbutsushū* 念佛宗] and called his teachings the exclusive *nembutsu*. 'You should do nothing more than utter (the name of) Amida Buddha. Do not undertake the esoteric or exoteric practices of the eight schools,' he would say. Ignorant or unenlightened lay priests and nuns [*guchi muchi no ama nyūdō* 愚癡無智ノ尼入道] of questionable circumstance delighted in his teaching, and it began to flourish beyond expectation and to gather strength. Among them was a monk named Anrakubō ... Upon ordination Anrakubō became an adherent of the exclusive *nembutsu*, and in association with Jūren (d. 1207) he advocated singing the praises (of Pure Land) six times a day (*rokuji raisan*), which is said to have been the practice of master Shan-tao.[11] There were numerous people, among them nuns, who turned to this teaching and placed their trust in it. They were given to believe that, once they became followers, then even if they indulged in sexual relations or ate meat or fish, Amida Buddha would not regard it as a wrongdoing in the least, and that, once they had entered into the single-hearted and exclusive way and had faith in nothing but the *nembutsu*, then at the end of their life Amida would come without fail to usher them into the Pure Land. As people in both the capital and countryside turned to this, a lady-in-waiting at the detached palace of the retired emperor, along with the mother of the imperial priest of the Ninnaji temple, also placed their faith in it. Secretly they summoned Anrakubō and the others to have them share their teachings with them, and so he proceeded there, together with his companion, and even spent the night there. Such a thing is unspeakable, so in the end Anrakubō and Jūren were beheaded. Also Hōnen was exiled, driven from his residence in Kyōto.

---

work, the *Senchaku-shū*. Another possible supporter could be Kanezane's son Yoshitsune who was regent at that time (Kleine 1996: 53).

11   Already in 1205, Hōnen had removed Anraku-bō together with another follower from the group of his disciples (Kleine 1996: 53).

This affair was dealt in such a way that it seemed in a short time that things were under control. Hōnen, however, had not been an ally in the plot, so he was pardoned, and eventually he died at Ōtani in the Higashiyama section of Kyoto.

DOBBINS 1989: 15–16; NKBT 86: 254–255; cf. BROWN AND ISHIDA 1979: 171–172

Jien first characterizes the wider circle of Hōnen's followers as "ignorant and stupid" nuns and novices.[12] He then remarks that the movement around him "began to flourish beyond expectation and to gather strength," and that it attracted people in the capital and countryside. These characterizations conform more or less to those of the *Kōfukuji Petition*. Now, concerning the event in 1206 causing the persecution, due to lack of historical sources we cannot determine precisely what really happened in the palace. It occurred at a time when the Retired Emperor Go-Toba was not in Kyōto but on pilgrimage to Kumano.[13] What is safe to say is that the retired emperor perceived this incident as an intrusion into the inner realm of his authority. The *Kōfukuji Petition* raised already the fear that Hōnen's teaching of the exclusive *nenbutsu* practice subverts the socio-religious hierarchy and that it damages the relationship between the Buddhist establishment and the government. It is the intrusion into the inner circle of imperial authority that unleashed the harsh reaction by the court, resulting in prohibition and persecution of Hōnen's movement.

As we have seen, the conflicts surrounding Hōnen's doctrines first had been triggered by intra-monastic struggles of the Tendai school, then developed to an inter-monastic and public affair because of the *Kōfukuji Petition*, and finally reached the political plane of an open conflict between the court and a new religious movement which in the span of only a few years had entered the stage of Japanese history.

4 The Socio-Economic Implications of Hōnen's Teachings

In Chapter 3 of his main work *Senchaku-shū*, Hōnen provides a concise summary of the interplay between Buddhist doctrine and the socio-economic situation of believers according to his own Pure Land teaching. Here he writes:

---

12   *Nyūdō* are lay people who had taken Buddhist vows but continued to live at home. In any case, such novices and the nuns are socially located on the lowest level of the Buddhist clerical hierarchy, just above ordinary lay people.

13   For the political significance of Kumano pilgrimages of retired emperors during the transition from the Heian to the Kamakura period, see Moerman (2005: 139–180).

Because the *nenbutsu* is easy (to practice), it is open (or relates, *tōsu* 通す) to all [people]. Because the manifold practices are difficult [to master], they are not open to the diverse [human] capacities. However, was it not [the aim of Dharmākara's] Basic Vow (*hongan* 本願)[14] to abandon the difficult and take up the easy [practices] in order to enable all sentient beings to attain birth in equality (*byōdō ni ōjō* 平等に往生)?

If the Basic Vow required to make Buddha images or to build pagodas (or stupas), poor and destitute [people] certainly would have to give up hope for birth. However, the rich and noble people are few and the poor and low people are extremely numerous. If the Basic Vow required wisdom and high intelligence, the foolish and dull certainly would have to give up hope for birth. However, the wise are few and the foolish are extremely numerous.... If the Basic Vow required to observe the precepts and to keep the monastic rules, the people who break the precepts or do not [know] the precepts certainly would have to give up hope for birth. However, the people keeping the precepts are few and the people breaking the rules are extremely numerous. One should know that it is the same with the other practices.

One should understand this correctly. If the Basic Vow would have required the various practices [mentioned] above, the people being able to attain birth would be few and those not attaining birth would be numerous. However, Amida Nyorai, when long ago he was the monk Dharmākara, being moved by compassion of equality (*byōdō no jihi* 平等の慈悲) in order to grasp all [people] comprehensively, did not make the Basic Vow for birth by requiring the various practices such as making Buddha statues or building stupas. He made the Basic Vow requiring only the one practice of reciting the *nenbutsu* (*tada shōmyō nenbutsu no ichi-gyō* ただ稱名念佛の一行).

> HSZ: 320; OHASHI II: 198–199; cf. Senchakushū English Translation Project 1998: 77–78

Hōnen argues here on the basis of the Pure Land doctrinal distinction between easy and difficult practices. As examples of the latter, he takes up donations as one of the main practices of lay followers thought to produce merits for ultimate liberation, keeping the precepts both by lay people as well as by monks and nuns, and studying sutras and treatises as the monastic cultivation of

---

14 *Hongan* is normally translated as "Original/Primal Vow." However, Hōnen's discourse on this vow suggests the translation offered here. The term denotes the 18th Vow among Dharmākara's 48 vows.

wisdom. Then he argues that those who are able to practice and master these paths are very few, and those who fail to accomplish them are by far the majority. Over against these practices, Hōnen explains the *nenbutsu* as an easy practice which was chosen by Amida Buddha in his previous state as bodhisattva since he was motivated by his "compassion of equality." His compassion of equality aims at the one goal of enabling all sentient beings to attain "birth in equality" (cf. Section 4.1.4). Beginning with concrete applications of this term of "equality," the following part (4.1) will elaborate some of the socio-religious implications of Hōnen's teachings. The subsequent part (4.2) then will deal with its consequences for the 'religious economy.'

4.1 *Socio-Religions Impacts of Hōnen's Teachings*

To begin with the quotation of the *Senchaku-shū*, "equality" (*byōdō*) is for Hōnen a religious term and certainly does not bear the social, legal and political meaning in the modern sense. The expression "compassion of equality" is an attribute of Amida Buddha, therefore it is a metaphysical term. And the expression "birth in equality," characterizing the way of ultimate liberation, is a soteriological term.

Thus, when Hōnen uses the term "equality," he does not directly aim at reforms of contemporary feudal society, as modern readers may be looking for. This world is for him the realm of immeasurable suffering from which human beings have to be liberated (*shutsuri* 出離, *gedatsu*) for sure and as fast as possible. However, even though Hōnen does not develop social, legal or political concepts of "equality" in the human world, his two religious terms exert certain effects in the human world. He is critical of the basic worldview of his time according to which social status and mundane value systems predetermine religious liberation. As such he also challenges the existing monastic-institution that had been structured according to social differences and mundane hierarchies.

Hōnen frequently mentions the basic human differences between men and women, young and old, wise and fool, and good and bad, but also the socio-economic differentiations between rich and poor, or between high and low. As an opposite term to equality, he uses the word *shabetsu* 差別, which means difference or distinction.[15] The subsequent sections will elaborate Hōnen's doctrinal treatment of human and social distinctions.

---

15   This meaning has to be distinguished from the modern Japanese usage (read *sabetsu*) which clearly means social discrimination.

4.1.1 Wise and Stupid: the Question of Intellectual Facilities

Contemporary attacks by Tendai, the *Kōfukuji Petition* and Jien's *Gukan-shō* share the criticism that the *nenbutsu* movement around Hōnen consisted mostly of stupid people. This section will examine such criticism from the point of view of Hōnen and his followers.

In the *Yōgi mondō* 要義問答, a didactic conversation on Pure Land practice and doctrine between Hōnen and an unknown interlocutor, the latter asks the question as to how "stupid persons (*oroka naru mono*) like us" can hope for birth into the Pure Land (HSZ: 615). The underlying presupposition is that intellectual facilities are assumed to be factors for liberation. Hōnen responds first by referring to the present time of *mappō*, in which it is impossible to attain awakening. Then he quotes from Eikan (Yōkan) 永観, a monk of the Tendai Pure Land tradition of the Heian period, according to which Tendai esoteric practice (*shingon*) and contemplation (*shikan*) penetrate deeply into principles, but that they are difficult to practice in order to attain *satori*. And the teachings of the Nara schools Hossō and Sanron are extremely deep, but make it easy to get lost. However, after having been born in the Pure Land, it is easy to attain awakening (*yasuku satorase tamawan*) (HSZ: 615–616; Ohashi III: 183). In the *mondō Nenbutsu ōjō yōgi-shō* 念佛往生要義抄, a didactic conversation on birth into the Pure Land through *nenbutsu* practice, an interlocutor poses the question as to whether there is a difference (*shabetsu* 差別) between the *nenbutsu* recited by a stupid person (*gusha* 愚者) and that by a wise person (*chisha* 智者). Hōnen responds by stating: "If [our deliberation] is based on Buddha's Basic Vow, there is not a tiny bit of distinction (*shabetsu*)" (HSZ: 687; Ohashi III: 221). In another *mondō*, Shinkū 信空, a Dharma brother and later a disciple of Hōnen, asks the question whether wisdom (*chie* 智慧) would be a "condition for birth" (*ōjō no yōji* 往生の要事), in other words, whether one has to study the scriptures (*shūgaku* 修学) diligently. Hōnen responds that the karmic relevant practice for birth is reciting the *nenbutsu* since "neither wise nor ignorant [persons] (*uchi muchi* 有智无智) are detested" (HSZ: 669).

Now we have to examine which social groups may be concerned with the distinction between wise and fool. First of all, the question posed by the Tendai monk Shinku indicates that this was of concern in the monastic community which at that time was structured in a hierarchical order. The bottom of the pyramid consisted of the menial workers (*shuto* 衆徒) and the ordinary hall priests (*dōshū* 堂衆) who served in daily rituals, maintenance and lower administration. Further up were the scholar monks (*gakushō* 学生) who supplied the leadership of temples and the whole order (*sangō* 三剛) (Adolphson 2000: 55, 158, 415). Thus, the intellectual distinction between "wise" and "stupid" marked for monks a major social distinction within the order. Among scholar monks was much competition to achieve higher positions in the temple administration and in clerical ranks. The traditional way to climb the ladder was through the process of mastering the doctrines, participating in official disputations (*rongi* 論議, *ryūgi* 竪義), and then being appointed by the court for official clerical ranks.[16] Thus, ascending the hierarchy by way of cultivating wisdom decided not only about the respective position in the hierarchy of the order, it affected also public recognition in the mundane world and resulted in patronage as well. And since in the Heian and Kamakura periods the hierarchies of society, religious institutions, and the afterlife corresponded with each other, wisdom and its lack decided also about one's future fate in the world beyond.

There was also another group of people concerned with the problem of wisdom and ignorance, namely those religious *bushi* (warriors) who had intellectual ambitions. This issue is raised in an inquiry by Tsunoto no Saburō 津戸 の三郎 and Kumagai Naozane 熊谷直実, Hōnen's most famous *bushi* followers, both from the Kantō region. In a letter Hōnen responds to their problem that according to public opinion of the time the "*nenbutsu* is recommended especially for ignorant people (*muchi no mono* 无智ノモノ), whereas [religious practice] for wise persons (*uchi no hito* 有智ノ人) is not limited to the *nenbutsu*" (HSZ: 501; Ohashi III: 69). Hōnen first states that this is a grave mistake. Then he explains that the *nenbutsu* is not limited to wise or to ignorant people since Amida's Basic Vow (*hongan*) is for all sentient beings (*issai shujō* 一切衆生). He did not make a vow for ignorant people to recite *nenbutsu* and another vow for wise people to pursue "other deep practices" (HSZ: 501; Ohashi III: 69. Cf. HSZ: 572; Ohashi III: 116–117).

In another letter to a high placed person of the warrior nobility, Hōnen takes up this inquiry by Tsunoto and Kumagai, apparently in response to a previous question.[17] This letter is addressed to Hōjō Masako 北條政子 (1157–1225), Minamoto Yoritomo's wife and one of the most powerful women of the early Kamakura government (*bakufu*). Here, Hōnen partly repeats his previous answer (see above), but also elaborates it further when he writes:

> ... the *nenbutsu* practice, in principle (*motoyori*), does not select (or discriminate, *erabasu*) between wise and ignorant; the great vow (*daigan* 大願) sworn by Amida long ago was for all sentient beings comprehensively. It is not that he made a vow for the ignorant [to practice] *nenbutsu*

16　Since the second part of the Heian period, noble birth played an important role for a fast track to top positions.

17　In this letter it becomes also clear that the public opinion was that Hōnen had recommended the *nenbutsu* practice only for the ignorant people (HSZ: 527).

and not a vow for the wise [to perform] the other practices. It is for [all] sentient beings of the world of the ten directions. Without separating (*hedatesu*) wise and unwise, good and bad people, keeper and breaker of precepts, nobility and low people, or men and women, ... it is precisely the *nenbutsu* alone that is the prayer (*kitō* 祈祷) for this and the next world.

HSZ: 527–573; OHASHI III: 8–9

Since the intellectual distinction between ignorant and learned people implied social differentiation between low and high, Hōnen's teaching of the *nenbutsu* practice for all people equally had also social implications. Thus, when the criticism voiced by Tendai and Kōfukuji targeted especially the ignorance of Hōnen's disciples and followers at large, this certainly implied also critique of his leveling the socio-religious 'separations' or hierarchies. Cultivation of wisdom was a highly esteemed goal in contemporary society both religious and secular; as for the religious world, it is one of the three basic Buddhist practices (*sangaku* 三学) and of the six bodhisattva practices (*ropparamitsu* 六波羅蜜). When Hōnen did not emphasize the cultivation of wisdom, it contributed to the bad image of his doctrine as being suited for fools only, and to that of his movement as being a band of low and stupid people.[18] It should be kept in mind, however, that critics blamed Hōnen himself for various shortcomings and heresies, but never for being a fool. In the context of his movement of 'fools,' however, it may appear as an irony of history that early hagiographers called Hōnen "wisdom number one" (*chie dai-ichi* 智慧第一) of his time. Considering his doctrinal masterpiece, the *Senchaku-shū*, in which he coined the term "selection" (choice, *senchaku* 選釋) that expresses nothing less than the paradigm shift occurring between the Heian and Kamakura periods (cf. Repp 2005a: 513–519), such characterization seems to be no exaggeration.

4.1.2 Women and Ritual Taboos

As for the religious status of women, in his early explanation of the *Muryōju-kyō* 無量壽經, the *Muryōjukyō-shaku* 無量壽經釋, Hōnen treats at length Amida's 35th Vow which states that upon birth into the Pure Land the body of women will change into that of men. In modern perspective, this seems to be gender discrimination. However, before judging too quickly from hindsight, we have to view Hōnen's interpretation in its historical context and see which kind of

---

18 Considering the fact that among Hōnen's followers were also a number of middle class samurai, members of the warrior and court nobility as well as of the imperial family, the opponents' image portrays only one part of the reality.

SOCIO-ECONOMIC IMPACTS OF HŌNEN'S PURE LAND DOCTRINES 273

innovations he brought forth in his own time. First he refers to the 18th Vow (the "Basic Vow") concerning birth in the Pure Land through *nenbutsu* and states that this vow does not "detest" (*kirawazu* 嫌わず) men or women (HSZ: 75; Ohashi I: 91). In other words, this vow treats both genders equally in respect to the way towards liberation. Then he explains that Amida made the 35th Vow only because there were certain doubts (*utagai* 疑) concerning their possibility to attain birth (HSZ: 76, cf. 75; Ohashi I: 93, cf. 91). For elaboration of such doubts he quotes passages from sutras and treatises which state that women cannot attain liberation. Then, and this is characteristic for Hōnen's way of thinking, he proceeds from the abstract doctrinal level to that of concrete reality, namely that of Buddhist institutions at this time. First he mentions the sacred mountains, Mt. Hiei, the main Tendai monastery, where he practiced and studied as monk for many years, as well as Mt. Kōya, the Shingon center. The founders Saichō and Kūkai, Hōnen explains, established a ritual boundary (*kekkai* 結界) preventing women from entering the sacred ground (*reichi* 霊地) (HSZ: 77; Ohashi I: 95–96). As for Mt. Kōya he states that even though the moon of esoteric Buddhism is supposed to shine universally (*amaneku* 普ク), it does not enlighten the darkness of women with their religious incapacity to attain liberation (HSZ: 77; Ohashi I: 96). Furthermore, also temples located in cities, such as the grand state temple Tōdaiji in Nara, prevent women from entering the halls and pray directly before the Buddha. They are allowed to pay reverence only in some distance from outside the gate. "How distressing (*kanashiki kana* 悲キ哉)!" Hōnen exclaims, and "how embarrassing (*hazubeki kana* 恥キ哉)!" (HSZ: 77; Ohashi I: 96).[19] Then Hōnen draws the conclusion from this discourse through the harsh religious realities of the time: when there are for women these hindrances (*sawari, shō* 障) of sacred mountains in this defiled world (*edo* 穢土) and when they are not permitted to approach Buddha statues made from dirty material, how could they possibly be born in a pure land with real buddhas? (HSZ: 77; Ohashi I: 97). Thus, after having moved in his reasoning first from the teachings of scriptures to the concrete world of religious institution, Hōnen then shifts to the metaphysical world, thereby deepening considerably the doubts concerning possibilities of liberation for women.

Now, having dwelt so extensively in doctrinal obstacles and institutional impossibilities for women to attain liberation—in other words, having now reached this climax in practical and doctrinal discourse on such

---

19   Formulations of emotional feelings, as articulated here, are not so often found in Hōnen's writings. They indicate of his deep personal concern for the liberation of religiously discriminated women.

'doubts'—Hōnen proceeds by quoting a passage from Shandao, the Chinese Pure Land teacher, to whose writings Hōnen himself owed the spiritual liberation from deep personal doubts concerning possibilities of his own ultimate liberation. Shandao explains the 35th Vow as follows:

> Because of [A]mida's power of the great vow (*daigan-riki* 大願力), when women recite the Buddha's name, at the proper time of the death their female body will be able to change into a male body at once they will attain birth [into the Pure Land] and, when entering the Buddha's grand assembly (*dai-e* 大会), will realize awakening of the unborn (*mushō o shōgo* 無生を証悟; i.e. nirvana).
>
> HSZ: 77–78; OHASHI I: 97

Shandao adds explicitly that those who teach otherwise are promoting deluded explanations (*mōsetsu* 妄説), which must not be believed.

Hōnen then concludes the explanation of the 35th Vow with his own brief words as follows: "This is the benefit of birth [owing to] the vow with [Amida's] mind of compassion, which at once removes the suffering of women and provides women with comfort (relief, joy, pleasure; *raku* 樂)" (HSZ: 78; Ohashi I: 97). Traditional Buddhist teachings and practices, described here by Hōnen as rendering liberation of women in this lifetime impossible, caused much additional distress for them in this world of suffering. However, as Hōnen explains the 18th and 35th vows, Amida's compassion relieves women from such evil spells and gives them joy in this life as well as hope for the next. Elsewhere (cf. Section 4.1.4) he calls this matter "birth in equality" based on Amida's "compassion of equality." Thus, the difference between the traditional Buddhist schools and Hōnen's teaching clearly illustrates how certain religious doctrines deeply influence the daily life of people. Religious, especially metaphysical concepts, are not floating somewhere in the sky, but occur in mutual interplay with existential and social realities in this world. Thus far, we have elaborated how Hōnen's teaching of women's birth into the Pure Land affects their present situation here and now by relieving them from deep religious anxieties and providing great hope and joy. Such a message certainly counts to a considerable degree for the fast and widespread growth of Hōnen's movement. After all, women constitute half of the population.

While Hōnen is mostly concerned with ultimate liberation in the world beyond, he also deals with concrete issues of religious practice in this world. From the perspective of contemporary religious practice we now shall elaborate how his teachings further extend to socio-religious realities of women. In Hōnen's works is a lengthy *mondō* consisting of 145 brief exchanges between

Hōnen and an unknown interlocutor which contains much interesting information about contemporary beliefs and practices. Judging from the kind of questions, the interlocutor must be a woman of higher social standing. In the *Hyakuyonjūgo kajō mondō* 百四十五箇條問答 (henceforth abbreviated as *145 Mondō*), the following dialogues are recorded:

> Question: "During the time of menstruation (lit. "monthly fear," *tsuki no habakari*), are there problems with giving offerings to the *kami* or with reciting sutras?"
> Answer: "There is no fear in respect to *kami*, and in the Buddha Dharma (*buppō*) is no taboo (*imasu*, i.e. *monoimi*). Consult a diviner (*on'yōji* 陰陽師).
> ...
> Question: "Is it true, as [people] say, that there is avoidance (*habakari*) concerning visiting a *kami* [shrine] or Buddha [temple] (*shinbutsu* 神仏) during the hundred days after childbirth?"
> Answer: "Again, in the Buddha Dharma is no taboo."
> HSZ: 659; OHASHI III: 255

In these cases, Hōnen simply states that according to Buddhist teachings there is no taboo to be observed for women. Such a teaching, which conforms to his criticism of ritual borders (*kekkai*, see above), certainly is revolutionary for the religious world of the Heian and Kamakura periods. When the *Kōfukuji Petition* criticizes Hōnen for a lack of respect of the Japanese *kami*, this may imply concrete cases such as those quoted. Followers of the sole *nenbutsu* practice probably began to disregard ritual boundaries, such as those for women. Hōnen's leaving the monk quarters on Mt. Hiei and settling in Yoshimizu close to Kyōto at the slopes of the Eastern mountains, in my view, also has to be seen in the context of his endeavor to transcend the ritual borderline and make the Dharma available (*keta* 化他) to all people.

When Hōnen abolishes the borderline between ritual purity and impurity, this concerns not only women but also lay people in general. He applies such equalization also to the *nenbutsu* practice in daily life. When being asked in the *145 Mondō* whether it is permitted to continuously recite the *nenbutsu* after having eaten meat and other ritual unclean food, he replies: "For the *nenbutsu* are no [ritual] obstacles whatsoever" (HSZ: 650; Ohashi III: 242). In the same sense, he states in the aforementioned letter to Hōjō Masako:

> The practice of the *nenbutsu* in principle (*moto yori*) does not choose (*erabasu*) between walking, standing, sitting or lying down, between

the various karmic conditions (connections) of time and place; since it is a practice not discriminating the impurities (*fujō* 不浄) of body and mouth, it is called the birth [by] relieved (or joyful) practice (*rakugyō ōjō* 樂行往生).

HSZ: 531; OHASHI III: 14

Here, Hōnen applies the specific attribute *raku* 樂 of the transcendent Land of Utmost Bliss (*gokuraku* 極樂) directly to the religious practice in this immanent world; in other words, he existentializes a metaphysical concept. Since such a term bears considerable consequences for the daily life of believers, this again is an indication for the close interplay between doctrine and socioreligious reality. The same can be said of the feeling of *raku* (joy and relief) that women experience here and now in anticipation of their ultimate liberation as treated above.

4.1.3   Clergy, Lay People, and Religious Hierarchies

Above the ritual demarcation lines in respect to religious space (*kek-kai*) and human body (*monoimi, habakari*) were treated which were all removed by Hōnen's teaching. The following examples concern border lines within the Buddhist community, institution and path to liberation. Buddhism makes a fundamental difference between lay people (*zaike* 在家) and those who have left mundane life (*shukke* 出家) and dedicate themselves completely to religious practice. At the same time, this distinction marks a qualitative difference since the latter have accomplished a decisive step towards the ultimate goal whereas the former still have a long way to go, including leaving family, house and work. Whereas the Mahāyāna tradition had reevaluated lay people, for example, by admitting their potential to become bodhisattvas, actual Buddhist practice in Japan maintained the two-class system. In his teaching and practice, Hōnen recovers the basically equal treatment of both lay and clerics (monks and nuns).

In the *145 Mondō* the interlocutor asks: "Is it possible to attain birth [into the Pure Land] even if one does not leave the house (*shukke*)?" Hōnen replies by simply stating religious 'facts': "Those who have attained birth while being lay people (*zaike*) are many" (*zaike nagara ōjō suru hito ōshi* 在家ながら往生する人おほし) (HSZ: 662; Ohashi III: 259). Since Buddhist teachings stress the 'salvific' significance of *shukke* so much, the custom developed to have people take this step by the latest time possible, namely immediately before dying. From such a background, the lady raises the following question in the same *mondō*: "How is it when a man or woman dies and their hair is [still] attached [i.e. not shaved]?" In response, Hōnen states: "[Liberation] does not depend on the hair, but only the *nenbutsu* is regarded [as being its cause]" (HSZ: 662; Ohashi III: 259–260).

Since Amida's "great compassion of equality" (*byōdō no daihi* 平等の大悲) does not distinguish between *zaike* and *shukke* (HSZ: 684; Ohashi III: 216), this has for Hōnen also consequences for the liberating effect of the *nenbutsu* practice. In the *Nenbutsu ōjō yōgi-shō*, the interlocutor asks: "Is there [a difference of] superiority or inferiority (*shōretsu* 勝劣) between the *nenbutsu* recitation of a holy man (*shōnin* 聖人)[20] and the *nenbutsu* recitation of a lay person (*zaike*)?" Hōnen responds: "The merits of a holy man's *nenbutsu* and the worldly person's (*sekken-sha* 世間者) *nenbutsu* are the same (*kudoku hitoshiku* 功徳ひとしく); there is no difference whatsoever" (HSZ: 683; Ohashi III: 214). In the *Muryōjukyō-shaku*, Hōnen states: "If there would be a special vow (*betsugan* 別願) according to which abolishing one's house and discarding one's desire were [the condition for birth], monks and nuns (*shukke no ni-shū* 出家の二衆) would be born [in the Pure Land], but not lay men and lay women (*zaike no ryōhai* 在家の両輩)" (HSZ: 72; Ohashi I: 82). Thus, by removing the qualitative difference between lay and clerics in respect to the possibilities of liberation, Hōnen on the one hand raises the religious status of lay people while in a certain sense he degrades the high religious status of monks and nuns.

According to the medieval religious worldview mentioned above, the hierarchy of society corresponds with the monastic hierarchy, and again, the religious hierarchy of the various kinds of merits (*kudoku*) accumulated in this life-time correlates with the hierarchy in the transcendent world. In the Pure Land tradition, this transcendent hierarchy is represented by the pyramid of the nine classes (*kubon*) in which believers are born into the Pure Land according to their individual merits. An example for such belief is found in a hagiography of Genshin 源信 (942–1017), the most important Tendai Pure Land teacher of the Heian period. It provides first an impressive list of all his religious practices performed during his life which indicate the huge amount of his accumulated merits (*kudoku* 功徳). Then the hagiography contains a report by one of his disciples about a dream after Genshin's death. The dream was supposed to reveal Genshin's destiny in the world beyond. Thus, in view of his impressive *kudoku*, he was expected to be born in one of the higher levels of the Pure Land. However, to the disappointment of his disciple, in the dream conversation Genshin revealed that he was born in the "outermost circle" (Rhodes 1996: 56, 65). That is, he was not even born on the lowest of the

---

20   At this time, *shōnin* designates a religiously distinguished monk. In later times it became a formal title within monastic institutions.

nine levels. I understand this story and similar other accounts (see Fujiwara Michinaga's case below) as an indication that the traditional worldview of the correspondence between accumulated merits in this world and the fate in the next world began to erode since the middle of the Heian period.

In view of this traditional worldview, Hōnen in his Pure Land doctrine not only leveled the qualitative difference between lay and clerics, the most important demarcation line within the Buddhist institutional hierarchy in this world, but he even attempted to equalize the hierarchical system in the world beyond. It is significant that in his main work *Senchaku-shū* Hōnen refrains from elaborating the nine classes of birth in concrete terms, as earlier Pure Land teachers had done. Moreover, he explicitly questions the validity of the notion of the nine grades. In one *mondō* the following exchange between an anonymous interlocutor and Hōnen is recorded:

> Question: "Was the distinction (*shabetsu*) of the nine classes (*kubon*) in the [Land of] Utmost Bliss designed (or established) by Amida Buddha?"
> Answer: "The nine classes of the [Land of] Utmost Bliss are not [contained] in [A]mida's Basic Vow (*hongan ni arazu* 本願ニアラス), they are also not [found] in [in any of his] 48 vows, they are Śākyamuni's skillful words. If one would say that good persons and bad persons are born in the same place, then those with evil karma (*akugō* 悪業) would become lazy; for this reason, he created the differences (*shabetsu*) of the classes (*hon'i* 品位) and taught that good persons would ascend to the higher level (*jōbon* 上品) and bad people would descend to the lower ranks (*gebon* 下品). Go quickly, then you can see [for yourself]!"
> HSZ: 633; OHASHI III: 172

As this and other passages show, Amida's Basic Vow is for Hōnen the only criterion according to which any religious idea and practice have to be judged. Because the nine grades are not mentioned in the Basic Vow, they must not be perceived as true reality in the world beyond. However, he proceeds to argue pragmatically, since such a teaching may invite abuse. According to the *Kanmuryōju-kyō* 觀無量壽經 (cf. T 12.344c–346b), Śākyamuni taught birth in nine grades in order that bad people will not become lazy in their religious efforts. Hōnen's negation of the nine classes here is nothing else than his teaching of "birth in equality." In this *mondō* we observe that Hōnen's religious concept of equality, to be more precise, his soteriological concept of "birth in equality," extends even into the metaphysical realm of the Land of Utmost Bliss when declaring that it has no hierarchical structure whatsoever. Before discussing Hōnen's notion of equality in the concluding section of the part dealing with

SOCIO-ECONOMIC IMPACTS OF HŌNEN'S PURE LAND DOCTRINES 279

socio-religious implications of Hōnen's Pure Land doctrines (see Section 4.1.4), one more important element of hierarchical thinking has to be examined.

The elevated status of *shukke-sha* in Buddhist tradition implied also that priests served in the important function of *mediating* ultimate liberation for the religiously less qualified lay people. It is this role of mediation that renders the clerics a *conditio sine qua non* for the liberation of ordinary people. At the same time, it provides monastic institutions with the task and authority as *Heilsanstalt* (salvational institution) in society. This issue appears in concrete form, for example, in two questions of the female interlocutor of the *145 Mondō* as follows: "As for sutra[-readings], should one receive them by a priest (*sō* 僧)?" Hōnen pragmatically answers: "If one is able to read [sutras], it is not necessary to receive [readings by] a priest" (HSZ: 655; Ohashi III: 250). For Hōnen, sutra readings are not a question of a presupposed elevated status of a cleric which would qualify a ritual as valid and effective, but simply the practical issue of whether a lay person can read sutra texts in classical Chinese or not. Whereas this *mondō* pertains to the individual mediation by priests, the next exchange refers to the institutional mediation by temples. "Is it necessary to visit [temples] (*monomōde*) to listen [to the Dharma] (*chōmon* 聴聞)?" Hōnen answers: "It is alright not to go, but this is rather bad. You should recite only the *nenbutsu* quietly" (HSZ: 655; Ohashi III: 250). Hōnen deprives here the priesthood and the temples of their crucial role in the process of religious liberation. This led apparently to the situation, which critics later blamed Hōnen for, that temples were neglected and priests deserted monasteries. At the same time, Hōnen endowed practitioners of the *nenbutsu*, be it lay or clerics, with a new sense of being subjects of their religious liberation, he elevated them to the status of agents of their religious salvation. This is certainly one of the most significant implications of Hōnen's teachings.

The contemporary notion that a priest is absolutely necessary for lay people to attain ultimate liberation is personified in the *zenchishiki* 善知識, a spiritual advisor in the final hour of a believer. In Pure Land literature, the *zenchishiki* originally appears in the *Kanmuryōju-kyō* (T 12.345c–346a) as the one who assists people of the four lowest of the nine ranks to attain birth in the time before dying. With the popularization of the Pure Land tradition during the second part of the Heian period, this figure came to play a crucial practical role for those hoping to attain birth into the Pure Land. The lady asks Hōnen in the *145 Mondō*: "Is it possible to attain birth owing to the daily *nenbutsu* even though one does not meet a *zenchishiki* in the last hour (*rinjū* 臨終)?" Hōnen replies: "Even if one does not meet a *zenchishiki* and even if the last hour does not [occur] in the way as one hopes, if one recites the *nenbutsu*, one will be able to attain birth" (HSZ: 658; Ohashi III: 253).

Hōnen had become the spiritual advisor for a lady from the imperial family, who had renounced the world and assumed the clerical name Shōnyo-bō 正如房. When the nun s last hour approached, she sent Hōnen a letter requesting to come and act as her *zenchishiki*. He replied by writing, "abandon the thought [wish] for an ordinary person as spiritual advisor (*bonbu no zenchishiki* 凡夫の善知識) and rely on Buddha as spiritual guide (*hotoke no zenchishiki* 佛の善知識)" (HSZ: 545; Ohashi III: 54). This clearly marks the decisive shift from mediation of ultimate liberation by a religious professional to the new approach of direct agency by an ordinary religious individual. Thus, Hōnen enhances the religious status of women (including nuns) and lay people at large.

At another place, he explains the same issue in different terms: birth into Pure Land does not occur because of the "power (*chikara*) of a *zenchishiki*" in the last hour, but because of "reliance (*tanomi*) on the vow power of the other-power (*tariki no ganriki* 他力の願力) in daily life" (HSZ: 562–563; Ohashi III: 153). Here, Hōnen significantly shifts the focus in the salvational process from the role of another person outside to the inner attitude of the person concerned, from a professional religious mediator to the believer's own subjecthood or agency. The significance of Hōnen's emphasis of "entrusting" or "believing" (*shinjin* 信心) lies precisely in the (re-)discovery of the individual as an agent of the own liberation. In such a way, Hōnen removes individual and institutional mediators of ultimate liberation for ordinary people and enables believers to immediately approach this goal. Hōnen's doctrinal notions, such as Amida's other-power, the *nenbutsu*, Amida's compassion of equality and birth in equality, caused such widespread and profound change in contemporary perceptions of lay people, priests and Buddhist institutions. At the end of this part on the socio-religious implications of Hōnen's Pure Land doctrine, a brief review of his concept of "equality" is in order since it is the doctrinal backbone for his reshuffling the socio-religious system of his time.

4.1.4 The Notion of Religious Equality

Since the middle of the Heian period, a tendency towards socio-religious equality can be observed in Tendai Buddhism.[21] This tendency becomes especially apparent in the Pure Land tradition within Tendai. Hōnen had studied intensively the first major Pure Land work of this time, Genshin's *Ōjō yō-shū* 往生要集 (984) (NST 6; cf. HSZ: 3–26). In his early interpretations of this work,

---

21 An indication for such a tendency can be found, for example, in formulations of the *setsuwa* (edifying tales) collection *Hokke genki* 法華験記, such as "priest and lay ('worldly'), noble and commoners (*sōzoku kisen* 僧俗貴賤)" which string different classes in one row (NST 7: 140).

Hōnen quotes Genshin's expression (NST 6: 250) that the *nenbutsu* practice does not distinguish (*erabazu* 簡ばず) between men and women (*nannyo* 男女), between noble and commoners (*kisen* 貴賤), or between (religious practices while) walking, standing, sitting or lying down (*gyōjū zaga* 行住坐臥), and it does not dispute (*ronzezu* 論ぜず) the various karmic conditions of time and place (*jisho shoen* 時処緒縁). Hōnen quotes this passage later also in his main work, the *Senchaku-shū* (HSZ: 320; Ohashi II: 197).

According to this passage, the Pure Land practice disregards any difference in gender or social class. With the formulation "does not distinguish" Genshin remains in a negative description and does not arrive at a positive expression. Yet, Genshin's formulation indicates that the Pure Land tradition of the mid-Heian period implied already a tendency towards socio-religious equality. This trend probably was first triggered by itinerant monks such as Kūya 空也 (or Kōya, 903–972), who transformed the *nenbutsu* from a monastic practice into that of commoners in their secular life (cf. NST 7: 29; Repp 2005a: 164–165). In such spirit, Genshin writes in the introduction to his work the following: "Teaching and practice of birth into the Pure Land are the eyes and feet of the defiled world and final period. Priests and lay people, noble and commoners (*dōzoku kisen* 道俗貴賤), is there any person who would not take refuge in it?" (NST 6: 10). Such kind of formulation suggests that Genshin considered particularly the Pure Land teaching and practice to be suited comprehensively for different religious and social classes.[22]

Whereas Genshin remains in a negatively formulated egalitarian notion, with the term "equality" Hōnen introduces a positive expression into the

---

22   This egalitarian trend is found also in contemporary Pure Land *setsuwa* literature, the *ōjō-den* collections, which are records of people believed to have achieved birth into the Pure Land. The first of such collections, the *Nihon ōjō gokuraku-ki* 日本往生極樂記, was compiled by Yoshishige no Yasutane 慶滋保胤. (ca. 913–1002), a young scholar, who was a founding lay member of the Kangaku-e 觀學会 (965), a circle of lay and monks devoted to Pure Land and Lotus practice; later he became monk (685) under Genshin. In the preface of his *Nihon ōjō gokuraku-ki* he uses the expression "priests and lay people, men and women" (*dōzoku nannyo* 道俗男女) (NST 7: 11; cf. the same expression in the preface of Miyoshi no Tamefusa's *Shūi ōjō-den*; NST 7: 353). Whereas this formulation expresses two pairs of religious and gender distinctions ("priests and lay people, men and women"), previous quotations from *Hokke genki* and Genshin have two pairs of religious and social differences ("priests and lay people, noble and commoners") and those of social and gender ("men and women, noble and commoners"). Among the stories Yasutane compiled are first those of monks (of various ranks) and novices (*shami* 沙弥), then nuns, noble lay people and finally female commoners. Thus, on the one hand the composition of this work follows the socio-religious order of his time from top to bottom, and on the other hand it expresses the egalitarian tendency of Heian Pure Land tradition.

Japanese Pure Land tradition.[23] This raises the question where he derived this term from. In one of his letters he first quotes from the *Kanmuryōju-kyō*, which states that "Buddha's mind (*busshin* 佛心) is precisely great compassion" (*dai-jihi* 大慈悲) (HSZ: 572; Ohashi III: 117; cf. T 12.343c). Then he quotes Shandao's commentary of the *Kanmuryōju-kyō* as follows: "With this compassion of equality (*byōdō no jihi* 平等の慈悲) [Amida] grasps all [sentient beings] universally" (HSZ: 572; Ohashi III: 117; cf. T 37.268a).

When tracing the genesis of Shandao's compound "compassion of equality," he seems to have combined the term "great compassion" from the *Kanmuryōju-kyō* with the term "equality" from the *Muryōju-kyō*. According to this sutra, Buddha in his awakened state of mind realizes that dharmas neither arise nor perish, in other words he awakens to the "Dharma of equality" (*byōdō hō* 平等法) (T. 12.266b). Since Shandao refers to this expression earlier in his commentary of the *Kanmuryōju-kyō* (cf. T. 37.253a), it is most likely that he combined the two compounds "compassion" and "equality." It is significant to observe, however, that in his reception of the two sutras Shandao made two modifications. First, in his quotation of the *Kanmuryōju-kyō* above, which speaks of the mind of the buddhas (Ch. *zhu fo xin* 諸佛心). he just drops the indicator for plural (諸) and thereby applies the accompanying expression "great compassion" to one Buddha only, namely Amida. The second modification concerns his reception of "Dharma of equality" from the *Muryōju-kyō*. This compound signifies a metaphysical term, namely the true character of reality as perceived by a buddha in the state of awakening. When Shandao now removes the term "equality" from its original context and places it in the new context of Amida's "compassion of equality," he changes the meaning of "equality" from a metaphysical to a soteriological term. Equality now characterizes the unbiased attitude of Amida as the Buddha who intends to save all sentient beings. Thus, Shandao shifts from a metaphysical characterization of true reality in itself towards the compassionate attitude of a Buddha in relation to sentient beings in this mundane reality. Thereby Shandao arrives in his commentary at the following formulation: "The essence of [Amida] Buddha's

---

23 It should be mentioned, however, that Hōnen uses also negative expressions, for example, when writing in the *Juni kajō no mondō* 十二箇條の問答 that for birth into Pure Land there is no choice (*erabazu*) between men and women or nobility and commoners (low people), and no distinction (*wakatazu*) between good and evil people (HSZ: 673; Ohashi III: 224).

SOCIO-ECONOMIC IMPACTS OF HŌNEN'S PURE LAND DOCTRINES 283

mind is compassion (Ch. *cibei* 慈悲), and with this great compassion of equality (Ch. *pingdeng daci* 平等大慈) he grasps all [sentient beings] universally" (T 37.268a).[24]

When Hōnen inherits Shandao's notion of Amida's compassion of equality, he automatically follows the decisive shift from a metaphysical dimension towards the immanent world. According to this line of thought, in the *Senchaka-shū* Hōnen spells out the concrete impact of Amida's compassion for religious practice in this world. Here, Hōnen first quotes from Genshin's *Ōjō yō-shū* the (aforementioned) passage saying that in respect to *nenbutsu* practice there is no difference between men and women or between noble and commoners (HSZ: 319; Ohashi II: 197–198). In his own subsequent discourse Hōnen then transcends Genshin's negative expression of equality through Shandao's positive term. Hōnen first states that the *nenbutsu* is an easy practice available to all people, whereas the manifold practices are difficult and therefore to be mastered only by few. For this reason, he then says, Amida made the Basic Vow abolishing the difficult and choosing the easy practice so that "all sentient beings attain birth in equality (*byōdō ni ōjō*)" (HSZ: 320; Ohashi II: 198).

To my knowledge, this term "birth in equality" is coined by Hōnen himself. In all likelihood it was formed according to the model of Shandao's term "compassion of equality" which Hōnen also uses a few lines later. By coining such term, Hōnen considerably extends Shandao's tendency towards this world (Amida's compassion is directed impartially to all sentient beings) because he shifts "equality" from Buddha's attribute to the characterization of the human beings' salvational process in transition from death in this world to birth in the world beyond. Still, apart from Shandao also the influence of Heian period Pure Land tradition must be acknowledged since it is also marked by a trend towards socio-religious equality. It may be assumed here that Hōnen gave this trend a positive and concise expression through his term "birth in equality." In summary, the journey of the term "equality," as we observed, began as metaphysical designation of true reality in the *Muryōju-kyō*, was transformed by Shandao into an epithet of Amida's compassion directed towards sentient beings, and finally was changed again by Hōnen into a characterization of the salvational process in transition from this defiled world into the Pure Land. The circle closes when we consider, as observed above, that Hōnen even questions

---

24   Hōnen inherits also the notion of Amida's "impartial mind," when stating, for example, in the *Gyakushu seppō* 逆修説法 that Amida with his "mind of compassion of equality" (*byōdō jihi no mikokoro* 平等慈悲の御意), established the *nenbutsu* practice because it is easy to practice for people such as fools (*guchi* 愚痴), old people (*rō* 老) and young people (*wakaki* 少き) (HSZ: 253; Ohashi II: 81).

the hierarchical structure of the nine classes (*kubon*) in the transcendental dimension. This is a consistent, or radical, application of his notion "birth in equality." Hōnen's reception of Shandao's term as well as his own new coinage clearly characterize his concern for the concrete realities of sentient beings.

The long passage of the *Senchaku-shū* quoted above (in Section 4) follows the Genshin quotation mentioned before. Two sentences from this *Senchaka-shū* passage may be recalled here:

> Amida Nyorai, ... being moved by compassion of equality (*byōdō no jihi*), in order to grasp all [people] comprehensively, did not make the Basic Vow for birth by requiring the various practices, such as making Buddha statues or building stupas. He made the Basic Vow requiring only the one practice of reciting the *nenbutsu* (*tada shōmyō nenbutsu no ichi-gyō*).
>
> HSZ: 320; OHASHI II: 199

Here Hōnen connects Amida's compassion of equality directly with the concrete conditions of religious practice. In other words, he counter-balances the classified differences of human beings, their religious practices, and all their possible impact on ultimate liberation, by the notion of Amida's impartial compassion, the one practice of the *nenbutsu*, and the concept of birth in equality. In his early exposition of the *Muryōju-kyō*, the *Muryōjukyō-shaku*, Hōnen explains the significance of Amida's "compassion of equality" (*byōdō no jihi*) to be such that the "ten thousand [human] capabilities (*manki* 万機) are embraced by the one vow (*ichi gan* 一願), and the thousand conditions (or classes; *senbon* 千品) are accommodated by the ten *nen[butsu]* (*jūnen* 十念)" (HSZ: 73; Ohashi I: 83).

Thus, Hōnen spells out the concrete impact of Amida's compassion for religious practices in this world as for liberation in the world beyond. The genesis of the notion of "birth in equality" makes it clear that it is not a trivial matter when Hōnen's attention is so much directed to concrete socio-religious realities. It is a final achievement at the upper end of a long and intricate process, beginning with the sutras, their interpretation by Shandao, and changes in the worldview of the later Heian period Pure Land tradition.

4.2 *Impacts of Hōnen's Teachings on the Religious Economy*

According to Hōnen's teaching, only the exclusive *nenbutsu* practice enables liberation from the world of suffering and transmigration for sure, whereas all other religious practices *may* have the same result, but not with certainty (Repp 2005b: 16–21). Thus, he does not completely negate the other practices, however, he considers them to have only limited value. They have practical

SOCIO-ECONOMIC IMPACTS OF HŌNEN'S PURE LAND DOCTRINES

merits in this world, such as keeping the rules maintains morality or giving donations prevents laziness, but they cannot bring forth liberation with certainty.

In this section I will treat the impact of Hōnen's teaching on the economy of monastic institutions. In particular, I deal with his teachings about (1) donations (*fuse* 布施; *dan* 檀) in general, (2) contributions for the construction of temple buildings, pagodas (stupas) and Buddha statues (*kiryū tōzō tō* 起立塔像等) in particular; (3) sponsoring religious services (*kuyō* 供養) (sometimes connected with dedication of sutras, statues, etc.); and (4) the accumulation of merits (*kudoku* 功徳) through religious practice and good deeds which are believed to bear results in the world beyond.

4.2.1 Donations (*Fuse*)

In Buddhism, donations (*fuse*) for religious purposes are counted among the basic forms of religious practice. According to Mahāyāna Buddhism, this deed is the first in a canon of the six basic bodhisattva practices or *pāramitā* (*ropparamitsu*) to enable the attainment of awakening. The other practices are keeping precepts, perseverance, endeavor, meditation and cultivating wisdom. For Hōnen, these "six (basic practices for) deliverance" as well as all other (more specific) "numerous practices" (*rokudo mangyō* 六度萬行), including donations (*fuse*), are difficult to practice and therefore cannot cause liberation for certain (HSZ: 523; Ohashi III: 40; cf. 97; I: 100). After all, they do not correspond (*sō'ō* 相応) with Amida's vow, his basic criterion (HSZ: 524; Ohashi III: 41; cf. 98). Hōnen states that Amida did not establish a special vow according to which donations would bring forth birth into the Pure Land (HSZ: 70; Ohashi I: 77). In the *Muryōjukyō-shaku* (HSZ: 78; Ohashi I: 98–99) Hōnen lists some of the "immeasurable" (*muryō* 無量) kinds of donations (*dan*), covering the broad spectrum not only of material offerings (*saibutsu* 財物), i.e. objects "outside of one's body" such as countries, castles, wife or child, slaves, fields, houses, gardens and forests, horses, cars and precious treasures, but also parts of one's own body, like eyes, ears, tongue, etc.[25]

---

25 The *Muryōjukyō-shaku* is a lecture Hōnen gave 1190 at the Tōdaiji in Nara upon the invitation of the monk Chōgen 重源 (1121–1206). Chōgen was commissioned by the imperial court to rebuild the temple complex through *kanjin* 勧進 (collecting alms) campaigns after the Taira had burnt it down in 1180 (cf. Goodwin 1994: 67–106). Chōgen belonged to the *nenbutsu* movement of this time, and being in charge for financing the reconstruction of the state temple, he invited Hōnen to give these lectures. They were held in the second month of 1190, and the ceremony for raising the framework of the temple was held shortly later in the tenth month of this year (Ohashi I: 66; Nara Kokuritsu Hakubutsukan 2005: 269). After having listed the different kind of donations in his exposition of the sutra (mentioned above), Hōnen discusses the difference between the manifold practices (to which donations belong) and the sole *nenbutsu* practice and then he concludes that

In the *Senchaku-shū* Hōnen explains the merits of donations when elaborating that there are various pure lands in which people are born owing to donation or the other five basic bodhisattva practices. However, according to Hōnen's fundamental criterion of Amida's Basic Vow, this Buddha abolished all these practices and chose only the one of reciting the *nenbutsu* for achieving certain liberation (HSZ: 319; Ohashi II: 193–194). In his main doctrinal work Hōnen elaborates the principle of Amida's choice (*senchaku*) of this Basic Vow, and concludes that also believers have to choose between the *nenbutsu* and the other practices, including donations.

In the *Muryōjukyō-shaku* Hōnen discusses concrete consequences when stating that if Amida would have made a special vow (*betsugan*) according to which donations were the condition for birth, only a king would be able to attain it, but none of "all the poor people" (*issai hinkyū no hito* 一切貧窮之人) (HSZ: 72; Ohashi I: 82). In the *Gyakushū seppō*, Hōnen explains the immediate results already in this life: if donations conditioned liberation, poor people would have to "give up hope for birth" into the Pure Land (FISZ: 253; Ohashi II: 81). Thus, Hōnen criticizes here donations as being a biased way for ultimate liberation and therefore abolishes them for socio-economic reasons. Here the economic consequences of his concept of "birth in equality" become apparent.

One of the *145 Mondō* provides a concrete example of Hōnen's attitude towards donations. Upon the lady's question "Is it sin (*tsumi*) [for a priest] to receive donations from a believer (*shinse* 信施)?" Hōnen replies: "There is no problem when the priest (*sō* 僧) eats [received food] after he has performed religious service (*tsutome*). If not, [the sin] is grave" (HSZ: 659; Ohashi III: 256). Hōnen considers here donation as part of a mutual exchange between priests and lay persons. He denies the necessity of donations if priests have not earned it through religious service.[26]

The significance of such a principle of mutuality in religious economy becomes clear when we compare it, for example, with the *Mappō tōmyō-ki*

---

according to Amida's Basic Vow only the sole *nenbutsu* practice leads to ultimate liberation. This implies an indirect criticism of Chōgen's *kanjin* campaign. See Section 4.2.2 for Hōnen's direct criticism.

26   Donations in Buddhism were not a one-way transaction from lay to monks, but priests performed also donations, as Gyōki's case from the early Nara period illustrates. For example, his construction of roadside shelters called *fuseya* for the porters, who had to carry supplies to the capital, clearly indicates the reverse side of donations by monks (Augustine 2005: 84–96).

SOCIO-ECONOMIC IMPACTS OF HŌNEN'S PURE LAND DOCTRINES 287

末法燈明記 (Candle of the Latter Dharma)[27] which claims that in the time of the "Final Dharma" (*mappō*) patrons should continue to support the monastic community even though monks break the rules, and this includes the neglect of service they were expected to perform. When Hōnen quoted from this work, he employed the contemporary idea of Buddha's Final Dharma in his argument that in such a desperate period only the *nenbutsu* is able to bring forth ultimate liberation.[28] However, the main intention of the *Mappō tōmyō-ki* is not so much concerned with expounding the *mappō* teaching as such, as most interpreters since Hōnen until today seem to assume, but with the justification for the claim that monks breaking the precepts rightly deserve donations from lay people precisely in such a time. Its background apparently was increased criticism of monastic decadence by patrons resulting in considerable decrease of economic support.

According to the *Mappō tōmyō-ki*, now during the period of *mappō*, when Buddha's Dharma has perished and practice (including keeping precepts) and awakening have become impossible, "monks in name only," or "nominal monks" (*myōji no biku* 名字ノ比丘; *myōji no sō* 名字ノ僧), who break the precepts, deserve the same respect and support as the precepts-keeping monks of the previous periods of the True Dharma (*shōbō* 正法) and Semblance Dharma (*zōbō* 像法).[29]

Consequently, this work argues, the monks breaking the rules in such a time deserve unchanged respect and support: "The Buddha, with insight into the destiny of this age [of the Latter Dharma], praised the nominal monks as the merit-field[30] for the people of the world in order to save the people of the Latter

---

27   The *Mappō tōmyō-ki* (DDZ 1: 415–426; Rhodes 1980 and 1994) is traditionally attributed to Saichō, the founder of Tendai. However, because its contents fundamentally contradict Saichō's emphasis on maintaining the monastic discipline and other reasons, modern research assumes that it was compiled much later (Rhodes 1994: 2; cf. 1980: 81–82). Hōnen was the first to quote from this work which provides the *terminus ante quem* of its compilation.

28   The *mappō* idea was popular especially in Tendai circles since the mid-Heian period. One date for the beginning of *mappō* was assumed to be the year 1052. For a brief overview of this concept and its history, as well as for relevant literature, see Repp (2005a: 182–194).

29   Thus, this work attributes to the monks and nuns of the *Mappō* period a kind of *character indelebilis* which resembles that of the Catholic clergy in medieval Europe. Quoting from the *Great Collection Sutra*, it states for example: "The crime of striking and reproaching a monk who wears a robe but breaks or does not keep the precepts, is the same as causing a trillion Buddhas to shed blood" (Rhodes 1994: 17). In other words, any criticism against members of the monastic order based on criteria derived from the Dharma valid in the previous period becomes impossible.

30   The term *fukuden* 福田 (Sk. *puṇya kṣetra*) designates the Buddhist community which produces good fruits. Rhodes (1980: 92 note) explains: "The field in which one plants the

Dharma" (Rhodes 1994: 16; slightly revised). Quoting from the *Great Collection Sutra*, it further states: "Suppose there is a nominal *bhikku* in the Latter World to come who has, within my Dharma, shaved off his hair and beard and donned a robe. If there is a donor [*danotsu* 檀越] who gives donations to him in faith [*shinse* 信施] and gives offerings [*kuyō* 供養], the donor will gain an immeasurable and limitless amount of merit" (Rhodes 1994: 16, slightly revised). Another sutra-quotation serves the same purpose: "If one gives alms to one evil *bhikku* [*akubiku* 悪比丘, cf. evil monk, *akusō* 悪僧] who resembles a true monk, one will gain immeasurable merit" (Rhodes 1994: 19–20). Thus, the *Mappō tōmyō-ki* addresses those people who economically do not support the Buddhist congregation because of abuse among monks:

> If, furthermore, there are people who construct stupas and temples and venerate the Three Treasures but do not arouse a feeling of respect and honor toward them; who invite monks to reside in temples but do not offer them drink or food, clothing or medicine; who, furthermore, turn right around to beg and borrow these things from the monks, and eat the monks' food; who, whether rich or poor, desire in all they do to work solely against the interest of the Sangha, impairing and causing distress in it, such people will fall into the three evil paths [the realms of beasts, hungry ghosts and hell] for a long time.
>
> RHODES 1994: 19

The compiler applies this passage immediately to the own present situation as follows:

> Right now, surveying the secular world, we find that such deeds are widespread. But this is simply the destiny of the age; it is not due to the people [i.e. evil monks]. Donors [*danotsu*] do not have the true intention [*kokorozashi* 志] of donors to begin with. Who can censure [or criticize, *soshiru* 誹ル] the monks for not practicing as monks?
>
> RHODES 1994: 19

Here, the *Mappō tōmyō-ki* reveals its true intention: While it excuses the abuse in the Buddhist community owing to the bad time of the absence of the Dharma, it blames the donors for not supporting it due to lack of respect. In other words, while defending the law-breaking monks, it urges the donors,

---

seeds of future merits; in this case, it indicates a monk who is recipient of the veneration and alms of the laity."

the lay people, to refrain from criticism and to continue their economic support of the—admittedly—corrupt monastic establishment.[31] What may be the reason for writing such a treatise—designed with a kind of *salto mortale* logic—to justify monastic abuse by warding off any criticism by lay people? It seems that the economic situation for monks, nuns and whole monasteries must have become really bad because lay followers had severely criticized widespread abuses in the Buddhist community of the time and subsequently reduced their economic support considerably.

The use of the term *akubiku* and their justification suggest that the *Mappō tōmyō-ki* was compiled during the Insei period (i.e. before Hōnen quotes from it) when monastic institutions began to engage their "evil monks" in violent actions and even warfare in order to protect economic and other interests, such as the landed estates (*shōen* 荘園). Apart from the *Mappō tōmyō-ki*, also the contemporary Tendai literature of the *hongaku hōmon* 本覚法門 (Dharma gate of inherent awakening) tries to justify the widespread abuse by *akusō* through the concept of "inherent awakening" which renders "acquired awakening" through keeping precepts and other practice unnecessary.[32] Thus, the intentions of *Mappō tōmyō-ki* and the *hongaku hōmon* on the one hand, and those of Hōnen differ considerably. Whereas the former attempt to justify the abuse in monasteries and thereby to argue for the necessity to continue economic support for the Buddhist community, the latter argues with the *mappō* concept requiring the exclusive *nenbutsu* practice which subsequently renders the donation as not essential for religious liberation! Another decisive difference is that Hōnen maintains the principle of mutual religio-economic exchange between monks and lay people, as mentioned above, whereas the *Mappō tōmyō-ki* suspends it which might not be convincing for ordinary lay people with a common sense. Finally, the sense of economic emergency expressed in the *Mappō tōmyō-ki* indicates the possibility that Hōnen's teachings and movement were not the only factors to be blamed for the decay of temple buildings, as Nichiren portrayed it, but that there may be also reasons such as the decadence of the monastic institutions themselves.

Hōnen's occasional affirmation of donations under certain conditions may seem to contradict his basic doctrinal stance expressed in his systematic work, the *Senchaku-shū*. However, we have to take here into account the different contexts. Whereas in doctrinal works teachings are formulated in general and

---

31 For a case that the *mappō* belief did not necessarily neutralize criticism of lay people against decadent monks, see Gernet (1995: 198–199).

32 Vivid descriptions of the *akusō* can be found, for example, in Jien's *Gukan-shō*. In subsequent times, the *akusō* were called *sōhei* 僧兵 (warrior monks). Cf. Adolphson (2007).

abstract terms, in sermons and didactic conversations (*mondō*) the concrete situation of the addressee is taken into account. Such kind of communication necessarily accommodates the basic teachings to the respective situation, even if modern observers may consider this to be a compromise.[33] We shall encounter these seemingly inconsistencies also in the subsequent section.

4.2.2   Constructing Pagodas, Temples and Buddha Statues (*Kiryū Tōzō Tō*)

Next, Hōnen's attitude towards sponsoring the construction of pagodas (or stupas; *tō* 塔), Buddha halls (*butsudō* 仏堂) and Buddha statues (*butsuzō* 仏像) will be treated, both in respect to his basic doctrinal stance as well as to his practical application. First, as for his basic teachings, he follows the principles encountered before. In a structurally similar way as his treatment of donations (see Section 4.2.1), in the *Muryōjukyō-shaku* he argues: If there would be a special vow (*betsugan*) according to which the construction of pagodas conditions birth into the Pure Land, only a king would be able to attain it, but none of the "whole company of destitute people" (*issai konbō no rin* 一切困乏之倫) (HSZ: 72; Ohashi I: 82). The significance of such a statement derives from its context. The *Muryōjukyō-shaku* is a lecture on the *Sutra of Immeasurable Life* which Hōnen gave in 1190 on the occasion of the reconstruction of the state temple Tōdaiji (cf. Section 4.2.1). He was invited by the monk Chōgen, whom the imperial court had commissioned to head the *kanjin* campaign to collect alms for the reconstruction. In my view, this is an open criticism of the *kanjin* campaign in the name of the sole *nenbutsu* practice.

Hōnen criticizes here the funding of religious construction work for socioeconomic reasons. This does not mean that he intends to discourage people with sufficient economic assets from doing so, as we shall see later. However, as a means to attain ultimate liberation such practice has no validity since its results are biased. The notion of equality as a principle for universal liberation is presupposed in this passage and subsequently the term appears in the conclusion of his deliberations (HSZ: 73; Ohashi I: 83).

In order to understand Hōnen's stance in historical context, an example from the mid-Heian period may illustrate the religious thought and practice he is critical of. Fujiwara no Michinaga 藤原道長 (966–1027/8), the most powerful regent during the height of the Heian period and also a generous patron of Buddhism, ordered the construction of the Hōjōji 法成寺, the most lavish Amida temple of the time. The *Eiga monogatari* 栄華物語 (ca. 1092) narrates an

---

33   Some modern critics (see, for example, Tanabe 1992: 85–89) judge such inconsistencies or contradictions as "double standard," because they neglect the different contexts into which the various statements belong and from where they have to be understood.

SOCIO-ECONOMIC IMPACTS OF HŌNEN'S PURE LAND DOCTRINES   291

anecdote of the rehearsal before the dedication ceremony of the Hōjōji (1022) as follows: A crowd of young and old people watched these preparations since they knew they were excluded from the official dedication ceremony the next day. When Michinaga saw the "common crowd," he exclaimed "They aren't an attractive sight," and ordered "Move them back a little" (McCullough and McCullough 1980: 546). This anecdote illustrates the class-oriented Pure Land beliefs of Heian aristocrats. The underlying presupposition was, of course, that good works like constructing temples would bring forth religious liberation for sure. Thus, the *Eiga monogatari* subsequently narrates that when Michinaga died he also achieved birth into the Pure Land.[34] The comparison with this example illustrating the religious world view of aristocrats during the Heian period puts Hōnen's way of thinking in historical perspective. Their kind of Buddhism is a religion for rich and powerful aristocrats, whereas Hōnen offers a Buddhist way to liberation in equality.

Whereas in the previously quoted passage of the *Muryōjukyō-shaku* Hōnen criticizes the funding of religious construction work 'simply' for socio-economic reasons, in the *Gyakushū seppō* he argues doctrinally. This is a re-cord of Hōnen's sermon at a funeral ceremony held in advance (*gyakushu*), i.e. before the actual death of a person. This particular seven-day ceremony, sponsored by the father of Anraku-bō (cf. Section 3), included also the dedica-tion of a Buddha statue (Ohashi II: 2). In this sermon, Hōnen negates religious construction work as a valid means to attain liberation by arguing as follows: Even though the *Muryōju-kyō* explains the other practices (*yogyō* 餘行) such as building pagodas, making statues, etc. (*kiryū tōzō tō*), but in its concluding section (*ruzū* 流通) it praises only the *nenbutsu* as having unsurpassed merit (*mujō kudoku* 無上功德) and great benefit (*dairi* 大利) (i.e. birth into the Pure Land), but it does not praise the other practices as having the same effect (HSZ: 245; Ohashi II: 50). Thus, while accepting the invitation to preach during this ceremony, Hōnen used his sermon to teach the Pure Land doctrine in a way that contained also indirect criticism of the sponsor's actual religious practice.

After these two statements concerning doctrinal principles, a case of Hōnen's practical application shall be mentioned. In the letter to Hōjō Masako, he recommends (*go-susume sōrō beshi* 御ススメ候ベシ) to construct Buddha halls, carve Buddha statues, copy sutras, and perform *kuyō* (cf. Section 4.2.3)

---

34   However, to the disappointment of the family, after his death his daughter, an empress, received the dream message that he was born only on the lowest of the nine ranks and not on one of the upper ones, as everybody expected! (McCullough and McCullough 1980: 770; cf. 560). This reminds very much of the disappointment of Genshin's disciples after his death, as we saw above.

for priests (*sō*), because such practices prevent the heart from becoming lazy (*kokoro midarezu shite* ココロミダレズシテ), foster compassion (*jihi o okoshite* 慈悲ヲオコシテ), and create "mixed good roots" (*zō-zengon* 雑善根) (HSZ: 530; Ohashi III: 13). The addressee of this letter was a powerful woman in the Kamakura government, who certainly had more than sufficient economic means to perform such good deeds. However, in the subsequent part of his letter Hōnen does not forget to instruct her about the sole *nenbutsu* practice as well. Thus, Hōnen guides this woman from her traditional religious world-view to that of the *nenbutsu* practice. This method is known in Buddhist tradition as *taiki seppō* 対機説法 (expounding the Dharma according to human capabilities).

4.2.3 Sponsoring Religious Services (*Kuyō*)

The word *kuyō* (Sk. *pūjanā*) is frequently translated as memorial service for the dead, but it has the broader meaning to venerate the Three Treasures (Buddha, Dharma and sangha) through offerings (*sonaemono* 供物, *fuse*), such as food, medicine, clothes, and housing. Thus it combines religious practice (*gyō* 行) with financial or material (*sai* 財) donations (JSDJ: I, 342; cf. Sections 4.2.1 and 4.2.2). Apart from the Three Treasures, also parents, teachers and spirits can be the recipients of *kuyō*. Hence *kuyō* may be rendered generally as "sponsoring religious services" or "giving offerings," but an adequate translation depends also on the particular context. In the letter to Hōjō Masako Hōnen pragmatically affirms that priests should receive offerings (*sō o kuyō semu* 僧を供養せむ) since it prevents lay people from becoming lazy and fosters compassion (HSZ: 530; Ohashi III: 13).

In medieval Japan, sponsoring religious services was a widespread practice among those who had sufficient economic means. Right from the beginning of the *145 Mondō*, the lady of high social status raises the issue of *kuyō* five times in her questions addressed to Hōnen:

Question: "When having repaired old [Buddha] halls and pagodas (stupas), should one perform *kuyō* (ceremony with offerings)?"

Answer: "It is not entirely necessary to perform *kuyō*; again, it is not a bad thing to perform *kuyō* since it would [produce] merit (*kudoku* 功徳); again, it is also not a sin or a bad thing not to perform *kuyō*" (HSZ: 647–648; Ohashi III: 237).

Question: "Should one gild an image of Buddha and perform *kuyō*?"

Answer: "It is not necessary" (HSZ 653; Ohashi III: 247).

Question: "When enshrining a Buddha statue in an altar, should one perform *kuyō*?"

Answer: "Not at all!" (HSZ 653 f; Ohashi III: 247).

Question: "Is there a problem when one (reads) a sutra and does not perform *kuyō*?"

Answer: "Only read it" (HSZ 654 f; Ohashi III: 249).

Question: "When reading 1,000 sutra volumes (*kyō senbu* 経千部), is it necessary to perform *kuyō*?"

Answer: "No, it is not" (HSZ: 655; Ohashi III: 249).

Most of Hōnen's responses here show his inclination to consider a believer's own religious practice more important than the additional *kuyō*, which includes material offerings and remuneration for one or more priests performing the ceremony. In Hōnen's view, it is sufficient for lay people to recite sutras, repair Buddha halls and install statues, but it is not necessary to supplement such practice with material offerings or expensive gilding of Buddha statues. Thus, Hōnen's responses indicate his reservation towards lavish offering ceremonies as well as his inclination towards religious simplicity and frugality. At the same time, such an attitude conforms perfectly with the aforementioned immediate communication between lay believers and Amida Buddha which elevates the agency of the individual believer and renders the role of the priest as salvational mediator obsolete (cf. Section 4.1.3).

Criticism of the economic side of the *kuyō* can be found also in pictorial depictions of the Insei period. The first scroll of the *Chōjū giga* 鳥獣戯画, probably drawn by Toba Sōjō Kakuyū 鳥羽僧正覚猷 (1053–1140), a renowned artist and abbot of Miidera, depicts in its second last scene a Buddhist funeral performed by a 'monkey priest' (clad in a Buddhist robe) in front of a 'frog Buddha' on a Lotus seat. Then the last scene shows the reverse side, the 'monkey priest' receiving lavish offerings (cf. Repp 2006: 188–192). These caricatures are very likely directed against the practice to turn religious service into business, in other words, against commercialization of Buddhism.[35]

4.2.4 Producing and Accumulating Merits (*Kudoku*)

Religious deeds are believed to bear good results for one's future destiny in this world as well as for one's ultimate liberation (*gedatsu*). Since this karmic mechanism is not only perceived in terms of the quality of such deeds, but also in terms of their quantity, *kudoku* bears the inherent necessity to accumulate merits as much as possible. Consequently, the notion of *kudoku* is structured

---

35 In the *setsuwa* literature, criticism of commercialization of Buddhism can be found as well. See, for example, Genshin's hagiographies according to the *Hokke-genki* and the *Konjaku monogatari* (Dykstra 1983: 105; and 1998: 352–353).

in the form of a pyramid: if includes a broad variety of good deeds on various horizontal levels, as well as on the qualitative and quantitative vertical line ascending towards the top. Hence, the hierarchical structure of accumulating merits corresponds with similar pyramids in society, religious institutions and the world beyond.

In the *145 Mondō*, the lady also raises twice the issue of virtuous deeds (*kudoku*) as follows:

> Question: "Is it good to produce *kudoku* during one's lifetime?"
> Answer: "This is very good (*niedetashi*)" (HSZ: 654; Ohashi III: 249).
> Question: "Is it true, as people say, that one should [accumulate] *kudoku* as much as one (lit. one's body) can bear?"
> Question: "It should not go so far that it becomes a problem; it should be [done] to the extent of one's strength (*chikara*)" (HSZ: 657; Ohashi III: 252).

Whereas the first *mondō* treats the problem of the quality of *kudoku*, the second one raises the question of the quantity in accumulating merits. The second exchange implies that there was no definite goal or upper limit for the constant effort to produce and collect merits, and that for this reason the religious subject felt overtaxed. Hōnen responds to this objective problem of "merit accumulation without limits" by the pragmatic consideration that one's subjective strength, abilities and assets constitute definite limits. Here again, Hōnen shifts the focus from abstract norms and doctrines to the existential situation of the individual. As mentioned before, the structure of accumulating merits corresponds with the hierarchies in contemporary society, religious institutions and the world beyond. The problem raised here in the lady's question, however, indicates that there is also a significant difference since the three hierarchies mentioned clearly have a definitive apex, whereas the notion of accumulating merits does not know an upper limit. Because requirements for collecting merits are "immeasurable" (cf. Section 4.2.1), they leave the believer in a restless state of mind and overtaxed condition. They do not provide a settled mind (or mind at peace, *anjin* 安心) as, according to Hōnen, the *nenbutsu* practice does (cf. HSZ: 333).

Now, how does Hōnen relate his Pure Land teaching and practice to the question of merits? In a letter to Hōjō Masako (titled *Jōdoshū ryakushō* 浄土宗略抄), he quotes Shandao's following question: "What kind of innerworldly (*gense* 現世) merit and benefit (*kudoku riyaku* 功徳利益) is there if one recites [the name of] Amida Buddha, keeps him in mind, venerates and contemplates

SOCIO-ECONOMIC IMPACTS OF HŌNEN'S PURE LAND DOCTRINES   295

him?" (Ohashi III: 101). This question implies the general belief that any religious practice causes not only good results in one's afterlife, but also during one's lifetime. Hōnen then quotes Shandao's response saying that the recitation of the *nenbutsu* causes the extinction of an immeasurable amount of sin and that believers receive protection against evil deities and spirits from Amida and those who accompany him. Finally, Hōnen summarizes the quotation with his own words by stating that those who deeply trust in Amida's vow and recite the *nenbutsu* will receive protection from Amida and his company against evil spirits, sufferings and disaster in this life, and then they will attain birth into the Pure Land (HSZ: 604; Ohashi III: 101–102).

In the same letter Hōnen writes:

> ... also the prayers (*inori*) for matters of this world as well as the merits transferred to any direction [or purpose] should all be redirected (lit. "recovered," *torikaeshite* とり返して); now one should transfer (*ekō* 廻向) them all straight towards [the Land of] Utmost Bliss and wish to be born [there]. When saying to transfer all merits (*kudoku*) completely towards [birth in the Land of] Utmost Bliss, [it means that] except of the *nenbutsu* there is no producing and accumulating deeds (*wazu*) and merits in order to transfer. However, this means that also the merits previously accumulated should now be transferred straight (*ikkō ni* 一向に) to the [Land of] Utmost Bliss, as well as those to be produced from now on, such as giving offerings (*kuyō*) to priests (*sō*) and donating (*hodokoshi*) material things (*mono* 物) to other people, [both] as far as one is able to do—all should be transferred to birth [into the Pure Land].
>
> HSZ: 599; OHASHI III: 94

This passage shows Hōnen's characteristic way of teaching when accommodating to the situation.[36] On the one hand he principally negates any kind of merit production and accumulation except of the *nenbutsu*, and on the other hand he offers 'compromises' for the addressee to redirect the accumulated merits only to one's birth into the Pure Land. In the latter case, again he follows the didactic principle of *taiki seppō*, whereas in the former he maintains the position that only the *nenbutsu* produces the ultimate merit of birth into the Pure Land.

---

36   A similar passage appears also in another letter (HSZ: 583–584; Ohashi III: 135–136).

5 Conclusion

This study did not follow the normal order of historical development but undertook the reverse approach by investigating possible causes in light of their results. Following the Japanese expression *sakunoboru* 遡る (go upstream, retrace the past or origin) for heuristic reasons, our deliberation began with criticism of the socio-economic effects which Hōnen's Pure Land doctrine bore and arrived at an investigation of possible socio-economic impacts of his doctrine.

When Nichiren saw temple buildings in decay and monasteries deserted, he blamed Hōnen's main doctrinal work for such a socioeconomic disaster having occurred in the span of about 60 years. The earlier admonition by the Tendai abbot and the petition of the Kōfukuji monks, both issued when Hōnen was still alive, did not yet clearly express possible economic effects of his teaching. However, its social and political impact was definitely realized. They perceived his Pure Land doctrine and the movement around him as a threat to the monastic establishment as well as for the delicate relationship between Buddhist order and the state. The immediate danger for religious institutions consisted first of all in decrease of monks, nuns and lay believers, but the massive change of religious affiliation by lay patrons also implied a considerable loss of economic income.

In the subsequent part, I attempted to re-read Hōnen's doctrinal works as well as his personal, occasional communications through the glasses of our main topic. Hōnen's only concern was to offer a sure way out of this world of suffering. Therefore he was not interested in soliciting economic support for the Buddhist establishment in this world, nor did he write any treatise to proof to authorities that his teaching was supporting and 'protecting' the state, as other founders of new schools, such as Kūkai, Eisai and Nichiren, did. Nevertheless, Hōnen's teaching of the exclusive *nenbutsu* practice posed a danger for the social, political and economic order of his time. Certainly, Hōnen was not a revolutionary intending to turn the established order upside-down. Judging from his recorded conversations and letters, his own personality seems to have been very conciliatory. Hence, attacks were not so much focused on his person, but on his doctrine and his followers. However, his teachings contained explosives resulting in social and economic consequences which in all likelihood he had not anticipated. The doctrine of the sole *nenbutsu* practice deprived the temple establishment of economic support, and his notions of Amida's "impartial compassion" and "birth in equality" leveled basic distinctions in the contemporary socio-religious order. In particular, this was caused by Hōnen's reevaluation of ordinary people (*bonbu* 凡夫) when endowing them with the hitherto unknown self-confidence of being agents of their own liberation. Subsequently, these ordinary people appear now on the stage of

Buddhist history in Japan as subjects of their own right. Paradoxically, it was his teaching of the "other-power" that provided individuals with this new sense of subjecthood. The treatment of the role of intellectual facilities for Buddhism (Section 4.1.1) indicated already that we may also detect here emerging conflicts between the established elite and the masses of ordinary people. Thus, Hōnen's teaching polarized society between those who adhered to traditional doctrine and order and those who gained a novel hope for their own salvation.

The spread of Pure Land belief and practice among ordinary people outside the temples had already begun in the later part of the Heian period and seems to have gathered momentum by the beginning of the Kamakura period. It grew into a movement by the time when Hōnen was active, and this movement found a focus and crystallized in Hōnen's 'simple' yet profound teachings fitting for ordinary people as well as for higher echelons of society. When Hōnen leveled the fundamental distinction between clerics and lay, he enabled lay people to become agents of their own liberation. At the same time, his doctrine of religious equality tore down the hierarchical monastic structure, and the teaching of the sole *nenbutsu* practice and Amida's "other-power" deprived temples of a considerable part of their income. It also undermined reconstruction work of temples which were burned down in political and military conflicts, as we saw from Hōnen's statements in the context of Chōgen's *kanjin* campaign.

The present findings suggest viewing this particular case in the broader perspective of Japanese history. The *Wirkungsgeschichte* (history of effects) of Hōnen's religious concept of equality probably can be found more in Jōdo Shinshū than in Jōdoshū.[37] Hōnen's disciple Shinran 親鸞 (1173–1262) coined the expressions *dōbō* 同朋 (fellow companion) and *dōgyō* 同行 (fellow practitioner) for the followers of the Pure Land path, thereby drawing the religious idea of equality further into the social realm of religious communities. When addressing his followers through such expressions, Shinran refused to function in the traditional role as master, thereby abandoning the hierarchical relationship between teacher and follower; instead, he "placed himself on an equal footing with his followers" (Dobbins 1989: 64). Another aspect of Shinran's equalitarian thoughts was that he abolished for himself the distinction between priest and lay follower (*hisō hizoku* 非僧非俗).

This trend continued in Jōdo Shinshū history, when the idea of social equality was applied in the formation of its congregations (*sō, kō*) (Pauly 1985: 266–268). Subsequently, the egalitarian way of thinking contributed to a certain

---

37   I am indebted to Galen Amstutz for making me aware of the *Wirkungsgeschichte* of Hōnen's concept of equality in Shinran's thought and Jōdo Shinshū history.

degree to the development of the *ikkō ikki* 一向一揆 peasant rebellions.[38] Through the "legacy of Rennyo" and other factors, even today *dōbō* has become "a key term in the language used by the various reform movements in the two Honganji, and in their insistence on the need to shape a society based on fellowship" (Dessi 2007: 105; cf. 28; 110; 166).

All of these religio-social developments in Jōdo Shinshū were initially triggered by Hōnen's notion of religious equality. Here, only a few indicators for the interaction among doctrine, religious community and society are mentioned. It would certainly be a rewarding task to analyze in more detail these interactions in the history of Jōdo Shinshū. Moreover, the observations of this study suggest that future research will investigate the close interplay among the basic factors of doctrine, society, and economy in other areas and times as well. This would permit comparisons with other cases in religious history and enable the formulation of some theories concerning this matter.

At the end of this essay I would like to return to the methodological deliberation from the beginning. As mentioned in the introduction, modern academic disciplines tend to compartmentalize the reality of our world by increasingly specialized research. This tendency has to be counterbalanced by increased interdisciplinary efforts. The method used in this study attempted to grasp the interplay between seemingly heterogeneous subjects, such as religious doctrine, economy and society. Thereby, a broader cosmos comes to light which consists of mutual interactions between numerous elements and factors. If applying static terms, such as interconnection, interrelation, relation(ship), correlation, correspondence, and the like, it will be difficult to comprehend the real dynamics emerging and occurring among the multiple and diverse factors which thereby create new phenomena and constellations. It is my hope, though, that such methodological approach contributes not only to a more comprehensive understanding of Hōnen and his time but also to interdisciplinary research in general.

References

Adolphson, Mikael S. 2000. *The Gates of Power: Monks, Courtiers, and Warriors in Premodern Japan*. Honolulu: University of Hawai'i Press.

Adolphson, Mikael S. 2007. *The Teeth and the Claws of the Buddha: Monastic Warriors and Sōhei in Japanese History*. Honolulu: University of Hawai'i Press.

---

38 Pauly (1985: 361). Since Pauly seems to rely on Jōdo Shinshū historiography, he fails to recognize the fundamental role of Hōnen's concept of equality for Shinran and the subsequent Jōdo Shinshū history.

Augustine, Jonathan M. 2005. *Buddhist Hagiography in Early Japan: Images of Compassion in the Gyōki Tradition*. London and New York: RoutledgeCurzon.

Brown, Delmer and Ichirō, Ishida. 1979. *The Future and the Past: A Translation and Study of the Gukanshō. an Interpretative History of Japan Written in 1219*. Berkeley, Los Angeles and London: University of California Press.

Dessi, Ugo. 2007. *Ethics and Society in Contemporary Shin Buddhism*. Berlin: Lit Verlag.

Dobbins, James C. 1989. *Jōdo Shinshū: Shin Buddhism in Medieval Japan*. Bloomington and Indianapolis: Indiana University Press.

Dykstra, Yoshiko K. (trans.). 1983. *Miraculous Tales of the Lotus Sutra from Ancient Japan: The Dainihon Hokekyōkenki of Priest Chingen*. Honolulu: University of Hawai'i Press.

Dykstra, Yoshiko K. 1998. *The Konjaku Tales: Japanese Section (Honcho-Hen) (I) from a Medieval Japanese Collection*. Hirakata City: Kansai Gaidai University Publication.

DZ = Hieizan Senjūin 比叡山専修院 and Eizan Gakuin 叡山学院 (eds.). 1984 [1926]. *Dengyō Daishi zenshū* 伝教大師全集. Tōkyō: Seikai Seiten Kankō Kyōkai.

Gernet, Jacques. 1995. *Buddhism in Chinese Society: An Economic History from the Fifth to the Tenth Centuries*. New York: Columbia University Press (translation of the original French version [1956] by Franciscus Verellen).

Goodwin, Janet R. 1994. *Alms and Vagabonds: Buddhist Temples and Popular Patronage in Medieval Japan*. Honolulu: University of Hawai'i Press.

HSZ = Ishii, Kyōdō 石井教道 (ed.). 1991 [1955]. *Shōwa shinshū Hōnen Shōnin zenshū* 昭和新修法然上人全集. Kyōto: Heirakuji Shoten.

JSDJ = Jōdoshū Daijiten Kankōkai 浄土宗大辞典刊行会 (ed.). 1964–1982. *Jōdoshū daijiten* 浄土宗大辞典. 4 vols. Tōkyō: Sankibō Busshorin.

Kleine, Christoph. 1996. *Hōnens Buddhismus des Reinen Landes: Reform, Reformation oder Häresie*? Frankfurt am Main: Peter Lang.

Kuroda, Toshio. 1996a. "The Development of the *Kenmitsu* System as Japan's Medieval Orthodoxy." *Japanese Journal of Religious Studies* 23 (3–4): 233–269.

Kuroda, Toshio. 1996b. "The Imperial Law and the Buddhist Law." *Japanese Journal of Religious Studies* 23 (3–4): 271–285.

Kuroda, Toshio. 1996c. "Buddhism and Society in the Medieval Estate System." *Japanese Journal of Religious Studies* 23 (3–4): 287–319.

McCullough, William H. and Helen Craig McCullough. 1980. *A Tale of Flowering Fortunes: Annals of Japanese Aristocratic Life in the Heian Period*. 2 vols. Stanford: Stanford University Press.

Moerman, D. Max. 2005. *Localizing Paradise: Kumano Pilgrimage and the Religious Landscape of Premodern Japan* (Harvard East Asian Monographs). Cambridge: Harvard University Asia Center.

Morrell, Robert E. 1987. *Early Kamakura Buddhism: A Minority Report*. Berkeley, California: Asian Humanities Press.

Nara Kokuritsu Hakubutsukan 奈良国立博物館 (ed.). 2005. *Dai-kanjin Chōgen* 大勧進 重源 (exhibition catalogue).

NKBT 86 = Okami, Masao 岡見正雄 and Akamatsu, Toshihide 赤松俊秀 (eds.). 1967. *Gukan-shō* 愚管抄 (Nihon Koten Bungaku Taikei, Vol. 86). Tōkyō: Iwanami Shoten.

NSI = Risshō Daigaku Nichiren Kyōgaku Kenkyūsho 立正大学日蓮教学研究所 (ed.). 1991 [1952–1959]. *Shōwa teihon Nichiren Shōnin ibun* 昭和定本日蓮上人遺文. 4 vols. Minobu: Kuonji.

NST 6 = Ishida, Mizumaro 石田瑞麿 (ed.). 1970. *Genshin* 源信 (Nihon Shisō Taikei. Vol. 6). Tōkyō: Iwanami Shoten.

NST 7 = Inoue, Mitsusada 井上光貞 and Ōsone, Shosuke 大曾根章介 (eds.). 1974. *Ōjō-den. Hokke-genki* 往生伝. 法華驗記 (Nihon Shisō Taikei, Vol. 7). Tōkyō: Iwanami Shoten.

NST 15 = Kamata, Shigeo 鎌田茂雄 and Tanaka, Hisao 田中久夫 (eds.). 1971. *Kamakura kyū Bukkyō* 鎌倉旧仏教 (Nihon Shisō Taikei, Vol. 15). Tōkyō: Iwanami Shoten.

Ōhashi, Shunno 大橋俊雄 (ed.). 1989. *Hōnen zenshū* 法然全集. 3 vols. Tōkyō: Shunjūsha.

Pauly, Ulrich. 1985. *Ikkō-Ikki: Die Ikkō-Aufstände und ihre Entwicklung aus den Aufständen der bündischen Bauern und Provinzen des japanischen Mittelalters*. Ph.D. dissertation, Rheinische Friedrich-Wilhelms-Universität Bonn.

Repp, Martin. 2002a. Review of: Jacqueline I. Stone. *Original Enlightenment and the Transformation of Medieval Japanese Buddhism* (Kuroda Institute. Studies in East Asian Buddhism, Vol. 12. Honolulu: University of Hawaiʻi Press 1999). *Japanese Religions* 27 (1): 105–110.

Repp, Martin. 2002b. Review of: Brian Bocking, *The Oracles of the Three Shrines: Windows on Japanese Religion* (Richmond, Surrey: Curzon Press 2001). *Japanese Religions* 27 (1): 113–117.

Repp, Martin. 2002c. "Hachiman: Protecting Deity (*kami*) of the Japanese Nation." In: Klaus Antoni et al. (eds.), *Religion and National Identity in the Japanese Context* (Bunka, Tübingen Intercultural and Linguistic Studies on Japan, Vol. 5). Hamburg, Münster, London: Lit Verlag, 169–192.

Repp, Martin. 2005a. *Hōnens religiöses Denken: Eine Untersuchung zu Strukturen religiöser Erneuerung*. Wiesbaden: Harrassowitz Verlag.

Repp, Martin. 2005b. "How to Ascertain One's Birth Into the Pure Land? An Investigation into Developments during the Heian and Kamakura Periods." *Shinshūgaku* 111–112: 9–24.

Repp, Martin. 2006. "Buddhism and Cartoons in Japan: How Much Parody Can a Religion Bear?" *Japanese Religions* 31 (2): 187–203.

Rhodes, Robert (trans.). 1980. "Saichō's *Mappō Tōmyoki*: The Candle of the Latter Dharma." *The Eastern Buddhist* 13 (1): 79–103.

Rhodes, Robert (trans.). 1994. *The Candle of the Latter Dharma by Saichō* (BDK English Tripitaka 107–III). Berkeley: Numata Center for Buddhist Translation and Research.

Rhodes, Robert (trans.). 1996. "Pure Land Practitioner or *Lotus* Devotee? The Earliest Biographies of Genshin." *Japanese Religions* 21 (1): 28–69.

Senchakushū English Translation Project (trans. and ed.). 1998. *Hōnen's Senchakushū: Passages on the Selection of the Nembutsu in the Original Vow (Senchaku Hongan Nembutsu Shū)*. Honolulu: University of Hawai'i Press, and Tōkyō: Sōgō Bukkyō Kenkyūjo, Taishō University.

T = Takakusu, Junjirō 高楠順次郎 et al. (eds.). 1924–1932. *Taishō shinshū daizōkyō* 大正新修大蔵経. 85 vols. Tōkyō: Taishō Issaikyō Kankōkai.

Tanabe, George J. Jr. 1992. *Myōe the Dreamkeeper: Fantasy and Knowledge in Early Kamakura Buddhism*. Cambridge: Harvard University Press.

Yampolsky, Philip B. (ed.). 1990. *Selected Writings of Nichiren*. New York: Columbia University Press.

PART 4

Shinran's More Radical Turn to the Enlightenment Gift as an Involuntary Emergent Property

∵

Faith: Its Arising

Alfred Bloom

Faith as a gift of Amida Buddha.—We now come to a discussion of one of Shinran's most significant insights which certainly qualifies him for a place among the great religious thinkers of the world, and clearly comparable to the Protestant Reformers, Luther and Calvin, in whose thought faith as the gift of God's grace worked a revolution in Christian theology. It should be pointed out here that the understanding of faith as a gift of the deity and determined by that deity does not inhibit preaching for conversion or the necessity of decision to accept the way of salvation. In this Shinran stands on common ground with thinkers in Christianity and Islam. For though Amida Buddha is the source of faith, Shinran continues to preach. In religious thought of this type, it is believed that the proclamation of the message affords the opportunity for salvation to be realized by the individual. The point at which conversion is achieved is considered the time when the deity grants salvation. Thus we find also an idea of conversion in Shinran which is the decisive moment for the individual.

This insight into faith on the part of Shinran extends its influence to every doctrine which he taught. Already in our discussion we have seen that the point at which Shinran departed from traditional thought was determined by his desire to emphasize the fact that faith, or salvation, is not due at all to the contriving action of man, but solely through the power of Amida Buddha. He reconciled the apparent contradiction between the theological interpretation of faith as the work of Amida Buddha and the human experience in which a man actually appears to make the decisive act of faith. He did this by indicating that what one is aware of as his act of faith or believing is actually the manifestation of Amida Buddha's gift of faith in his mind.[1]

The principle that faith is a gift of Amida Buddha is set forth in the volume on faith in the *Kyōgyōshinshō* where Shinran takes up in detail the essential nature of faith. In the course of his writing, he gives a very concise statement of the theory:

Source: Bloom, Alfred, "Faith: Its Arising," in Alfred Bloom, *Shinran's Gospel of Pure Grace*, Tucson, AZ: University of Arizona Press, 1965, pp. 45–59. Reprinted with permission of the Association for Asian Studies, (www.asian-studies.org).

---

1 Ibid., 48 for a paradoxical statement of these two aspects of faith.

The mind of the Buddha is difficult to understand, but if we may infer concerning his mind, (we might say) that the whole sea of sentient beings, from the beginningless past even until the present time, are defiled, impure and stained. Their minds are not pure, and being false, they do not have a mind of truth. For this reason, the Tathagata had compassion on the whole sea of suffering sentient beings. For incomprehensibly infinite kalpas he performed the disciplines of a Bodhisattva, and never for even a single moment were his practices of the mouth, mind or body, impure, or untrue. By his pure, sincere mind, the Tathagata perfected his completely harmonious, unimpeded, mysterious, inexpressible, incomprehensible, supreme virtue. *He transferred the sincere mind of the Tathagata to all the sea of sentient beings who are passionridden, evil in deed and in mind.* Hence this manifests the true mind for helping others therefore it was never mixed with doubts. Hence this sincere mind has his virtuous name as its essence.[2]

However, in order to clarify more adequately the importance of this insight we must first briefly indicate the nature of faith in the general Buddhist tradition. It is evident in this tradition that faith is regarded as an act of the will, aroused by the individual and directed toward the Buddha, his teaching and his community of followers. Thus a leading Western expositor of Buddhism describes the act of faith in Buddhism:

> In Theravada Buddhism faith is the faith of a traveller in a famous guide. The Guide has pointed the way which he has trodden and the traveller, nothing doubting, follows in that Way.[3]

A modern Theravada Buddhist also expresses a similar understanding:

> A man first learns about the Buddha's teaching by hearsay. Then he tests what he has heard as far as he can. When he has done this enough to feel convinced that it is reliable, he outwardly expresses his conviction by pronouncing the three Refuges, the *Saranattaya* or *Tissarana* as they are

---

2 Yamabe and Akanuma, op. cit., 1, 87–89 gives a detailed discussion of Ekō, Shinran's reinterpretation and his textual supports.

3 Humphreys, *Buddhism*, op. cit., 61.

FAITH: ITS ARISING

called in Pali. And afterwards, whenever he has the occasion outwardly to reaffirm that inner conviction, he does so by pronouncing them aloud.[4]

Recently a Japanese Buddhist in a discussion of faith in Buddhism and Christianity, has defined the faith of a Buddhist in terms of a strong resolve:

> Faith through understanding is to listen to a teaching, understand it, and then come to a decision that there is no other teaching than this on which one can depend. Thereupon he becomes converted, and fervently tries to follow the teaching. He no longer looks to right and left, but turns to one direction, singleminded. This state of mind is faith. A sutra says: "*Bodhisattva* (Buddha-to-be), at his first conversion, earnestly seeks bodhi (wisdom) and is too firm to be moved." This is the faith through understanding. His faith is firm and intense, based on understanding and conviction.[5]

In the declaration of refuge in the three treasures, the traditional mark of Buddhism: "I take refuge in the Buddha: I take refuge in the Dharma, I take refuge in the Sangha," the devotee reveals his resolve to place all reliance on the Buddha and his teaching as the way to liberation. There is no question that faith has always been an essential element in the Buddhist religious life, but it has generally been a faith which is the result of inquiry and decision cultivated by the devotee himself.

Faith has always played a particularly conspicuous role in the aspiration for birth in the Pure Land. Faith was always considered a necessary prerequisite to the discipline and practices which would bring that birth. Nagarjuna, who was considered by Shinran as the first patriarch in the Pure Land tradition, wrote:

> If good men and women hear that Buddha's name and obtain deep faith, then they do not regress from (the state of) anuttara samyaksambodhi.[6]

Nagarjuna also distinguished the "easy practice of the means of faith (Shinhō-benigyō)"[7] from the difficult practices in Buddhism. Vasubandhu also

---

4   Bhikku Nanamoli, *The Three Refuges*, tract, *Bodhi Leaves*, #5, (Buddhist Publication Society: Kandy, Ceylon), 1.

5   Fumio Masutani, *A Comparative Study of Buddhism and Christianity* (Tōkyō: Young East Assoc., 1957), 68–79.

6   *SSZ.*, I, 255.

7   Ibid., 254.

308

called men and women to arouse faith and practice the five gates of devotion.[8] For himself Vasubandhu declared:

> O World-honored One, I, singleheartedly, take refuge in the Tathagata of Universal, unimpeded Light, and desire to be born in His Land of Bliss.[9]

The character of faith was discussed in T'an-luan's commentary to Vasubandhu's treatise on the Pure Land. T'an-luan declared that the content of faith was singlehearted refuge (reliance, faith) in Amida Buddha and desire for birth in this Pure Land.[10] This singlehearted faith was to be manifested in continuous and uninterrupted thought on the Buddha and his land.

When T'an-luan discussed the hindrances to true practice, he explained that they were the lack of ardent faith, the lack of deep faith and the lack of continuity (steadfastness). These factors were all interrelated so that the lack of any-element meant the lack of all. The presence or absence of these aspects of faith determined the condition of the devotee's singlehearted faith.[11]

T'an-luan placed the greatest stress in his understanding of faith on the aspect of continuity. He pointed out that the continuous repetition of the name of the Buddha would cleanse the devotee of eighty millions of kalpas of sins as the *Kammuryōjukyō* taught.[12] In his discussion of the number of recitations that were needed to assure birth in the Pure Land, he held that the important thing was that the recitation, or thought of the Buddha, be continuous and one need not be concerned greatly with the exact number itself.[13]

We can observe in T'an-luan's conception of faith that he stood deep within a meditative tradition. In this tradition the condition of the mind in approaching meditation was all-important in achieving the goal of meditation. In the meditative approach, purification of the mind and steadfastness (singleheartedness) were essential in the realization of the goal of insight and enlightenment. Purification preceded insight; concentration and unification of the mind preceded contemplation. In the traditional system of discipline it was no problem to justify the necessity for the purification of the mind as a preliminary step in the path of meditation. A problem arose in the Pure Land tradition as to how mediocre, evil mortals who commit the five deadly sins and ten evil acts could attain the required purification or steadfastness of mind. T'an-luan

---

8   Ibid., 270.
9   Ibid., 269.
10   Ibid., 282.
11   Ibid., 314.
12   Ibid., 282.
13   Ibid., 311.

FAITH: ITS ARISING

did not clarify the dilemma, but he was outstanding in calling attention to the nature of the faith needed to gain rebirth in the Pure Land through the practice of recitation. After him the concept of single-hearted faith became an important focal point of Pure Land doctrine.[14]

Shan-tao, as we have seen previously, also analysed in detail the mind of faith required for birth in the Pure Land. In his commentary on the *Kammuryōjukyō*, he taught that the practice of recitation was to be performed with a sincere mind, deep faith and strong desire for birth. According to him sincerity must pervade all practices. One must believe deeply that he is a sinner chained to the wheel of transmigration, as well as believing deeply that he can be saved by Amida Buddha's Vows. All the devotee's merits in practices are to be directed toward birth in the Pure Land.

It is clear from our survey of Buddhist tradition that faith is conceived as an operation of the human will in which the individual in full sincerity turns his aspirations and his efforts toward the attainment of Buddhist ideals.

Shinran's personal religious experience caused him to diverge widely from the Buddhist tradition. So compelling was his insight that he had to rend the grammar of the sutra in order to get an authoritative, textual basis for it.

Shinran read his epoch-making insight into the text of the *Muryojukyo* where it relates the fulfillment of the Eighteenth Vow by Amida Buddha. He was enabled to do this through the application of certain Japanese principles of grammar devised for reading Chinese texts. When he applied the Japanese grammar to the Chinese text, he implied that faith and the thought of Amida Buddha were transferred to beings by the Buddha himself. According to the Chinese text read strictly, the sutra reads:

> If all those beings hear that name, believe and rejoice even for one thought (moment), and sincerely transfer (the merit of the thought) desiring to be born in that Land, then they will obtain rebirth and abide in the state of non-retrogression. Only those are excluded who have committed the five deadly sins and slandered the Dharma.[15]

However, Shinran read the text according to his insight in the following manner:

> If all beings who hear that name, believe and rejoice, even for one moment, as a result of the fact that (Amida) has sincerely transferred (His

---

14　Keishin Nagata, "The Commentary on Singleness of Heart in the Ronchu," *Indogaku Bukkyōgaku Kenkyū* III-2 (6) (March 1955), 532–533.

15　*SSZ.*, I, 24.

Name), and desire to be born in that country, they will obtain birth and abide in the state of non-retrogression, excluding those alone who have committed the five deadly sins and slandered the Dharma.[16]

The problem in the alteration of the grammar of this text revolves about the term Shishin Ekō. Shishin Ekō normally means to "transfer with a true or sincere mind." In traditional Buddhism, transfers of merit are usually made by a devotee toward some spiritual object or benefit which one desires. When the practice of recitation is viewed as a means to salvation, the salvation comes about when the merit acquired through the recitation is directed toward the goal of birth in the Pure Land.

In Shinran's thought the perspective is entirely reversed. *All transfer of merit comes from Amida Buddha to man.* From our discussion of the degenerate nature of beings in his thought, it is clear that beings have nothing to transfer since they are deeply evil. Yet Amida Buddha as the absolute source of salvation has the merit to give to beings to bring about their salvation. Thus Shinran's insight overpowered the normal grammatical interpretation of the text.[17] This can be evidenced from the fact that the verbal ending Seshimetamaeri is put into the mouth of the Buddha. As an honorific form, one would not use it of himself or of persons below himself. Shinran, however, desired to point out clearly that all spiritual benefit proceeded from Amida Buddha. He alone is the source of

---

16 Ibid.

17 Another interesting example of Shinran's subjectivity in the treatment of traditional texts can be found in the way in which he employed Shan-tao's description of Amida Buddha's sincerity in his volume on faith in the *Kyōgyōshinshō* and in the volume on the transformed land. In the volume on faith, Shinran quoted the part of the passage giving the three minds as outlined by Shan-tao. It is significant, however, that Shinran deleted a passage dealing with ethical and religious exhortation. The material which was deleted in the faith volume was later used in the volume on the transformed land to typify the ideal of the devotees of self power.

The question is raised why did Shinran cut up the passage in this way? The answer lies in his endeavor to show in the faith volume that the three winds, (sincerity, deep mind and the mind of transfer and aspiration) were given as gifts to men from Amida Buddha, as a result of his aspiration to save all beings. Any text which could be made to imply this transfer on the part of Amida Buddha was appropriated by Shinran for the faith volume. In the case of the initially deleted portion which was used in the volume on the transformed land, the grammar and content were such that it clearly referred to beings and not to the activity of the Buddha. Therefore, it could not be used in the faith volume.

These examples of the arbitrary dividing of passages indicates that Shinran imposed his insight on the text and employed the text as subordinate to the insight. Throughout he shows great freedom in the handling of traditional texts. See *ssz.*, II, 52 and 149; compare with I, 533–534. Also Yamabe and Akanuma, op. cit., II, 607–608.

FAITH: ITS ARISING   311

virtue and merit. Further the grammatical relation of the phrase Shishin ni
Ekō Seshimetamaeri and the phrases preceding and following are not clear.
The disruption of the thought of the Chinese is due to Shinran's insight and
his desire to stress the fact that Amida Buddha is the ultimate ground of salva-
tion. This interpretation is further clarified in the *Ichinentannenmoni* where
Shinran gives a word interpretation of the passage in question;

> The term Shoushūjō signifies all the beings in the universe. Mongomyōgō
> (hearing that name) is to hear the name of the Original Vow (i.e. the name
> of Amida). "To hear" means to hear of the Original Vow and not to have
> a doubting mind. Further "to hear" is the principle that manifests (the
> meaning of) faith. (In the phrase) Shinjinkangi naishi ichinen, Shinjin
> (faith) is to hear of the Vow of the Tathagata without any mind of doubt;
> Kan (joy) means to cause to rejoice with the body; Ki (joy) is to cause
> to rejoice in the mind. Previously the mind of rejoicing meant "not ob-
> taining (now) what one will obtain (in the future)." Naishi signifies both
> many or few, far or near, before or after. It is an inclusive term. (The term)
> Ichinen reveals the smallest fraction of time when faith is obtained. In
> the phrase Shishin Ekō, Shishin is the word for truth (Shinjitsu). Truth
> is the mind of Amida Nyorai. Ekō is the principle in which (Amida) has
> given his name of the Original Vow to all the beings of the Universe.[18]

Shinryū Umehara points to several other passages which indicate Shinran's
view of absolute Other Power, or the fact that Amida Buddha bestows ultimate
salvation on man.[19] Shinran's treatment of the Chinese character reveals his
insight into Other Power. In a passage from the *Muryōjukyō*[20] which Shinran
interpreted in the *Songōshinzōmeimon*[21] he wrote that beings who heard of
the Vow Power and Amida Buddha's name, and desire to be born into the
Pure Land, "naturally" attain the unretrogressive state. The term Ji (自) was
interpreted as "naturally" and meant that the individual attained without any

---

18   *SSZ.*, II, 604–605. For discussion of this point the reader may be referred to Suzuki.
   Miscellany on the Shin Teaching of Buddhism, op. cit., 23; 61–63. Also Umehara, op. cit., II,
   46–50. Karasawa, *Shinran no Sekai*, op. cit., 138–141, shows that Shinran read this insight
   into passages which he quoted also from T'an-luan and Vasubandhu. Wherever the term
   Ekō appears, he interpreted it to refer only to the activity of Amida Buddha. Yamabe and
   Akanuma, op. cit., I. 87–89 give a detailed discussion of Ekō. Shinran's reinterpretation
   and his (textual supports).
19   Shinryū Umehara. *Shinran Kyōgaku* (Toyamaken; Senchōji Bunsho Dendōbu, 1952).
   66–79.
20   *SSZ.*, I, 26.
21   Ibid., II, 579.

striving or calculating on his part. Rather the individual *is caused* to arrive there through the operation of nature which is the working of Amida Buddha and symbolized by his Vow.

Similarly Shinran saw the principle of absolute Other Power in the (横) Ō which appeared in the *Muryōjukyō*.[22] In the *Songōshinzōmeimon*,[23] this term has the sense of "crosswise," "transverse." In its use in such terms as Ōshi (横死), "violent death," Ōryō (横領), "seizing," and Ōbō (横暴), "oppression," there is implied the sense of suddenness. This sense of suddenness pointed to the instantaneous aspect of salvation for Shinran, and he saw in it the operation of Buddha's Vow apart from the individual's striving or contrivance. Thus he wrote:

> Ō (横) means "crosswise." "Crosswise" means that *it is not the contrivance of the devotee* because he believes in the Vow Power of the Tathagata. The five evil paths are "naturally" cut off and one is liberated from the four (types of) births. This we call "Crosswise," "Other Power." This is "Crosswise Transcendence" (横超 Ōchō).[24]

Shinran also found similar significance in the term Soku, Sunawachi (即) which also appeared in the *Muryōjukyō*[25] and was interpreted in the *Ichinentannenmoni*[26] Here, he saw the word having the sense of principle, law or rule. It also had the meaning "thereupon" or "accordingly," and conveyed the idea that the succeeding statement followed the previous as its "natural," inevitable outcome. All contrivance or calculation on the part of the individual was again set aside. Thus he wrote:

> Soku (即) means Sunawachi (thereupon) or Nori (rule). When one believes in the Original Vow of the Tathagata for one moment, he is assuredly *caused to receive* unsurpassed virtue without soliciting it. Unconsciously he receives profound blessing. It is the law which manifests therefore various insights (Satori) naturally (Jinen).[27]

It is clear that the central point of Shinran's teaching concerning faith is not only that he made faith the primary cause for salvation, but that he insisted

---

22   Ibid., I, 31.

23   Ibid., II, 580.

24   Ibid.

25   Ibid., I, 46. "Therefore, these are endowed with the highest virtue."

26   Ibid., II, 611.

27   Ibid.

FAITH: ITS ARISING 313

that *faith is not the result of human resolution to believe* or the cultivation individually of a sense of dependence. Other Pure Land teachers, and Buddhists through all periods had talked of the faith that was required for embarking on the discipline that would lead to release from the stream of birth and death. There is, however, a qualitative difference between Shinran's understanding of faith and that found in the Buddhist tradition before him. Shinran maintained that faith was aroused through the operation of Amida Buddha in the heart and mind of the individual, and this faith was the true cause of salvation. It was precisely because Amida Buddha gave the faith that faith, and faith alone, could be the true and only cause for birth in the Pure Land for defiled beings. From this significant change in the understanding of faith flow the important contributions of Shinran's thought.

Factors in the Appearance of Faith.—The belief that faith is a gift from Amida Buddha raises the question about the process by which faith becomes manifest in beings. We are not concerned here with the psychological characteristics of the appearance of faith, but with the theoretical understanding of its origin. The description of the actual arising of faith within man does not greatly differ in Shinran's thought from the traditional view, except in the qualification that what appears to us as "our" faith and sincerity is really the result of Amida Buddha's work in our minds. Shinran, therefore, can employ traditional descriptions of faith when depicting the nature of faith in man. It is his philosophical understanding of the origin of faith and its implications for religious existence that distinguishes his thought so sharply from previous Pure Land thinkers.

These are several aspects to Shinran's view of the process of the arising of faith in sentient beings. In the first place our attention is drawn to the significant interpretation which he placed on the Seventeenth Vow of Amida Buddha.[28] Secondly, we must discuss the operation of the name of Amida Buddha and his Light as the cause and condition for the appearance of faith in beings.

In order for Shinran to establish his insight into the absolute Other Power faith firmly, it was necessary for him to discover materials in the sutras and commentaries which he could use as evidence. The realization that faith was a gift from Amida Buddha and beyond human achievement naturally prompted the question: How does this faith arise? In his answer to the question, he made the Seventeenth Vow a central point in his explanation. In this Vow he discovered the universal basis for the origin of Other Power faith. In the operation of

---

28   See above p. 156 for text of the Vow.

the name of Amida Buddha and his Light. Shinran saw the immediate causes of faith.

The Seventeenth Vow.—According to Shinran, the Seventeenth Vow was the universal source which declared the dissemination of Amida Buddha's name among sentient beings. Although this Vow was one of the forty-eight Vows given by that Buddha when he began his striving to save beings, it had never gained an outstandingly prominent place in the teachings of the earlier Pure Land teachers. T'an-luan had taught that the Eighteenth, Eleventh, and Twenty-Second Vows were the central Vows.[29] Shan-tao referred to the Seventeenth Vow in his discussion of deep faith, but he used it only to indicate the fundamental identity of all Buddhist teaching.[30] However, Shinran saw deep spiritual meaning in the Seventeenth Vow that escaped previous teachers. For him it revealed the link between the effect of the fulfillment of Amida Buddha's Vows in the ideal realm and the historical appearance of that teaching in the time-space realm of sentient beings. It provided an absolute basis for the historical tradition.

Attention was drawn to the work of Sakyamuni Buddha because he came into the world in order to reveal the work of Amida Buddha to beings in accordance with the Seventeenth Vow.[31]

The proclamation of this teaching by Sakyamuni Buddha was in accord with the original intention for the appearance of a Buddha in the world as stated by Sakyamuni Buddha to Ananda in the *Muryōjukyō*. He declared that a Buddha appears in the world out of the infinite compassion for the beings of the three worlds and out of a deep desire to bestow real benefit on beings.[32] In fulfillment of this intention Sakyamuni Buddha, according to Shinran, taught the *Muryōjukyō*. *Kammuryōjukyō* and *Amidakyō* which fully revealed the way of salvation established by Amida Buddha and was the basis for Pure Land teaching in India, China and Japan.

By stressing this interpretation of the intention for the appearance of the Buddha in the world, Shinran reversed the traditional relationship between the "Holy Path" and the Pure Land school. In the earlier tradition Pure Land doctrine was considered merely as an expedient way in Buddhism for inferior people. However with Shinran, the "Holy Path" became completely instrumental and subsidiary to the Pure Land teaching. The difficult practices

---

29   *SSZ.*, I, 9–10.

30   Ibid.

31   Ibid., II, 43–44.

32   Ibid., I, 4. Shinran's interpretation is given in *Ichinentanenmoni*, Ibid., II, 614–615, 618.

and teachings were expedient doctrines in order to bring finally the devotee to faith in Amida Buddha's Vow.[33]

The titles which Shinran uses to describe the Seventeenth Vow also reveal to us other aspects of the theological importance of this Vow for him. In the *Kyōgyōshinshō* where he discusses the titles of this Vow, two are instructive. On the one hand, he called it "the Vow of the Transfer (of Merit) for Going (to the Pure Land)." On the other hand, he termed it "the Vow of the Selected (practice of) the Recitation of the Name." In the first title he wished to show that the foundation for the Other Power way of salvation was given in this Vow through the declaration of Amida Buddha's way of salvation by all the Buddhas in the universe. In the second title, Shinran taught that the Seventeenth Vow was the true basis for the practice of recitation which had traditionally been based on the phrase Naishi Junen, "till ten thoughts," of the Eighteenth Vow.[34] The significance of his view lies in the fact that the Eighteenth Vow was released from its traditional connotation of the Vow of practice,[35] by distinguishing the Seventeenth Vow as "the Vow of True Practice" i.e. the "Vow in which the Buddhas Recite the Name." The Eighteenth Vow was then designated "the Vow of True Faith" i.e., the "Vow of Sincere Faith." The center of Shinran's interest in the Eighteenth Vow was shifted from the consideration of the practice of that Vow in its traditional sense to the contemplation of the faith that was promised in the Vow.

Through his interpretation of the Seventeenth Vow, Shinran was able to explain the existence and meaning of the Pure Land tradition, and he was able to root the process of the arising of faith in beings to the cosmic process of the realization of Amida Buddha's compassion and desire to save all beings. It was an important concept contributing to the consistency of Shinran's interpretation of Pure Land doctrine.

The Name and Light: The Immediate Causes of Faith.—In tracing Shinran's thought on the way in which Amida Buddha's gift of faith is realized among men, we come now to take up the immediate causes for the arising of faith which he regarded as issuing from Amida Buddha's compassion and finding fulfillment within the human consciousness. In this process he pointed to two factors. The active cause he designated as the name of Amida Buddha and the passive cause he termed the Light of Amida Buddha. His interpretation of this process is mainly philosophical since the name and Light of Amida Buddha are

---

33   Umehara, *Kyōgyōshinshō Shinshaku*, op. cit., I, 39–40.

34   *SSZ.*, II, 5.

35   Ibid., 42–43.

regarded as transcendental realities embodying Amida Buddha's compassion and wisdom.

Shinran's conception of the name of Amida Buddha is rooted in the theory developed in the Pure Land tradition. T'an-luan was the first of the Pure Land patriarchs to present a theory of the name. As we have observed earlier, the name, according to his theory, embodied the total reality of the nature of Amida Buddha. Therefore, when it was repeated, it had the power to cleanse and purify evil beings and to bring them great benefit.[36] Hōnen also formulated a significant conception of the virture of the name which he stated in the *Senjakushu*:

> ... the Nembutsu is superior and all other practices are inferior, because all virtues are wrapt up in the one sacred name. There are the four wisdoms, the three bodies, the ten faculties, the four fearlessnesses, and all other virtues of the inner faculties, external signs, light rays, sermons, the benefitting of others—indeed all outward activities. These. I say. are inherent in the sacred name of the Buddha.[37]

Shinran was also influenced by these ancient ideas concerning names. Nevertheless his use of the idea was quite different from preceding teachers, and his use purged the conception of any magical overtones. He would agree that the name of Amida Buddha contained the whole virtue of the Buddha within itself. But this name and its power were not to be conceived merely in terms of the practice of the recitation done by sentient beings as an effort to gain salvation.

The name as conceived by Shinran is that name. Amida, sounded forth by the Buddhas of the universe in accordance with the Seventeenth Vow. It is the true cause of salvation as it mysteriously arouses faith in sentient beings when they hear it and become aware that it embodies Amida Buddha's compassionate intention to save all beings. Conceived in this manner, the name of Amida is no longer the merely vocal element in the practice of recitation, but it is the mysterious activity of Amida Buddha within the minds of men.

Shinran, thus speaks of the name as the "efficient cause of rebirth."[38] or as a "father"[39] signifying the positive activity of the name in bringing about salvation.

---

36   See the study of T'an-luan above pp. 7–11.

37   Coates and Ishizuka, op. cit., II, 343.

38   Suzuki, *Miscellany on the Shin Teaching of Buddhism*, op. cit., 145.

39   *SSZ.*, II, 33–34. 694.

FAITH: ITS ARISING   317

Before moving on to discuss the second factor in the arising of faith we must call attention to an important aspect of the conception of the name. Shinran's understanding of the activity of the name must be considered from both objective and subjective standpoints. The transfer of the name of Amida Buddha to beings as represented by the Seventeenth Vow is the objective aspect. However, when the transfer of the name is analyzed, discussion must move immediately to the subjective aspect. Although the name is spoken of as an objective existence, in reality it only manifests itself as the subjective factor of faith when that faith is expressed in the practice of recitation. The name is thus never separate or apart from beings, but intertwined in their existence as faith or recitation, as the manifestation of faith in mind, word or deed.[40] This is a very difficult point for Westerners to comprehend in Buddhist thought even beyond Shinran's thought. That is, that objective reality appears to be dissolved into the subjective awareness. Frequently fundamental concepts pointing to transcendental realities are described by Buddhists, but they immediately qualify their thought by indicating that the realities that they refer to do not exist outside the mind of the believer as a self-subsisting, objective reality. Rather what is spoken of as apparently existing objectively, because of the way in which men must express their thought, is, in reality, to be discovered within one's consciousness. Hence for Shinran, the name of Amida Buddha is not some metaphysical entity or some objective existence somewhere in the world, nor truly are the Buddhas who speak this name some type of objective existences located in the universe. The name, spoken by the Buddhas, or heard by people in whom the faith is to be aroused, is the name heard upon the lips of ordinary people, or the content of teaching in which Amida Buddha's intention is praised, or even as the historical tradition of the Pure Land itself which has consistently proclaimed Amida Buddha's compassion for men.

The second factor which Shinran singled out in the process of the arising of faith is the Light of Amida Buddha. The Light of the Buddha stands for the aspect of wisdom in a Buddha or a Bodhisattva, and it is usually portrayed in the mythology as a stream of light which illumines every aspect of reality and shows its true nature. The *Muryōjukyō* gives a picture of the Light generated by Amida Buddha as the result of the perfection of the austerities which he carried out.[41]

Amida Buddha's nature as Infinite Light is based on the fulfillment of his Twelfth Vow[42] in which he promised that there would be no place in the

40   Umehara, *Kyōgyōshinshō Shinshaku*, op. cit., I, 62–63.
41   *Sacred Books of the East*, XLIX, op. cit., 28–30.
42   See above p. 2.

universe which would not be illumined by his Light, that is, his wisdom. Wisdom in Buddhism means to see things as they really are, to apprehend the true nature of things and oneself.

The Light of Amida Buddha, as the passive cause for the arising of faith in men. interpreted by Shinran, refers to that religious experience when the individual feels himself to be illumined, when the significance and meaning of the teaching becomes real to him. According to Shinran, the Light of Amida Buddha is promoting faith in men when "they feel the darkness of Ignorance gradually fading in them and are ready to see the seed of good karma germinate."[43] The experience of Amida Buddha's Light in his thought was attended by the double insight into the sinful condition of beings and the complementary insight that trust in Amida Buddha's Vows will result in liberation from the bonds of finitude.

What we have said above concerning the subjective-objective relation of the name in Shinran's thought also applied to his conception of the Light of Amida Buddha. This Light approaches the sense of the "glory" of divinity as perhaps seen in the beauty or order of nature. However, its function is not to indicate something of the nature of the universe, but to point directly to man's nature as a sinner, and to make him aware of the compassion of Amida Buddha. In this way the Light stimulates men to faith in Amida Buddha's Vows.

In connection with the concept of Light. Shinran developed a theory which shows again how his sense that salvation is completely the work of Amida Buddha influenced his treatment of traditional Pure Land themes. He placed great emphasis on the fact that in the experience of salvation "one is accepted and protected by unimpeded Light of Amida Buddha's mind."[44] This is the concept of the "acceptance (by Amida's Light) which does not reject."

One important aspect of Shinran's own spiritual experience was his sense of being accepted and not abandoned by Amida Buddha. This experience within his consciousness countered his sense of spiritual incapacity and lostness, because he recognized that Amida Buddha was the sole source of salvation. Through this experience, and its formulation into a key doctrine in his thought. Shinran found strong evidence for his understanding of faith as a gift of Amida Buddha. According to him. the moment in which faith arises is the moment when beings receive Amida Buddha's acceptance. Thus he declared:

> True faith is caused to arise through the efforts of the two Honorables, Sakyamuni Buddha and Amida Buddha. When we say that faith is

---

43   Suzuki, *Miscellany on the Shin Teaching of Buddhism*, op. cit., 45.

44   SSZ., II, 670.

FAITH: ITS ARISING

determined, it means the time when one is given "Acceptance." After that one abides in the status of the company of the truly assured, and it will be so until he is born into the Pure Land.[45]

Through Shinran's frequent reference to the Light of Amida Buddha we could describe his theology as a theology of Light. For according to him it is in the embrace of Light that passion-ridden beings are granted the status of salvation realized in the awakening of faith. On its cognitive side the Light reveals to man his true nature as passion-ridden and shows him the way of faith in Amida Buddha. However, this knowledge is not factual datum, but inner awareness of one's spiritual condition and the simultaneous awareness that in effect Amida Buddha, by fulfillment of his aspirations, has already deigned to save such beings. This is faith itself. On its transcendental side, the embrace of Light points to the fact that the sole ground of salvation is Amida Buddha. Thus Shinran extolled that Light, for as one is illumined by this Light he senses that his sins are cleansed, that karmic bonds are broken, and all illusions are dispelled. Surrounded by Amida Buddha's Light faith grows and there is joy. Thus Shinran calls all men to submit themselves to this Light and share its wondrous blessing:

> Wisdom's light is infinite.
> Of all finite beings, there are none
> That light have not received.
> Let us take refuge in the True Light![46]

Shinran's concept of salvation through the embrace within Amida Buddha's Light represents a significant change in emphasis from the traditional Pure Land doctrine based on his insight into the nature of absolute Other Power. According to previous Pure Land doctrine, the Light of Amida Buddha shone only on those who recite the name. The basis for this view was the *Kammuryōjiikyō*:

> Buddha Amitayus has eighty four thousand signs of perfection, each sign is possessed of eighty-four minor marks of excellence, each mark has eighty-four thousand rays, each ray extends so far as to shine over the

---

45   Ibid., 673–674. See also 678–679.
46   Ibid., 486.

world of the ten quarters, whereby Buddha embraces and protects all beings who think upon him and does not exclude (any of them).[47]

Shan-tao's interpretation of the text makes it clear that to think on the Buddha means to recite Amida Buddha's name. He shows also that the degree of spiritual benefit of the practice is directly dependent on the intensity and constancy of the devotee's effort.[48] He stresses the fact that the illumination of the Buddha is attained only by those who think on Amida Buddha's name and not by those who employ other practices or devote themselves to other Buddhas.[49]

The concept of Amida Buddha's Light in traditional Pure Land thought was connected entirely with the merit acquiring process, and was received as a result of intense spiritual endeavor in the practice of the recitation of the Buddha's name. Thus experience assured the devotee of his union with the Buddha and no doubt was an experience of great spiritual depth.

It can readily be seen that Shinran differed sharply from this narrow understanding of Amida Buddha's Light which restricted its operation to only an effect of discipline. For Shinran, the idea was elevated to a cosmic or universal level as the precondition for the salvation of all beings. For him it was the spiritual basis whereby the Buddha acted to make known to beings their sinful and degenerate condition and to assure them of his compassionate intention in his Vow. In other words the Light, as understood by Shinran, was the source or cause of faith, rather than the visionary effect of meditative discipline.

We bring our discussion of the two causes of the arising of faith in beings to an end by stating that the function of these two concepts, the name and Light of Amida Buddha, is to give further support to Shinran's theory that salvation comes about entirely through the work of Amida Buddha. In order to substantiate this insight, Shinran had to develop these concepts in his distinctive manner to indicate the universal process through which faith is realized in beings.

Further, the Seventeenth Vow establishes the connection which explains the emergence of Amida Buddha's salvation into the historical world, while the name and Light serve to establish the connection between Amida Buddha's compassionate activity and the experience of faith in the individual.

Conversion.—We have pointed out that the activity of the name and the Light relate primarily to the experience of faith in the individual. The idea that faith is a gift of Amida Buddha and also the understanding that it arises and is manifested when a man is aware of his sinful state and the availability of

---

47 *SBE.*, LXIX, op. cit., 180. *SSZ.*, I, 57.

48 *SSZ.*, I, 521–522.

49 Ibid., 628–629.

FAITH: ITS ARISING

the Buddha's compassion, both point to the fact that there must be a decisive time when this salvation is effected. In other words there is a concept of conversion in Shinran's thought. This concept of conversion will naturally reflect his own experience as he achieved this insight under the tutelage of Hōnen and thereby put an end to futile religious striving. The concept of conversion as developed by Shinran is completely consistent with his understanding that salvation comes about through the work of Amida Buddha. Conversion is not a matter of human effort.

Shinran's concept of conversion is based on the term Ōchō, translated as transverse transcendence. In our discussion of the term Ō (横)[50] we pointed out that it implied an instantaneous achievement of salvation, which meant that no human contrivance was involved. In the *Songōshinzōmeimon* he wrote that "since one has attained faith, therefore, we must know that we have transversely cut off the five evil paths. As for the term Ōchō, Ō speaks of the Tathagata's Vow Power, Other Power. Chō (超) signifies that we pass over the sea of births and deaths easily and enter the capital of the unsurpassed great Nirvana."[51]

In a similar vein, Shinran employed the term Eshin (回心) which may be translated as "turning the mind" and is taken as the conversion experience itself. According to Shinran, conversion means to reverse the mind of self power. That is to reject the way of works, good deeds, purifying exercises, and turn in faith to Amida Buddha's Vow.[52]

In both terms Ōchō and Eshin the aspect of discontinuity which occurs at the moment of the arising of faith was interpreted by Shinran as the result of the activity of Amida Buddha, and this activity was manifested in the individual's experience as the rejection of self effort and reliance on the Buddha. Thus it was a decisive experience which took place once and for all.[53]

Shinran's understanding of conversion permitted him to give a deeper theological basis for the religious life. Following the critical classification of doctrines in the Tandai school, he maintained that faith in Amida Buddha conferred upon the devotee immediate and total salvation. Thus for him the Pure Land doctrine was the ultimate of Mahayana doctrine because it promised the sudden, instantaneous, complete and perfect salvation which was the ideal of Buddhist tradition. We must turn our attention next to this status which the devotee received in this life as he attained faith in Amida Buddha.

---

50   See above pp. 50–51.

51   *SSZ.*, II, 562, 576. Also 632.

52   Ibid., 628.

53   Ibid., 787–788. According to Yuiembo, conversion occurs only once.

"Rely on the Meaning, Not on the Words"
Shinran's Methodology and Strategy for Reading Scriptures and Writing the Kyōgyōshinshō

Eisho Nasu

When Śākyamuni was about to enter *nirvāṇa,* he said to the *bhikṣus,* "From this day on, rely on dharma, not on people who teach it. Rely on the meaning, not on the words. Rely on wisdom, not on the working of the mind. Rely on the sūtras that fully express the meaning, not on those that do not."[1]

∴

1 Introduction

The *Kyōgyōshinshō*[2] is the most significant work by Shinran (1173–1262), the founder of the Jōdo Shin-shū, upon which the doctrinal foundation of the school has been established. The text of the *Kyōgyōshinshō* has been studied almost exclusively by Jōdo Shin-shū scholars whose primary focus is on doctrinal issues within their own tradition, with little concern for historical context. This focus has produced a rather rarefied view of Shinran. It is understandable

---

Source: Nasu, Eisho, "'Rely on the Meaning, Not on the Words:' Shinran's Methodology and Strategy for Reading Scriptures and Writing the *Kyōgyōshinshō*," in Richard K. Payne and Taigen Dan Leighton (eds.), *Discourse and Ideology in Medieval Japanese Buddhism,* 1st Edition, New York: Routledge, 2006, pp. 240–262. © Routledge, 2016; reproduced by arrangement with Taylor & Francis Books UK.

---

1 *Dazhidu lun* (Jpn. *Daichidoron,* Commentary on the Mahāprajñāpāramitā sūtra) cited in *The True Teaching, Practice, and Realization of the Pure Land Way* (*Kyōgyōshinshō*), in *The Collected Works of Shinran* (hereafter *CWS*), 2 vols, Kyoto: Jōdo Shinshū Hongwanji-ha, 1997, 1:241.

2 The full title of the *Kyōgyōshinshō* is *Ken Jōdo shinjitsu kyō gyō shō monrui* (A Collection of Passages Revealing the True Teaching, Practice, and Realization of the Pure Land Way). During the thirteenth and fourteenth centuries, the text was called as the *Kyōgyōshō* or the *Kyōgyōshinshō monrui.* The *Kyōgyōshinshō* is an abridged title of the text that became popular around the time of the eighth abbot of Hongwanji, Rennyo (1415–1499). See Shigemi Kazuyuki, *Kyōgyōshinshō no kenkyū,* Kyoto: Hōzōkan, 1981, pp. 32–33.

© KONINKLIJKE BRILL NV, LEIDEN, 2020 | DOI:10.1163/9789004401501_014

"RELY ON THE MEANING, NOT ON THE WORDS" 323

that a religion should seek to extract the founder's ideas and teachings from their own particular historical context—religious teachings, if they are to survive, after all, must have some sort of universal currency. But when these same scholars then look back to describe the founder, they are then liable to attribute to him an originality or uniqueness that seems to place him outside of his own time. Such is the case with Shinran. He is described by the tradition as an "original" thinker,[3] and, according to one even more extreme critique, his readings of Buddhist scriptures in the *Kyōgyōshinshō* are "completely arbitrary and audacious in the extreme."[4]

As a result of recent developments in studies of the medieval Japanese Tendai school,[5] however, we are beginning to uncover that Shinran's readings of the texts are perhaps "audacious," but neither "arbitrary" nor "unique." Shinran, in the *Kyōgyōshinshō*, systematically applied the *kanjin* (mind-contemplation) style of scriptural reading popularly practiced among medieval Japanese Tendai scholastics.[6] Historical evidence suggests that Shinran was schooled in *kanjin*-style reading, particularly that of the Eshin school (Jpn. Eshinryū),

---

3 The editors of the *Collected Works of Shinran,* in their introduction to the *Kyōgyōshinshō,* however, acknowledge the problem regarding the originality of the text as follows: "The greater part of Shinran's 'collection of passages' is made up of quotations from the sūtras and the treatises and commentaries of the masters, and there is little of his own comment. It is certainly striking that an original thinker of Shinran's stature should, in the single systematic presentation of his thought—unquestionably his lifework—bury his own words with quotations from the works of others. Moreover, these quotations are not always cited faithfully ... a number of them are greatly altered in meaning" (CWS, 2:23).

4 The critique goes on to focus on Shinran's methodology of reading texts, saying that "It is difficult to recognize them as quotations; they are basically nothing more than original passages. In order to set forth his own views, he borrowed passages from the sūtras, treatises, and commentaries that suited his own purposes." Mochizuki Shinkō, *Ryakujutsu Jōdo kyōrishi,* Tokyo: Nihon Tosho Center, 1977, p. 431. The passages are translated and cited in the CWS, 2:23–24.

5 A historical review and the scholarly updates of the Japanese scholarship on medieval Tendai studies and other related topics are available in Jacqueline I. Stone, *Original Enlightenment and the Transformation of Medieval Japanese Buddhism,* Honolulu: University of Hawaii Press, 1999, pp. 3–95.

6 Jacqueline Stone, in her recent study on medieval Japanese Tendai, summarizes the principle of *kanjin*-style reading as follows: "The *kanjin*-style interpretive mode found in many medieval *kuden* [oral transmission] texts aims at retrieving hidden meanings held to embody the most profound insights of religious liberation. Such hidden meanings, it was thought, could be accessed only by those with enlightened insight and transmitted only to the properly initiated; they were not part of common doctrinal understanding. This mode of interpretation has been characterized by modern scholars as undermining orthodox doctrinal understanding by encouraging the proliferation of arbitrary, private readings.... In large measure, this dismissal may be traced to a profound epistemological gap that separates the way scholars read texts today from the way they were read by scholar-monks of medieval period"

while he was a monk on Mt. Hiei. It is also noteworthy that the Eshin lineage was transmitted to the Kantō (Eastern Regions) during the mid-thirteenth century,[7] which coincided with the period when Shinran was completing an early draft of the *Kyōgyōshinshō*. By applying the *kanjin* style in his readings of scriptures in the *Kyōgyōshinshō,* Shinran kindled the spirituality of the other power (Jpn. *tariki*) *nenbutsu* at a time when the Pure Land teaching of Hōnen (1133–1212) Was under tight scrutiny by the medieval religio-political powers.

Despite the fact that there is ample evidence demonstrating the influence of medieval Tendai doctrine on the development of Shinran's thought,[8] the significance of this fact has yet to be examined in detail. This chapter is one such attempt to reposition Shinran's thought in a broader doctrinal and historical context. It focuses on how Shinran employed the *kanjin*-style method of reading texts to construct his *Kyōgyōshinshō*. First, I situate Shinran in his position as a disciple of Hōnen, in order to examine the historical context that led him to compile the *Kyōgyōshinshō*. I look particularly at the evidence for his interactions with, or knowledge of, Hōnen's other followers who were also composing texts at that time. Second, I examine Shinran's adoption of the Eshin school's *kanjin*-style reading for the composition of the *Kyōgyōshinshō,* re-evaluating the significance of Shinran's background as a Tendai monk who witnessed the rise of the popularity of the Tendai studies, especially in the Kantō region. Third, I revisit the significance of Shinran's unique understanding of the other power *nenbutsu* in the *Kyōgyōshinshō* by focusing on his *kanjin*-style re-reading as applied to the concept of the directing of virtue (Jpn. *ekō*). Although Shinran's understanding of Pure Land thought, as Shin scholars maintain, might spiritually transcend history, the significance of his act of writing the *Kyōgyōshinshō* must also be appreciated in the concrete historical context in which the text was written.

(Stone, p. 156). For the detailed discussion on the *kanjin*-style interpretive mode, see Stone, pp. 165–167.

7   For the transmission of the Eshin school lineage to Kantō, see Stone, pp. 148–150 and 306–314.

8   Tendai's influence on Shinran's thought has been suggested by several scholars, such as Shimaji Daitō, *Nihon Bukkyō kyōgakushi,* 1933, reprinted Tokyo: Nakayama Shobō, 1976, p. 464; Hazama Jikō, *Nihon Bukkyō no tenkai to sono kichō (jō): Nihon Tendai to Kamakura Bukkyō,* 1948, reprinted Tokyo: Sanseidō, 1968; Fugen Kōju, *Nihon Jōdokyō shisōshi kenkyū,* Kyoto: Nagata Bunshōdō, 1972, pp. 535–549; Uryūzu Ryūo, "Shinshū kyōgaku no shūso katen no ichi benken," in Uryūzu Ryūo, *Zoku Shinshū tenseki no kenkyū,* Kyoto: Nagata Bunshōdō, 1992, pp. 302–316.

2   Shinran's Writing of the *Kyōgyōshinshō*: Historical Contexts

In order to understand the purpose of Shinran's writing of the *Kyōgyōshinshō*, it is often suggested by Shin scholars that "gratitude" was the primary "motive force" for his writing of the text, as clearly demonstrated in the postscript of the *Kyōgyōshinshō*.[9] In the conclusion of his postscript, Shinran expresses his joy in compiling the text:

> How joyous I am, my heart and mind being rooted in the Buddha-ground of the universal Vow, and my thoughts and feelings flowing within the dharma-ocean, which is beyond comprehension! I am deeply aware of the Tathagata's immense compassion, and I sincerely revere the benevolent care behind the masters' teaching activity. My joy grows even fuller, my gratitude and indebtedness ever more compelling. Therefore, I have selected [passages expressing] the core of the Pure Land way and gathered here its essentials. Mindful solely of the profundity of the Buddha's benevolence, I pay no heed to the derision of others.[10]

Shinran's motivation in writing the *Kyōgyōshinshō*, however, cannot be simply attributed to his gratitude for the compassion of Amida Buddha. Before this humble but passionate statement, he also makes very specific references to a few historical incidents that are political rather than spiritual. He begins the postscript with a brief account of the government persecution in 1207 waged against Hōnen and his major disciples, in which they were punished with a sentence of five years of exile from Kyoto. This is followed by a brief note on Hōnen's death in Kyoto a few months after his pardon in 1211.[11] In the next section of the postscript, Shinran then records in detail how he received a transmission of the *Senchakusū* directly from Hōnen in 1205, followed by his praise of the book with a note that the text was compiled at the request of the Chancellor Kujō Kanezane (1149–1207).[12] What is the significance that such notes are included in the postscript of the *Kyōgyōshinshō*?

---

9   See, for example, the introduction to the *Kyōgyōshinshō* in cws, 2:15.

10   cws, 1:291.

11   cws, 1:289–290.

12   cws, 1:291. Shinran's mention of Kujō Kanezane in the postscript as the person who requested that Hōnen compile the text could be read as a political statement. During the persecution against Hōnen and his disciples, two politically influential Tendai monks, Jien and Ryōkai, intervened in the dispute over Hōnen's followers to restore order within the Tendai school. Jien was a younger brother of Kanezane. Ryōkai was Kanezane's son. See Taira Masayuki, *Shinran to sono jidai,* Kyoto: Hōzōkan, 2001, p. 188.

Shinran's postscript clearly reflects the historical situation Hōnen's disciples encountered after the death of their master. Trouble began almost immediately after they published the *Senchakusū* in 1212, within a year of Hōnen's death. The publication of the *Senchakushū* almost immediately encountered criticism by the eminent scholar-monk Myōe Kōben (1173–1232) of the Kegon school, who wrote the *Saijarin* (The Wheel of Obliterating the Heresy) in 1213.[13] Major disciples of Hōnen, such as Ryūkan, Seikaku, Kōsai and Shōku, were quick to respond to Myōe's critique in the *Saijarin* by writing numerous texts to defend the master's work.[14] Myōe's criticism of Hōnen, although raising a very serious doctrinal challenge, did not seem to have any potency in silencing Hōnen's disciples. After Hōnen was pardoned, his disciples quickly became active again in propagating the Pure Land teaching in Kyoto. During this period, Shinran was living in Hitachi province in the Kantō and is thought to have been preparing for writing the *Kyōgyōshinshō*.

Hōnen's disciples, who were actively engaged in the propagation of their master's teaching, were, however, hit hard again in 1227 (Karoku 3) by another persecution waged against them.[15] This persecution originated with a Tendai scholar in the Kantō named Jōshō who in 1225 wrote a text titled *Dan Senchaku* (Denouncing the Selection [of *Nenbutsu*]) criticizing the *Senchakushū*. Ryūkan, who read Jōshō's work, which had been brought into Kyoto in the same year, responded to the critique by writing *Ken Senchaku* (Revealing the Selection [of

---

13   Scholars generally agree that Myōe's criticism of the *Senchakushū* "centers on Hōnen's rejection of the necessity of the mind aspiring for enlightenment (Skt. bodhicitta) for the practicer of the nembutsu. Hōnen considered beings of the latter age (Jpn. mappō) incapable of awakening the mind of enlightenment and classified it with the various practices of the Path of Sages, which were to be put aside in favor of simply saying the Name in accord with the Primal Vow." "Introduction to Teaching, Practice, and Realization," in *CWS*, 2:17.

14   Among the leading disciples of Hōnen, for example, Ryūkan wrote the *Gusanshingi* in 1216 and the *Gokuraku Jōdoshūgi* in 1220, Seikaku (1167–1235) wrote the *Yuishinshō* in 1221, and Kōsai (1163–1247) wrote the *Gengibunshō* in 1218 to defend Hōnen's Pure Land teaching expounded in the *Senchakusū*. In the same year, the Shingon scholar Jōben (1166–1224) wrote the *Zoku Senchakumongiyoshō*. Another distinguished disciple of Hōnen and the founder of the Seizan branch of the Jōdoshū, Shōku (1177–1247), lectured on various writings of Shandao from about 1215 though 1226. His lectures were later published in a series of works as the *Kangyōsho kanmongi*. The above are the only extant texts from before the persecution in Karoku 3 (1227). For an overview of Hōnen's disciples literary activities, see Ishida Mitsuyuki, *Hōnen shōnin monka no Jōdo kyōgaku no kenkyū*, 2 vols, Tokyo: Daitō Shuppansha, 1979, 2:398–406.

15   This persecution is often referred to as the Karoku persecution (Jpn. Karoku no honan). For an overview of the presecution, see Taira, *Shinran*, pp. 168–213. For a more detailed historical analysis, see Taira Masayuki, *Nihon chūsei no shakai to Bukkyō*, Tokyo: Hanawa Shobō, 1992, pp. 329–387.

"RELY ON THE MEANING, NOT ON THE WORDS"

Nenbutsu]) in 1227. According to a historical record, one of Ryūkan's followers, named Okamoto Gyōren, distributed the *Ken Senchaku* in the Kantō, and the tract received strong support there.[16] In order to suppress the rising popularity of Ryūkan's work, Jōshō sent his *Dan Senchaku* and Ryūkan's *Ken Senchaku* to the administrators of Enryakuji on Mt. Hiei to settle this doctrinal dispute. Unsurprisingly, Jōshō's position was upheld, and the Enryakuji's administrators issued a request to the imperial court and Bakufu to suppress the activities of Hōnen's disciples in both Kyoto and Kamakura.[17]

The resulting suppression was particularly damaging to Hōnen's disciples, who were allowed to remain in Kyoto only under the supervision of the administrators of the Tendai school. The court ordered that Ryūkan, Kōsai, and Kūamidabutsu (1155–1228) be exiled from Kyoto. Disregarding the restraining order from the imperial court, Tendai priests raided the residences of Hōnen's followers and vandalized Hōnen's grave. Upon the request of the administrators of Enryakuji, the imperial court confiscated the printing blocks of the *Senchakushū* and turned them over to Enryakuji to be burned. Although Ryūkan escaped arrest by fleeing from Kyoto quickly, he died in 1227 in Sagami province under the protection of his follower Mōri Suemitsu.[18]

The disciples of Hōnen, however, did not stop propagating the Pure Land teaching through their writings. Soon after the persecution in 1227, Hōnen's disciples who escaped the persecution, such as Benchō in Kyūshū, and Shōku, Genchi, and Chōsai in Kyoto, remained active throughout this period.[19] In 1239, the *Senchakushū* was published again and distributed among Hōnen's followers. All this historical evidence suggests that, though Hōnen's disciples encountered severe persecutions, they were very active in publicly defending the criticism waged against the *Senchakushū*. Despite the Tendai school's attempt to suppress the distribution of the *Senchakushū*, the text continued to circulate among Hōnen's followers.[20]

16 The document is found in the *Kinkoshū* compiled by Nikō (1253–1314), a disciple of Nichiren. The text is cited in Taira, *Nihon chūsei,* p. 332.

17 Taira, *Shinran,* pp. 184–190. For a detailed analysis of the historical documents related to the Karoku persecution, see Taira, *Nihon chūsei,* pp. 331–361.

18 Taira, *Shinran,* p. 190.

19 Benchō (1162–1238) wrote the *Matsudai nembutsu jushuin* in 1228. He also wrote the *Tessenchakuhongan nembutsushū* in 1237. Shōkū's *Kangyōsho tahitsushō* was completed around 1235. In the same year, another of Hōnen's disciples, Genchi (1183–1238), wrote the *Senchaku yōketsu* (1237) in Kyoto. It is also noteworthy that there was another direct disciple of Hōnen, Chōsai (1184–1266), who remained active in Kyoto throughout this period. See Ishida, 2:401–405.

20 Tsukamoto Zenryū, "Kamakura Shin Bukkyō no sōshisha to sono hihansha," in *Honen,* Tuskamoto Zenryū, ed., *Nihon no meicho,* vol. 5, Tokyo: Chūō Kōronsha, 1983, p. 64.

For a historical placement of the *Kyōgyōshinshō* it is significant that the period during which Shinran was compiling the *Kyōgyōshinshō* clearly overlaps with the literary activities of Hōnen's disciples, especially after the 1227 persecution. A prototype of the *Kyōgyōshinshō* is considered to have been completed some time after Shinran returned to Kyoto in his sixties (around 1232) and at latest before he allowed his follower Sonren to copy the manuscript in 1247.[21] Therefore, it is not difficult to imagine that Shinran was well aware of the activities of Hōnen's other disciples in both the Kantō and Kyoto while he was compiling the *Kyōgyōshinshō*.

It is in this light that we can understand the final remarks in the postscript. Shinran is alluding to the very sensitive political situation of the surviving disciples of Hōnen who dared to defend their master's teaching after the persecution in 1227:

> May those who see and hear this work be brought—either through the cause of reverently embracing the teaching or through the condition of [other's] doubt and slander of it—to manifest *shinjin* within the power of the Vow and reveal the incomparable fruit of enlightenment in the land of peace.[22]

Shinran's final statement in the postscript is, however, not completely original to him. Shinran borrows a passage found in the final section of Seikaku's *Yuishinshō*.[23] A very ironic historical reality behind this passage is that Seikaku, who was one of the most revered disciples of Hōnen, was in fact one of the

---

21 James Dobbins, *Jōdo Shinshū: Shin Buddhism in Medieval Japan*, 1989, reprinted Honolulu: University of Hawaii Press, 2002, pp. 31–32.

22 *CWS*, 1:291.

23 Seikaku concludes the *Yuishinshō* with the following remarks (see also *CWS*, 2:15): "Although there are many important doctrines concerning the nembutsu, they can be summarized in the preceding way. Some people who read this will surely ridicule it. Nevertheless, both belief and slander will become a cause for each one's birth in the Pure Land. With the pledges of friendship in this life—brief as a dream—to guide us, we tie the bonds for meeting before enlightenment in the coming life. If I am behind, I will be guided by others; if I go first, I will guide others. Becoming true friends through many lives, we bring each other to the practice of the Buddha-way, and as true teachers in each life, we will together sunder all delusion and attachment" (*CWS*, 1:697). The last sentence of Seikaku's conclusion borrows a passage from Tao-ch'o's *An-lo-chi* that, interestingly, Shinran cites after the passage quoted above. "*Passages on the Land of Happiness* states: I have collected true words to aid others in their practice for attaining birth, in order that the process be made continuous, without end and without interruption, by which those who have been born first guide those who come later, and those who are born later join

"RELY ON THE MEANING, NOT ON THE WORDS" 329

Tendai administrators who requested the imperial court to suppress the activities of Hōnen's disciples led by Ryūkan in 1227,[24] After Hōnen died, Seikaku, as the leader of the Agui lineage of Tendai preaching, returned to Enryakuji to pursue a career as a scholar administrator. He was serving as a *tandai* (a judge of Tendai doctrine) when Jōshō submitted his complaint about Ryūkan's work. Seikaku was even invited to visit Kamakura just before the persecution in 1227 took place.[25] Therefore, there is little doubt that Seikaku was aware of the activities of Hōnen's disciples in both Kyoto and the Kantō before the persecution.

In the Kantō, Shinran must have witnessed the development of tensions between Jōshō and Ryūkan's supporters, which eventually dragged in Seikaku, and resulted in the untimely death of Ryūkan, who fled to Sagami province in the Kantō. Shinran's final remark in the postscript, hoping that "either through the cause of reverently embracing the teaching or through the condition of [other's] doubt and slander of it" others might be brought to attain "enlightenment in the land of peace," was not a rhetorical embellishment but a reflection on a historical reality.[26] In this social and political context, Shinran wrote the *Kyōgyōshinshō* in order to clarify and transmit Hōnen's teaching expounded in the *Senchakushū*.

those who were born before. This is so that the boundless ocean of birth-and-death be exhausted" (CWS, 1:291).

24   Stone, pp. 148–149, and Taira, *Shinran*, pp. 203–207.

25   Taira, *Shinran*, pp. 193–194.

26   Taira Masayuki believes that Shinran did not know of Seikaku's role behind the Karoku persecution, because later Shinran continuously recommended his followers to read Seikaku's *Yuishinshō* (Essentials of Faith Alone). In particular, in 1230, three years after the Karoku presecution, Shinran is known to have made a copy of the *Yuishinshō* from Seikaku's original manuscript (see Taira, *Shinran*, pp. 212–213, and *Nihon chusei*, p. 330). However, considering the fact that the Karoku persecution was initiated by the Tendai scholar Jōshō in the Kantō, it is difficult to imagine that Shinran, who was living in the area as a disciple of Hōnen, was not informed about the details of the persecution. Why Shinran became interested in the *Yuishinshō* after the Karoku persecution is not clear. How he got hold of Seikaku's original manuscript, while he was presumably still living in the Kantō, is also not known. It is, however, clear that Shinran never lost faith in Seikaku's understanding of Hōnen as expounded in the *Yuishinshō*. The ambivalent characteristics of Seikaku, one of the most eminent Tendai scholars of the Kamakura period, is an issue that needs further attention.

3 The Tendai Eshin School's Influence on the Writing of the *Kyōgyōshinshō*

As demonstrated in the postscript discussed in the previous section, the *Kyōgyōshinshō* reflects the very concrete historical situation faced by a disciple of Hōnen after the 1227 Tendai persecution. This historical context is likewise reflected in Shinran's style of writing. His choice of the *kanjin*-style textual analysis, developed in the medieval period by the Eshin scholars, is yet another sign that Shinran was a man of his time.

The *Kyōgyōshinshō* consists mainly of passages cited from more than sixty different sūtras and commentaries.[27] But Shinran's free and creative method of explicating the texts often goes beyond the original meaning of the passages. These facts tend to cause some consternation among Shin scholars:

> The greater part of Shinran's "collection of passages" is made up of quotations from the sūtras and the treatises and commentaries of the masters, and there is little of his own comment. It is certainly striking that an original thinker of Shinran's stature should, in the single systematic presentation of his thought—unquestionably his lifework—bury his own words with quotations from the works of others. Moreover, these quotations are not always cited faithfully; ... [a] number of them are greatly altered in meaning. We must consider his intent in choosing to present his thought in this way.[28]

Although Shin scholars praise Shinran for compiling a text defending his master Hōnen and thereby "express[ing] in detail a highly original and dynamic

---

27   Shinran's writing style of the *Kyōgyōshinshō* is influenced by one of the Chinese Buddhist literary genres, called *monruishū* (collection of passages). Modern scholars agree that Shinran most likely adopted the style from the *Lo-pan wei-lei* (Collection of Passages on the Land of Bliss, Jpn. Rakuhō monrui, T. vol. 47, no. 1969) published in 1200 by Zongshao (1151–1214) in Song China, which was introduced to Japan during the Kamakura period. It is also noteworthy that Shinran cited novel Chinese works such as the Commentary on Yuanzhao's Commentary on the Contemplation Sūtra (Jpn. *Kangyōsho shōkanki*, written in 1181, included in the *Jōdoshū zensho*, Tokyo: Sankibō Busshorin, 1970, vol. 5) and the Notes to Yuanzhao's Commentary on the Amida Sūtra (Jpn. *Amidakyō monjiki*, published in 1217, included in the *Jōdoshū zensho*, vol. 5) by Jiedu (d. c. 1189); the *Kanmuryōjukyō gyōsho* (abbreviated title, *Kangyōsho*, in T. vol. 37) and the *Amidakyōsho* (T. vol. 37) by Yuanzhao (1048–1116). These texts are thought to be some of the many texts that Shunjō (1166–1227) of Sennyūji brought back from China. Zongshao's text was probably also included in that collection. See CWS, 2:14, and Ishida Mitsuyuiki, *Shinran kyōgaku no kisoteki kenkyū 2*, Kyoto: Nagata Bunshōdō, 1977, pp. 154–179 and 259–264.

28   CWS, 2:23.

"RELY ON THE MEANING, NOT ON THE WORDS"

vision of the Pure Land way,"[29] they are also a little uneasy about the method he employed to explain his interpretation of the Pure Land teaching:

> Chief among his [Shinran's] methods is his controversial use of the Japanese practice of punctuating and annotating Chinese texts in order to recast them into Japanese sentence structure and grammatical form and to interpret the Chinese characters. He added such reading notes to all the passages in his collection, but at a number of points he chose to depart from the accepted readings and to impose new interpretations, some clearly at variance with the literal meanings of the texts.[30]

Recent studies on medieval Japanese Buddhist hermeneutics, however, show that the methodology of reading Shinran applied in the *Kyōgyōshinshō* was not as controversial as modern Shin scholars seem to think.[31] Shinran simply adopted an exegetical method very commonly employed within the Japanese Tendai school. This is the *kanjin* style of reading, best known for its liberal parsing of the scriptures through skillful application of *kunten* (Japanese-reading notations) to a Chinese text in order to reinterpret the text without altering the order of the characters. Jacqueline Stone, in her recent work on medieval Tendai studies, describes the methodology *of kanjin*-style reading:

> *Kanjin*-style readings frequently employ elaborate forms of word play. One common device is the creative "breakdown" (Jpn. *yomikudashi*) of a text written in literary Chinese text to produce a Japanese reading unrelated to, or even at odds with, the sense of the Chinese original. Syntactical markers and phonetic syllables indicating grammatical inflections were also added to a Chinese text so that it could be read in Japanese word order. Most Chinese characters are not in themselves nouns, verbs, or modifiers but function as such according to their syntactical placement; thus the creative use of such indicators can rearrange, even subvert, the Chinese text to produce a Japanese reading radically different in meaning from the original yet still technically "faithful" to it in the sense that every character is preserved and accounted for. Thus the text is made in effect to testify against itself; its authority as a classic document is appropriated to legitimate an interpretation quite different from what it actually says.[32]

---

29 Ibid., 2:18.
30 Ibid.
31 For medieval Japanese Buddhist hermeneutics, see Stone, pp. 97–236.
32 Ibid., p. 159.

332   NASU

Let us look at some specific examples of Shinran's use of the *kanjin* method. (See the appendix for English translations of Shinran's text, followed by the *kanbun* texts and his *yomikudashi* (breakdown reading) based on the notation. The *kanbun* and *yomikudashi* texts are also added to the English translation of the standard reading to demonstrate the differences of the readings.) The following passage from Confucius' *Analects,* which Shinran placed as the last citation before the postscript, is typical of how Shinran alters the meaning of the original passage by applying his own reading notes. Shinran's reading of the text is as follows:

> 1 The *Analects* states: Chi-lu asked, "Should one worship spirits?" Confucius said, "One should not worship spirits. Why should people worship spirits?"[33]

Now compare the standard reading of this passage:

> 2 Chi Lu asked how the spirits of the dead and the gods should be served. The Master said, "You are not able even to serve man. How can you serve the spirits?"[34]

In the context of the *Analects,* Confucius critically responds to Chi Lu's concern about the spirits of the dead and the gods. Considering the popularity of the *Analects* in Japanese culture, there is no doubt that Shinran knew the original intent of the passage. Indeed, the point here is that anyone seeing it would know the original meaning—that is, an important premise of the *kanjin* method is that both writer and audience are aware of the facts of interpretation. The writer demonstrates his mastery of both classic texts and the latest doctrinal trends through his new interpretation. Thus, in the above example, Shinran alters the reading without changing the word order of the passage to extract a meaning that confirms his own opinion that "Buddhists should not worship non-Buddhist deities."[35] Shinran's reading might not have pleased the Confucian scholars serving in the imperial court, but in the context of medieval

---

33   *CWS,* 2:289.

34   Confucius, *The Analects,* Book XI, 12, D. C. Lau, tr., New York: Penguin Books, 1979, p. 107.

35   Shin scholars often defend Shinran's readings: "It is not that he ignored their original intent; rather, he rendered the authors' intent more plainly and profoundly than the authors' original expression. He quotes the scriptures and yet changes the readings because, while receiving the tradition, he went beyond it. By delving to the very depths of the Pure Land teaching he transcended it and, at the same time, brought about a revolutionary development within the Pure Land tradition itself" (*CWS,* 2:27).

"RELY ON THE MEANING, NOT ON THE WORDS"   333

Tendai studies, this kind of doctrinal manipulation was perfectly understandable and acceptable among medieval Tendai scholars.

The following is another straightforward example of how Shinran applies the *kanjin* style of reading in the *Kyōgyōshinshō*. Here, Shinran reformulates the simple noun phrases found in Shandao's *Commentary on the Contemplation Sūtra* into sentences to demonstrate that meditative (Jpn. *jō*) and non-meditative (Jpn. *san*) practices are skillful means to guide practitioners to entrust Amida's Primal Vow and sole practice of *nenbustu*. The doctrinal position genuinely reflects the Pure Land teaching advocated by Hōnen. However, the methodology of reading that Shinran employs is clearly that of the medieval Tendai.

Shinran's reading:

> 3 Further, he [Shandao] states: Meditative good is a means to lead one to discernment [of the Primal Vow].

> Further, he [Shandao] states: Non-meditative good is a means to lead one to the practice [of the *nenbutsu*].[36]

The source text:

> 4 Passages on meditative good introducing the contemplation [on Amida and the Pure Land].

> Passages on non-meditative good introducing the practice [of good in everyday life].

Although Shinran spiritually converted to the Pure Land teaching of Hōnen in 1201, he seems to have remained faithful to the methodology of Tendai studies which he learned as a monk on Mt. Hiei. Modern historians generally agree that, before he became a disciple of Hōnen, he was a priest at Jōgyōzanmai-dō in Yokawa.[37] Some also suggest that he had close ties with Mudōji at Tōdō.[38] While it is not clear exactly what lineage Shinran was affiliated with when he was practicing on Mt. Hiei, it is clear that both the Yokawa and Mudōji areas

---

36   *CWS*, 1:217.
37   Dobbins, pp. 22–24.
38   Asada Masahiro, "Hieizan jidai no Shinran Shōnin," in Asada Masahiro, *Ikasareru inochi wo mitsumete,* Kyoto: Nagata Bunshōdō, 2003, pp. 159–231.

were strongholds of the Eshin school lineage of Tendai studies during the Kamakura period.[39]

There is also circumstantial evidence that Shinran's association with the Eshin school scholars probably continued while he was compiling the *Kyōgyōshinshō* in Kantō and then in Kyoto. According to research on medieval Japanese Tendai studies, the early to mid-thirteenth century is the period when the Tendai school, particularly the Eshin school lineage, began to establish its institutional foundation in all provinces in the Kantō. By the late thirteenth century, "growing Tendai presence in the east eventually gave rise, within that tradition, to distinction between the Tendai of the capital (Jpn. *miyako Tendai*) and eastern or provincial Tendai (Jpn. *Kantō Tendai,* or *inaka Tendai*)."[40]

Although it was after Shinran's time that the Kantō Tendai established an extensive network of seminaries called *dangisho* (centers for doctrinal studies) in all the Kantō provinces, there is ample historical evidence that Tendai priests were very active in the Kantō from the early thirteenth century, when Shinran was living in Hitachi province.[41] Even after Shinran left the Kantō, financial support for his living in Kyoto was brought from the Kantō regions by his followers.[42] Therefore, it is not difficult to imagine that Shinran remained well informed about developments in Tendai studies there, particularly those of the Eshin school, through his followers' continuous visits and letters.[43]

The effectiveness of the *kanjin*-style readings in the *Kyōgyōshinshō* is demonstrated by the fact that Ryūkan's *Ken Senchaku* received strong support from the Kantō followers, while Jōshō's *Dan Senchaku* was rejected. Although today neither text is extant, the differences of these two scholars' doctrinal lineages within the Tendai school are well known. Jōshō was a disciple of

---

39 Stone, p. 106.

40 Ibid., p. 148.

41 Ibid., pp. 148–150.

42 Dobbins, pp. 38–46.

43 Stone also notes that it has been suggested that Shinran's adoption of the Eshin school method of Tendai studies is evidenced not only by the *kanjin*-style reading of texts. The structure of the text of the *Kyōgyōshinshō* might also have been inspired by the teaching of the Eshin school, which was eventually systematized as the "threefold seven great matters" (Jpn. *sanjū shichika no daiji*). The "threefold" aspects are three categories of transmissions, teaching (Jpn. *kyō*), practice (Jpn. *gyō*), and realization (Jpn. *shō*), which corresponds with the full title of the *Kyōgyōshinshō, Ken Jōdo shinjitsu kyō gyō shō monrui* (A Collection of Passages Revealing the True Teaching, Practice, and Realization of the Pure Land Way). See Stone, pp. 187–188, and Asada, pp. 235–239.

"RELY ON THE MEANING, NOT ON THE WORDS" 335

Hōchibō-Shōshin, who was a "scrupulous exegete" and a critic of the *kanjin*-style interpretive mode.[44]

The Japanese historian Taira Masayuki, in examining the 1227 persecution of Hōnen's disciples, concludes that those who arranged to bring Jōshō's complaint to the Tendai administration were also disciples of Shōshin. Among them Shūgen, who succeeded Shōshin's lineage, was a die-hard critic of Hōnen.[45] On the other hand, Ryūkan is known to have been a successful Tendai scholar who studied with two Eshin school scholars, Kōen and Hangen, before becoming a disciple of Hōnen.[46] Ryūkan was clearly an advocate of the *kanjin*-style interpretation of texts, as demonstrated in his *Gusanshingi*:

> 5 Rely on the words, not on the meaning. That is what ignorant people love to follow. What a shame![47]

In 1227, Jōshō was able to suppress Ryūkan's advocacy of Hōnen's teaching by appealing to the ecclesiastical authorities on Mt. Hiei. However, in a broader historical context, he was fighting a losing battle over the *kanjin* style of interpretation developed within medieval Tendai studies. The *kanjin* hermeneutics, based on "personal insight" (Jpn. *kanjin*)—extracting the meaning—rather than "fidelity to texts" (Jpn. *kyōsō*)—adherence to words—prevailed in both Kyoto and the Kantō during the Kamakura period, despite efforts to preserve traditional Tendai scholasticism by Shōshin and his disciples.[48] Considering this historical context of Shinran's background as a Tendai monk, his adoption of *kanjin*-style exegesis in the *Kyōgyōshinshō* was very natural and reasonable.

4   The Uniqueness of Shinran's Thought Revisited

Shin scholars often laud as one of Shinran's most significant accomplishments his courageous effort to maintain the momentum of Hōnen's teaching of other power—even after numerous persecutions against the advocacy of the "sole"

---

44   Stone, pp. 38–39. Stone also notes an interesting episode in Shōshin's life which reflects his personality as an "ivory-tower" scholar: "According to a tradition, Shōshin was so absorbed in his doctrinal studies that he knew nothing about the fighting between the Taira and Minamoto." Stone, pp. 38–39, and 224; see also Taira, *Shinran*, p. 198.

45   Taira, *Shinran*, pp. 197–198.

46   See Ishida, *Hōnen*, 1:197, and Shimaji, p. 474.

47   *Gusanshingi*, cited in Ishida, *Hōnen*, 1:209.

48   Hazama Jikō, *Nihon Bukkyō no tenkai to sono kichō (ge): Chūko Tendai no kenkyū*, 1948, reprint, Tokyo: Sanseidō, 1968, pp. 11–94.

practice of *nenbutsu* (Jpn. *senju nenbutsu*)—by writing the *Kyōgyōshinshō*.[49] It is noteworthy that prior to the 1227 persecution, Hōnen's disciples such as Ryūkan, Seikaku, Kōsai and Shōkū all strongly emphasized in their writings the aspect of the Pure Land teaching as "single" or "sole" *nenbutsu* practice of recitation of the name through Amida Buddha's other power, as Hōnen demonstrated in the *Senchakushū*. After the persecution, however, Hōnen's position of single and sole practice of recitation of Amida's name through other power almost disappears from the writings of Hōnen's disciples such as Benchō, Genchi or Chōsai—undoubtedly to avoid unnecessary confrontations with the Tendai authorities on Mt. Hiei.[50]

Contrary to this general tendency among Hōnen's disciples, however, Shinran, in the *Kyōgyōshinshō*, further elaborated Hōnen's understanding of the Pure Land practice in the *Senchakushū*, boldly stating that one should cast aside the sundry self-power practices of the path of sages and practice solely the single practice of *nenbutsu* through other-power. Shinran's doctrinal position emphasizing other power corresponds to the same general attitude of disciples immediately after Hōnen's death, particularly that of Ryūkan.[51]

In order to express his "personal insight" on the other power of Amida Buddha, Shinran systematically applied the *kanjin* method to the texts he cited in the *Kyōgyōshinshō*. Following are three such examples found in the *Kyōgyōshinshō*, in which Shinran rereads the passages to express his understanding that in the Pure Land teaching the subject of the directing of virtue (Jpn. *ekō*) does not originate in the *nenbutsu* practitioner but is directed from Amida Buddha, which is other-power (Jpn. *tariki*).

The first example is from Shinran's "Chapter on *Shinjin*," citing a passage of the *Larger Sukhāvatīvyūha Sūtra*, which Shinran identifies as the passage of the fulfillment of the eighteenth vow.[52] The following is a comparison of Shinran's reading and the standard reading.[53]

---

49   cws, 2:17–18, and Ishida, *Hōnen*, 1:166–180, and 2:424–428.

50   Although this generalization is somewhat oversimplified, we can safely say that at least this tendency is recognizable in the extant writings of Hōnen's disciples after the Karoku persecution. For the details of Shinran's doctrinal position *vis-à-vis* Hōnen's other disciples, see Ishida, *Hōnen*, 2:529–534.

51   Ishida, *Hōnen*, 1:195–241, and 2:530.

52   This example is cited and explained in Alfred Bloom, *Shinran's Gospel of Pure Grace*, Tucson: University of Arizona Press, 1977, pp. 48–49. Jacqueline Stone also mentions this passage, pp. 159–160. She, however, mistakenly calls the passage "the eighteenth vow." Also Shinran's addition of a honorific verb is wrongly identified as *shitamaeri*, which should be corrected to *seshimatamaeri*.

53   Where Shinran alters the readings has been underlined in the English translation. The translation is followed in the appendix by the *kanbun* text and his *yomikudashi* (breakdown reading) based on the notation. The *kanbun* and *yomikudashi* texts corresponding

"RELY ON THE MEANING, NOT ON THE WORDS" 337

Shinran's reading:

> 6 The passage declaring the fulfillment of the Primal Vow in the [*Larger*] Sūtra states:

> All sentient beings, as they hear the Name, realize even one thought-moment of *shinjin* and joy. [**Amida Buddha**] **shall direct** [**his**] **sincere mind to them** (**Jpn.** ***shishin ni ekō seshimetamaeri***). If they aspire to be born in that land, they then immediately attain birth and dwell in the stage of non-retrogression. Excluded are those who commit the five grave offenses and those who slander the right dharma.[54]

Standard reading:

> 7 If all sentient beings, as they hear the Name, realize even one thought-moment of *shinjin* and joy, sincerely direct their merits to [others], and aspire to be born in that land, they then shall immediately attain birth and dwell in the stage of non-retrogression.[55]

In this citation, Shinran takes the four characters in the middle of the sentence, *shishin ekō,* out of the flow of the passage and adds the honorific verb *seshimetamaeri* so that the reader cannot identify the subject as the *nenbutsu* practitioner. The word *seshimetamaeri* is the highest honorific form of the verb *su,* implying that the subject of the directing of virtue (Jpn. *ekō*) is the most venerable "person" in the text, who, in this context, is Amida Buddha.[56]

The next example, from the *Kyōgyōshinshō's* "Chapter on Practice," is a citation from Tanluan's *Commentary on the Treatise on the Pure Land.*

Shinran's reading:

> 8 How is directing of virtue accomplished? It is by [Amida Buddha, who] never abandons any sentient being in suffering, but constantly aspires for [the salvation of the suffering beings] in [his] heart, and **venerably**

---

with Shinran's alterations are also included in the appendix, complementing the English translation of the standard reading to demonstrate the difference in the readings.

54   *cws*, 1:80, modified.

55   Ibid., 2:259, modified.

56   *Shime* in the word *seshimetamaeri* is a variant of *shimu* which is most commonly used to make the causative form of a verb. When it used with another honorific verb ending, such as "verb+*shime*+*tamaeri*," the word becomes a higher honorific form than the original honorific. See Nakada Norio, Wada Toshimasa, and Kitahara Yasuo, eds, *Kogo daijiten,* Tokyo: Shōgakkan, 1983, p. 803.

fulfills (Jpn. *etamaeru*) the mind of great compassion by taking the directing of virtue as foremost.

The directing of virtue has two aspects: that for going forth to the Pure Land and that for returning to this world. "Directing for going forth" means that [Amida Buddha] gives [his] own virtues to all sentient beings and **has vowed (Jpn. *sagan shite*)** [as Dharmākara Bodhisattva] **to bring them all to birth (Jpn. *ōjō seshimetamau*)** in Amida Tathāgata's Pure Land of Happiness.[57]

Standard reading:

9 [Bodhisattvas] never abandon sentient beings in suffering, constantly aspire [for their awakening] in their hearts, and take the directing of virtue as foremost. That is because they wish to accomplish their mind of great compassion.

"Directing for going forth" means that [bodhisattvas] shall give their own virtues to all sentient beings and aspire to be born together with them in Amida Tathāgata's Pure Land of Happiness.[58]

In the context of Tanluan's *Commentary,* the subject of the directing of virtue (Jpn. *ekō*) is all bodhisattva practitioners who aspire to be born in Amida Buddha's Pure Land. Shinran, however, changes the subject of the directing of virtue (Jpn. *ekō*) to Amida Buddha by adding honorific endings to two verbs, *etamaeru* and *ōjō seshimetamaeru.* In the second half of the citation as well, he modifies the sentence structure to produce the meaning that Amida Buddha, when he was Dharmākara Bodhisattva, vowed to bring all sentient beings to the Pure Land. In the standard reading, the word *sagan* (aspire, or vow) is modifying the following clause. Shinran, however, changes the punctuation to make an independent clause with the word.

The third example, from the "Chapter on *Shinjin,*" is a citation of Shandao's *Commentary on the Contemplation Sūtra.*

Shinran's reading:

10 The third is the mind of aspiration for birth and directing of virtue.... Again, let **those who are to be born (Jpn. *shōzuru mono*)** [in Amida

---

57   *CWS*, 1:29, modified.
58   Ibid., 2:254, modified.

"RELY ON THE MEANING, NOT ON THE WORDS"   339

Buddha's Pure Land] with the mind of aspiration and directing of virtue to aspire [for attainment of birth] by unfailingly and **decidedly (Jpn. *ketsujō shite*) taking (Jpn. *mochiite*) the Vow (Jpn. *gan*)** which [Amida Buddha] **has directed (Jpn. *ekō shitamaeru*) *to them with [his] true and real mind.*** [59]

Standard reading:

> 11 Again, those who wish to be born [in Amida Buddha's Pure Land] by directing their virtue with the mind of aspiration [for attainment of birth] must unfailingly aspire to be born [in the Pure Land] by directing [their virtue] and aspiring [to be born] with the true and real determined mind.

In this example, Shinran not only adds an honorific to the verb *ekō*, but also substantially modifies the sentence structure by altering the parts of speech in the sentence so that readers will identify the subject of the directing of virtue (Jpn. *ekō*) as Amida Buddha, not the practitioner aspiring for birth in the Pure Land. [60]

As shown in these three examples, throughout the *Kyōgyōshinshō* Shinran consistently and systematically adds honorifics and modifies the sentence structure of passages discussing the concept of the directing of virtue to express his insight regarding Amida Buddha's other power. As for the practitioners' recitation of *nenbutsu,* in the "Chapter on Practice," Shinran says:

> Clearly we know, then, that the *nenbutsu* is not a self-power practice performed by foolish beings or sages; it is therefore called the practice of "not-directing virtue [on the part of beings]" [Jpn. *fuekō no gyō*]. Masters of the Mahāyāna and Hīnayāna and people burdened with karmic evil, whether heavy or light, should all in the same way take refuge in the great treasure ocean of the selected Vow and attain Buddhahood through the *nenbutsu.* [61]

Shinran's comment comes immediately after his citation of a passage of Hōnen's *Senchakushū* in which Hōnen explains why he recommends practitioners to

---

59   Ibid., 1:88, modified.

60   The altered parts of speech are *subekaraku* (adverb) > *mochiiru* (verb); *ketsujō* (adjective) > *ketsujō shite* (verb); *ganzuru* (verb) > *gan* (noun).

61   CWS, 1:53.

choose the recitation of *nenbutsu* over other Buddhist practices, for which Hōnen drew heavy criticism from the scholars of the other Buddhist schools.[62] In this passage, Shinran defends Hōnen's doctrinal position by pointing out that, in fact, the selection of the *nenbutsu* practice over other practices was not made by Hōnen but was selected in Amida Buddha's primal vow. Nor is the recitation of the *nenbutsu* selected because it strengthens the practitioners' power of the directing virtue, as other Buddhist practices often claim. Therefore, the *nenbutsu* is the practice of "not-directing virtue" (Jpn. *fuekō no gyō*) from the perspective of the practitioner.

By applying a *kanjin*-style reading to the cited passages in the *Kyōgyōshinshō*, Shinran skillfully defends Hōnen's advocacy of the sole practice of *nenbutsu* (Jpn. *senju nenbutsu*). By reconfiguring the scriptural passages, Shinran transforms the concept of directing virtue from an action originating in practitioners to one originating from Amida Buddha himself. He accomplishes his purpose without compromising Hōnen's doctrinal position by appealing to the highest authority, that of Amida Buddha, who undoubtedly supersedes the authority of scholars and administrators on Mt. Hiei.

5 Conclusion

Although Shinran's spiritual insights may be ahistorical, the *Kyōgyōshinshō* clearly is genuinely a product of medieval Japanese Buddhist thought. More importantly, Shinran's skillful use of the Tendai exegetical method reflects his strategy for defending *nenbutsu* communities developing in the Kantō, especially after the tragic death of a leading disciple of Hōnen, Ryūkan, as a result of the persecution of the *nenbutsu* practice in 1227 instigated by the Tendai school. Shinran compiled the *Kyōgyōshinshō* to defend the *Senchakushū* by applying the same methodology his opponents used and by appealing to the higher spiritual authority of Amida Buddha himself. Shinran's strategic adoption of *kanjin*-style reading perhaps aided his followers in the Kantō regions in

---

62 Hōnen's statement on "three choices" (Jpn. *sansen no mon*), cited in the *Kyōgyōshinshō*, reads as follows: "If you desire to free yourself quickly from birth-and-death, of the two excellent teachings leave aside the Path of Sages and choosing, enter the Pure Land way. If you desire to enter the Pure Land way, of the two methods of practice, right and sundry, cast aside all sundry practices and choosing, take the right practice. If you desire to perform the right practice, of the two kinds of acts, true and auxiliary, further put aside the auxiliary and choosing, solely perform the act of true settlement. The act of true settlement is to say the Name of the Buddha. Saying the Name unfailingly brings about birth, for this is based on the Buddha's Primal Vow" (CWS, 1:53).

"RELY ON THE MEANING, NOT ON THE WORDS"   341

defending their sole-practice *nenbutsu* against the rising presence of the medieval Tendai institution in virtually all Kantō provinces.

It is noteworthy that Shinran inherited Ryūkan's critical eye toward Tendai scholars who "rely on the words, not on the meaning." In the *Kyōgyōshinshō*, Shinran clarifies his position against these scholars' blind adherence to the literal reading of texts by drawing on the *Dazhidu lun,* citing a passage in which Śākyamuni Buddha instructs his disciples to "rely on the meaning, not on the words," when he was about to enter nirvāṇa. Śākyamuni explains:

> With regard to relying on the meaning, meaning itself is beyond debate of such matters as, like against dislike, evil against virtue, falsity against truth. Hence, words may indeed have meaning, but the meaning is not the words. Consider, for example, a person instructing us by pointing to the moon with his finger. [To take words to be the meaning] is like looking at the finger and not at the moon. The person would say, "I am pointing to the moon with my finger in order to show it to you. Why do you look at my finger and not the moon?" Similarly, words are the finger pointing to the meaning; they are not the meaning itself. Hence, do not rely upon words.[63]

Words can direct the reader to an insight, just like the finger pointing to the moon. However, words cannot reach the insight itself, as the finger cannot reach the moon. The act of reading by simply following the meaning of words is, as Shinran points out, just like staring at the finger without even bothering to look for the moon. Shinran is, of course, careful enough to cite this passage without altering its reading.

Shinran's strategy for compiling the *Kyōgyōshinshō* based on the insight of "relying on the meaning, not on the words," however, has yet to be understood properly by polemically charged modern scholars who are either too critical or too apologetic. Critical readers typically fault Shinran's method of reading scriptures in the *Kyōgyōshinshō*, saying, "if scripture is cited as proof, it is necessary to quote with sufficient care so as not to distort the meaning of the original."[64] Meanwhile, apologetic readers defend Shinran's reading:

> He did not alter the texts ignoring the original meaning as some have charged; quite to the contrary, he read the source meaning of the scriptures more deeply and clearly than the original authors, and in order to

---

63   *CWS*, 1:241.
64   Ibid., 2:23.

bring it out, he changed the traditional readings where he felt that they were inadequate.[65]

The reality, perhaps, falls somewhere between these positions. In order to express clearly his "personal insight" conceived through reading the scriptures, Shinran selectively and systematically altered the readings of the cited texts. His re-reading of texts, however, was a doctrinally acceptable method in the context of medieval Japanese Tendai studies. In this light, it is telling to note that in his own day Shinran may have been criticized for his ideas, but not for his methodology. His use of the *kanjin*-style reading was not simply a "leftover" from his days as a Tendai monk but was a historically necessary strategy to counter the criticisms against Hōnen's *Senchakushū* raised by Tendai scholars. Shinran must have been well aware that he too might receive harsh criticism from the traditional Tendai scholastics, as Ryūkan had. He must also have felt the trend of the time, that those who advocated traditional exegesis of strict adherence to words of the scriptures were rather in the minority and could not keep pace with the rapidly growing spiritual needs developing among medieval Japanese Buddhists.

Appendix

1   The Analects states: Chi-lu asked, "Should one worship spirits?" Confucius said, "One should not worship spirits. Why should people worship spirits?"

『論語』云、季路問、「事二鬼神一」、子日「不三 能二 事一、人焉能事二鬼神一」

『論語』にいはく、「季路問はく、〈鬼神に事へんか〉と。子のいはく、〈事ふることあたはず。人いづくんぞよく鬼神に事へんや〉」と。

2   Chi Lu asked how the spirits of the dead and the gods should be served. The Master said, "You are not able even to serve man. How can you serve the spirits?"

　「季路問事鬼神、子日、不能事人、焉能事鬼神」

「季路、鬼神に事へんことを問ふ。子のいはく、〈いまだ人に事ふるとあたはず、いづくんぞよく鬼神に事へんや〉。」

---

65   Ibid., 2:25.

"RELY ON THE MEANING, NOT ON THE WORDS"

3   Further, he [Shan-tao] states: Meditative good is a means to lead one to discernment [of the Primal Vow].

Further, he [Shan-tao] states: Non-meditative good is a means to lead one to the practice [of the nembutsu].

又云「定善示観縁」

又云「散善顯行縁」

またいはく、「定善は観を示す縁なり」と。
またいはく、「散善は行を顯す縁なり」と。

4   Passages on meditative good introducing the contemplation [on Amida and the Pure Land] (定善示観縁).

Passages on non-meditative good introducing the practice [of good in everyday life] (散善顯行縁).

5   Rely on the words, not on the meaning. That is what ignorant people love to follow. What a shame!

依文不依義、愚者之所好也。可恥乎。

文に依りて、義に依らざるは、愚者の好むところなり。恥ずべきかな。

6   Shinran's reading:

The passage declaring the fulfillment of the Primal Vow in the [*Larger*] *Sūtra* states:

> All sentient beings, as they hear the Name, realize even one thought-moment of shinjin and joy. [**Amida Buddha**] **shall direct [his] sincere mind to them (*shishin ni ekō seshimetamaeri*).** If they aspire to be born in that land, they then immediately attain birth and dwell in the stage of non-retrogression. Excluded are those who commit the five grave offenses and those who slander the right dharma.
>
> 本願成就文、經言、「諸有眾生、聞其名號、信心歡喜、乃至一念。

至心回向。願生彼國、即得往生住不退転。唯除五逆誹謗正法」。〔已上〕

本願成就の文、『經』にのたまはく、「あらゆる眾生、その名號を聞きて、信心歡喜せんこと、乃至一念せん。**至心に回向せしめたまへり**。かの國に生ぜんと願ぜば、すなはち往生を得、不退転に住せん。ただ五逆と誹謗正法とをば除く」と。以上

7　Standard reading:

If all sentient beings, as they hear the Name, realize even one thought-moment of shinjin and joy, sincerely direct their merits to [others], and aspire to be born in that land, they then shall immediately attain birth and dwell in the stage of non-retrogression.

諸有眾生、聞其名號、信心歡喜乃至一念、至心回向願生彼國、即得往生住不退転。

あらゆる眾生、その名號を聞きて、信心歡喜せんこと、乃至一念し、至心に回向して、かの國に生ぜんと願ぜば、すなはち往生を得、不退転に住せん。

8　Shinran's reading:

How is directing of virtue accomplished? It is by [Amida Buddha, who] never abandons any sentient being in suffering, but constantly aspires for [the salvation of the suffering beings] in [his] heart, and **venerably fulfills (etamaeru)** the mind of great compassion by taking the directing of virtue as foremost.

The directing of virtue has two aspects: that for going forth to the Pure Land and that for returning to this world. "Directing for going forth" means that [Amida Buddha] gives [his] own virtues to all sentient beings and **has vowed (sagan shite)** [as Dharmākara Bodhisattva] **to bring them all to birth (ōjō seshimetamau)** in Amida Tathagata's Pure Land of happiness.

云何廻向。不捨一切苦惱眾生、心常作願、廻向為首得成就大悲心故。廻向有三種相。一者往相、二者還相。往相者、以己功德廻施一切眾生、作願、共往生彼阿彌陀如來安樂淨土。

"RELY ON THE MEANING, NOT ON THE WORDS" 345

「〈いかんが回向する。一切苦惱の眾生を捨てずして、心につねに作願すらく、回向を首として大悲心を成就することを**得たまへるがゆゑに**〉（淨土論）とのたまへり。回向に二種の相あり。一つには往相、二つには還相なり。往相とは、おのれが功徳をもつて一切眾生に回施して、**作願して**、ともにかの阿彌陀如來の安樂淨土に**往生せしめたまへるなり**。

9 Standard reading:

[Bodhisattvas] never abandon sentient beings in suffering, constantly aspire [for their awakening] in their hearts, and take the directing of virtue as foremost. That is because they wish to accomplish their mind of great compassion.

不捨一切苦惱眾生、心常作願、廻向為首。得成就大悲心故。

一切苦惱の眾生を捨てずして、心につねに願を作し、回向を首となす。
大悲心を成就することを得んとするがゆゑなり。

"Directing for going forth" means that [bodhisattvas] shall give their own virtues to all sentient beings and aspire to be born together with them in Amida Tathāgata's Pure Land of happiness.

往相者、以己功德廻施一切眾生、作願共往生彼阿彌陀如來安樂淨土。

往相とは、おのが功德をもつて一切眾生に回施して、ともにかの阿彌陀如來の安樂淨土に往生せんと作願するなり。

10 Shinran's reading:

The third is the mind of aspiration for birth and directing of virtue.... Again, let **those who are to be born (*shōzuru mono*)** [in Amida Buddha's Pure Land] with the mind of aspiration and directing of virtue to aspire [for attainment of birth] by unfailingly and **decidedly (*ketsujō shite*) taking (*mochiite*) the Vow (*gan*)** which [Amida Buddha] **has directed (*ekō shitamaeru*)** to them with [his] true and real mind.

三者回向發願心〔乃至〕又回向發願生者、必須下決定真實心中回向願上作二得生想一。

〈三者回向發願心〉。乃至また回向發願して**生ずる**ものは、かならず**決定して**真實心のうちに回向したまヘル願を須ねて得生の想をなせ。

11 Standard reading:

Again, those who wish to be born [in Amida Buddha's Pure Land] by directing their virtue with the mind of aspiration [for attainment of birth] must unfailingly aspire to be born [in the Pure Land] by directing [their virtue] and aspiring [to be born] with the true and real determined mind.

又回向発願生者、必須決定真実心中回向願、作得生想。

また回向発願して生ぜんと願ずるものは、かならずすべからく決定真実心のうちに回向し願じて、得生の想をなすべし。